JOHANN EWALD
Jäger Commander

James R. Mc Intyre

A KNOX PRESS BOOK
An Imprint of Permuted Press
ISBN: 978-1-94849-606-3
ISBN (eBook): 978-1-68261-941-4

Johann Ewald:
 Jäger Commander
© 2020 by James R. Mc Intyre
All Rights Reserved

Permuted Press, LLC
New York • Nashville
permutedpress.com

Published in the United States of America

Acknowledgements

Too many people to count have helped me in the writing of this book, despite my best efforts to record them all, to make a point of listing them here. In the end, these debts are either professional or personal. It seems only sensible then to address them in that order.

First and foremost, Vincent Rospond at Pike & Powder Publishing Group who was willing to take on the project as publisher and wait patiently almost an additional year for the manuscript. I hope the final product was worth the wait.

This book would not have come together as it did without the assistance of Sue Yach, Interlibrary Loan Representative at the Moraine Valley Community College Library. Sue tracked down numerous obscure pieces for me and helped to locate materials that have greatly enriched the final manuscript. Thomas Gothe at the Landeskirchliche Archiv, Kassel, who guided me to some key materials at a critical juncture. Likewise, the National Archives of Denmark, Copenhagen, which furnished me with a digital copy of Ewald's first Treatise, here translated into English for the first time.

At Temple University, Russell F. Weigley introduced me to academic military history, and demonstrated through example what a great scholar and mentor should be. His memory lives on in these pages, as I hope does some of his professionalism.

At University of Illinois in Urbana-Champaign, John A. Lynn aided my growth as a historian by fostering in me a sense of academic rigor. Many editorial decisions concerning materials included in these pages underwent his litmus test.

Alexander Burns read the entire manuscript and provided insightful comments on the work in progress. He, along with the other members of the Seven Years' War Association, including Jude Becker, Ken Bunger, Paul Petri, Jim Purky and the late Dean West have often provided me with stimulating conversation, and at times important resources on the Hessian Army.

The word colleague does not begin to describe the relationships I have enjoyed with my coworkers at Moraine Valley Community College over the years. Kristine Van Baren and Merri Fefles have been remarkable friends as well as supportive colleagues.

My colleagues at the United States Naval War College, College of Distance Education, based in Newport, Rhode Island, K.J. Delamer and Stan Carpenter, have always provided stimulating conversation. It's always a pleasure to talk with two people just as passionate about the American War of Independence. In addition, the seminars I have been fortunate enough to lead through the College of Distance education, have allowed me to further refine ideas, and the astute criticisms of the students have at times forced me to revise my own views on the war, and the conduct of warfare in general.

My mother, Florence Mc Intyre supported my interest in history from the start, and never challenged my choice of the discipline as a career. Instead, she nodded and said it seemed the natural direction for me to take. Likewise, my older brother David, who took me to numerous historical sites and reenactments as a youth. They truly fanned the flames of my passion for history especially that of the nation's founding.

Finally, to my wife Catherine, and our children Jessica, Tara and Nathanael. Thank you does not even begin to cover it. You have all listened to me and shown more patience than I could ever hope to expect. I love you all.

A NOTE ON TRANSLATIONS

AND SPELLINGS

This work contains a significant amount of translated material. In some respects, I have relied on the works of others, such as Tustin's excellent translation of Ewald's *Diary* from his services in the American War of Independence, and Selig and Skaggs equally erudite translation of his *Treatise on Partisan Warfare*. In other instances, the translations are my own, either from German or from French. I have not attempted literal translations but instead sought to convey, to the best of my ability, Ewald's intent into English. I submit that this gives a more accurate rendering of Ewald's ideas as he would want his audience to understand them than a literal translation from the original Hessian German of the eighteenth century would make possible. In this regard, I follow the notions put out by the eminent historian Peter Paret concerning his and Sir Michael Howard's translation of Carl von Clausewitz's *On War*.[1] My goal throughout has been to render, as accurately as possible, the meaning Ewald hoped to communicate, based on extensive research into his life and experiences. Any errors in this endeavor are mine and mine alone.

In regard to spellings, I have kept German and French names and terms in their native spellings throughout, including in quotes from primary sources in order to facilitate understanding and maintain consistency. Where they are altered in titles of either primary or secondary works, I have left these as they appear on those works in order to aid in following my research.

TABLE OF CONTENTS

INTRODUCTION

I first came in contact with Johann Ewald's *Diary of the American War* shortly after giving my first conference paper, on tactics in the American War of Independence. My focus was on the Continental Army and how they evolved over the course of the war. It was suggested by the commentator that if I wanted to develop the topic further, I should read Ewald's diary.

I was at once struck by several things in Ewald's *Diary of the American War*. First, Ewald's keen and incisive style as he described the many engagements in which he played a part and the objective manner in which he recorded events. It seemed as if he were always working to distill lessons learned from his experiences. Finally, the sheer breadth of his military career impressed me deeply. All of these factors made me thing, "This man truly warrants a biography." At the time, however, it did not seem to be the "right" project.

Several years later, while reading the translation of a letter between Ewald and his former comrade, John Graves Simcoe, I thought once again about just how much his life and military thought warranted a thorough treatment. The following stands as just such a treatment.

Prior to launching into an account of Ewald's life it is important to establish certain analytical parameters. In order to establish these parameters, it is necessary to provide a brief overview of Ewald's military service.

Johann (later von) Ewald not only served in all the major wars of the latter eighteenth century, he distilled his experiences in them into workable lessons for subsequent generations of officers. Ewald became an expert in what is today referred to as irregular warfare. Despite this expertise he remains generally unknown, even in the realm of military history. Bringing his experiences and the lessons he derived from them to the broader public is the primary purpose of the following work.

Ewald was born in Hessen-Kassel in 1744 and began his military service in 1760 at the age of sixteen. As a result, he participated in the later campaigns of Prince Ferdinand of Brunswick in the Seven Years War. In 1776, he left Hessen-Kassel as part of that states contingent of troops in the British service and fought in the American War of Independence from 1776-1783, being captured at Yorktown and eventually returning to his hmeland. After a period of administrative postings, and a general halt to career advancement, Ewald received permission to enter the Danish service, which he did in 1788. In Denmark, he rose to the rank of brigadier general and acquired a title of nobility. Denmark initially chose to remain neutral during the Wars of the French Revolution and Napoleon. Ewald's initial service to the Danish, therefore, consisted in reforming and training their light infantry. His next combat experience came in the suppression of the uprising of Major Ferdinand von Schill.

Clearly, Ewald accumulated a vast store of military experience. Throughout his career, Ewald utilized a special form of tactics referred to by contemporary French and German authors as *petite guerre* or *kleinen krieg* respectively. The term partisan war was often applied as well.[1]

Partisan warfare consisted of the constant activity that took place between two armies in the field outside of and around major battles. It was the war of patrol engagements, intelligence gathering and foraging. In this type of warfare, a very junior commander wielded a great deal of authority. On his own, the officer determined when to engage an opponent and when to withdraw. He organized ambushes and remained wary of his opponent doing the same while patrolling in his assigned area.

Ewald developed all of these skills to a high degree. More importantly, he sought to transmit them to other practitioners of partisan warfare through his writings. As a result, writing a biography of Ewald demands certain things. First, a simple narrative of a life will not suffice. If this is all that is asked, Ewald himself provided a very detailed account of his time in the American War of Independence. His son, Carl, would provide the remainder from the short biography he composed of his father in the early nineteenth century.[2] Instead, telling Ewald's story requires a rehearsal of his actions combined with speculation on how these shaped him as a specialist at irregular warfare.

At the same time, the approach described above means that battles will tend to fall into the background. The war of major engagements was not Ewald's war. The aspect of warfare he most often observed and participated in consisted in that of the partisan.

It is my sincerest hope that the following pages accomplish these goals.

James McIntyre
July 2017

PROLOGUE

Somewhere in New York, 1776

The air was chill with the first inklings of winter as the green coated men formed up to the right and left, their one-eyed commander directing them with hand signals. The commander was Captain Johann Ewald, and these were his men of the Second Company, Hessen-Kassel Jäger Corps. They were beginning to move out, the van of the British march into the countryside in search of George Washington and his Continental Army.

The men began to march down the dirt track. As they moved out, they kicked up dust from the narrow path that passed for a road which hung in the still air like smoke. Suddenly, the hiss-crack of muskets filled their air, as the trees on the left exploded with fire. The Jäger had marched straight into an ambush!

Their captain tried to climb up a hill in order to get a better idea of what was going on from the height. At that moment, an intense fire exploded on his left. Hot lead was now flying through the air. The captain gestured half a platoon of his men forward to engage the attacking Americans.

They all ran up to find his advanced guards already caught in a fire fight with several battalions of ragged looking soldiers. For all their pitiful appearance, the enemy fought well. This would be something for the captain to consider at a later time. Not now. Now, he had to worry about his men, and determine if there were some way to extricate them from the predicament they had unwittingly marched into. Retreat was impossible. The enemy were too close, and there were too many of them. The Jäger would have to fight their way out!

Silently, the captain gestured to his men. He gave orders through hand signs, so as not to alert the enemy to his intentions, just in case any of them spoke or understood his Hessian dialect. The captain was trying to deploy his men to better adjust to their situation. As it was, they were spread out in a circular formation about an acre wide. Keeping his men in formation and under orders grew more and more difficult as the air quickly filled with the thick sulfuric smoke of musket and rifle blasts. With musket balls whizzing through the air and sheering off branches from the surrounding undergrowth, the situation looked bleak indeed. What an inglorious end to their first real action with the Americans, and so soon after their arrival in the colonies!

Suddenly, mounted on his brown steed, Colonel Karl Emil von Donop, proprietary commander of the Regiment von Donop, appeared with several cavalry as an escort. Spying Ewald, he shouted 'You want to conquer America in one day! You write rules and then violate them." The one-eyed captain winced, but only momentarily, at the admonishment from his superior. Inwardly he knew, if he were guilty of anything, it was being overzealous in the service of his Count.

At the sight of the Hessian reinforcements, the Americans broke off their attack and retreated. They fell back quickly so as not to be surrounded themselves. Ewald held his men back from any pursuit. They had seen enough action for the day. For his part, the captain resolved to write about this experience in his diary. It helped to think, to be better next time. He had already learned this lesson from the last great war he had served his count in back in Europe. Captain Ewald had no doubt that such reflection would serve him well in this new war as well, as would some of the experiences gained from the last one. Still, this was a new land and a new war. He had much to consider, but far from shrinking from the task, he looked forward to it with relish. Any chance the captain could find to hone his martial skills he grabbed at with enthusiasm. Such efforts had so far helped him rise to a captain in the service of the Landgraf of Hessen-Kassel, even without the noble pedigree so often seen as a necessity. They would no doubt help to continue his rise, and war was the great chance to distinguish himself in that service. These thoughts, mixed with a sense of relief at the rescue of his command, filled the captain's head as his men resumed their march…

CHAPTER I

A SOLDIER IS BORN IN KASSEL

Johann Ewald was born in Kassel, the capital of the Landgraviate of Hessen-Kassel on 30 March 1744. He was born into a state at war in an age of near constant conflict. It is necessary to examine the cultural and political milieu in which the young man grew up, as well as the influences of his family to understand the Ewald's path in life. In Ewald's case, the former is much more accessible than the latter, as there is very little information concerning his personal life that survives. The history of Hessen-Kassel in the eighteenth century, however, has received ample attention from historians.[1]

The state came into existence in 1567 as a part of the Holy Roman Empire.[2] Initially, it formed a portion of the territories of the imperial prince Philip I, originally called "Hessen". On Philip's demise, the state of Hessen-Kassel was created as a division of his patrimony. The other states formed out of the division of Philip's patrimony became Hessen-Darmstadt and Hessen-Rheinfels.[3] Hessen-Kassel was not contiguous. By the eighteenth century, it consisted of three separate regions, the largest of which lay around the capital city of Kassel to the northeast and Marburg to the southwest. A second area lay to the northwest of Wiesbaden and straddled the Rhine. The third, and smallest portion of the state was south of Fulda. In all, the three areas that composed the Landgraviate equaled out to roughly a third of the modern German state of Hesse. The division of the Philip's territory led to the establishment of the line of Landgrafs as well. The line began with the ascension of William IV, eldest son of Philip. Wilhelm IV thus became Wilhelm I of Hessen.

Prior to setting up the division of his patrimony, Philip converted to the Lutheran faith early in the great Reformation of the sixteenth century, and much of his polity followed suit. It is likely that Ewald was born into this faith, based on his later comments concerning religion. At the same time, as will be seen, he possessed at least a passing interest in other denominations. While serving in North America, he attended the services of several other Christian sects, usually leaving with his own religious ideals strengthened. The Lutheran faith had a profound influence on the development of Hessen-Kassel, as it served as an important factor in the policy decisions of the Landgrafs.

During the Thirty Years' War, for instance, Hessen-Kassel was a staunch ally of the northern Lutheran state of Sweden, which became the defender of continental Protestantism. Hessen-Kassel paid an enormous price for their support of their northern Protestant neighbor. The state was overrun on several occasions during the fighting and sustained significant damage as well.[4] Still, under the Treaty of Westphalia Hessen-Kassel acquired some additional territories, gaining the greater part of the County of Schaumburg as well as Hersfeld Abbey, considered at the time as an important site.[5]

Economically, Hessen-Kassel ranked among the poorer of the German states. There were several reasons for this lack of prosperity. The contributing factors included difficult terrain, a large and growing population that tapped already sparse resources, and a lack of industrial development. With regards to the terrain, Charles Ingrao notes, "Agriculture was handicapped by a hilly, heavily wooded terrain, generally infertile soil, and an inhospitable climate."[6] In addition, Hessen-Kassel had a high population density that reached one hundred twenty people per square mile by 1781. The density of the population only served to exacerbate the problem of the country's inability to provide for its subjects.[7] While the peasants were the most gravely effected by these conditions, the nobility were not immune either, and many Hessian nobles endured a standard of living below that of the average colonial freeholder in North America.[8] In addition to the large population and poor farming climate, there was little industry to help support the economy. While Hessen-Kassel had once boasted a growing textile industry, this never recovered from the ravages of the Thirty Years' War. By the middle of the eighteenth century, the state sustained only a small middle class. The lack of a middle class often manifested in the condition of the urban areas. Again, Ingrao observes, "Contemporary travelers passing through Hessen-Kassel usually commented on the wretchedness of its provincial towns and cities."[9]

Given the relative poverty of Hessen-Kassel, it should come as no surprise that the Landgrafs were constantly in search of some means of reducing the economic burdens on their state and people. One method of obviating the states' economic difficulties that developed during the seventeenth century involved the state essentially renting out its army to various other European powers.[10] Historians later christened this practice the *Soldatenhandel* or "soldier trade." There are a variety of interpretations of this practice as it emerged in the seventeenth century and continued well into the eighteenth.[11] Since the *Soldatenhandel* or *Subsidientruppen*, would have a profound impact of Ewald's life, and eventually bring him to North America, it warrants a detailed discussion.

It should be emphasized from the outset that this practice was not necessarily viewed as the outright hiring of mercenaries by either party. As Peter H. Wilson, one of the more thorough historians of early modern Germany, notes, "Traditionally, the German princes are regarded as having bartered their subjects as soldiers for subsidies to 'increase their revenues and satisfy their taste for luxury.'"[12] Wilson further observes, however, that the motivations for this practice were not always plain avarice. In his view, if a prince sought to fulfill their political and dynastic ambitions, which could include such things as territorial aggrandizement or a greater title, they needed a large army and robust treasury. If the prince in question did not possess these resources on their own, they had to find a new revenue stream to make up the difference. Concerning these factors, Wilson concludes, "The most important and politically significant form of such assistance was the subsidy treaty."[13] Further, he notes how the "princes regarded them (the treaties) as an opportunity to escape from political obscurity and to play a larger role on the international stage."[14]

Subsidy treaties themselves dated from the fifteenth century, however, they grew much more common in the period after 1660. While the use of mercenaries existed simultaneously, there existed a clear division between the outright sale of mercenaries and the subsidy treaty. Throughout much of this period, the determining factor on how their transactions were viewed depended upon whether the troops were placed in the pay of the Holy Roman Emperor.[15] Beyond the perceived economic benefit to the smaller state, the subsidy treaty served as a means to attract partners who could protect and possibly assist the smaller polity in realizing its ambitions.[16]

The above political, diplomatic and security issues drove the princes of the Holy Roman Empire to expand their armies. As on historian neatly summarized, "Subsidies undoubtedly enabled some rulers to maintain larger forces than they would otherwise have done: A number of princes raised new units directly following the signing of a treaty."[17] While the subsidy treaties themselves could vary widely in their financial and political details, according to Peter H. Wilson, they all included one basic characteristic, "one party provided military assistance in return for financial or political advantage from the other."[18] Thus, the subsidy treaties provided the various second and third tier princes of the Holy Roman Empire with a means to capitalize on the human resources of their territories as a means of enhancing their reputation in the international arena.[19] The subsidy treaties held important rewards for the smaller states involved in the practice. They aided the larger states as well.

The benefit to the larger power involved was that the "the hiring of auxiliary troops by great powers in the eighteenth century in the history of western warfare from the feudal levy to the modern conscript army."[20] This was a time when armies were becoming more organized, with training especially gaining greater emphasis. Emphasis on training required states to keep soldiers under arms in peacetime, a significant expense even for the great powers. Subsidy troops allowed a state to quickly expand its forces when necessary. Thus, they alleviated some of the expense of maintaining a standing army in peacetime, but still allowed them to take the field with a trained force when a war broke out. This was the theory at least. It is important to keep in mind, as one expert on the *Subsidientruppen* pointed out, that no state "raised an army solely for the purpose of hiring it to the highest bidder."[21]

Not all princes of the second and third caliber joined in the use of *Subsidientruppen*. Various factors could play a role in the decision, including the feelings of the prince themselves regarding the practice. Likewise, their ambition for aggrandizement and the relative wealth of the state exerted some influence. The location of the prince's territory played some role in their ability to provide *Subsidientruppen* as well.

Due to the historical controversy attached to the term *Soldatenhandel*, most contemporary scholars utilize the term *Subsidientruppen*. The latter is more descriptive of what was actually occurring and will be utilized hereafter in the current study.[22]

As will be seen later, public opinion on these treaties changed significantly over the course of the eighteenth century. The American War of Independence would stand as an important period of change in the way the public viewed subsidy treaties, both in the Holy Roman Empire, and throughout Europe more generally. A key factor in this shifting perception was where the men served. Many contemporary authors, soldiers and dramatists among them, were more than willing to lay down their lives in the defense of their homelands, but not on some distant foreign battlefield.[23] Due to this this sentiment, the distances involved in sending troops to put down the revolt in North American formed an important factor in changing the popular perception of the treaties. Still, these changes remained in the future. At the time of Johann Ewald's birth, most in Europe continued to see the subsidy treaties as necessary if not mutually beneficial. While some critics asserted that the treaties drove the proliferation of large armies by the numerous princes of the empire, no less a figure than Friedrich II of Prussia (r. 1740-1786) recognized their merits. The Prussian monarch noted both their importance in providing greater options to the rulers of the smaller states, and the options they gave the larger states of being able to quickly expand their armies in times of war. Frederick evidently comprehended the various options *Subsidientruppen* provided.[24] With the preceding overview of the subsidy treaties in mind, it is now pertinent to examine how these effected the state of Hessen-Kassel in particular.

The use of subsidy treaties by the Landgrafs Hessen-Kassel dated back to the late seventeenth century. Under Karl I (r. 1677-1730), for instance, Hessen-Kassel first entered the military-diplomatic exchange. It quickly became a major contributor of *Subsidientruppen*. Karl I, known as the barracks and church builder, sent thousands of his troops into foreign service. From a meager beginning of 1,000 troops to the Holy Roman Empire to fight the Turks in 1687, the number rose to 9,000 in 1702. Likewise, 11,500 went to Venice in 1706 as the Venetians were recognized for their high pay. These men were dispatched to fight against the Ottoman Empire, and so many in Europe perceived their service as a defense of Christianity. Another 12,000 went to George I of England after the Treaty of Utrecht in 1713. Likewise, with the ascendancy of George II, a treaty was negotiated under which England agreed to pay an annual subsidy to Hessen-Kassel for troops. This agreement held mutual benefits for both signatories. For Hessen-Kassel, it provided a guaranteed income to the state coffers for the length of the treaty and allowed for budgeting to take place based on the additional revenue. For England, it meant they had access to a manpower reserve to bolster their Hanoverian forces. Simultaneously, the treaty effectively removed these troops from the open market, meaning, they could not be acquired by an enemy.

In 1730, Landgraf Karl died. His eldest son was Friedrich, who was then king of Sweden stood next in lane to inherit the Landgraviate. While he was known as a gallant soldier, as well as for is romantic conquests, politically, he was only nominally the new Landgraf. Friedrich's brother Wilhelm, the Statthalter of Hessen held the real power in the state. He became the de facto ruler and sought to continue his father's policies. The connection to Sweden proved an enduring one. Between 1730 and 1751, there existed a personal union between the two states, with Wilhelm VIII remaining in control of Hessen-Kassel until he inherited the throne of his homeland in 1760.[26] In so far as the disposition of Hessen-Kassel's army went, Frederick I provided 24,000 troops to Sweden, however, this may be seen as simply shifting troops around within the family demesne in order to meet security needs. Wilhelm VIII likewise provided 6,000 soldiers to George II in 1743.[27]

The provision of *Subsidientruppen* did serve as a significant source of income for some of the German states, in particular Hessen-Kassel, during the eighteenth century. This should come as no surprise. Conflict stood as more the rule than the exception in Central Europe during the early modern period. Based on this fact contemporaries viewed warfare as an accepted part of life rather than an aberration. In the context of the times, their view held some merit. The eighteenth century witnessed numerous major conflicts, including the War of the Spanish Succession (1700-1715), the Great Northern War (1700-1725) the War of the Austrian Succession (1740-1748), and the Seven Years' War (1756-1763). In addition, there were the smaller conflicts, such as the War of the Polish Succession (1734-35) and the War of the Bavarian Succession (1786). All of these conflicts were later eclipsed by the cataclysm of the Wars of the French Revolution (1792-1799). Based on the preceding list, roughly forty-nine years, nearly half of the century was spent in conflict! These were only wars in which some of the major powers took part. There were numerous other, smaller, conflicts which did not draw in the great powers, and likewise, there were external conflicts, fought outside Europe over issues such as trade. A prime example of the latter would be the War of Jenkins' Ear.[28]

At the time of the Johann Ewald's birth, Hessen-Kassel, under its Landgraf Wilhelm IV of Hesse (r. 1730-1760), was engaged in the War of the Austrian Succession.[29] The conflict erupted when the newly minted king of Prussia, Frederick II (r. 1740-1786) violated the Pragmatic Sanction signed by his father and seized the Hapsburg province of Silesia from his contemporary, Maria Theresa. While Frederick attempted to justify the annexation through propaganda, much of Europe viewed it as nothing more than blatant aggression, with the consequence that Austria's allies came to her defense. Her foes, likewise, sought to benefit from the growing conflagration by seizing the opportunity to reduce Hapsburg power. The overall outcome was a dynastic struggle that pitted two coalitions against one another. On the one side stood Prussia and France, the latter no friend to the Hapsburgs. These two were joined by Spain, ostensibly a part of the Bourbon Family Compact, but reality fighting to achieve her own ends.[30] Austria, the traditional foe of France, and England, made up the opposing side. The two coalitions drew on agreements with the smaller German states of central Europe that composed the Holy Roman Empire to broaden their respective coalitions. The princes themselves took part in the hopes of gaining territory or prestige, or both at the end of hostilities.

The overlapping subsidy treaties entered into between the great powers in Europe and the smaller German states to meet the manpower needs of the former during the War of the Austrian Succession gave rise to a truly bizarre situation. As noted above, Wilhelm had a preexisting agreement with Great Britain, who was opposed to Prussia and allied with the Austrian Hapsburgs. The latter had refused to recognize Hessen-Kassel's claim to the state of Hanau, and instead supported that of Darmstadt.[31] There were already six thousand Hessian troops in British pay, when Wilhelm concluded an agreement to support the aspirations of Charles VII of Bavaria with a corps of 6,000 men in return for his granting of electoral status to the state, as well as some territorial acquisitions. This corps fought against the Austrian army in Bavaria in 1744 and 1745, creating a situation where Hessian troops served on both sides simultaneously. They garrisoned fortresses in the Low Countries for Britain, while they served with the Bavarian army in southern Germany.[32] A secret clause existed in both agreements, which, in theory at least, prevented the two contingents from ever coming into direct conflict.[33] Still, the simultaneous existence of the two treaties with states on opposite sides of the conflict did not help Hessen-Kassel's image among the more powerful states of Europe. Nor did the fact that the treaty with Charles VII contained provisions that stipulated rates to be paid to Hessen-Kassel for every soldier killed or wounded seriously enough to be incapable of further service. The same stipulations were included concerning horses as well. These clauses came to be known as blood money by many contemporaries. These "blood-money" clauses were unpopular at the time and have since served to fuel the pens of critics who coined the term *Soldatenhandel.*[34] Once Charles died, Wilhelm quickly had the Hessian forces in the pay of the Bavarians declare neutrality, thereby ending the precarious situation.[35]

Clearly, for someone interested in a military career, there were numerous opportunities to enter the profession of arms. Given the environment in Hessen-Kassel, the boy was exposed to the pomp of military life from his earliest days. This would not be surprising, since according to the most recent study throughout the eighteenth century, one in every fifteen males in Hessen-Kassel served in some military capacity at some point in their lives.[36] Playing in the streets of the city, he would have seen numerous soldiers passing to and fro, and he was likely struck by the color and richness of their uniforms, which were far more eye-catching than the drab garb of most civilians. All of this exerted an effect on the boy and would play a prominent role in his decision of which career path to follow. As he later recalled, "Watching the bustle in Kassel, Ewald took it into his head to be a soldier and officer of the Landgraf."[37] Initially, at least, his family sought to dissuade him form a military life. They went to great lengths to try and awaken the youth to the dangers attendant in the choice of a military vocation. Growing up in the martial atmosphere of militarized city of Kassel, social pressures would have encouraged men of the merchant class to seek a military career where they could possibly become officers—a path not open to the lower classes. As noted by a traveler through Hessen-Kassel later in the century:

> *For many years the Hessian knows that he is born to be a soldier; from his youth he hears nothing else. The farmer who bears arms tells the son his adventures, and the lad, eager to tread in the footsteps of the elder, trains his feeble arms in the use of weapons; so when he has reached the size necessary to take a place in the valiant ranks, he is quickly formed into a soldier.*[38]

These words, while written later in the century, were in all probability very descriptive of the Kassel in which young Ewald grew up. Certainly, the martial environment of Kassel during and just after the War of the Austrian Succession exerted some influence on him during his formative years. These influences would become abundantly clear as he became a young man.

Johann's father was George Heinrich Ewald, a bookkeeper, who worked for the general post office in Kassel. His mother was Katherine Elisabeth, née Breithaupt, the daughter of a Kassel merchant.[39] George Ewald oversaw the early years of the boy's education, until his death later in the decade when Johann was about eight years old. At that point, responsibility for the boy's nurturing then fell completely on the shoulders of his mother. Katherine worked diligently to educate the boy and keep him safe.

She died soon thereafter, and the boy moved in with his grandmother. In the words of Ewald's son, she attempted to bring him up with good morals and according to the *Golden Rule*, however, she could not divert him from his martial interest.[40] His grandmother continued to see to other aspects of his education as well. She made certain he was literate. That and his middle-class origins held the potential to open new opportunities for the youth. Still, the boy seemed determined on a military career, and the as the years passed following the Treaty of Aix-la-Chapelle, it became clear that Europe stood poised on the brink of another major conflict. Too little had actually been settled by the treaty for the continent to remain peaceful for very long.

CHAPTER 2

A YOUNG MAN GOES TO WAR

While his name is most often brought up in connection with the American War of Independence, Johann Ewald actually began his military service in the army of Hessen-Kassel during the Seven Years' War. It is therefore necessary to examine that earlier conflict to gain a better understanding of the formative influences on his development as a soldier.

The spark which ignited the global conflagration known alternatively as the Seven Years' War, the Great War for Empire, or French and Indian War exploded in the backwoods of Pennsylvania.[1] A young George Washington, ambitious to enhance his real estate holdings, as well as make his mark with the elites of Virginia colony, took part in an international incident that essentially placed the colony at war with the Kingdom of France. The mother country decided to back her New World colony, and it grew increasingly clear that the conflict originating in North American would spread to Continental Europe. In 1756, there followed what historians term the diplomatic revolution, in which alliances which had stood for nearly a century shifted over the course of months. The shifting alliances resulted in an entirely new power dynamic dominating the European continent.

Specifically, France now allied with her traditional continental foe, Austria. These erstwhile allies turned their collective military might against Great Britain and the sometime supporter of the House of Bourbon, Prussia. In her desire to seek vengeance on Prussia, and regain her lost province of Silesia, Maria Theresa of Austria sought additional allies in central Europe as well. Her diplomatic endeavors succeeded in drawing in both Russia and Sweden as added members of the growing coalition ranged primarily against Prussia on the European continent. All the aforementioned powers save France saw Great Britain more as a secondary foe.[2]

Many of the smaller states in central Europe, members of the Holy Roman Empire, joined either faction depending upon several factors. These included existing agreements, familial connections between respective ruling houses, and political interest. Religion exerted an influence as well, with, the Roman Catholic states in western Europe taking up arms against Protestant antagonists. Thus, Saxony, under threat of Prussian invasion in 1756, threw in her lot with Austria, while Hanover and Hessen-Kassel joined in with Prussia.

The fighting in Europe erupted on August 29, 1756, when Prussian troops invaded the Imperial State of Saxony. The first major engagement on the continent occurred shortly thereafter with the battle of Lobositz on October 1, fought between the forces Frederick II of Prussia, and Maria Theresa of Austria. Lobositz stood as a tactical victory for the Prussians, but proved to be more of a strategic success for Austria in that while the Frederick's troops held the field of battle at the end of the day, the Austrian commander, von Browne, succeeded in stopping Frederick's advance, and allowed his own force to continue crossing the Elbe River.[3] Due to the timing of the invasion, Lobositz stood as the only major engagement in Eastern Europe in 1756.

The year 1757 began with a series of defeats for Prussian arms, both tactically and strategically, which included such clashes as the battle of Prague, on May 6, 1757, and the battle of Kolin, fought on June 18, 1757. Recovering his equilibrium from these blows, Frederick struck back with force. Late in the year, he fought, and won two battles, Rossbach on November 5, and Leuthen on December 5 respectively.[4] These victories, both gained against significant odds, were brilliant tactical and strategic successes for Prussian arms. Not only did Frederick succeed in defeating two forces that were every much superior in numbers to his own, but in doing so, he demonstrated to all of Europe that Prussia was still able to maintain the continental war effort. These victories strongly influenced George II of England's desire to support an Allied Army in the west to fight against the French. Thus, these two victories restored the fortunes of the House of Brandenburg, at least for a time.[5]

In the West, where a young Johann Ewald would soon see his first military service. Frederick's brother-in-law, Ferdinand, Duke of Brunswick-Wolfenbüttel, received command of a revamped force known as His Britannic Majesty's Army. This army is intimately connected with Ewald's earliest, formative military experiences.

Ferdinand (January 12, 1721-July 3, 1792) was a close confidant to the Prussian king Frederick II. He was born at Wolfenbüttel, the fourth son of Ferdinand Albert, Duke of Brunswick. The young duke received a military education, as befit someone of his station. At age 26, he was placed in command of the Brunswick regiment in the Prussian service. He saw action in the War of the Austrian Succession (1740-1748), taking part on the battles of Mollwitz (April 10, 1741) and Chotusitz (May 17, 1742). Due to his solid performance in this conflict, Ferdinand was placed in command of the Life Guard Battalion of the Prussian Army. It was at the head of this unit that he crashed through the Austrian center at the battle of Soor in 1745.[6]

By the beginning of the Seven Years' War, Ferdinand was a lieutenant general. As such, he took part in the opening campaign of that conflict against the Saxons which led to their surrender at Pirna.[7] He likewise played a significant role in the battle of Lobositz discussed above. In 1757, he took part in the battle of Prague and saw service at Rossbach.[8] After the latter, Ferdinand was placed in command of the Allied Hanoverian Army nominally under the leadership of the Duke of Cumberland, the son of King George II of England and Elector of Hanover. This force had previously submitted to the humiliating Convention of Kloster-Zeven, signed on September 10, 1757. This document amounted to a virtual withdrawal of the Allied army in the west from the war, and the opening of Hanover to the French. It was quickly repudiated by the British government.[9] A substantial part of Ferdinand's assignment therefore involved the restoration of the Army's morale and potency as a fighting force in the western theater.[10]

Ferdinand rapidly succeeded in this mission. He rebuilt his new command in late 1757. In a brilliantly conducted campaign of maneuver in February and March 1758, he succeeded in evicting the French from Hanover. He completed this turnaround in the fortunes of the allied army by leading the force to victory over the French at Krefeld on June 23, 1758. After suffering a significant reverse at Bergen the following year, Ferdinand led his army to the stunning victory at Minden on August 1. The battle itself was a decidedly uneven contest, with 51,000 French troops under the combined command of Marshals Contades and Broglie facing off against 41,000 allied troops. In the event, Ferdinand seized the initiative and marched his troops forward on the French. The German and English troops of His Britannic Majesty's Army marched forward boldly and withstood a number of French cavalry charges in order to win the day.[11]

Ferdinand's army spent the remainder of 1759 in maneuvers designed to outflank their French adversaries. Due to these movements, His Britannic Majesty's Army did not go into winter quarters until January of 1760, with the British contingent camped at Osnabruck and the main army with Ferdinand at Fritzlar. The two contingents remained in these positions until June of 1760.[12]

The actual campaign of 1760 would be crucial in the West. In response to the heightened morale after Minden, Ferdinand had received

substantial reinforcements from the various states that composed his coalition in that theater. Unfortunately, he soon had to part with some of
these troops to reinforce Frederick after the latter's defeat at the battle of
Maxen on November 20, 1759.[13]

As spring approached, Ferdinand, ever the aggressive commander,
approached the start of a new campaign season with a fresh operational
goal.[14] He sought to drive the French out of the German states, and prevent them from again occupying the area, on which they had subsisted
their war effort for several years.[15] If he succeeded, he would effectively
undermine their strategy to take Hanover as a bargaining chip which they
could use to take back virtually any of the territories taken by British forces elsewhere around the globe.[16] Further, he would remove the heavy burden of French exactions from some of his allies, while placing additional
strain on French logistics.

To accomplish his goals, however, Ferdinand required fresh troops.
Units depleted in the previous years' fighting and maneuvering had to
be brought back up to strength. The resultant recruiting provided young
Johann Ewald with the opportunity to follow his vocation.

By all accounts, Johan Ewald showed a desire to join the Hessian
army throughout his youth.[17] In a last-ditch effort to dissuade the young
man from a military career, an uncle took him to the bloody battlefield
of Sandershausen shortly after the battle fought there on July 23, 1758.[18]
The older man's hope was that if the boy witnessed the carnage of the
battle first hand, it would free him from any romantic notions concerning warfare and rid him from any thoughts of making the military his
profession.[19] By some accounts, young Ewald was supposed to have cried
out "Oh, how happy are they who died for their country in such a way!"[20]
While this story is likely apocryphal, it is in keeping with his character.
Ewald seemed to believe that military service to the state encompassed the
highest calling an individual could follow. Later he would write concerning an officer who fell at the battle of Velllinghausen "Happy is the little
one who can finish his life in such a glorious place and sell his life so dearly
to his prince!"[21] In any case, all attempts at dissuading him from joining
the army were thrown by the wayside. Indeed, by then it would likely have
been pointless to try to dissuade the youth.

On June 23, 1760, at the age of 16, around the same time that most
young men embarked upon their chosen profession, Johann Ewald enlisted in the infantry Regiment von Gilsa.[22] This was not unusual for a male
in this period. As Daniel Krebs has recently pointed out, "Most young
men in the Holy Roman Empire started learning their trades around the
age of fourteen." Young Ewald's decision becomes even more understand-

able given the percentage of men who served in the army of Hessen-Kassel over the course of the century.[23] The recent victories of His Britannic Majesty's Army under the Duke of Brunswick would further attract a young man, already enamored with the military life, to enlist in one of its regiments. Finally, Ewald's desire may have been further kindled by the idea that Ferdinand's Army was the shield of Hessen-Kassel against the invading French. Thus, began what would eventually be a twenty-four-year career with the Hessian army.

To better understand the influences recruit Ewald encountered during his early military service, it is worth taking a few moments to describe the Hessian army that fought in the Seven Years' War. The Hessian army contained about 12,000 troops at the outset of the conflict. Given the size of Hessen-Kassel, it constituted impressive force, one that equaled roughly three percent of the state's population.[24] Both Wilhelm VIII and his successor Friedrich II were admirers of Friedreich II of Prussia, and they patterned the Hessian army on the Prussian model. In 1756 the army was organized into eighteen battalions of infantry and seven cavalry regiments. The line infantry regiments of the Hessians consisted of single battalion units. The terms regiment and battalion will therefore be used interchangeably in describing the Hessian infantry formations of the Seven Years' War. Each battalion held ten companies of 70 men, giving a total of 770 men on paper.[25] At the outset of the conflict, the Hessian infantry consisted of one Guard and eleven Line regiments. There were a further three garrison and land battalions as well as two standing and two garrison grenadier battalions.[26]

The demands of the conflict drove the expansion of the army to the point that, by 1760, the force consisted of two Guard, two fusiliers, nine musketeers, and two grenadier regiments. The augmentation drove some reorganization of the army along with further expansion and resulted in the creation of seven grenadier battalions composed of the companies from various infantry regiments, as well as three garrison and one frei-korps as well as a Jäger battalion. Each regiment included its own battalion guns manned by trained artillerists. In addition, by 1760, due in part to Prince Ferdinand of Brunswick's enthusiasm for light troops, Hessen-Kassel had added two squadrons of mounted Jäger.[27] Clearly, the demands of the war forced a significant expansion of the Hessian army.

It should be noted that in 1760, the Hessians would go campaigning with a major handicap, as their new elector, Friedrich II, had doubled the size of his forces. He accomplished this feat by cutting the effective strength of his units in half. In reality, therefore, he managed to simply double the number of units in his army. This move by the elector has often been depicted as an attempt to bluff the French as to the actual manpower of his army. If that was his goal, the move stood as a monumental failure.[28] In his defense, the reforms of Frederick can be attributed to his inexperience.

Frederick only became Landgraf in 1760.[29] The Regiment von Gilsa was undergoing some significant changes as well. The preceding year, the commander of the regiment changed, leading to the unit being renamed from the Regiment von Fürstenberg to the Regiment von Gilsa. In addition, the reforms set in motion by Friedrich II of Hessen-Kassel transformed the unit from a standard line regiment into a fusilier regiment. The uniforms of the unit were altered to reflect this change, with the facing colors going from yellow to black accordingly.[30] Hessian uniforms of the Seven Years' War closely followed the patterns of those of Prussia. The young recruit, then, would not likely have worn a dark blue coat with red lapels and stocks. The preceding description is of the uniform as it existed in 1759. Changes were adopted in 1760.[31] In his biography, Ewald's son recorded that a great deal of attention was given to finding recruit Ewald the proper uniform before he was presented to the other officers.[32] It seems likely, therefore, that he was issued the newer uniform, which would not be in as great a supply. The new uniform consisted of a blue coat with black cuffs and facings and red turnbacks. The britches were buff.[33] Proper attire was important as Ewald was considered something of a junior officer, and therefore had to look the part. This constituted the first step in the recruit's indoctrination into the regiment as well.[34]

After joining the Regiment Gilsa, Ewald left from the gates of Kassel at dawn on June 24, 1760.[35] As his son Carl later noted in a biography of his father, the young Johann Ewald waited at the city gates with "the calm of a veteran."[36] He arrived at the regimental bivouac at Neustadt the following day.[37]

Ewald would later paint a vivid picture of his early days serving in the unit and the discomforts of his new military life, "In the ranks of the Hessian Regiment von Gilsa marched 16-year-old *Freikorporal* Johannes Ewald, whose weary feet could hardly move forward, weighed down by the heavy, chunky musket on his shoulder, which, with the intersecting bandoliers on his chest, left the boy hardly able to breathe."[38] In his description, Ewald presents an image to which anyone who has endured military basic training can relate. His designation as *freikorporal* meant that Ewald was essentially a gentleman volunteer, or someone who was serving unattached until a junior officer's billet could be found for them.[39] Summing up, he observed, "It was a hard school, which he had chosen, more than once it was with teeth clenched against loosing heart that he marched on."[40] Ewald did not keep any thorough record of his experiences in the war. What follows is a reconstruction of his involvement based on several sources.[41]

As a Freikoroporal, he was presented to the other officers of the unit. Ewald was initially assigned to Major von Keudel's company, in which a Lieutenant Schlemmer took the new recruit under his wing.[42] This was often the case in armies of the period. Officers would partner a recruit with a trusted veteran. The veteran would teach the new soldier the basics of military life, from the elements of drill to the proper organization and care of their uniform and equipment. Essentially, Schlemmer was indoctrinating Ewald into the rigors of military life through what historian Don Higginbotham referred to as the tutorial method. This training was much more humane in the German armies of the eighteenth century than is generally appreciated. The officers and NCOs generally sought to educate the new recruits rather than brutalize them.[43]

Indeed, Lieutenant Schlemmer seemed paternalistic and protective of his young charge. For instance, the first time the regiment Gilsa went into combat after Ewald joined, the Lieutenant ordered him to remain with the baggage until he was trained.[44] This was not an uncommon practice, still it upset Ewald, who greatly wanted to take his place in the line. In the young man's view, it was a matter of honor to take his place alongside the veteran soldiers.[45]

Young Ewald's determination to take his place in the line no doubt impressed his superiors. Making such an impression and standing out was important since through most of the eighteenth century any real chance of becoming an officer remained closed off to all but the noble class. However, the Seven Years War was a great consumer of manpower, and many noble families across Europe lost numerous male members to the conflict. Thus, the officer corps of various European forces stood in need of officers. These vacancies opened a window of opportunity, albeit briefly, for some whose origins lay outside the nobility to have a chance at becoming officers.[46]

As the Regiment von Gilsa took in new recruits at Neustadt, it prepared to rejoin the His Britannic Majesty's Army, as the larger force prepared to embark on its 1760 campaign season.[47] In fact, given the time at which Ewald enlisted, he likely underwent much of the basic training as the army moved into the field. Schlemmer's injunction that he stay with the baggage likely saved the young recruit until he acquired the necessary skills to stand some chance of survival in his first taste of combat. Still, Ewald's baptism of fire would not be long in coming.[48]

Since Ewald fought primarily on land through his long career, before discussing his first combat experiences, it is fitting to discuss the basics of land warfare in the eighteenth century.[49] Eighteenth century European armies were divided into three main types of troops: the artillery, cavalry and infantry. At the time, these were considered separate elements of the army, with specific and distinct roles to play on the battlefield.[50]

The artillery was usually parceled out between the various infantry regiments, instead of being concentrated in batteries. This was done as it was believed that sounds of the guns going off around them would stiffen the infantrymen's resolve. On the battlefield, the artillery performed two functions. First, it engaged the enemy artillery in the hopes of destroying or disrupting it. Second, it would be turned against enemy infantry.

The guns came in a variety of calibers, distinguished by the weight of the solid shot they threw. These included 3-, 4-, 6-, and 12-pounder guns. The last stood as the largest piece usually used in the field. Likewise, there existed a variety of different types of ammunition developed for specific uses. Solid shot could be used both for bombardment of fortifications and other structures and for anti-personnel work. In addition to the solid shot, cannons in the field often fired canister as well. This took the form of a tin can filled with projectiles slightly larger than musket balls. Canister had the effect of turning the gun into a giant shot gun and was employed solely for anti-personnel work. There were several other, less frequently employed, types of shot for land warfare, and numerous types that were used at sea as well.[51]

The cavalry of the eighteenth century remained the decedent of the knights of Medieval Europe, sometimes in a very literal sense. The officers of the mounted arm often hailed from the nobility, which was useful, since they often had to pay for their own mounts and equipment. While the troopers were often commoners, they did have to know how to ride. Ideally, the most decisive role of the cavalry encompassed driving a defeated foe from the field, turning a retreat into a route, though this rarely occurred in practice.[52] The army that possessed the more effective cavalry in this period was therefore most often the one that tasted victory.[53]

Finally, there was infantry, the queen of battle in the eighteenth century. The infantry composed the bulk of the land forces in European armies of the period. Contrary to popular myth, the men were generally volunteers, though depending on the prevailing conditions in a particular time and place, the voluntary nature of their enlistment could be quite questionable. The infantry's role was to engage their opposite and drive them from the field of battle, often at the point of the bayonet. A prized, if seldom achieved, goal of the period lay in breaking the enemy's will to hold the field and then having the cavalry swoop in to complete their destruction. Such a complete triumph involved the combination of fire and shock to disrupt an enemy formation.

During the eighteenth century, there existed three types of infantry. The bulk of the men were the line infantry (sometimes called fusiliers after their weapon), who composed the majority of companies in any infantry regiment. These troops received their designation as they took their place in the line of battle and engaged the enemy in musketry actions. They could be called upon to charge the enemy with the bayonet as well. These men were of average height.

The grenadiers were selected from the taller recruits. Each regiment in a European army usually possessed a grenadier company. They derived their name from the fact that in the seventeenth century, they had been armed with primitive hand grenades, and tasked with attacking enemy defensive works. While they no longer carried grenades, many units kept alive the heritage by having grenade insignia on their cartridge boxes and hats with no brims. Likewise, these troops continued to serve as the shock troops and the grenadier companies of various regiments were often brigaded together to form an assault unit.

Finally, the eighteenth century witnessed a revival of the light infantry. These were men trained to serve as skirmishers, to conduct raids behind enemy lines, and to set up ambushes of enemy patrols. They were often recruited from the borderlands of the various states, beginning with the Austrian Empire. They could be of average height, even somewhat shorter. At the same time, they were expected to be athletic, and to possess some skills as hunters as these were seen as necessary for them to conduct their operations. Often, these men had to demonstrate some skills as marksmen as well.

The primary infantry weapon in the eighteenth century was the flintlock musket and bayonet combination. Most of these guns ranged between .60 and .70 caliber, firing a one-ounce lead projectile. Their range lay somewhere in the vicinity of one hundred yards or less, however, they were truly effective at less than eighty yards. As for accuracy, since the weapons were smoothbore, the projectiles left the muzzle and went where they would. In order to try and compensate, armies began to mass their troops in large blocks. This process began earlier with the advent of the first firearms, when slow reloading times exacerbated the general inaccuracy and thus ineffectiveness of the weapons.[54]

By the eighteenth century, the musket had evolved significantly, and their emerged a debate among military professionals as to its exact role on the battlefield. The discussion centered around the question of whether the musket was a fire weapon, to be used primarily for the hail of bullets it could throw out or was it a mainly a shock weapon for use in storming enemy positions with the addition of the bayonet. The former led to the development of what are referred to as linear tactics, with units arraying themselves on the battlefield in long lines between two and three ranks deep if fighting on the defensive where they would await the approach of a foe. When the enemy grew close enough, eighty yards or less, the troops would unleash devastating volleys of fire. These volleys would be let loose by smaller sub-units, such as platoons or companies, with the idea being that the regiment, the basic unit of maneuver, would be presenting a near-constant fire. Sub-units which had already given their fire would immediately begin the process of reloading with the objective being that by the time the last company or platoon had fired, the first would be fully reloaded and able to begin the process all over again. By following this method, they could work to deplete their opponents before the latter came close enough to engage with the bayonet.[55]

In the case of assault with the bayonet, troops were often grouped in large assault columns, which would make their way across the battlefield. They would cross the field of battle as quickly as possible, especially after they had entered the eighty-yard or less killing zone of their opponent. Military practice in the eighteenth century dictated that the men refrain from firing their weapons and put all their efforts into closing with the enemy. Once inside the killing zone, therefore, the men on the attacking side would quicken their pace accordingly so as to reduce the time they were exposed to enemy fire before closing with the bayonet. The advance would end with a melee of hand-to-hand combat, in which one side would almost literally push their opponent from the field. At least that was the theory. In many instances, one commander or the other would determine to cut their losses and retreat, trained soldiers standing as a valuable commodity of the state.[56]

The bayonet was a long, pointed, metal shaft generally triangular in shape. The addition of the bayonet transformed the musket form a fire into a shock weapon. It essentially acted as a sort of spike, designed to skewer an opponent. Since most bayonets were triangular, they tended to leave deep puncture wounds that required long periods of convalescence for the wound to heal, if the victim survived. Likewise, if the man was wounded in the abdomen, he stood a good chance of developing an infection. If so, then a lingering and painful death awaited as the state of medical knowledge was incapable of saving him. Much the same could be said of wounds from musketry.

Even with their inaccuracy, if someone were wounded by a musket ball, their injuries could be crippling if not life-threatening. Low muzzle-velocity and large caliber meant that if the person were hit in a limb, any bones in the path of the ball were likely to be pulverized. The only treatment in that case was amputation, which required speed and skill on the part of the doctor, less their patient succumb to shock. Nothing was available in the realm of antiseptics, or anesthesia for that matter. If the patient did not go into shock, the danger of infection loomed as a very real possibility during their convalescence.

While the preceding stood as the stark reality of combat in the eighteenth century, much of this would have been obscured from the young Johann Ewald as he grew up amongst the bustle of soldiers and couriers passing through the capital city of Kassel. If he did see the occasional invalid, he likely heard a great many tales of glory in the service of the Landgraf. Regardless of whatever views the young man held of military service, he would soon encounter the stark realities of the battlefield.

On June 22, the French army under Marshal Broglie stirred from their long winter lethargy and began an advance towards the town Giessen. This was just two days after Ewald had joined the Regiment von Gilsa and marked the opening of the campaign of 1760.[58]

Given these circumstances, it seems likely that one of the first engagements Johann may have taken part in as a soldier was the battle of Korbach fought on July 10, 1760. While it remains unclear whether he took any part in the actual fighting, he was certainly present with the Regiment von Gilsa.

The goal of the predominantly Anglo-Hanoverian force, under the command of Prince Karl Wilhelm Ferdinand, the Hereditary Prince of Brunswick was to clear the French off the Heights of Korbach (sometimes given as Corbach) in order to clear them out of the area. The Allied army numbered between 15,000 to 20,000 troops. The French force under Gen. St. Germain numbered some 12,000 at the commencement of the fighting but rose to some 20,000 as reinforcements arrived on the field.

On this occasion, the French launched their advance ahead of the Allied army. The result was the bloody repulse of Karl Wilhelm's force, with the loss of between 800 and 1,000 men, which stood slightly higher than the French losses of 700 to 800. More important to Ferdinand, the overall allied commander, was the loss of 18 to 19 guns from his artillery park. In addition, it seemed that the campaign season was off to a poor start in the West.[59]

Several days later, on July 16, the Allied army as well as the Hereditary Prince, grabbed a chance for revenge at the battle of Emsdorf. The French

and Allied forces were roughly equal in number, each about 3,000 strong.
The engagement itself developed when elements of the allied army sought
to disrupt the French supply lines by taking the city Marburg, which the
latter used as a supply base. The Hereditary Prince and his forces managed
to surprise the French as they were sitting down to lunch. The French
cavalry were quickly driven off by the allied cavalry. Several French infantry regiments managed to form and meet the attack but were eventually
driven in by the Hessian troops. In the end, some 1,650 French troops
were captured on the field. Meanwhile, Hereditary Prince's forces lost
only 186 men.[60]

Before he had even served in the army for one calendar month, the
young Ewald had, at the very least witnessed, if not served in, two battles.
Truly he lived through a baptism of fire.

The next major engagement in which Ewald's regiment participated
occurred at Warburg on July 31, 1760. The clash came about as the result
of a series of maneuvers in which both Ferdinand and his French opponents sought to gain the operational advantage in the theater through
movement as opposed to a direct clash of arms. With 62,000 troops under
his command, Ferdinand faced off once again against Duc de Broglie,
who led a force of 130,000. The numerical difference gave the French
a better than two to one advantage over Ferdinand's composite army.
Forced to retreat in the face of Broglie's superior numbers, Ferdinand fell
into a desperate situation. Broglie had him cornered in a rough triangle
formed by the junction of the Diemel and Weser Rivers. Ferdinand's base,
the city of Kassel, lay on the left bank of the Weser, and was therefore
threatened by the French troops. The actual battle involved only a portion
of the overall armies, pitting some 20,000 French against 16,000 German
and British troops.[61]

In the end, the French lost 1,500 men to the allies 1,200. More in-
dicative of the magnitude of their defeat, they lost 1,200 prisoners and
ten guns. Warburg stood as only a tactical win for Ferdinand. He was
unable to exploit the victory further since on the same day, Prince Xavier
of Saxony and Lusatia captured Kassel when its small corps of defenders (11,000) under the command of General Georg Ludwig von Kiel-
mannsegg abandoned the city, which was important as a supply depot for
Ferdinand's troops. The next day, Prince Xavier captured Münden, thus
completing the French conquest of Hessen-Kassel.[62] After some additional clashes, Xavier managed to open the way to Hanover, but Broglie
was unable to exploit this due to logistical difficulties. The result of this
impasse was that for over a month, both forces remained idle. During this
time, young Ewald may have completed some additional training. More

importantly, he had now taken part in several engagements and likely had direct experience of combat. In late 1760, one event occurred far from Johann Ewald and the Allied Army, but which would exert a profound effect on their fighting capacity for the remainder of the conflict.

On October 25, George II of England died and was succeeded by his son the peace-oriented George III. Consequently, both the English and Hanoverian commitment to the war effort on the Continent began to wane. Eventually, it ended altogether. Still, this diminution of the war effort on the part of Great Britain and Hanover took some time. There remained some minor engagements in 1760, in which Ewald may or may not have taken part before the two armies once again went into winter quarters. For the Allied army, however, this was not to be a long respite.

The campaign of 1761 began with Ferdinand launching His Britannic Majesty's Army on a winter offensive. The drive began on February 9, much earlier than anyone had expected. The reason for this early start to the campaign stemmed from Ferdinand of Brunswick's hope to drive the French completely out of Hessen-Kassel, which they had occupied the preceding year. The French had established several supply magazines in this area, protecting them with strong garrisons. The garrisons were large enough to threaten Ferdinand's lines of communications. This meant that the garrisons had to be defeated before he could launch his offensive in earnest. The main objective of the Allied offensive stood, then, as the capture of the capital city of Kassel. To take the city, Ferdinand divided his force into three columns.[63]

The right flank of his force consisted of 17,000 men under his nephew, the hereditary prince of Brunswick. This force would advance from the Deimel in two columns. A second, weaker prong in the center, composed of 5,000 troops and under the command of Hessian general Ludwig Karl von Breitenbach would advance on Marburg from Brillon. Finally, a corps of 12, 000 men under General Spörcken made up his right flank. The right flank was to assemble east of the Weser near Duderstadt. Ewald, with the Regiment von Gilsa, served in the center portion of Ferdinand's army under the command of the Count von Wilhelm von Schaumburg-Lippe-Bückeburg, often referred to simply as LaLippe.[64]

The ensuing offensive quickly deviated from the plans. Breitenbach's advance was initially successful, capturing some substantial French supply magazines. He reached Marburg on February 14 and immediately launched an attack on the city. The assault encountered stiff resistance, with Breitenbach himself being killed at the outset of the engagement. The French repulsed the Allied attack forcing the army to beat a hasty retreat across the Eder River. Still, in other areas the offensive gained ground.

During this stage of the campaign, one engagement in particular seems to have stuck in Ewald's memory - the assault on the city of Kassel on the night March 6-7, 1761. The attack came about as part of an overall attempt by Ferdinand aimed at driving the French from the territory of Hessen-Kassel. Strategically, Kassel, the capital of Hessen-Kassel, was of great importance to the Allied army. Likewise, it probably held some special significance for Ewald himself as it was his birthplace. In any case, his son describes Ewald's being chilled to the bone in the siege trenches as the troops got into position. Before the Hessian assault troops reached their positions, they were surprised by a sudden attack by the French garrison. The unexpecrted assault threw back the Hessian and Hanoverian troops. The Hessians only restored their equilibrium when General von Gilsa himself assumed command. The Count von Schaumburg-Lippe led the overall counterattack. An intense clash developed between the two forces. There were many wounded on the Hessian side, including Freikorporal Ewald, who received a musket ball through the thigh. Due to the seriousness of his wound, he was admitted to the main hospital at Iringhausen.[65]

The wound kept him in hospital recuperating for some time, and he missed the battle of Grünberg on March 21, a French victory which forced Ferdinand to raise the siege of Kassel. Young Ewald was quite lucky, however, in that if the ball had hit the thigh bone itself, the only treatment would have been to amputate the leg, which stood as the standard practice of the time.[66]

After surgery and a period of convalescence, Johann Ewald returned to the line, though his wound still bothered him. One morning on the march, the regimental adjutant greeted him, saying, "Good morning, Mr. Ewald officer cadet! I congratulate you!" Later, at the next stop, Ewald conferred with the adjutant and confirmed, the bravery he had shown in the fighting outside Kassel had earned him a spot as an officer in the regiment.[67] He later reflected, "The first objective was achieved, Ewald was an officer of his Highly Serene Highness the Landgraf of Hessen." Likewise, for his valor, Johann Ewald received the decoration, *pour la vertu militaire* for valor in his conduct during the siege. This was a rare honor for someone without a noble lineage. Still, the fighting continued, and with it, more dangers and opportunities for the newly minted officer to gain further military laurels. In the campaign that followed Ewald's return to his unit, the Regiment Gilsa took part in the battles of Unna, Villingshausen, Kloster Bredlar, and Hoxter.[69]

The first major engagement Ewald took part in as a non-commissioned officer was the Battle of Villingshausen, fought on July 15-16, 1761. The clash came as the result of the efforts of the Duc de Broglie and the Prince de Soubise coordinating their armies in an attempt to force Ferdinand out of Lippstadt, another important depot town. While some much-needed reinforcements led by general von Spörcken brought Ferdinand's army up to 65,000 the two French armies combined to field a total of about 90,000 men. Ferdinand deployed his troops in a line along a series of hills, with their left anchored by the Lippe River and the Asche River in their center.

The battle opened with a French attack on the northern sector of Ferdinand's line, which was held by the British under John Manners, Marquis of Granby. These forces held their ground through the day against repeated attacks. Allied reinforcements arrived during the night and Ferdinand deployed these so as to strengthen his left at the expense of his right flank.

Ewald's first participation in the battle came in the skirmish at Unna fought on July 15. His unit fought a delaying action against the French attempt to cut the road to Hamm.[70]

The following morning, Broglie continued his attacks again Ferdinand's left, expecting Soubise to move on the weakened enemy right. Soubise, however, only launched a few spoiling attacks over the course of the day. The key problem for the French lay in the fact that both commanders were of equal rank and were therefore unwilling to take orders from one another and no superior even attempted to impose any sort of chain of command between the two. This, in turn, led to a lack of coordination in their efforts. When additional troops arrived on the Allied side, Ferdinand was able to halt and turn back Broglie's attack, thus making Villingshausen a victory for him.[71]

Ewald, with the Regiment von Gilsa, was stationed on the left wing of Ferdinand's army, in Lieutenant General von Gilsa's Brigade, which constituted a part of Lieutenant General von Wutginau's Corps, under the overall command of the Marquis of Granby.[72] Thus, Johann Ewald was in the thick of the fighting at Villingshausen, and it clearly left an imprint on his memory.

Ewald recalled, "The hill was attacked by a company of French chasseurs, some of whom were thrown on the boards, which they had thrown over the ditch as they ascended the hill."[73] He went on to record how

> *The unit was commanded by a Hanoverian major, a man who was dizzy at the moment when the attack came. Their enemies (the French) carried it out with great liveliness. So the major permitted the hill to be given over to the French. He let shame beat him and I did not miss him much;*[74]

The situation changed, however, when general von Gilsa arrived and took command. He inspired the men with his words, and his example, leading a counterattack in person, with sword in hand. His actions, as well as those of the Hanoverian major, made a significant impression on Ewald. He would later draw on this episode when discussing the defense of redoubts in his first book.[75]

The preceding makes clear that by now, Ewald was something of a veteran soldier. He had seen combat on several occasions, been wounded, and routinely took part in intense combat. Furthermore, it seems that he was already developing the trait that would differentiate his later professional writings from those of many contemporaries. He would support his ideas not only with examples from other conflicts he had read about, but with his own real-world experience. This factor would later single out his writings for positive comment from the great Prussian military theorist Carl von Clausewitz.[76]   Still, there remained some hard fighting to be done, and experience to be gained in the current conflict.

While the Allied army under Brunswick won a tactical victory at Villingshausen, it did not alter their strategic situation. The French sustained some 5,500 casualties at Villingshausen, 2,000 of them prisoners, as opposed to the Allied army's 311 killed and roughly 1,000 prisoners. This did not alter the fact that Ferdinand was forced to retreat before his opponent's superior numbers, fighting smaller actions near Kassel on July 31 and at Kloster Bredlar on August 5. One significant outcome of Villingshausen emerged in the French marshal Broglie's subsequent reluctance to give battle with Ferdinand. Much the remainder of the campaign season of 1761 was therefore spent in maneuvers between the opposing forces.

The battle of Wilhelmsthal, fought on June 24, 1762, constituted the last major engagement of the Seven Years War in which Ewald took part. With the French once again threatening Hanover in a last desperate bid to occupy it and try to mollify the verdict of the war. At the same time, the allies under Brunswick sought to defend the territory. Ferdinand, pitted against the Duc d'Estries and Prince de Soubise, maneuvered around the French invasion force, surrounded it, and forced the French to retreat.[77]

As stated, Ferdinand managed to outflank both of his French opponents by occupying the heights of Calle or Calden in their rear. In addition, the marquis of Granby attacked the French commander, lieutenant general Stainville, in the flank. mThe combined attacks inflicted significant casualties on Stainville's command though he did manage to extricate two battalions from the fighting. The remained of his force broke and retreated.

While Wilhelmsthal stood as the last major engagement of the war in which Ewald took part, there remained other, smaller clashes before the final peace. Some of these could be quite intense and certainly left an imprint on the young soldier's mind. One of these was an action fought on September 21, 1762.

The last battle of the war in which Ewald saw action was at Brücker Muhle. The engagement is sometimes referred to as the battle of Amöneburg as well.[78] The clash came about as a result of Ferdinand's attempt to unite his dispersed columns and force an engagement with a part of the French army under favorable circumstances. The larger strategic goal was, once again, to drive the French back across the Rhine, and deny them any territorial bargaining chips in the German states. Territories which they could utilize in the ongoing negotiations in order to achieve the return of at least some of the overseas empire.[79]

Unfortunately for Ferdinand, his French adversaries both managed to thwart his plans, and to achieve a union of their forces. As his opponents bore down upon him, Ferdinand, for his part, took up a strong position in the area east of Ohmverlaufs, occupying the area from Mount Gemünden to Cölbe. In seizing this position, the duke occupied all of the bridge and river crossings as well.

Ferdinand realized that the French would direct their main effort against him and reacted accordingly. He placed his English troops on the Amöneburg itself. The force amounted to roughly 600 men. In addition, on the day before the battle (September 20, 1762) he received a reinforcement of some six battalions of infantry and eight of cavalry, as well as six companies of heavy artillery. He placed these forces in the area east of Ohmübergangs. In addition, the duke ordered earthworks and barricades constructed on the Ohmbrück in order to strengthen the defensive capabilities of that position. Likewise, Ferdinand placed his artillery, which consisted of eight of Bückeburg's six-pounders, on the heights on the Ransberges. Finally, the duke mustered the remainder of his troops behind the heights in reserve.[80] The extreme left wing of His Britannic Majesty's Army stood at Homberg/Ohm. They were supported by battalions stationed at Dannenrod and Schweinsberg.[81]

On the opposing side, the French placed their main force at Schönbach, with other supporting units under the command of Prince Xaver of Saxony to the right of the Lahn. The prince made his command post to the southwest of Homberg/Ohm. Meanwhile, in village of Amöneburg, the French general Castries brought his troops into position. In addition, the French raised several batteries on the night of September 20-21 with

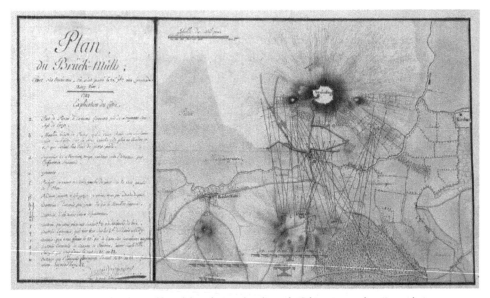

Figure 1: Plan of Bruker Muhle with legend. Digital Archives of Marburg. Internet http://www.digam. net/document.php?dok=5374 Last accessed December 2, 2016.

the intent of taking Amöneburg. They threw up a small breastwork at the Brücker Muhle, along with a trench to secure the entrance.[82]

The French constructed a series of entrenchments to the west of Ohmbrücke. In addition, they sited their guns on the heights above on the eastern slope of Amöneburg. They placed a battery to the west of the city as well. General de Castries positioned the greater number of the French and Saxon troops to southwest of Amöneburg in Rossdorf, Mardorf and Erfurtshausen respectively.[83]

The French began the engagement with a bombardment of the city which commended at 5 am on 21 September. Soon after the preparatory bombardment, they launched an infantry assault against Ferdinand's position. The assault broke down however, as it encountered heavy resistance. Zastrow's artillery crews worked feverishly, sending solid shot into the advancing French formations. As he received information on the hard fighting in this sector of the field, Ferdinand dispatched guns from his own artillery reserve to bolster the pieces in this area. By 8 o'clock, six Hessian 12-pounders were in position by Ziegelhütte. Over the next few hours, the French launched a series of additional assaults against this part of the line, however, these were broken up with heavy artillery fire.[84] Interestingly, at this point during the battle, the French infantry units were given permission to advance in open order, so as to reduce their casualties from enemy fire.[85] It is interesting to speculate, given Ewald's subsequent career, whether he observed this movement during the battle, and if so, what impression it had on his fertile mind.

To maintain the pressure on the French during the afternoon, Ferdinand dispatched six more Hessian 12-pounders to provide additional fire support. The fighting was so intense that these guns ran out of ammunition and had to be replaced with a battery of Hanoverian 12-pounders.

Towards the late afternoon, the French redirected their efforts at the hills behind the bridge leading into the town. The regiments von Gilsa and von der Marlsburg occupied this section of the battlefield. Ewald and his unit were about the feel the full weight of the final French assault!

The action began at roughly seven in the evening, with the French columns advancing rapidly on the allied positions. Heavy firing ensued on both sides as a desperate struggle erupted for control of that portion of the field. The fighting only broke off with the coming of night roughly an hour later. Ewald reported that the fighting over the hill occupied by his regiment was so intense, "The parapet on the hill was so shaved by cannon fire, that if one stood up, it would not cover them above the knee." He further recorded how the men used the bodies of the fallen to create an improvised barrier to protect themselves from the fire of their assailants.[86] This was during the defense of the Brücker Mühle, a post which the Allied army sent reinforcements to in various detachments. The fighting was so intense, Ewald would later describe it in his first treatise, "The hill was only held with a hundred men, who were replaced every half an hour."[87] The men were likely rotated out as they spent all their ammunition in that time. He further noted how great exhortations were made to the von Dittfurth and von Knyphausen Regiments as the men of these units moved in to defend the position. Confirming his experience, Ewald stated "I myself was witness to this murder-hole."[88] Clearly, for the young officer, this was an intense fight.

Still, for a battle which lasted roughly fourteen hours, the resulting casualties were surprisingly light. The Allied army lost roughly 745 killed and wounded, while the French sustained 350 killed and 730 wounded. On the French side, De Castries himself was among those wounded. The disproportion between the killed and wounded testifies in some measure to the ferocity of the fighting in this engagement.[89]

On the following day, September 22, the French renewed their assaults. In the fighting, they succeeded in gaining the castle of Amöneburg and driving off the garrison.[90] However, the French failed to gain full possession of the town, though they did manage to breach the walls of Amöneburg.[91] While the French and Saxons had gained some key positions, the battle is usually seen as constituting a victory for Ferdinand's forces.[92]

Figure 2: Modern view of Amöneburg in thebackground. The bridge that was a central feature in the fighting Ewald engaged in is no longer visible. Source: Anonymous "Militär in alten Mauern" September 13-14, 2003 Internet. https://web.archive.org/web/20031005141352/ http://www.hessenmilitaer.de/amoeneburg.htm Last accessed September 28, 2016.

Later, on September 23, the two sides entered into negotiations. These culminated in a truce between the two armies, making Amöneburg effectively the last battle in the western theater.[93]

However, during the same month that the two armies clashed at Amöneburg, France and Great Britain entered into negotiations to end the war. Due to these diplomatic actions, a ceasefire came into effect. While both armies regrouped and prepared for further action should the negotiations break down, there was no need in the end. On November 3, a preliminary peace agreement was signed at Fontainebleau.

In the final Peace of Paris of February 10, 1763, several things were readily apparent. France was most certainly the loser. They forfeited their territory in North America, their trading posts in Africa and their interests in India all to Great Britain. Consequently, Great Britain stood as the clear winner of the contest for empire. At the same time, this victory had caused the island nation to rack up an enormous debt, and some means were necessary to begin paying down the colossal expense.

Finally, Prussia was the survivor. It had survived in the face of concerted efforts by Catherine and Maria Theresa to obliterate it. Frederick II, though he had clearly initiated the conflict on the European continent to conserve and protect Prussia, seemed more than happy with the prospect of an end to the tumults of military life. Prussia, through endurance, due somewhat to the temerity of her king, came out of the war as the closest the continent of Europe had to a victor in the conflict. Her territories were intact, Frederick and his generals having thwarted the goals of their adversaries.[94]

rich's embrace of the movement in Hessen-Kassel something remarkable and unique.

Friedrich's avid support of the Aufklärung stood as something notable for a much more practical reason as well. In order to fully appreciate the Landgraf's reforms, it is important to recognize that the endemic poverty that engulfed Hessen-Kassel effected the university towns as well. The university center at Marburg, for instance, often "appalled its visitors."[29] Thus any investment made in the institutions of higher learning constituted a major outlay on the part of the state. Given this context, Ewald's entrance into the Collegium came as a high honor.

The young officer was well prepared well for his time at the institution, as he spent much of his time while convalescing from the duel in "ferocious military studies."[30]

While attending the Collegium, Ewald studied economics and military theory under Jakob Mauvillon (1743-94). Mauvillon was a well-known author in both disciplines. He is described in the work of Ferdinand Zwenger as a captain and professor of military studies.[31] He may have taught one of Ewald's future comrades, Captain Johann Heinrichs as well.[32] Under Mauvillon's tutelage Ewald published his first military treatise, *Gedanken eines hessichen Officier uber das, was man bey Fuhrung eines Detaschements im Felde zu thun hat. (Thoughts of a Hessian officer about what he has to do when Leading a Detachment in the Field.)* in 1774. As indicated by the title, the work concerned the command of detached forces, in other words, small units operating under the command of a junior officer. His work was therefore dedicated to *petite guerre*, or *kleinen krieg* which had been attracting the attention of military theorists across Europe since just after the War of the Austrian Succession.[33]

Petite guerre, sometimes known as the war of posts, consisted of the constant operations of small units around the main armies. These activities included raids, patrols to gain information or simply disrupt the rear areas of an opponent, and the seizure of goods through what were referred to as contributions. Such operations required a great deal of initiative on the part of junior officers. For this reason, they offered junior officers a forum in which they could make a name for themselves. It was this issue which Ewald addressed throughout his work.[34]

Ewald's *Thoughts* is worth some scrutiny at this juncture as it was his first contribution to the literature of the military profession. In that vein, it provides a snapshot of how Ewald understood his profession at a relatively early point in his career, though he possessed over a decade's worth of experience by the time he composed the work. Likewise, it established him as at least a minor contributor to the Military Enlightenment.

One of the most respected scholars of the movement, Azar Gat, describes emergence military enlightenment as follows, "In the middle of the eighteenth century a sharp upsurge in the volume of military literature—reflecting an intense and unique intellectual activity—took place in Europe, spreading from France to the rest of the continent."[35] To some extent, this trend emerged in a profound increase in the number of works published on military matters. Of greater importance in the current context, however, were the intellectual underpinnings which exemplified the majority of these works. Gat notes, "The scientific model was perceived by them as a general method for the foundation of all human knowledge and activity on an enduring basis of critical empiricism and reason."[36] For many of the authors, both military and civilian, who now began to analyze warfare, it was ruled by tradition and prejudices handed down from previous ages. The solution, then, was to apply the predominant outlook of the period to the military field.[37] As Gat summarizes,

> *Indeed, the military thinkers of the Enlightenment maintained that the art of war was also susceptible to systematic formulation, based on rule and principle of universal validity which had been revealed in the campaigning of great military leaders of history. At the same time, it escaped formalization in part, while the rules and principles themselves always required circumstantial application by the creative genius of the general.[38]*

As will be shown below, Ewald's *Thoughts* or Gedanken thoroughly conformed to the parameters set out in the preceding description.

Ewald opened the work by giving thanks to the Landgraf: "This little effort from my studies and experience is here laid at your feet. I would not have dared to see the heights to which this manuscript has risen by your giving it permission to be printed."[39] While such an acknowledgement was customary, it indicates the author's gratitude for the Landgraf's permission to print the work, as well as some lingering gratitude on Ewald's part for the leniency shown him by his sovereign after the dueling incident.

Following the dedication, there is a foreword. The first paragraph establishes quite plainly Ewald's reason for writing and is therefore worth quoting at some length:

> *Since man first encountered the dangers of war, a deceptive prejudice has developed, as if it only is in the war itself that one could learn. To a large extent, in this century, many have enlightened us and*

delivered into the hands of men the finest works in the science of war.
They have excelled at accommodating us with a systematic knowledge
of the war. They have started us on the way, to see the art of war as
a science.[40]

It is readily apparent from the preceding that Ewald perceived war
to be a science, something that could be studied and understood, as opposed to some mystical activity that only those with a certain gift could
in engage in with any real hope of success. It follows then, in Ewald's
framework, that if war could be understood, certain principles could be
found that when applied, would allow one belligerent to defeat the other.
War therefore became, at least to some extent, a sort of equation. Success
would be more likely if one belligerent applied these principles while the
other neglected them in full or in part. At the same time, he is far from
reductionist. Time and again throughout the work, Ewald stresses the importance of experience and careful observation of surroundings. All of this
may seem abstract in the extreme. Ewald, however, does not dwell on such
abstracts, he is infinitely practical in the work, providing examples of how
a detached force should be led in day to day operations.

The main section of the work opens with a discussion of how a commander should govern his troops on the march, and in the attack and defense of various fortifications. In explaining his recommendations, Ewald
routinely makes use of examples, both from the Seven Years' War just
passed and from other historical conflicts. Thus, not only did the *Thoughts*
demonstrate that he had read significantly in the other contemporary authors on *petite guerre*, it contained Ewald's original ideas as well. In the
"Vorrede" or "Forward" of his *Thoughts*, Ewald cites La Cointe, Grand-
masion and Jenny specifically as inspirations.[41] It would not have been
very difficult for Ewald to read these works, as there were several German
publications that aided in their dissemination throughout the German
States.[42] Concerning his reading of the various military works available to
him Ewald noted that "it benefits and officer a great deal if he develops
a knowledge of such works in peacetime."[43] Essentially, he was mixing
together the ideas of these men with his observations from his own military experience. This was an approach Ewald would utilize throughout his
writing career, the only exception being his diary of his experiences during
the American War of Independence.

For instance, in his first chapter, on "How an officer behaves when
leader of detachments on the March," Ewald cites as an example, a patrol
led by Marshal Schomberg during the War of the Spanish Succession.
The use of this somewhat obscure example demonstrates Ewald's depth

of reading in military history.[44] Likewise, it is clear that he had at least begun to acquire some facility with French as well. In later years, he often used French to communicate with English officers while serving in North America.[45]

As important as his growing intellectual ability, Ewald demonstrated growing practical skill as a solider as well. For instance, he noted the importance of reconnaissance and a solid knowledge of the terrain one was operating in for the successful conduct of the march. At one point, in the first chapter, he observes that when operating in a strange locale, a detachment should be sent out ahead, composed of about fifty men. These men should be ordered to "…search everything exactly look around at all times so that nothing evades their eyes"[46]

Gathering intelligence on local conditions stands as a theme throughout the work as well. Later, Ewald notes "When we find ourselves in places such as villages, manner houses, mills or mountains we must at all times send some man forward to inquire with the residents about the enemy."[47] He follows up this injunction with the admonition to officers that "It is essential before you march your troops through [an area] to gain information about its layout yourself."[48] As will be seen subsequently, a personal reconnaissance prior to bringing his troops into an area was a habit Ewald would routinely practice during his service in North America.

The second chapter deals predominantly with the construction and defense of field fortifications. It is therefore for the most part fairly technical. Ewald opened the chapter with the reflection "There are thousands of cases that occur in the field, which create a need for the construction of such works."[49] This declaration served to underscore the importance of possessing a thorough knowledge of these works, and especially their defense. Ewald spends little time of the actual construction of the works, observing, "I have often talked with many sensible officers about the defense of field works, the greater part would rather strengthen the work than actually defend it."[50] He does, however, tell his readers to consult one of the specific works on military engineering he cites. He then went on to discuss how it was possible to defend works successfully. In doing so, he drew upon his personal experiences at several of the engagements of the Seven Years' War including the siege of Kassel, and the battles of Velllinghausen and Amöneburg. The details of Ewald's experiences at all of these engagements were discussed in the preceding chapter. Again, his experiences in these battles clearly exerted a profound influence on the development of his military thought.

As noted above, Ewald described what he perceived to be the important characteristics of an officer in these endeavors. One quality that held a high rating for the lieutenant was honor. This concern over honor emerges in the third chapter when he discusses the defense of redoubts by a detachment. Ewald begins with the assertion that the staunch defense of a redoubt, even if unsuccessful in the end, should win laurels for the defenders.[51] He then proceeds to describe what he perceived to be the key elements in the defense of a redoubt, citing historical examples and the works of other contemporary military writers where relevant. Interestingly, Ewald often changes sides in the work. In other words, he discusses the defense of field works in the third chapter, then looks at the same situation from the opposite side in the next.

In the fourth chapter Ewald discusses the attack of field works. Here again he stresses the role of the officer, observing "An officer, who is in such a commanding position, cannot be vigilant enough, inasmuch as the peace and security of a whole army are based on it, without earning the reproaches which he receives when he loses his post by his own guilt."[52] He likewise reinforces the importance of reconnaissance and intelligence gathering, especially with respect to the terrain, "Before proceeding to the attack, one must try to find out the position and the lay out of the entrenched post, either with his own eyes, which is the best, or by spies, in order to the develop a thoughtful plan of attack."[53] Ewald further provides a number of points the commander should consider in planning an attack,

> *It is necessary to know all the approaches and paths leading to these posts, and how they are to be made. Second, one must know the strength of the crew who defend it. Thirdly, we must know how far the next post of the line, which may come to its aid, is separated from it. Fourthly, whether the post is provided with foxholes, pallisades, and sally-ports, and whether there are wolf-pits and chaff-mines in the same.*[54]

In the fifth chapter, Ewald address the fortification of various posts. These include such important points as manner houses, churches and castles. First, he addresses how to take such positions. Then, when discussing their defense, he notes,

> *But if one intends to make a stand at the position which is to be defended, it is also well to dig a trench around it. Then proceed as I have mentioned above regarding how to put your men around the wall.*[55]

He goes on to admonish his readers,

We must take care, however, to cut down all the trees in the hedges, so that when the enemy arrives, he is exposed from head to foot. Close all exits, as already mentioned, as well as the lowest windows. The staircase on the lower floor must not be forgotten, and to climb up, a ladder is to be used, which after being ascended, is drawn up behind.[56]

Finally, he observes that the commander should

Then his men were put into the rooms, so that he might find adversaries in every place. These men could fire out of the windows, and when they load, they place themselves on the walls, when they are sufficiently covered from the small arms fire.[57]

The fortification of these posts served as important prelude to the topic of the following chapter.

The sixth chapter, then, focused on the defense of churches, manner houses and like posts, Ewald notes "The arrangements for the attack and taking of these positions are precisely adapted from those for the attack on redoubts."[58] The preceding illustrates an important point concerning Ewald's writing style. He tried to keep his explanations as concise as possible. Rather than engage in an extended explanation of why he advocated a certain approach, he often left that task to the supporting examples he provided. Again, in this chapter, Ewald draws on the French theorist and author Folard as support for some of his own ideas. The Hessian lieutenant seemed particularly influenced by Folard at this point in his career, as he often cited the Frenchman's works.[59]

He went on to observe "that for a brave officer, considering the attack as well as the defense of a post, must think and meditate on a thousand means, how he can thwart those who would oppose him, and how a happy stroke can be obtained."[60] The defense is more than simply a matter of the placement of troops however. For Ewald, bravery and honor always constituted core values. For instance, shortly after the preceding, he noted, "For one must be bold in war, but do not call the fearful intentions of exaggerated caution the advice of prudence."[61]

In the seventh chapter, *On the Fortification and Defense of Villages,* Ewald moves beyond the main subject and indicates that he is going to develop more of an overall system.[62] Again, he sets out his thesis for the chapter clearly, "I will show in this section of the treatise on the defense of the fortresses and houses how one should behave to counter the enemy with a stubborn defense in one of these posts."[63] He further observes "It will be seen from this that the security of the armies is based on the defense which is associated with the proper vigilance, insight and determination."[64] If these attributes are employed in the defense of a post, then an officer in charge of such a post is his own "commander-in-Chief, he understands his craft and thereby attains the greatest fame."[65] The concern for reputation and advancement in the service through honorable conduct again serving as a theme in the writing.

As he wraps up this section, Ewald refers to several plans he had drawn and included in the work in order to better clarify his ideas.[66]

Ewald begins the eighth chapter, on the defense of villages, building on ideas already set out. He notes,

Since the fortification and defense of villages requires many of the same insights as that of the small post, it is important to keep in mind that it is precisely in the attack of the on those places which many of the hardships and obstacles which cannot be foreseen or avoided lie.[67]

Building on this assertion, Ewald returns to one of his key concern, the acquisition of local knowledge. This is the first thing the commander of a detachment should do when they enter a village to defend it. Intelligence can come from a number of sources, especially if the commander is willing to use money to acquire it.[68] As will be seen, Ewald would often put this idea into practice when he deployed to North America. Once intelligence is gathered, "one must design his plan and carry out the enterprise with due intelligence, courage, and determination.[69]

Ewald further details the manner in which to launch an attack on a village occupied by the enemy,

All the units must have an officer with twenty men at the front, who undertakes the beginning of the attack with the greatest vivacity, and which the rest of the team follows fifty steps to the rear. The men in advance sneak up as near as possible, and with those supporting, double their steps, and seek with them at the same time those of the enemy entrenchment. The small units, which are supposed to march at the head, must be six men deep and as closed as possible, so that the attack has the proper strength and force.[70]

Stealth, speed, force and solid planning on the part of the commander all come together in the prosecution of a successful assault.

The ninth chapter of *Thoughts* covers retreats. Ewald begins by building on previous concepts, observing that "If an officer follows the fundamentals I introduced in the first chapters, it will be impossible for him to be surprised."[71]

Finally, in the tenth chapter, Ewald addresses the topic of actual partisan actions. He begins by noting the success of these groups in the recent Seven Years' War.[72] He goes on to note how these troops are best suited to operations in wooded areas, questions the use of cavalry, especially dragoons, in this role, as was sometimes practiced.[73] Ewald again stresses the acquisition of intelligence by the commander. The leader of a partisan corps in an area "must, as I have stated, know exactly all areas of the country where he will operate."[74]

In his *Thoughts*, Ewald reveals himself as a budding soldier-intellectual, with a keen analytical mind. His scrutiny of events in the war in which he had so recently served stood as harbinger of the approach he would take in his diary, as well as his latter professional writings.

Ewald would approach a topic, the defense of redoubts for instance, and discuss what he perceived to be the best practice on the subject. He would then support his ideas with examples from both the Seven Years' War, and the ideas of various military authors cited above. He also drew upon other historical examples where applicable in support of his ideas. While his reading in military history was far from complete, he did deploy a remarkable breadth of examples in his *Thoughts*. These characteristics combine to bestow on Ewald's treatise an internal cohesion which makes it more of an extended argument.

Among the topics Ewald address repeatedly in his work is the leadership of troops on detached service, fitting given the title. Throughout *Thoughts*, Ewald advocates for certain qualities a successful leader of troops on detached service should possess. These include an eye for terrain, and concern for regular reconnaissance and posting of reliable sentries. He frequently gives examples of how a leader should balance caution and boldness in his operations. Ewald was a supporter of the notion of calculated risk in military actions. Likewise, he routinely stresses the determination of troops to put up a courageous resistance even against superior odds to preserve and enhance their personal honor. He began to develop the importance of a soldier's honor in combat as a key role from the outset. Using examples from recent conflicts he hoped would resonate with his readers. For instance, he described how serving with the Regiment von Gilsa in 1762, they had met and defeated an enemy force, taking numerous prisoners.[75] Likewise, he noted how during the allied army's feint in the attempted relief of Kassel, "the Prince Ferdinand of Brunswick had to make a false attack on Krassberg before Kassel, which the French had entrenched with great skill."[76]

The scientific aspect of Ewald's views on war reappears shortly thereafter in his discussion regarding the defense of posts. He observes a number of precautions incumbent on the commander, chief among them being the gathering of intelligence from the local population, "It is necessary, however, to inquire, on one's arrival about the region which is leveled in the back and sides [of the detachment]; whether a hollow path, gorge, or otherwise hidden place, whereby the enemy can secretly sneak in, is nearby…"[77] He further notes particular geographical features the commander should be aware of in setting out his camp, such as sudden drop offs near the campsite. He observes, again drawing on his own military experience, "such sloping angles must either be guarded, or they should be blocked with trees and deep trenches, so that the enemy could not possibly advance without the greatest difficulties. I have once found myself, in one of these cases in the wretched war."[78]

Certainly, there were some topics Ewald consciously avoided. For instance, concerning the war of posts he was addressing in the *Thoughts*, he notes, "I am not going to go into details as what the service is called by different armies, and what an officer has to do to disengage those detachments or to have the fall back. For these things, every officer has his predetermined set of rules."[79] Ewald was not one to let himself get bogged down in minutia.

Small unit tactics would be the focus of much of Ewald's subsequent military career, especially in North America. Prior to that time, however, it is important to note that his work had been only theoretical. The treatise was dedicated to the Landgraf, who in turn sent Ewald a letter of appreciation.[80] This marked a significant step forward for the young second lieutenant as it began what would become a long and respected career as a military author and analyst. In a more concrete sense, on March 6, 1774, Ewald received a clear indication of the Landgraf's approval in the form of promotion from second lieutenant to the rank of captain and was reassigned to the Hesse-Kassel Lieb Jäger Corps, which was based on the town of Waldau, and later moved to Müllertor (now near Holländischer Platz) in Kassel.[81] The unit was initially designed to be a full corps, however, in keeping with the pervasive economies in post-war Hessen-Kassel, the unit remained limited to a company.[82]

Several factors distinguished the Jäger from the other line troops. One was their distinct uniforms, with green coats as a reminder of the origins among the huntsmen. The Jäger carried a short hunting rifle, also known as a Jäger, as well as a sword from the foresters of the state. Third, the

Jäger were considered experts at irregular warfare, the small war that raged constantly between armies in the field, in part because they were used to tracking prey in the forests. This was the war of posts, comprised of ambushes, raids and rapid movement by small forces.[83]

The use of these units expanded dramatically with the outbreak of the War of the Austrian Succession. At the outset of this conflict, hard pressed for troops, the empress Maria Theresa had called up contingents from her border with the Ottoman Empire and sent them to fight against Prussia and France. Since the type of fighting these troops regularly engaged in encompassed the so-called war of posts, they, in turn, brought this form of combat with them to central Europe.[84] Both France and Prussia responded to the threat posed by these troops by raising contingents of similar troops. It is worth noting, that not all troops designated as Jäger or chasseurs (their equivalent in French) truly deserved the title. Still, the Hessian Jäger seemed to be authentic enough.[85]

With the outbreak of the Seven Years' War, the Hessian state once again turned to its Hunter and Forester guilds to supply men adept in woodcraft.[86] As before, a primary skill of these troops was marksmanship, and these men were supposed to be able to hit a mark at 300 paces.[87] While this description is certainly lacking in clarity, if a pace is taken to be roughly one yard, then hitting at 300 yards remains an impressive feat considering the real killing zone for a contemporary musket was eighty yards or less.[88] The aimed fire of the Jäger stood as their chief contribution to the war effort, as during this period most regular troops were trained to point their weapons in the direction of the foe rather than take careful aim.

Beyond marksmanship, the Jäger were expected to possess a "familiarity with the woods and fields as well as combat readiness at all times and in all conditions..."[89] Tactically, they fought in open order. This implied that the men serving in the Jäger Corps were expected to have greater self-discipline and individual initiative than the men in the regular line units. These qualities undoubtedly served to enhance the combat value of the Jäger who were considered elite troops. The fact that, initially at least, each Jäger brought along his own weapon, certainly contributed a great deal to this sense of esprit d'corps.

The most recent incarnation of the Jäger was founded as a special unit of the Hessian army, the Chasseurs d'Armee, by Major Johann Gottlieb Rall in 1762.[90] It was recruited from the elite of the other Hessian regiments. Once formed, the men were trained by the Jäger of the state in the techniques of light infantry warfare. This was significant in that it helped to integrate the Jäger into the regular standing army, a process one historian has referred to this as domestication. At the same time, it reduced the burden of service on the actual hunters on the royal lands, who could now return to their forest work with the end of hostilities. Finally, it enhanced the discipline necessary for the successful conduct of irregular operations.[91] According to one source, the French soon began to fear the Hessian Jäger.[92]

For the remainder of the war, the Jäger were utilized predominantly for flank protection or to support and attack with their targeted rifle fire. Their other duties included acting as the rear guard when the army was on the march, serving as escorts during foraging operations and providing sniper fire during sieges.[93]

For the Hessen-Kassel Jäger, their baptism of fire in the Seven Years' War came at the battle of Sandershausen, on July 23, 1758.[94] Ironically, this took place at the same battlefield Ewald's uncle took him to in a last-ditch effort to dissuade him from a career in the military. In one of the Jäger more desperate actions, they took part in the defense of Kassel against the French invasion under Marshal Soubise. During this operation, the Hessian Jäger served under the command of Prince Ysenburg, who had the Jäger hold their position valiantly until the prince withdrew the remnants of the unit.[95]

During the Seven Years' War, the Jäger consisted of two companies of mounted and two companies of foot Jäger. After the war, however, as another facet of the Landgraf's attempts at economy, the corps was reduced to only the Lieb-Jäger Company. This small force was returned to its prewar duties as foresters and game wardens.[96] As noted, in 1774, the force was reconstituted, with a second company added with Ewald made its captain.[97] As noted, Ewald's appointment stood as a clear sign of the Landgraf's esteem for him, and the impact of this treatise, especially given Ewald's common ancestry. For Ewald, on the other hand, his promotion constituted a high honor, and it came with many benefits. Not least among these advantages was that he now had a unit with which he could test out the theories he had developed in his studies in actual practice.[98]

Ewald's new command was stationed by Waldach, where there was also a school of forestry. The proximity to the school encompassed one of the reasons for the units being stationed there as all the recruits for the corps were required to be skilled foresters.[99] The unit was composed of 102 men under the command of Ewald and a Lt Lorey.[100] The promotion came at an opportune time, as Ewald had significant debts to pay his creditors.[101]

The period after the Seven Years' War was thus one of great professional development for Ewald. He continued in his career in the army of

Hessen-Kassel, even attaining promotion twice. This stood as quite an accomplishment considering the control exercised by the Hessen nobility over positions in the officer corps. In addition, he continued to grow in his chosen profession, first attending the Collegium, and then publishing his own treatise. As Ewald pursued his career goals, half a world away, events were taking shape that would soon sweep the newly promoted captain up in their maelstrom. He would once again smell the smoke of battle and encounter a whole new set of military adventures from which he would draw later lessons.

With the end of the Seven Years' War, or French and Indian War (In America) in 1763, most of Britain's North American colonies saw themselves as proud subjects of the empire won in the contest. This perception would soon alter rapidly, and for the worse. The beginning of the decline can be traced back to the short-sighted policies of General Jeffrey Amherst while he was commander of British troops in North America. In an attempt to reduce the expenses of his command in the aftermath of the war, Amherst curtailed the practice of gift-giving as part of Indian diplomacy. The result—an uprising by various Native American groups known as Pontiac's Rebellion.[102]

While British arms successfully put down the rebellion, the new king, George III issued the Royal Proclamation of 1763, halting westward settlement of the colonists until a more peaceful and cost-effective method of expansion could be developed. Likewise, it was decided to maintain a force of roughly 10,000 regular troops in North America to provide for colonial defense. The London ministers further reasoned that it was only logical to expect the colonies to foot at least a part of the bill for their own defense.

There followed a whole series of measures, beginning with the Sugar Act of 1764 designed to offset, at least in part, the cost of colonial defense. The response of the colonies was as unexpected in London as it was drastic. Committees of Correspondence, especially active in the New England colonies, organized protests. Simultaneously, groups of laborers and craftsmen calling themselves the Sons of Liberty rioted in the streets.

The policies of Great Britain's ministry towards her North American colonies generated ever greater protests, culminating in the Boston Massacre of March 5, 1770. In the months following the violence in the streets of Boston, the British ministry and the instigators of American protest both stepped back from the looming precipice of civil war. Still, the home country and the colonies had already crossed a fateful line in the colonial relationship.

The Tea Act of May 10, 1773 launched a renewed wave of colonial protests, with the Sons of Liberty resuming their coercive tactics against merchants attempting to sell the tea. These activities reached their greatest manifestation in the Boston Tea Party of December 16 that same year. The better part of three shiploads of tea were dumped into Boston Harbor by the Sons of Liberty.

Responding to what was perceived as a direct challenge to his control of the colonies, George III determined to make an example of Boston, and dispatched additional troops, as well as guiding through Parliament a series of measures known as the Coercive Acts (Intolerable Acts in North America). These closed the port of Boston until the value of the Tea was repaid, imposed a virtual martial law on the colony, under the governorship of General Thomas Gage, commander of British troops in North America. In addition, they removed the trial of all capital crimes from the colony.

These actions, meant to break the back of colonial resistance seemed to have the opposite effect, stiffing the resolve of the colonists to resist British efforts at control. The colonists came together for the first time in the Continental Congress and worked to protest against what they perceived as the ministry's repressive measures. At the same time, the militias in various colonies began to drill again. Tensions were building, and many perceived a military confrontation as a fore drawn conclusion.

Within less than a year of assuming his post as military governor of Massachusetts, on April 18, 1775, Gage ordered troops into the countryside to arrest two known leaders in the rebellion, John Hancock and Samuel Adams, as well as to seize some valuable military stores he had learned about from loyalist informants. These orders sparked the confrontations at Lexington and Concord on April 19. On that day, a political confrontation grew into a military one. Receiving the news in London, the king determined to crush the rebellion as quickly as possible.[103]

Great Britain had developed a fairly solid machinery for waging war over the course of the eighteenth century. They possessed good local recruiting grounds in Ireland and Scotland. Likewise, their ties with continental powers, especially the smaller German principalities, allowed them to rent ready-trained military forces until those of the British Empire were recruited and brought up to combat readiness. Thus, Great Britain once again resorted to the time-honored tradition of subsidy treaties to provide some of the troops necessary to suppress the colonial insurrection.

This policy grew more urgent after the fighting outside Boston at Breed's Hill on June 17, 1775. While the British regulars managed to take the tactically important territory, they only accomplished their mission at the cost of nearly a thousand casualties. In order to launch subsequent operations, trained reinforcements were needed in North America.

Shortly after Bunker Hill Colonel William Faucitt went to Hanover and began inquiring after troops from the various German princes. Some of these rulers had previously contacted the British King and offered the services of their troops, since Britain had often utilized continental forces in its previous wars in the eighteenth century.[104] Faucitt was directed to offer generous terms to the various German rulers in order to secure the largest numbers of troops as swiftly as he could and in so doing to provide an army with which Britain could crush the American rebellion as quickly as possible.[105]

The treaty signed between Faucitt and the Hessian Minister Schlieffen reaffirmed the previous agreements between the two states, as well as providing for mutual aid in case either were attacked. The second point held great value for a smaller European state such as Hessen-Kassel. Under the terms of the treaty, Hessen-Kassel was to provide a corps of four grenadier battalions, fifteen line infantry battalions and two Jäger companies. Each of the battalions would bring along its organic artillery pieces as well. These amounted to two three-pounder guns and their crews per battalion.[106]

In order to ensure prompt delivery of the troops, the Landgraf gave orders that some thirteen battalions be ready to march on February 15, 1776, before the treaty had even be ratified in Great Britain.[107] The first division left their garrisons in Hessen-Kassel in February and March of 1776 and marched in easy stages. They had rest breaks every fifth day. They made their way through Hanoverian territory to an encampment near Bremerlehe.[108] Ewald was with the Jäger in the second division based in the vicinity of Kassel under the command of General von Knyphausen. This unit was given orders to march on May 9, 1776.[109]

They marched past Gottingen, Hanover, and through Hadeln and Rittzenbuttel and arrived at Luxhaven on June 3. Their march took twenty-one days. The units composing the second division were then inspected by Colonel Faucitt.[110]

From this point, the second division boarded ships for the remainder of their journey to North America. Ewald's Jäger Company, numbering some 125 men was berthed on a Dutch ship named *The Three Sisters*. They were joined on board by 175 men from the Wissenbach and Stein Regiments. Beginning on June 9. The ship sailed down the Elbe River, and then made a thirteen-day voyage for Spithead off Portsmouth in England, where it joined a larger convoy that included troops from the second division of Brunswickers and the Waldeck Regiment. The entire convoy composed of sixty-one transports and three frigates for escort set sail for New York on June 28.[111]

They were driven back into post shortly thereafter by adverse sailing conditions. The convoy remained in harbor until July 20.[112] Finally, they set sail for America.

CHAPTER 4

COMING TO AMERICA, THE 1776 CAMPAIGN

To their great relief the Hessian Jäger aboard their British transports sighted land on October 17, 1776. While it had not been a particularly rough crossing, it should be remembered that many of these men had not even ridden on a small river craft before, much less crossed an ocean. Thus, their sense of relief only grew as they entered the Hudson estuary at around noon on the following day. As news of the military situation began to make its way to the transports, it likely seemed to Ewald and his men that they had arrived just in time to gain some combat experience since at this point, the military fortunes of the Americans were close to their nadir.

After the British evacuated Boston, both sides prepared for a new encounter.[1] Both armies set their sights on New York City. Strategically, New York encompassed the most logical target. After all, the city possessed a number of advantages that Boston simply did not. It was centrally located along the east coast of North America, and it possessed a deep-water port making it an ideal anchorage for the transports and warships of the Royal Navy. As one recent history summarized, "There was adequate anchoring ground in Raritan Bay and plenty of beach space on Staten Island and Long Island to land and protect an army."[2]

Of the two rivers that flowed passed the city, the Hudson offered access to the interior of the continent as far as Albany. From there it would be possible to open communications with other Crown troops stationed in Canada. If a link could be made with the Crown forces in Canada, it could serve to cut off the remainder of the colonies from what was rightly perceived as the center of the rebellion in New England. In addition, the city and its environs were home to substantial numbers of loyalists. These people could aid the British in the restoration of Crown authority in the region. Once secured, therefore, New York would make an excellent base of operations, a lynch pin to swing the door closed and shut off the supply of manpower and material going to fuel the rebels in New England. All of these factors combined to make New York a much more appealing target than Boston from the British perspective.

The Americans perceived these same strategic assets as well. John Adams of Massachusetts called it a "kind of key to the whole continent."[3] Both Congress and Washington understood the importance of preventing British forces from securing a deep-water port on the coast, especially one that provided such access to the interior of the Continent. Defending the port against a British incursion would be a difficult proposition, however, as the colonists had no navy to speak of, and thus would have to rely on land batteries to try and prevent the enemy from gaining a foothold on the continent.[4]

While most historians maintain that Washington sought to interdict the British in their attempt to take New York City, few had addressed how he planned to accomplish his goal. Mark Kwasny observes that by this time Washington had adopted the strategy of that revolved around defending strongpoints, explaining "By using fortified positions to guard key locations, Washington hoped to weaken the enemy army as it took each successive post."[5]   This war of posts comprised the type of fighting in which light troops, such as the Jäger, were designed to engage.

For the British, gaining control of the city would require additional forces. The necessary troops were already on their way as the British government set out to crush the rebellion in a single campaign through overwhelming force, the quick decisive victory. In pursuit of this goal, the ministry raised and dispatched a force of some 32,000 troops to North America, escorted by seventy-three Royal Navy warships, nearly half the strength of the fleet at the time.[6] Many of the troops sent to North American came from central Europe. Along with the advantages of this method already described, the services of these troops allowed the British to maintain important garrisons in their empire as well. In this instance, Britain, through the activities of their agent Colonel Sir William Faucitt, drew on troops from the states of Hessen-Kassel, Anhalt-Zerbst, Brunswick-Wolfenbüttel, Hessen-Hanau, Ansbach-Bayreuth, and Waldeck.[7]

The first Crown troops landed on Staten Island on July 2. The troops spent several weeks Staten Island, regaining their health after the long sea voyage. The commanders took the time to reconnoiter the area and plan their next move.

That next move came on August 22, when British and Hessian troops were moved from Staten Island to Long Island. By August 27 the overall commander, General William Howe, believed he had amassed sufficient troops and supplies. He then unleashed his forces against the

Americans with devastating results.[8] The Continentals were outflanked and driven into their fortifications on Long Island, where the Royal Navy could prevent their escape while the British land forces moved in for the final assault.

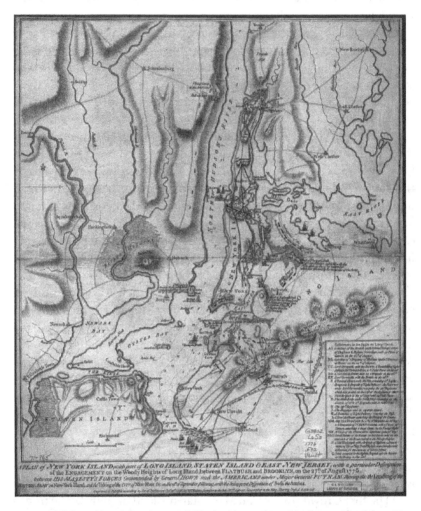

Figure1: William Fadden, A plan of New York Island, with part of Long Island, Staten Island & east New Jersey, with a particular description of the engagement on the woody heights of Long Island, between Flatbush and Brooklyn, on the 27th of August 1776 between His Majesty's forces commanded by General Howe and the Americans under Major General Putnam, shewing also the landing of the British Army on New-York Island, and the taking of the city of New-York &c. on the 15th of September following, with the subsequent disposition of both the armies. Scale ca. 1:85,000. Hand colored. Relief shown by hachures. Depths shown by soundings. Shows information to Sept. 23, 1776. Pictorial map. Annotated in lower right corner in pencil: 3rd impression. Includes "References to the battle on Long Island." LC Maps of North America, 1750-1789, 1144 Available also through the Library of Congress Web site as a raster image. Vault AACR2

Boldness, ingenuity, the sheer physical strength of a Massachusetts unit known as the Marblehead Mariners, along a thick fog combined to provide the Continental Army with an escape from Long Island to Manhattan.[9] While not a victory in and of itself, the evacuation of Washington's forces prevented them from being penned in and annihilated on Long Island.[10] The Continental Army's travails did not end once they were across the Hudson. Defending a city constructed on a series of islands against an opponent with a clear naval superiority proved impossible for Washington's green troops.

The action halted for the first few weeks in September, while the Howe brothers, acting in their role as peace commissioners, attempted to negotiate with the Continental Congress. While they did meet with representatives John Adams, Benjamin Franklin and Edward Rutledge on September 11, the discussions collapsed over the issue of independence.[11]

During this lull in the fighting, Washington, afraid that he might he trapped by the British in lower Manhattan, placed 5,000 troops there, and withdrew the remainder of his force to Harlem Heights. With the farce of negotiations ended, General William Howe soon launched his forces at the Americans. He began by landing 12,000 troops on Manhattan at Kip's Bay on September 15, leading to a small engagement with the Americans. The following day, September 16, occurred the battle of Harlem Heights. Finally, after some additional maneuvering as Howe sought to outflank the Continentals, came the battle of White Plains on October 28. Except for Harlem Heights, these battles were all American losses, and the cause, which had become one of national independence in July, began to look impossible.

Shortly after arriving, Ewald rode with a patrol out in search of fresh provisions, though his body was not as yet able to digest them after growing accustomed to the salt provisions on ship.[12] In this respect his experience was similar to that of many of the troops after making the Atlantic Crossing, they needed to become re-accustomed to life on land. At the same time, as he explored New York City, he noted that "More than a thousand houses which had formed the most attractive part of the city lay in ashes."[13] This devastation resulted from a major conflagration that engulfed the city shortly after the Americans abandoned the city and the British took possession of it on September 15. The fire broke out on September 21 and burned through most of the night. Between 10 and 25% of the Manhattan was destroyed in the fire which the British and many Loyalist who remained in the city blamed on American incendiaries. This belief was so prevalent that several people were killed in the streets of the city by angry mobs of citizens and British troops.[14]

Shortly after his initial reconnaissance, Ewald and his Jäger were assigned a camp on the perimeter of the main army. Once the Hessians made their camp, Ewald noted that numerous animals from the surrounding area were procured and the men began preparing their meals. He observed, "From this one can see how easily a good soldier knows his way about."

It was not long after his arrival that Ewald's company, which composed a part of General Knyphausen's Corps took part in their first action. On the morning of the 23rd, Ewald was ordered to headquarters, escorted by the English adjutant General Payne. At headquarters, Ewald's Jäger Company was inspected by Colonel Count Carl Emil von Donop, another veteran of the Seven Years War, known for his bravery in combat.[15]

Donop rose quickly during the previous conflict, becoming the personal adjutant to the Landgraf. He led the elite troops of the Hessian contingent, including the grenadiers and the Jäger. He was known for his impetuous nature, a trait that will be discussed in greater depth in connection with subsequent operations.[16] He was sometimes accused of being less than kind to enlisted men, but one Johann Conrad Dolha, who remained a private throughout his service in America called him as "an excellent man, experienced in war; above all polite and compassionate towards the officers and men."[17] By the same token, Donop was sometimes abrupt with subordinate officers. It was not an uncommon trait for superiors to be kind to the enlisted men, but less so towards inferior members of their own class.

Following the inspection, Ewald was ordered to follow the road he was on until he met with Captain Wreden and the 1st Jäger Company, which had preceded Ewald to America having sailed with the first division. He was to wait there for further orders, but Donop informed him "General Howe would reconnoiter the enemy position at Mile Square today and I would be used for the task."[18] As Ewald noted, "I was delighted with the message, for there was nothing I dreaded more in this world than a rest camp, and I wished for nothing more than to get to know the enemy." He added, "My wish was fulfilled within five hours."[19]

During this period, the British were in the process of driving the remains of Washington's Army from New York. William Howe, in overall command of British ground forces, along with his brother, Admiral Lord Richard Howe, overall commander of the fleet in North America also served as peace commissioners. The brothers insisted upon the dual appointments prior to agreeing to serve in North America. Their dual roles exerted significant influence on how the campaign developed.[20]

After receiving his orders, Ewald marched his men forward to rendez-vous with the First Jäger Company. As soon as the two companies met, they began to march, Ewald noting "The colonel ordered that as soon as the 1st Jäger Company drew up on the right side of the road I should proceed on the left side and try to keep abreast." The Jäger were being used as a screen for the remainder of the British and Hessian forces as they advanced against Washington's Continentals.[21]

Ewald's conduct during his first campaign in North America reveals his inexperience as a company grade officer. For instance, when "The colonel asked me whether it would not be better to intermix the two companies during the march, since the 1st Company had some knowledge of warfare in this county and knew the enemy." Ewald replied, "I requested, however, that this should not be done, because I wished to get acquainted with my men." While his request possessed some merit in that he hoped to get to know his men better, doing so under combat conditions may not have been the most opportune time. Colonel Knyphausen echoed this sentiment, "The colonel seemed to be disgruntled over this and exhorted the Jäger to demonstrate their good conduct, since they would get their first test today."[22]

Soon the men were on the march. They had been on the move for only a few minutes when shots rang out on their left.[23]

> *As I tried to gain a hill from which I could look around, our left wing suddenly came under fierce fire. With the half of the platoon I had taken with me I rushed toward the sound of the firing, where I found a handful of Jäger engaged with several battalions of Americans. I could not retreat, especially as I assumed that I was supported, and I could not advance with my few men, since I caught sight of a company nearby which must have belonged to the enemy.*
>
> *I maneuvered as well as I could to cover both my flanks, which had formed into a circle lying an acre's length apart under heavy fire. I discovered a house on a hill to the right toward which several jägers were crawling. Through their fire I gained some air on the right flank, but on my left I was completely hemmed in.*[24]

Ewald was saved from this near disastrous deployment of his troops by the timely arrival of Colonel Donop and some dragoons. Donop ordered Ewald to retreat, and he initially refused, causing Donop to remark, "You want to conquer America in one day! You write rules and then you violate them."[25] This second rebuke likely stung Ewald the most, as it referenced his own book on tactics. In this case, Donop was likely thinking of Ewald's oft-repeated injunction to reconnoiter the terrain an officer would be operating in prior to bringing his troops forward.[26]

Donop rode off, but returned shortly thereafter with some English light infantry, and two guns. These reinforcements provided Ewald with the opportunity to extricate himself from the situation his lust for action created.[27] While Ewald's handling of his men in the above encounter reveals his lack of experience in command at the company level, he did analyze his conduct afterwards. In Ewald's view "the entire misfortune had resulted from the fact that what the 1st Company took for an advance was, in my opinion, more of a retreat. Thus, I continued to move forward while the rest withdrew."[28] Therefore, he misunderstood the role his troops were to play in the action. While he may not have written that proceeding with a green company unsupported by more experienced troops had likely contributed to his predicament, the Jäger captain was at least drawing lessons from his experiences. These lessons came at some cost, Ewald reported that his losses in the engagement were six dead and eleven wounded. The latter included a Lieutenant Rau who was wounded in the foot and taken prisoner by the Americans.[29]

For his conduct in the engagement, Ewald received a sharp rebuke from General Heister, the commander of Hessian forces in the campaign.[30] General William Howe mollified this criticism by expressing his satisfaction with Ewald's actions through an adjutant.[31] This divergence in responses between Ewald's superiors likely stemmed from the riff already developing between them.[32] Howe did not care for Heister and would eventually have him removed from command of the Hessian contingent. For his part, Ewald derived satisfaction from the fact that on his first operation he managed to gain the attention of his superiors.

Soon after this initial encounter, a new deployment was announced. On October 25, it was decreed that the Donop Jäger Company would thereafter cover the right wing of the army on the march. Ewald's company would cover the left flank. Ewald continued, "Moreover, when the army marched in wing formation, or in two columns, a Jäger company was to serve as the advanced guard, supported by a battalion of light infantry."[33]

The Jäger were ideally suited to this sort of role, which included probing forward of the main force, searching for enemy traps, and reporting back any intelligence they came across concerning the enemy's whereabouts, number, movements or intentions. Simultaneously, the advanced troops served to screen the movements of their own forces from the enemy, denying him the same types of information they were hoping to collect. Posting in such a position further provided Ewald with an ideal command from which to hone his skills in independent leadership. At the same time, command of one of the advanced guards provided him with further opportunities to distinguish himself to his superiors.

As the British and Hessians moved out, Ewald led the advanced guard of the left column, under Hessian general von Heister. Prior to leaving camp, Ewald received orders to occupy a farm on the main road from East Chester. This placed him in an independent command for the first time. Ewald accepted this post with enthusiasm, "Here I was left alone for the first time with my own theory of partisan warfare, which I had acquired through much reading."[34] Now he would have the opportunity to test his theories under the conditions of actual combat.

Ewald took up a position in an apple orchard, surrounded by a stone wall, "behind which, since it lay on a hill, I thought I could defend myself well against an enemy attack."[35] Here there is the close eye on the terrain, and how to utilize it to the best advantage. His appreciation of the importance of terrain, something he already discussed in his first treatise, would mark much of Ewald's subsequent service in North America. Likewise, it would manifest in his later writings as well.

Once he had personally inspected his position, Ewald deployed his troops in order to take advantage of the terrain, "I placed two pickets on two knolls from which we could see far around, and dispatched constant patrols as far as Mile Square."[36] Here was an example of making the most out of the troops at his disposal.

Shortly after he occupied his new position, Ewald's Jäger again served as the advanced guard. On this occasion, they fought as the tip of the spear for a raid on a rebel supply depot. Ewald launched his company on the approach march. They had been on the move "scarcely an hour when we encountered an enemy patrol of riflemen which gave fire and ran back."[37]

The riflemen serving in the Continental army were considered elite troops by both sides. They were recruited from the backcountry of Pennsylvania, Maryland and Virginia and armed with a weapon alternatively known as the Pennsylvania and later Kentucky long rifle. The weapon most likely developed in the region of Lancaster, Pennsylvania during the 1720s. In fact, a local gunsmith named Martin Meylin is often credited with its invention. The long rifle he devised combined the length of the English fowling piece with the rifling of the central European rifle. The firearm created was long, possessed a narrow bore, using less powder, itself an important consideration on the frontier, where provisions were scarce. At the same time, it possessed extreme accuracy, being used by frontiersmen for hunting small game, both to supplement their tables, and for the value of the pelts thus acquired. As the rifle proliferated through the frontier, shooting contests became local events, and many men grew quite proficient in the use of the long rifle. Many of those who enlisted in 1775 were quite capable marksmen, being able to place a round in a target the size of a man's nose at the distance of 150 yards.[38] These troops, when properly deployed, could serve as excellent light infantry. The chief drawback to the long rifle as a military weapon was the fact that it could not mount a bayonet due to the shape of the barrel and the lack of a bayonet lug. This deficiency, combined with the rifle's slower reloading time, could leave a rifleman dangerously exposed between rounds.[39]

As the American riflemen retreated, several dragoons gave chase, but were unable to overtake them.[40] The column continued its march through the day. About six in the evening they came upon a farm the Americans were using as an outpost. The Jäger deployed in preparation for the attack, supported by the British light infantry and with the dragoons in the rear.[41]

The Jäger launched their attack and had a short skirmish with the American pickets. "Nearly everyone was struck down, and only a few officers and men were taken prisoner. The loss on our side was not over thirty men.[42] Once they had disposed of the defenders, the Jäger moved forward along a road leading to the American camp to take their true prize, the supply depot. "As much as possible, was carried away on wagons, and what could not be transported was destroyed."[43]

The above mission constituted the sort of work that the Jäger were initially recruited for in Europe and something they clearly excelled at in North America. Raids such as the one described above served several purposes simultaneously. They deprived the enemy of valuable logistics, and at the same time, contributed to the material support of the attacking force, a double-win. Likewise, they helped to undermine an opponents' morale and sew confusion in their ranks. Nothing can deprive an army of its desire to fight more than a lack of food, clothing, or other basic necessities.

Ewald and his men withdrew after midnight and covered the rear of the raiding party. They returned to camp and rejoined the remainder of the army on the 27th. The raid was quite successful, and it is with some pride that Ewald recollected "I had the honor to receive a compliment from the commanding general."[44]

Certainly, forays such as the one above provided Ewald with the opportunity to test out his ideas concerning partisan warfare. It should be recalled, that many of these ideas were developed based on a mixture of his own previous experiences combined with the writings of the other military theorists he had read back in Hessen-Kassel.[45] Now, for the first time, Ewald had the opportunity to put his theories into practice as the commander of a company, often serving as the vanguard, and so essential-ly on detached service. From the outset, Ewald's time in America offered him ample opportunity to test and refine his ideas on partisan warfare in the school of combat on an almost daily basis.

One aspect that stands out in Ewald's diary is his attention to terrain, a factor he often commented on in his *Thoughts*. This comes across clear-ly in his description of the area in which they were fighting. "The area was intersected by hills, woods, and marshes, and every field was enclosed with a stone wall."[46] At the same time, it should be noted that this was grueling fighting. Even after his return from the raid around midnight, Ewald and his men were expected to take their place on the march the following day.

The next morning, the British and Hessians set out. The right col-umn, under the command of General Sir Henry Clinton, was composed of the Donop Jäger Company, half of the 16th Dragoon Regiment, the 1st and 2nd Battalions of English Light Infantry under Colonel Abercromby, the three Hessian grenadier battalions, von Linsing, von Minnigerode, and von Block, commanded by Colonel von Donop.[47] The English Light Infantry Battalions were actually composed of the light companies of sev-eral regiments each. Ewald's company was posted to the left column under General Heister, and included the 17th Dragoon regiment, the 1st and 2nd English brigades, eight six pounders, and the von Lossberg and von Mirback brigades. A group of provincial troops covered the right flank of this column.[48]

The Army had been on the march for only about two hours when it came into contact with the advanced units of the Continental Army. Ewald's company engaged this advanced guard with the aid of the British Light Infantry.[49] Thus, over the course of twenty-four hours, Ewald and his troops took part in two engagements and returned with a quantity of enemy material!

The first major operation for the Crown forces following Ewald's ar-rival was the attack on White Plains on October 28. Ewald meticulously details the skirmishing that occurred as the two forces came into con-tact. As the armies came into position, Howe found Washington in a strong defensive posture on some high ground behind the Bronx River. The key feature of the American position was a rocky elevation about 180 feet high.[50]

Howe deployed his force of some 13,000 troops and had them march before the American position in full view, hoping to unnerve his oppo-nents. When this tactic failed, he ordered the Hessians troops forward.[51] Ewald described the role of the Hessian forces in the engagement,

The first assault by the Hessians on the American position was made on the left. While this assault by the left column was taking place, Colonel Donop hurried around from the right wing with the Hessian grenadier brigade to support the mounting attack, and tried to keep in alignment as much as possible. The two Jäger companies had to work their way under the heaviest enemy canon fire, through the ravines and marshes which lay between the two wings. Here we came upon a number of riflemen who were hiding in these ravines and only withdrew when they caught sight of us after sharp firing.[52]

The fighting continued through much of the day, when "Toward six o'clock in the evening, the enemy gave way on all sides. But since we could not pursue him further because of the extremely intersected terrain, he was able to take up a new position in the mountains within an hour's distance."[53] The reason for the American collapse was that Count von Donop managed to locate an unguarded pass that allowed them to attack the Americans in the flank. Much like the battle of Long Island, the Americans were defeated by the adroit use of a flanking maneuver on the part of the Crown forces. Donop personally led his men forward, and took the height, though at great cost.[54]

Ewald noted that "I think the losses were nearly equal on both sides. When I rode over the battlefield the next day, I counted about one thousand dead."[55] This is in keeping with estimates from both sides. One other British source claimed 349 killed and wounded out of their troops alone. Recently, David Hackett Fischer presented a total of about 313 killed and wounded for the battle, which amounts to a slightly conservative version of the above British figure.[56] British accounts notoriously downplay their own losses while inflating those of the Americans and ignoring those of the Hessians altogether. David Mc Cullough gives the very low figure of 250 casualties for the British and Hessians, however, he does point out that the victory did not give them any advantage either.[57]

After the fighting, Howe's army camped on the battlefield. Knyphausen's corps moved off in the direction of New Rochelle and took possession of the passes at King's Bridge. For his part, Ewald noted that Washington entrenched his camp and enclosed the center with an abatis. Howe sought to prevent this through frequent attacks on the American fatigue parties, resulting in "constant hard skirmishing."[58]

These small clashes between fatigue parties and raids sent to disrupt them continued through the night. "On the morning of November 3rd, the left wing under General Heister made a demonstration against the enemy's right, during which the right wing under General Clinton prepared for action." While Clinton engaged in this feint "Two battalions of English light infantry, which I joined with fifty Jäger, tried to seize a wood in front of the enemy's right wing."[59]

The result of these maneuvers was a skirmish that cost both sides several casualties. After the fighting, Ewald took up a post in an orchard a mere thousand paces from the enemy.[60] Again, this placed him in an excellent position from which to observe the movements of the enemy and gather intelligence concerning their intentions. At the same time, his proximity to the American forces meant that his troops were constantly exposed to attack and would be the first line should the Americans turn and snap at their pursuers.

On the morning of November 6, just before daybreak, the British army began a retrograde motion away from the Americans. Ewald reports that while the first units moved out in the predawn hours, due to the bad roads, the artillery and baggage could not be got off until three in the afternoon. Ewald's company marched as part of a third column under the command of Heister and served as the rear guard for the army.[61] The reason for this seeming retreat was the hope that General Howe could draw the Americans out of their camp and into a pitched battle. In this regard, the move was unsuccessful.[62] On November 7, the army camped on some heights near Dobbs Ferry, with its left flank resting on the Hudson River. In this position, the main army gave cover to the forces besieging Fort Washington.[63]

This was a newly-constructed fort situated on the northern end of what is now Manhattan Island. At the time, it stood as the last remaining American post on Manhattan Island. While Fort Washington was impressive in some respects, with outer works that were more than a mile in length, it was actually very weak. Its size meant that it was in fact too large for its 3,000-man garrison to adequately defend.[64] Fort Washington, and its counter-part, Fort Lee on the New Jersey side were intended to deny the British access to the Hudson River, however, their artillery was of insufficient weight to interdict the movements of the larger British vessels in the river. The British had already demonstrated this by sailing past the forts out of range of their guns. Though the forts could not achieve their intended purpose, several of Washington's subordinates, most notably Nathanael Greene, urged that they be retained as a means to prevent the British from moving on Manhattan. The primary responsibility for holding Fort Washington fell to Colonel Robert Magaw of Pennsylvania, the garrison commander. Magaw believed he could hold the post against a British attack as well. The garrison of the post contained many of the best troops of the Continental Army, including several units of Pennsylvania riflemen. In addition, it possessed strong artillery and contained large quantities of supplies. The essential problem lay in the fact that there existed no secure way to reinforce and resupply the fort across the Hudson, especially with British shipping in control of the river.[65]   If the defenders were to hold the fort, they would have to do so without hope of aid from the remainder of the army. Bit by bit, the noose began to tighten on the outstretched neck of Fort Washington, and Ewald with his Jäger played a major role in pulling the halter.

On the afternoon of the November 7, the Jäger went out and engaged American pickets in a sort of running skirmish, and occupied territory as the Americans fell back. During this fighting, Ewald observed that the Continentals had burned the houses of some Loyalists as they retreated, a practice of which he did not approve.[66] While Ewald certainly recognized the necessity of force to achieve goals in war, he routinely condemned attacks against civilians or their property. Perhaps the experiences of his native Hessen-Kassel in the Seven Years' War influenced his views on this point. Whatever their source, Ewald was quite candid regarding his feelings on this point in his diary, another facet that makes the work so invaluable for gaining an understanding of a Hessian perspective on the war.

In driving back the Continentals, Ewald and his men forced them into Fort Washington, preparing the way for operations to take the post. The attack on Fort Washington stood as the first major operation of the Jäger since their landing in North America. For the Crown forces, launching a frontal assault on a fortified position stood as a costly proposition, even if the post were cut off from resupply and reinforcements. While the Americans had often run from British and Hessians troops in the field, since the fighting at Bunker Hill the preceding year, they had maintained a reputation for making a staunch defense of fortified posts.

On the American side, the problems of defending the fort were compounded when the adjutant, on William Demont, deserted to the British and provided them with a complete plan of the works. Demont's intelligence placed General Howe in an excellent position to assault the works.[67]

Howe did not accept the information gained from Demont's treason at face value, and the low-level probing between the two forces continued for several days. It served as a means for both sides to get an idea of their adversary and his intentions. Likewise, it allowed the British commander to check his intelligence without committing to a full-scale attack. As a part of these maneuvers, on the 14th, Ewald was asked by von Donop to reconnoiter the "debauches to Fort Washington as closely and as carefully as possible, without risking capture or loss of life."[68] Entrusting the probe to Ewald gives some idea of the esteem in which he was held by von Donop.

Ewald took a Captain Pauli of the artillery with him along with two Jäger to serve as guards. He described their approach to the American post "We tried to crawl along the bushy bank of the North [Hudson] River without being discovered by the enemy." Once in position, Ewald and Pauli, "could see a long way off and observed the following."[69]

> *The fort is situated on a steep hill between the Hudson River and the Harlem Creek, where a single road winds. The terrain has been leveled for the distance of rifle or grapeshot range. The road runs up the hill through a wood which is cut through with rocks and deep ravines, and which has been made completely impassable by many abates. Several small works lie in the wood on the steepest height in front of the fort, one behind the other, which can fire upon the entire road.*[70]

In the above, Ewald demonstrated his fine attention to the details of terrain. Where one of Ewald's contemporaries described the post as "erected on a high rocky elevation, which seemed fortified by nature itself," Ewald presents much more thorough, technically detailed account, the sort of information to be expected from someone who planned possible assaults on the post as he observed its contours.[71] Returning with this description of the terrain and dispositions of the Americans around the fort, Ewald contributed in no small measure to William Howe's developing plan of attack on the post.

Howe thus concentrated more than 13,000 troops in all against the fort, more than four times the garrison. Still, this stood as an accepted ratio of forces for attacking an enemy in an entrenched position. In addition, William Howe had the support of some of his brother's ships in the Hudson River. The fort could now be attacked from all sides.

After observing the proper protocols and dispatching an officer with a demand for the fort's surrender on November 15, Howe prepared his attack. The Americans within the works rejected the call to surrender, and Nathanael Greene even sent in reinforcements to the post from Fort Lee.[72] General von Knyphausen was chosen to lead the attack against the post and divided his assault force into two columns accordingly.

The attack began on November 16. As British troops made their way into position using boats to cross the Harlem River, four thousand Hessians attacked the post on the landward side.[73] The two sides met outside the fort, and a fierce firefight ensued.

The fighting grew especially intense where the Hessians collided with American riflemen. The well-aimed fire of the latter exacted heavy casualties from the attackers. Eventually, however, the sheer weight of the combined assault drove the defenders into the center of the fort.[74] As Ewald noted, "All obstacles including the almost inaccessible cliffs and an abatis two hundred paces deep were overcome successfully, and one outwork after another was captured under the heaviest grapeshot and small-arms fire."[75]

Surrounded and cut off from any hope of further reinforcement or evacuation, Colonel Magaw surrendered the remainder of his garrison. In the ensuing confusion, the Hessians put some of the riflemen to death even after they had surrendered.[76] In all, the Americans lost some fifty-nine killed and ninety-six wounded. Additionally, 2,837 officers and men lay down their arms when the fort surrendered.[77] Conversely, the British placed their losses at eighty-four killed and 374 wounded. Ewald placed the losses at between seven and eight hundred, "among whom were very many officers."[78]

Just as damaging to the Americans as the losses in manpower were the material losses suffered in the capture of the fort. Ewald placed these at four 32-pounder cannon, two 18-pounders, seven 12-pounders, five 9-pounders, fifteen 6-pounders, eight 3-pounders and two howitzers. Likewise, large quantities of ammunition and other supplies were taken.[79]

The British invasion of New Jersey followed quick on the heels of the capture of Fort Washington. On the evening of November 19, British troops under Earl Charles Cornwallis crossed into New Jersey, making a night amphibious landing. Something which David Hackett Fischer lauds as an "extraordinary feat of soldiering."[80] Ewald and his Jäger took part in this operation, along with the English and Hessian grenadiers. They were accompanied by five English brigades. The units made their way to Phillipsburg on the Hudson River, and crossed into New Jersey on flatboats the following morning.[81]

Once on the New Jersey side, "We climbed ashore along a steep bluff and scaled the rocky and bushy height as quickly as possible."[82] As they emerged, the men came across several farms, or plantations as Ewald called them. The troops deployed in a semi-circle behind some stone walls on these properties and established a perimeter. Once they were joined by the grenadiers, the troops began to advance towards the town of New Bridge.

As they proceeded, Ewald discerned a farmhouse in the distance and took some of his Jäger forward to gain intelligence from the residents. During his conversation with the farmer, an event occurred that even years later kindled excitement in the author as evidenced by his reporting,

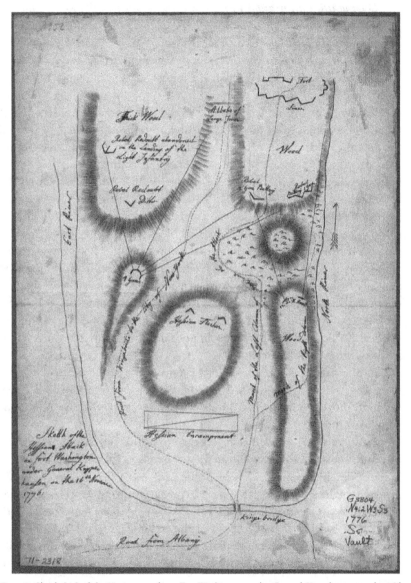

Figure2: Sketch [sic] of the Hessian attack on Fort Washington under General Knypehausen on the 16th November 1776. Scale not given. Manuscript, pen-and-ink (black and red). Relief shown by hachures. Shows route of march from Kingsbridge to the fort. LC Maps of North America, 1750-1789, 1164 Available also through the Library of Congress Web site as a raster image. Vault AACR2.

*During this conversation I discovered a great glitter of bayonets and
a cloud of dust in the distance. - Who is that? - That must be the
garrison of Fort Lee! - Can't we cut them off from the bridge? - Yes,
you have only two English miles from here to there! - I ran back to
Captain Wreden and told of my discovery.*[83]

Wreden, for his part, believed that the column Ewald observed was
actually the second column of the British army. Ewald recalled, "I wanted
to know the truth and took several Jäger with me to draw near this column
in the flank..." They went forward, "crawling from stone wall to stone
wall, and discovered that it was American."[84] The Americans, under the
command of General Nathanael Greene and in full retreat, were in the
process of making their escape down the western slope of the Palisades
through the area then known as English Neighborhood.[85]

On confirming the identity of the troops, Ewald, "began to skirmish
with them and sent back a Jäger to fetch more men, but instead I received
an order from Lord Cornwallis to return at once."[86] Since Cornwallis was
the overall commander of the force, Ewald had no choice but to comply.
Still, he did inform the Earl of his discovery. He was told, "Let them up
my dear Ewald, and stay here. We do not want to lose any men. One Jäger
is worth more than ten rebels."[87]

In accordance with these orders, Ewald broke off his skirmishing activity and waited as the reminder of the British army came ashore. They
began to move out again about four in the afternoon, with Ewald's company covering the right flank.[88]

As they moved forward, Ewald began to notice the rear of the retreating Americans. As they came into view, "I moved further to the right in
hopes of catching some baggage." Again, this was a classic element of the
petite guerre in which the Jäger were experts, capturing supplies and materials from the enemy, including officers, which could be valuable both
at the time for information then later for exchange. On this occasion, "A
coach and four with several men actually fell into my hands, but I hardly
wanted to pursue my game further, and I received orders to keep closer to
the column."[89]

These orders pushed Ewald to a new awareness of the parameters of
the American War. As he recalled, "Now I perceived what was afoot. We
wanted to spare the King's subjects and hoped to terminate the war amicably, in which assumption I was strengthened the next day by several
English officers."[90] Ewald's suspicions are supported by the testimony of

an American in Greene's command, a Sergeant White, who reported that the British "let us march by them, leaving all the camp equipage."[91]

By dusk on that day, Ewald reached Fort Lee. He reported that the army camp around the post "in great disorder." In addition, due to the precipitous nature of the American retreat, "a huge magazine of forage, flour, and biscuit," were left at the post.[92] Not only did the British and Hessian forces come into this windfall of supplies, but "During the night all the plantations in the vicinity were plundered and whatever the soldiers found in the houses was declared booty."[93] It is telling that Ewald did not differentiate between the property owned by Loyalists or Whigs in his account, which seemed to be the contemporary practice. Hessians troops were recognized for indiscriminate looting in areas they passed through during the advance into New Jersey. More recent investigation has shown that the British were culpable as well. This practice would have grave repercussions on the Crown efforts to the subdue the colonies in the near future.[94]

For Ewald, this was a time he had prepared for throughout his years of garrison duty. He was now often in command of his own detached force as his Jäger were routinely in the advanced guard of the army. As a result, he was very much responsible not only for the safety of his own troops, but for the security of the army as well. In one instance, he was posted about seven miles from Tappan in New Jersey. He later recalled that during this assignment, "On the 22d I was notified by headquarters that a corps of riflemen and horsemen had arrived at Tappan, and that I should be on my guard…" He went on to describe the challenges of his assignment, "since I now had no communication with the army and my post hung in the air." Still, Ewald arrived at a clear understanding of what he had to do, "Thus my entire safety depended upon reports of the enemy and constant patrolling which crossed around my outposts."[95] In many ways, Ewald's characterization of his post and its responsibilities resonates with any junior officer who has ever held a detached command. Likewise, it accords well with the ideas he had set out in his *Thoughts*. Thus, he was now putting those concepts into practical application.

The young captain likewise confronted the question of how he and his troops should conduct themselves in the conflict. As he noted concerning the civilian dwellings in his area of operations, "To be sure, I could plunder these prosperous inhabitants according to our rules…" What Ewald meant by the above was that standard European practice, especially for partisans was to live off the land in the areas where they operated, so plunder was tolerated. Some, such as the Pandour leader Francicus von der Trenck had made almost a profession of plunder until it led them into conflict with their own superiors. However, in the present conflict, Ewald recognized that such behavior came with serious negative repercussions, "but to convince these people that there were humane persons in our army, and to invite their good will and gratitude, I gave them every protection, and they forfeited nothing by my visit but several dozen chickens and one young ox."[96] While it was important to extract supplies form the local population, Ewald held back the hard hand of war from the civilians he came in contact with in New Jersey. He seemed to grasp that in the conditions of the civil conflict in which he was serving, winning the allegiance of the people constituted an important element in achieving final victory.

Now began the pursuit of Washington's beleaguered Continentals across New Jersey. From Fort Lee, the Americans retreated through Aquackanonk, Second River, Newark, Piscataway, down through Brunswick, Kingstown, and Princetown. They made their way through Maidenhead, and finally to Trenton by early December.[97] During this phase of the campaign, the British and Hessians hounded the Americans across New Jersey, and much of Washington's force, demoralized and their terms of enlistment growing short, simply abandoned the cause.[98]

Continuing with the pursuit of the retreating Americans, Ewald pushed on towards Tappan to attempt to gain information. He took twenty-four Jäger with him on the patrol, and left orders with senior officer of the company to follow him with the remainder when they heard only footsteps. This second detachment was to provide a covering force should one be necessary for Ewald's withdrawal.[99] This patrol led to a short skirmish in which Ewald had one Jäger wounded but inflicted some casualties on the enemy as well. These sorts of clashes composed the day to day routine of troops such as the Jäger at this time. It was hard, dangerous service tat exacted a heavy toll on the men.

During their operation, Ewald observed "Since all the plantations I passed were abandoned by their occupants and were plundered and destroyed, and I was not fortunate enough to take a prisoner, which was my intention, nothing much was accomplished."[100] His remark is telling in that it speaks to his growing professionalism. Ewald concerned himself more with gaining prisoners and the intelligence they could provide than with taking plunder, though, as noted above, it was his right under the conventions of war as he knew them form his experience in Europe.

The next day, the army marched again, and the Jäger skirmished with the Americans near a river crossing which the latter had destroyed behind them on their march southward. Soon Cornwallis arrived with the main British force and drove off the remaining Americans. The Jäger then ford-ed the river and took up a position on a nearby high ground from which they could simultaneously defend the crossing of the rest of the army and skirmish with the American rear guard as it retreated. That night, the army camped near Acquackannonck, with the Jäger posted ahead of the main army and to the right, along the road to Newark. Ewald noted the difficulties posed by the terrain, "The area was very woody and hilly." As a result, "The posts were so distant that our security depended upon vigilance and patrolling around us."[101]

Shortly after establishing their posts, Ewald and the Jäger Captain Wreden went out on a patrol, again to try and gain greater intelligence of their area of operations. In the course of their exploration, their forces became engaged with several American units at different times. While they managed to extricate themselves from each of the skirmishes, Ewald noted soberly, "This foray for refreshment could have been very costly for us if the enemy had retained his composure." Still, the value of the experience was not lost on the Jäger captain, "Meanwhile this stroke taught us novices in the art of partisan warfare what resoluteness can do."[102] It is interesting, as well, that Ewald continued to perceive himself as a novice in partisan warfare. Clearly, during his first campaign in America, Ewald seemed as if he were constantly learning how to conduct the operations of *petite guerre*, and the challenges to look out for as well.

Soon after Ewald's reconnaissance, the Jäger determined to set up an ambush in case the enemy should try to launch an attack on them. The ambush was composed of some thirty volunteers "whose hearts were not strengthened with wine and beer."[103] The force lay in wait until evening, but on this occasion no new fighting broke out.

On November 28, the army once again marched, this time in the direction of Newark with Ewald entrusted with the security of the right flank. As they progressed through the region, Ewald and his men witnessed "a deplorable sight." As he noted, "The region is well cultivated with very attractive plantations, but all their occupants had fled and all the houses had been or were being plundered."[104]

The topic of plunder by the Crown forces, whether British or Hessian, has already been touched on several times. It is clear from Ewald's account that the practice did take place. While he remained careful in his diary to refrain from laying the responsibility for plunder on any one group, it is commonly understood that the Hessians were most often the culprits. In their understanding, all Americans were rebels, and therefore, following the dictates of accepted European practice, their property was forfeit.[105] For his part, Ewald did not fully subscribe to this notion. In fact, it is clear he saw it as working against the strategic goal of the Crown forces. At one point, as the army continued its pursuit of Washington's Continentals across New Jersey, Ewald was given the Whig Governor William Livingston's house as his headquarters. He was informed "that this man was one of the first and most fiery rebels." Thus, his property was clearly forfeit, "But I was not inclined to turn robber, and everything was left undisturbed save for a few provisions."[106]

Shortly after this interlude Ewald earned a de facto detached command as the army began to march to the left. His corps, along with that of Major Maitland, was tasked with guarding the right flank and rear of the army, especially from American mounted forces. These partisans harassed the British rear through the entire march.[107]

While carrying out this assignment, Ewald sounded a lament familiar to any junior officer placed on detached command. "To perform this little feat for the first time was no small task. I received neither further instructions nor guide, except that I was told this road would lead there, and I would no doubt find someone on the way." Thus, he was dispatched with only the vaguest of guidelines for accomplishing his mission. Ewald went on, "I had nothing but my theory from which I could obtain advice." Here referring to the work he had written while attending the Collegium Carolinum in Hessen-Kassel, he now had the opportunity to put his ideas into practice. Not only was he bereft of clear orders but Ewald "knew the heavily intersected country only by a miserable map." Thus, one of his key principles, clear knowledge of the terrain in which one was operating, remained out of his grasp.

If this litany of problems were not enough, they were compounded by the fact that "My officers were young and inexperienced in this kind of warfare."[108] Finally, summing up his predicament, Ewald opined, "Honor was not to be gained with them, for what I did no one would see. But should I suffer a reverse, I would lose my honor and the good opinion which they had of me."[109]

Having set out his circumstance, Ewald began his march with his ninety-three men in dispersed order. He chose this formation as the "country was greatly cut through with defiles."[110] By choosing such a deployment, he could hope to gain some warning if American forces were laying in ambush anywhere in his vicinity. Looking back through the lens of the past, Ewald may have added a touch of bravado to his description, as he asserted, "I was determined to resolutely attack any of the enemy I encountered, and to sell my life dearly should I be defeated..." Ewald held this view as he "had no safe retreat as the army was marching to the left and I to the right."[111]

During this operation, Ewald captured an American rifleman from the Continental Army Rifle Corps.[112] He interrogated the man, attempting to gain information from him as to the whereabouts and intentions of the Continental Army, "The captured rifleman resolutely declared he was my prisoner but not my spy." Ewald in turn noted "I admired this worthy man."[113] This incident provides some insight into Ewald's views concerning honor. He was impressed by the soldier's refusal to provide information, and this engendered a feeling of respect for the prisoner. David Hackett Fischer notes that over the course of the New Jersey campaign, especially after the battles of Trenton and Princeton that many of the British and Hessians serving in America began to develop a grudging respect for their American adversaries. Perhaps this encounter constituted one of the first steps down that path for Ewald. On the other hand, it may simply have been the respect of one soldier for another. As will be seen, Ewald would echo the rifleman's sentiments himself in the then distant future.[114]

As Ewald continued his operations in pursuit of Washington's retreating forces, the next day, during the afternoon, he heard gunfire in the distance. Following what would become one of Napoleon's dictates, he "encouraged his men to march faster so that we would not arrive too late."[115]

Ewald and his men joined the main army towards evening and found them deployed on the heights overlooking the Raritan River. The British and Hessians had erected batteries and were cannonading the Americans on the opposite bank. The Americans were returning fire across the river. Both sides had deployed light troops, riflemen for the Americans and Jäger for the British, into the twenty or so houses that made up the town. To slow the British assault, the Americans demolished the bridge across the river. It seems clear that the Jäger were coming up against an American rear guard whose duty it was to slow their advance and buy time for Washington's main Continental Army to put greater distance between itself and the pursuing British.

The Jäger were commanded by Captain Wreden, whom Ewald joined shortly after reporting to Colonel Donop. The skirmishing in the town was intense, and both sides took casualties. One Hessian casualty was a close friend of Ewald's a Captain Weiterhausen of the Hessian grenadiers who was hit in the spine by a rifle-ball.[116]

Just below the town, the Jäger captured two sloops loaded with wine and clothing. Of special importance to Ewald were the stocks of shoes and long trousers on board, "which came at the right time, because our men could no longer proceed in their own boots."[117] This is significant in that it demonstrates that not only the Americans were subject to shortages in equipment and clothing during the War of Independence. As the tempo of operations increased, the movements of the army often outstripped logistics on the British side as well. As a result, shoes and other articles of clothing could become scarce for periods of time.[118]

After the Americans retreated from Raritan, the British remained in the area for five days. This halt in the pursuit led Ewald to question their motivation for inaction. He questioned their letting the Americans escape unscathed from Fort Lee, the slow pursuit across New Jersey which allowed them to cross two rivers unmolested. If they had caught the Americans in the process of crossing either body of water, the British would have had their enemies at a great disadvantage. Finally, he questioned their escape from Raritan, and the lack of any pursuit thereafter. The explanation Ewald reached was that "One had to conclude, therefore, that we had hopes of ending the war amicably, without shedding the blood of the King's subjects in a needless way."[119]

The British and Hessians began marching again on December 6. Around nine o'clock that evening, Ewald was summoned to a meeting with Lord Cornwallis, where he was given the mission of going to the house of one Van Veghten and bringing him back to the army. He was to take two reliable Jäger with him, as well as a guide and to remain on the alert as a unit of American partisans was known to be on the move somewhere in the vicinity as well.[120] Van Veghten, apparently, held Loyalist sympathies, and could provide Cornwallis with intelligence concerning the Morristown area. The British general assured Ewald that if he were captured, steps would be taken for his quick exchange. Ewald further reported, with a clear note of pride, that "I was selected for this task because he relied on me fully."[121] Ewald carried out the mission successfully and returned with Van Veghten to Lord Cornwallis.

Following his escort of Van Veghten in the British lines, before daylight on the morning of December 7, Ewald was once again in action. He accompanied Quartermaster General Erksine on a foraging raid. For his part, Ewald was to arrest a Whig near Blacker's Copper Mine. He did not apprehend the man whose wife and family were at the residence. Nor did he plunder their home. As he noted, "She gazed in astonishment when I marched off again, leaving her wagons and coach standing, and contenting myself with forty-five bottles of Madera wine which I divided among my men, and for once drank myself."[122] Again, the Jäger captain's restraint towards civilians is clear in the above incident. At the same time, it gives the impression that the captain rarely indulged in alcohol, a rarity during his time. Perhaps Ewald's youthful reveries and their consequences made him somewhat hesitant about imbibing.

Following the above actions, the pursuit of Washington's army re-sumed. The two columns of the British force re-united at Princeton. Skir-mishers kept the Jäger, who were deployed in a wood outside the town, under arms through the night. The following day, they continued their pursuit of the dwindling American force and chased them to the banks of the Delaware River. At this point, the Jäger were assigned to Falls Ferry, to cover the crossing point of the Delaware located there.[123]

Ewald commented on what appeared at the time to be the final stage of the 1776 campaign, "On this two-day march, which could have been done in twelve hours by an army that carried so little artillery, it became clearly evident that the march took place so slowly for no other reason than to permit Washington to cross the Delaware safely and peacefully."[124] He further stated that "Lord Cornwallis had orders from General Howe to proceed in such way."[125] Ewald attributed this approach to the fact that both Howe brothers opposed the war politically, and therefore showed restraint in the hopes of reaching a negotiated conclusion to hostilities.

At this point, the British and German forces operating in New Jersey were divided into various smaller contingents. These forces were placed in garrisons across the state both to ensure the security of the British gains to that point in the campaign, and to reduce the burden of supply req-uisitions on the area. In addition, the posts were sited so as to provide mutual support for one another in case of attack. There did exist the pos-sibility that once the Delaware River froze, as it regularly did in the winter months, the British Army would simply march across and destroy the remainder of Washington's army or capture the Continental Congress in its Philadelphia meeting place, or both. The fear of such an occurrence permeated the Americans on the west back of the Delaware. For its part, the Continental Congress abandoned Philadelphia and headed for An-napolis, Maryland.

In reality, however, this marked a period where Howe would husband his resources. He had his opponent on the ropes and could easily finish the dwindling American forces off in the spring, when the conditions were more conducive to campaigning. This cautious approach made sense in that it spared men and horses both the rigors of a winter campaign. Since Washington's army had dwindled significantly from its summer high of roughly 19,000 down to about 2,000, and with so few new recruits en-tering Washington's camp, it seemed time was on Howe's side. Thus, the British and their Hessian auxiliaries went into winter quarters, occupying a string of posts that stretched from close to the main British base in New York City at Perth Amboy in the North with the other end of the line anchored on Bordentown, New Jersey.

Contrary to popular assumption, their going into winter quarters did not lead to a period of passivity for the British and German forces stationed in New Jersey. During this time, Ewald held post with his Jäger company near Lewis Mill to protect the communication between Blackhorse and Bordentown.

One event of crucial importance to the Americans occurred on December 12. The General Charles Lee was captured having spent the previous night at White's Tavern in Basking Ridge, New Jersey. Many officers of the Continental Army, as well as many members of Congress saw Lee as their most experienced and therefore best general. It seems clear that Lee hoped to capitalize on Washington's failures over the preceding months and have himself promoted to the post of commander-in-chief of the Continental Army. Lee spent the next year and some months on parole as a British prisoner in New York City. During this time, he attempted to ingratiate himself with his captors by offering advice on how they could defeat Washington.[126]

On December 13, Ewald went on patrol with a hundred men. His force included both his own Jäger and some Scots highlanders. They clashed with an American foraging party, when Ewald attacked the enemy force, captured several men and some forty head of oxen.[127] Clearly, this was not the dull life of garrison duty.

On December 22, Ewald took post at the Bunting House. This was far from a quiescent cantonment as well. As the captain related, "I had scarcely arrived at this post when the enemy appeared in the wood, and I took the Jäger to reconnoiter him and to learn with whom I had to deal."[128] This was significant in that as Washington husbanded his meager troops, many New Jersey militia formations came out and began to skirmish with the British and Hessian forces occupying their state.[129] Ewald continued, "I skirmished with the enemy, who, since I attacked him quickly, withdrew toward Burlington with a loss of several dead and wounded. I pursued him a short distance, and after I was certain of his retreat I returned to my post."[130] No sooner had Ewald returned from the previous alarm than "I heard heavy small arms fire mixed with canon fire in the vicinity of Black Horse or Slabtown."[131] This time, the fighting seemed to be in Ewald's rear, a situation with which no soldier is comfortable. Ewald determined on a classic partisan response, "I decided to investigate the firing and to fall upon the enemy's rear during his own attack."[132] In this instance, even though Ewald hurried to the scene of the fighting as quickly as he could, by the time he arrived, the engagement had already ended.

While these skirmishes were not sufficient to hamper British efforts in New Jersey in and of themselves, their cumulative effect was to reduce the overall combat effectiveness of the Crown forces. They sapped the morale of the troops, who instead of being in a quiet winter cantonment, found themselves routinely turned out of quarters to deal with repeated alarms. These repeated alarms occurring in the winter weather sapped their physical strength as well. [133]

On the night of the 22nd, Ewald received orders to pull his men back behind the grenadiers, as the following day, Colonel Donop planned to seek out the enemy. On the 23rd, Ewald's Jäger served as the advanced guard as the Hessian force searched for the Americans. Ewald then established a new headquarters at Mount Holly, which he described as trading center that was "inhabited by many wealthy people."[134] This wealth produced its own problems as "Since the majority had fled and the dwellings had been abandoned, almost the whole town was plundered, and because the stocks of wine were found there, the entire garrison was drunk by evening."[135] However, the section of the town in which the Jäger were billeted had little alcohol, and so they remained fairly sober. Still, they did receive some supply from the grenadiers.

Ewald was next ordered to the town of Longbridge near Moorestown.[136] He had barely arrived before being directed to patrol as far as Burlington with his Jäger and some Hessian grenadiers. They were hunting for some rebel shipping that had come up the river and shelled the Hessian troops. As he patrolled, it began to snow, "I returned at midnight. The snow had risen so high since yesterday that we could hardly get through."[137]

On the 24th, Ewald reported an emissary coming into camp from Washington to propose a prisoner exchange. Ewald, however, described this as a ruse designed to get information as to Donop's whereabouts.[138] In the end, he was correct, the emissary was in fact a spy sent to gain information as part of the preparation for the American attack on Trenton.

The battle of Trenton stands as one of the crucial turning points of the American War of Independence, not for the numbers engaged, as these were fairly small. Rather, Trenton as well as the follow-up, the battle of Princeton was crucial in halting the British drive and restored some support to the revolutionaries. Given its significance, while Ewald was not present at the battle, it still requires some discussion.

As matters stood in late December 1776, Washington's force had fallen from a summer high of some 19,000 troops to barely 1,200. Many of these were sick and poorly clad, and therefore unfit to do duty. All of them were due to leave the army with the passing of the year. As a result of the defeats suffered in the late summer and fall, recruits were not coming in. As Thomas Paine's aptly titled pamphlet suggests, this was the American Crisis.

Even during the nadir of American military fortunes, or perhaps because of it, Washington planned a bold stroke—an attack on Hessian garrison at Trenton. The march began on December 25, 1776. Only one of three American columns that were to take part in the attack actually made it across the Delaware River, this being the one under the direct control of Washington himself.

Early on the morning of December 26, the Americans attacked the Hessian garrison. The men were in doors, not, as has been essential to American tradition, sleeping off a Christmas hangover, but instead being relieved from standard patrols due to the harshness of the weather. Colonel von Rall had determined that under the prevailing conditions, an enemy attack was highly unlikely and took the opportunity to relieve his men from the constant guard duty they had been mounting for several days previous.

Around eight o'clock in the morning, the Americans hit the town of Trenton from two sides and succeeded in capturing the bulk of the garrison with minimal casualties. The result was that over 900 troops out of a total of 1,200 were taken prisoner, along with their baggage, and equipment. While this was a small engagement in and of itself, Trenton had enormous strategic consequences.

Ewald and his Jäger, for their part, were nowhere near Trenton when the American forces attacked. On the morning of the 25th, he had been sent to New Mills, where an American Colonel Reynolds and two captains were said to be spending the night at Reynold's house. Ewald's mission was a partisan classic, sweep in and grab the officers and take them prisoner. He took eight Jäger and twenty Scots with him for the enterprise.

When he came to the house Reynolds was reportedly staying at, Ewald deployed his Jäger to surround it, and then deployed the Scots further out from the target in case an American relief party should attempt a rescue.[139] He then entered the house with two Scots and proceeded to a room where three men and four women were drinking tea. He knocked and was told to enter. Entering, he was offered a cup of tea, which he accepted, "They looked at me and did not know what to make of me for my uniform was covered over with snow which had been falling all night."[140]

As one of the women attempted to leave, she was forced back into the room by one of the Scots with Ewald, "At this instant I put an end to the affair, identified myself to the gentlemen, and announced the agreeable news that they were my prisoners." The officers attempted to defend themselves with their swords. Ewald, "advised the men to give me their swords or they would be cut down. They followed my advice, and I permitted them to take a tender farewell to their wives."[141] With his prisoners, Ewald was back in Mount Holly by midday.

Later in the afternoon, he went out on a foraging operation, which was interrupted by the news of the surprise at Trenton. The foraging expedition came to an abrupt end, and the Hessians had to return to their base. Years later Ewald recalled how this small but significant victory had changed the dynamic of the war, "Thus had the times changed! The Americans had constantly run before us. Four weeks ago we expected to end the war with the capture of Philadelphia, and now we had to render Washington the honor of thinking about our defense."[142] Likewise, he noted the effect on the morale of the troops, "Due to this affair at Trenton, such a fright came over our army that if Washington had used this opportunity we would have flown to our ships and let him have all of America."[143] He concluded, "Since we had thus far underestimated our enemy from this day onward we saw everything through a magnifying glass."[144]

He went on to mete our blame for the debacle, singling out Colonel Donop, whom he said had been "led by the nose to Mount Holly by Colonel Griffin and detained there by love..."[145] In addition, he singled out Lieutenant Grothausen whose troops were posted in the Dickinson house near Trenton as they constituted one of the pickets and failed to provide sufficient warning of the impending attack. Interestingly, for Ewald, the defeat at Trenton "surely caused the utter loss of the thirteen splendid provinces of the Crown of England..." Again, it is clear that this section was written years after the conclusion of the fighting in North America. It is still intriguing that in reflecting back on his experiences, Ewald viewed Trenton as such a major turning point.

In the short term, Crown units were quickly mustered and dispatched towards Trenton to try and salvage what they could of the situation. The tactical command once again fell to Cornwallis, Howe's able and aggressive subordinate. If they could catch Washington before he re-crossed the Delaware and force him to fight an action with exhausted troops and his back to the river, they might yet be able to turn the defeat into a resounding Crown triumph. At the very least, the presence of reinforcements could force the American general to reconsider attacking any additional British or Hessian garrisons.

CHAPTER 5

INTO THE CAULDRON:
THE 1777 CAMPAIGN

Ewald missed out on playing any major role in the January 2, 1777 battle of Princeton as well. Instead, he and his Jäger company were ordered to make a reconnaissance in the area farther south. As previously noted, in the aftermath of Trenton, the British forces occupying New Jersey had become overly suspicious that the Americans would launch another assault on their positions. As a result, the British and Hessians remained on heightened alert. They stepped up their patrols, though these were by no means lax prior to battle.

Washington, buoyed up by the success of the Trenton attack, began planning a follow-up against the British while he continued to hold the initiative. The key obstacle to any further activity by the Continentals lay in convincing his veteran troops, many of whose enlistments were set to expire on December 31, to remain with the army just a bit longer. This would give him the solid core of regulars essential to success in any offensive operations.

Personal appeals by the officers, including a direct appeal by Washington himself, combined with promise of payment of a ten-dollar bounty in exchange for a month's service initially had no effect. Finally, a second appeal by Washington himself led some troops to step forward and volunteer for the operation. The American Army re-crossed the Delaware back to the New Jersey side on December 31. On January 1, 1777, money from the Continental Congress arrived, and Washington's men received their bounties.[1] By then word reached the British garrison at Princeton that the Americans had re-crossed the Delaware, and Earl Charles Cornwallis led a force to intercept them at Trenton. As was often the case when Cornwallis commanded, the Jäger were deployed as part of the advanced guard.

The two forces clashed outside the town and a running engagement developed. As the two forces made contact, the Continental Corps of Riflemen switched from the advanced guard to defending the army's retreat, maintaining constant pressure on the British vanguard. Thus, the Jäger clashed with their American equivalents, the riflemen.

As Ewald relates, "The army was scarcely in motion when the advanced guard came upon an enemy outpost which withdrew into a small wood through which the highway ran to Trenton, where Lieutenant von Grothausen - fortunately for him - was shot dead along with several Jäger."[2] This may appear a harsh verdict, however, Grothausen's outpost had been surprised outside Trenton, and thus he had been dishonored in the eyes of this fellow soldiers, or at least in Ewald's. His death in battle was, in a sense, a way for him to redeem his lost honor, at least in Ewald's perception. This concept of honor stood as one Ewald held to and often commented on, especially in his first treatise.

The Americans withdrew from their positions gradually, only yielding a position to their foes when the pressure became too intense. They were therefore able to buy time for the remainder of the American force in Trenton itself.

Once in the town, "The Jäger and light infantry immediately attempted to occupy the houses on this side of the bridge. Since the enemy had likewise occupied the houses on the other side, which lay in front of the enemy army, a stubborn outpost fight occurred here whereby many men were killed and wounded on both sides."[3] This stubborn outpost fight Ewald refers to above was the Second Battle of Trenton, fought on January 1, 1777. During this battle the Americans skirmished with British under Cornwallis' forces throughout the day. The British pushed the Americans back across Assunpink Creek. By nightfall, the Americans held one side of the Creek and the British the other, with the certainty of a resumption of hostilities on the following morning. The British commander, Earl Cornwallis, sent for additional troops from Princeton, and planned to renew the fight with their arrival the next day.[4]

Following a council of war with his senior officers, Washington determined to leave his position that night and circle around behind the British forces via a back road and attack their post at the college town of Princeton the following morning.

The army moved out through the bitter January night, leaving only a skeleton force behind to stoke the fires of the former American camp. The men who remained behind had been ordered to make as much noise as possible to deceive the British into thinking that the entire Continental force remained in position, and so make good the ruse.

The following morning, the vanguard of the American forces engaged a British detachment on its way from Princeton to reinforce the troops at

Trenton in a classic encounter battle. In furious fighting, the Americans eventually drove the British back and managed to take more than 200 prisoners.[5] They broke off the attack and left the town as it became clear that Cornwallis, hearing the sounds of battle to his rear, initiated a counter-march on Princeton. Washington did not want to forfeit his hard-won victory by allowing himself to be caught between the two British forces.

Ewald described the return of the main British force to Princeton that same afternoon, stating that they marched "in and around the town like an army that is thoroughly beaten." He further noted that "Everyone was so frightened that it was completely forgotten even to obtain information about where the Americans had gone." Likewise, he noted the power of rumors in the absences of solid information, "But the enemy now had wings, and it was believed that he had flown toward Brunswick to destroy the main depot, which was protected by only one English regiment."[6]

While both of the forces engaged at Princeton were fairly small the sensation caused by the American victory contributed to a renewal of determination on the Whig side. As Ewald observed, "This brilliant coup which Washington performed against Lord Cornwallis, which raised so much hubbub and sensation in the world and gave Washington the reputation of an excellent general, derived simply and solely from Lord Cornwallis's mistake of not marching in two columns for Trenton."[7]

The above constituted an interesting reflection in that Ewald approaches the British defeat as an example of a "lessons-learned." In analyzing the battle in this way, Ewald examines the engagement from the perspective of what each commander did well as opposed to what they did poorly. His silence concerning Washington's conduct of the battle may indicate that he did not see that the American commander had done anything outstandingly well. On the other hand, Ewald noted a significant failure on Cornwallis' part. Cornwallis' failure, in turn, presented Washington with an opportunity which the American general took advantage of, something any reasonably adept commander would be expected to do.

When Ewald returned to Princeton, shortly after the fighting had ended, he "found the entire army under arms." He received orders to "draw biscuit and brandy from the depot for the men, and to continue marching to Maidenhead, where I found Colonel Donop with the Hessian grenadiers, the Jäger and the light infantry."[8]

After the British defeat at Princeton, they consolidated their line of outposts, and the troops in New Jersey realigned to better respond to the new operational situation developing in the state. Due to these realignments, Ewald received a new posting. His quarters were now set "at a house beyond New Brunswick on the road to Princeton." He described the features of his new quarters, "This house lay isolated on a hill and was constructed of brick, three stories high." Clearly, this position formed a good observation post, and being constructed of brick made it a solid defensible point. The actions he took on receiving this new post demonstrate the new defensive posture adopted by the British forces in New Jersey. "I had part of the apple and peach orchard near the house toward Princeton cut down and placed as many trees as were necessary at the three entrances to barricade them."[9]

Describing his new location, Ewald commented, "After a very exhausting campaign, these quarters where the soldier could not get straw for his bedding, were to serve for refreshing the troops." The problem was that "this whole region had been completely sacked" during the motions of the armies across New Jersey the previous fall. To compound the miseries of the troops, "The entire army had been stripped bare of shoes and stockings by the constant marching during the bad weather." In addition, "Uniforms were torn and the officers especially those of the Jäger companies, had almost nothing on their bodies."[10] In addition to the material discomforts suffered by the men, the winter grew more severe, compounding the problem.

As the British lines receded across New Jersey, local Whig militia forces moved forward to occupy the territory they formerly held. Thus, when Ewald conducted a patrol towards Princeton and Millstone on January 5, he learned that both places were now occupied by the enemy.[11] He was now posted at Raritan Landing, a small community that by 1740 possessed no more than one hundred inhabitants. Somewhat larger by the time of the War of Independence, it occupied an important point in the British communications network in New Jersey. Ewald was entrusted with covering the road between Brunswick and Boundbrook in New York. He again possessed a detached command and could further implement some of the ideas he set down in his Treatise.[12]

Ewald only had to maintain patrols to gather intelligence on enemy activity in his area, while active fighting continued as well. During this period, January through February 1777, there was a great deal of skirmishing in New Jersey. Continentals, aided by the New Jersey militia, attacked small foraging detachments and outposts. Several purposes underlie these actions by the Americans. First, it kept the troops active. Secondly, it kept the British off balance. Third, it provided new troops with the opportunity to gain in experience fighting the enemy, without risking a full-scale engagement. Finally, they continued to wear down the British and Hessian troops, though these minor engagements took their toll on the Americans as well.[13] This was *petite guerre* at its most intense, and it was the kind of war at which the Jäger excelled.

These skirmishes were often small affairs. For instance, on January 12, Ewald received information that the Americans were moving on Quibbletown (modern New Market) and Bond Brook (modern Bound Brook). From then on, Ewald and his Jäger patrolled constantly in the direction of these towns. This maneuvering led to some skirmishing on the 13th, when "the Americans entered Bound Brook and Quibbletown and visited us towards ten o'clock in the evening." The Americans goal was "to surprise my post nearby," however, Ewald and his men were prepared and "since they were greeted with shots from the same sentries they merely fired several shots in the direction of our pickets' fire and withdrew."[14]

The skirmishing between the two sides intensified, as Ewald relates, due to the fact that the British camp was less than an hours' march from the American outposts at Bound Brook and Quibbletown. As a result, "The teasing now occurred daily, and when they did not visit us, we rendered the honors to the Americans." The consequences of this constant activity were that "Not only did the men have to stay dressed day and night but they had to be kept together, the horses constantly saddled, and everything packed."[15] Thus the Jäger remained on continual alert.

One reason for this constant fighting with its heightened state of alert derived for the army's need for fodder. To provide fresh food for the horses represented a daily challenge to the men who were sent out to procure it. This often led to additional clashes as British and Hessian units foraged for fodder, and the Americans interdicted their efforts.[16]

The constant activity described above also wrought havoc with men and equipment, the latter of which was already in need of repair or replacement. This need was offset at least somewhat on January 23rd, when "the Jäger received the promised gift from Lord Cornwallis, which consisted of a complete uniform for each man."[17]   At the same time, the distribution of uniforms can and should be seen as a mark of esteem from the British general.

Soon after this welcome supply of new uniforms, Ewald and his Jäger were sent out to help cover a foraging mission. On the march they formed the advanced guard, and during the return, the formed the rear guard. The Jäger, therefore, remained almost constantly engaged with the Americans throughout the operation. Their conduct under these circumstances drew the approbation of British commander. As Ewald noted, "Lord Cornwallis honored me by publishing an order expressing his satisfaction with me and my courageous men..." Not only did Ewald receive recognition on this occasion, but "each Jäger received a gift of one piaster" as well.[18]

Not all was duty for the captain at this point, however. On January 30, 1777, Johann Ewald began a one-sided correspondence with a Miss Jeannette von Horne of Flatbush in New York. The letter was written while Ewald was stationed at Raritan. The captain sent her some sausages "made in the German manner" as a token of his esteem.[19] An interesting courting gift to be sure. Ewald continued writing to Miss van Horne through the winter and spring of 1777. Clearly, the Jäger captain was smitten with the young lady, for on June 10,

> *What a terrible desert this town has become for me, and what a lovely name* <u>*Flatbush*</u> *has become in my thoughts. But if I meet you there, then I shall have the greatest pleasure in the world seeing you again.*[20]

While there are no letters from Miss van Horne to Ewald, it seems likely that there existed some mutual feeling, as she took care of some equipment he forwarded to her at one point.[21] Ewald's letters to Jeannette van Horne do provide some potential insight into the officer's emotions. He expresses himself quite openly in his letters. Again, in the letter of June 10, he writes,

> *Pardon, my dear, if my letter is confused and if it is not in the state it should be. For the love of you, my mind finds itself in such a condition that if I wish to write three words, I have already forgotten two.*[22]

The last letter from Ewald dates from August 7, 1778.[23] Again, no letters from Jeannette van Horne have come to light. This does not necessarily mean that she did not return Ewald's messages. The letters may simply have been lost, or they may have been destroyed intentionally. They do demonstrate that while he served in North America, Ewald's not wholly focused on his profession.

The constant skirmishing exerted a mixture of morale effects on the British and Hessians. On the one hand, as Ewald observed, "Since the army would have been gradually destroyed through this foraging, from here on the forage was procured from New York." It still possessed some beneficial qualities, "a renewed spirit entered the hearts of the soldiers, who had become disheartened by the disasters of Trenton and Princeton."[24] Their success in some of these encounters allowed the men to recover from the initial shock of their previous defeats.

Sporadic raids continued through the late winter and early spring. At the same time, Howe had to drastically revise his plans from the preceding fall, when all indications stood in favor of a British victory in the following

88

JAMES R. MC INTYRE

years' campaign. Still, as the weather improved, the grueling war of posts resumed in earnest once again. For Howe's subordinate, Cornwallis, the answer always seemed to lay in aggressive action. He therefore determined to drive the American rebels from the area near his camp.

On April 12, Cornwallis determined to make a surprise nighttime attack on Bound Brook. Ewald and his Jäger assumed the advanced guard and the army moved out. He took a Lieutenant Trauvetter and thirty volunteers with him. Just about daybreak, "I came upon an enemy pocket on this side of the stone causeway which led to Bound Brook through a marsh along the Raritan River for five to six hundred paces over the two bridges." He attacked and, "The picket received us spiritedly and withdrew under steady fire." At this juncture in the fighting, Ewald, "tried to keep as close as possible to the enemy to get across the causeway into the town at the same time."[25] Ewald sought to remain in contact so that the enemy would not be able to interdict his crossing the bridge as determinedly as they would otherwise. He worried as well, as the American had erected a flying bridge (a sort of drawbridge), and if he allowed too much space between his troops and the retreating American picket, the defenders could simply raise the bridge and deny his force entrance to the town.

Ewald succeeded in gaining entrance to the town to the "extent that I arrived at the second bridge at a distance of a hundred paces from the redoubt which covered it and the flying bridge." At this point, things took a serious turn for the worse when as "day dawned I was exposed to a murderous fire." To compound matters, "When I looked around for my men, I saw that no one had followed me except the brave Lieutenant Trauvetter, my Hornblower Muller, Corporal Doesckel, and the Jäger Reichmeyer, Meister, Mergel, Haschell, Gurckel, Buchwald, and Ruppel."[26] At this point, Ewald commanded an advanced assault force of eleven men, against a now alerted garrison! Furthermore, of the men listed in his party, the last two were already severely wounded.

Ewald was cut off in front of his own troops and pinned down under heavy enemy fire. To some extent this demonstrates that he still had much to learn regarding the successful conduct of night attacks. His aggressive streak, likely a reason for his positive working relationship with Cornwallis, could still be the source of trouble for the Jäger captain.

Grasping the perilous nature of his situation, and the fact that, "We had no choice but to lie down on the ground before the bridge," Ewald reacted with boldness, "whereupon I ordered 'Forward' sounded constantly." This action alerted other nearby units to Ewald's position, and "Luckily for us, Colonel Donop's column appeared after a lapse of eight to ten minutes, whereupon the Americans abandoned the redoubt."[27]

Ewald's predicament demonstrates the difficulties incumbent on a night march or attack. At the same time, his reaction upon the realization that he was cut off from the main force demonstrates the sort of quick thinking and resourcefulness that he would later comment were integral to a successful commander on detached service. At the same time, it could be argued that his need for support in the attack resulted from the captain's own brash actions in pushing his advance too far. In either case, Ewald's relief did not bring an end to the fighting. He then set off in pursuit of the retreating Americans, "We arrived in the town with the garrison of the redoubt amidst a hard, running fight, and the greater part were either cut down or captured."[28]

This area remained hotly contested between the two sides, as evidenced by Ewald's orders on the 28th to maintain his post only during the day. "At night I was ordered to withdraw across the sunken road, where the remainder of the company was stationed under Lieutenant Hinrichs, because the enemy had reinforced the two posts at Bound Brook and Quibbletown."[29] In addition to maintaining his outpost only during daylight hours, Ewald fortified it to make it better able to withstand an enemy attack.[30]

This action paid off shortly thereafter when, on the afternoon of the 30th, "the enemy attacked my post." During the assault, "Captain Lorey fought with eight mounted and ten unmounted Jäger, while I tackled the enemy on his right." Ewald maneuvered his troops into position to "cut him off from the highway to Bound Brook behind a hill around his left flank," he then "fell on his [the enemy's] rear, cut down ten men and took six prisoners."[31]

Soon after this skirmish, on May 15, Ewald received intelligence that the Americans had evacuated Elizabethtown and Newark and had consolidated their forces around Basking Ridge. The following day, he learned that that the American posts at Samptown and Quibbletown had been abandoned as well. On May 24, he set out for headquarters to pass this information on to his superiors. While he was at Lord Cornwallis' headquarters, a report came in indicating that the Americans would evacuate Bound Brook at nightfall. Cornwallis ordered Ewald to go with an officer and twenty dragoons from the 16th Light Dragoon regiment and confirm the report.[32]

Ewald set out with the patrol, arriving near Bound Brook about ten in the evening. Concerning the British officer who accompanied him on the mission, Ewald commented, "He was a young man who seemed to have much good will, but no knowledge of this business."[33] They came upon a farm about six hundred paces for the outskirts of the town. A dragoon went ahead to take the owner of the farm and bring him back for questioning. It seems Ewald sought to confirm the American evacuation of the town via a local source rather than direct personal observation on this occasion. "The dragoon returned with the owner, who walked through the orchard and remained standing behind the railing. He assured me that Bound Brook was deserted, but he spoke in a low voice that I became suspicious."[34] Ewald was learning to read the body language of people, a vital skill for a partisan on detached service, and one which he would later comment on in his own writings.

Reacting to the farmer's strange behavior, "I then ordered him to climb over the railing and come to me, and when he refused I threatened him with a beating." Ewald's threat quickly brought action, "I had hardly uttered these words when rifle fire coming from the orchard made the air hot around my nose." He and the patrol had marched into an ambush. "We sprang back and received more fire in the face from the road."[35]

Reacting to their predicament, Ewald recoiled, "I reached the sunken road, where my horse fell down with me, and my groom and dragoon rode over me without ceremony, so that I was quite trampled down."[36] Ewald was also now quite alone, clearly outnumbered and pinned down by heavy enemy fire. At least he had managed to avoid being trampled under the precipitous retreat of his companions.

Some of Ewald's own men must have accompanied him on the patrol, as he reported, "Fortunately for me, the Jäger had caught my horse," Ewald having proceeded on horseback with the other dragoons. On catching his horse, "hornblower Muller, Jäger Bauer and Jäger Ewald decided to search for me, even if it meant risking their lives and liberty." This sort of loyalty on the part of junior officers and soldiers likewise constituted a trait that Ewald would later comment upon. It was necessary for survival and success in the sort of actions he and his men routinely engaged in. His gratitude was clear in his reaction when these troops came to his rescue, "To my great joy, these faithful fellows appeared and found me in my wretched situation."[37]

Not only did these men rescue their fallen commander from a very tight spot, but when they learned that he had lost his hat in the action, they volunteered to go and search for it. Responding to this, Ewald stated, "These men deserve a monument hewn in marble and I shall never forget it."[38]

Incidents such as the preceding served to reinforce the small unit cohesion that was so important to the success of partisan forces.[39] At the same time, the preceding demonstrates that loyalty and self-sacrifice clearly ranked high among the captain's values. Ewald previously commented on these qualities in his first treatise.

In so far as the injuries Ewald suffered that night, the next day he was transported to Brunswick, where he remained in bed for two weeks. Following his return to duty, he had to lead on horseback for over a year due to injuries to his legs.[40] During his convalescence, "all the general officers honored me with their visits and reproached me somewhat because I had not been ordered to go with the party." Still, Ewald disclosed a note of pride, recalling, "However, such reproaches are pleasant to hear when one has done more than his duty."[41] Still, convalescence from injuries, even fairly minor ones, could take some time without the aid of medicines and treatments that are fairly commonplace today.

It was June before the Jäger captain returned to partial duty. Shortly afterward, on June 8, a Lieutenant von Wangenheim arrived with a contingent seventy-five new recruits for the Jäger Corps. These men replaced those lost in the previous years' fighting and the opening skirmishes of 1777. Ewald was not overly impressed with the human material he was presented with, "The recruits for both companies consisted of a few adventurers and experienced Jägers, and they were generally fine-looking men."[42]

It should be recalled that the Jägers were considered an elite unit, and the men selected for service were expected to possess a very specific skill set. For instance, they were expected to be able to provide aimed fire, and to have some idea of woodcraft, or how to survive in the forest. Some among these recruits could lay claim to the skills in question, these were the "experienced Jägers" Ewald refers to. Others would require more training, and therefore time, before they could be considered to possess the necessary skills to contribute the unit. Until then, they would be considered a detriment in that they would require extra looking after when the unit served in the field.[43]

Along with the recruits, Waggenheim brought news of a reorganization in the Jägers Corps. The companies were to be augmented to the strength of 175 men and placed under the overall command of Lieutenant Colonel Ludwig von Wurmb. The Journal of the Jäger Crops places the official date for von Wurmb's assumption of command as June 23, 1777.[44]

In many respects, von Wurmb's career formed a rough parallel to that of Ewald. Born in 1736 to a noble family in Hessen-Kassel, he saw his first military service on the Seven Years' War as well. Like Ewald, he served first in a regular infantry regiment, the regiment von Ysenburg, with which he saw action at Hastenbeck, Sandershausen, and Lutterburg. Later, von Wurmb transferred to the Jäger Corps, with which he was wounded and captured at Lubeck in 1760. In his case, however, promotion came much more rapidly, with von Wurmb achieving the rank of captain by age 23. He was forty-one when he took over command of the Hessian Jäger Corps in North America.[45]

In addition, the cavalry Captain Ernst Carl von Prusechenk was to be made the corps major. Ewald responded to this stating, "Neither my friend Captain [Carl August von] Wreden nor I liked this view, because we would lose our independent commands." Beyond the personal effect of the change, the men worried for the unit, "Besides, we foresaw that such a large corps could not possibly consist of such excellent men as those of which both companies were now composed; hence less honor was to be gained."[46] Reacting to the situation, Ewald almost resigned his commission in the Hessian army and joined the English, "However, we let ourselves be deceived by good words and the *pour le merite* order."[47] The latter was a military award from the Hessian Army.

On June 12, General William Howe arrived at New Brunswick, with the Hessian general von Heister. On the following day, the army camped at Hillsborough. The army moved out on June 14, and the Hessen-Kassel and Anspach Jäger covered its left flank as it moved on Rocky Hill near Millstone.[48] It is sometimes stated that Howe's excursion into New Jersey was an attempt to draw Washington into battle and crush the Continental Army. This intereration seems likely, and there were definite rewards to such a maneuver.

If Howe were able to goad Washington into battle, then he stood a good chance of achieving a tactical success. If he could achieve the oft sought after but seldom achieved decisive battlefield victory, he might stand a greater chance of bringing an end to the rebellion on terms favorable to Great Britain.

By now, however, Washington grasped the importance of the army to the cause of American independence and would not oblige his opponent by risking his entire army on a single action. The result was an operational stalemate. For his part, Washington withdrew further south into New Jersey, and Howe decided not to follow him and further extend his lines of communication. To do so would be to make them a tempting target for American partisan activity. On June 19, the British Army began to retreat back in the direction of New York City. During the march, they vented their frustration with their opponents as "all the plantations of the disloyal inhabitants, numbering some fifty persons, were sacrificed to fire and devastation."[49]

Washington took advantage of the situation by sending out skirmishers to harass the British withdraw. As Ewald noted, when the army set out for Amboy on June 23, the outposts had been warned throughout the preceding night. Likewise, during their march, "a great number of riflemen, supported by light cavalry and guns, followed us so closely that we had to withdraw under constant skirmishing up to the vicinity of Bonhamtown." He further noted that Wreden's Jäger and the Queen's Rangers sustained heavy casualties in the fighting that ensued that day.[51]

Soon after covering the British retreat on Amboy, Ewald and his Jäger were sent once again, along with the British general Leslie, to the Scottish Mountains to defend against a possible American attack from that direction.[52] There ensued a series of small actions as the British and Hessian forces had to fight to gain control of the mountains. In the process, they captured some thirty American soldiers as well as several officers.[53]

After clearing the area, the British and Hessians, along with their prisoners, returned to the main army. They arrived about ten o'clock in the evening, and found the army camped in a crescent around the town, with both wings anchored on Prince's Bay. The Jäger took up a post on the road to Short Hills. Finally, Ewald and his men could enjoy a brief respite from constant marching and skirmishing.[54]

The following day, the 24th, Lieutenant Colonel Wurmb and Major Prusechenk arrived with the newly raised Jäger. They were still without horses and their arrival caused Ewald and his comrade von Wreden "to fuss and grumble again."[55] Ewald described the men who composed the mounted Jäger company as men "drafted from the Hessian hussar and cavalry regiments and deserters from all the services of Europe." In particular, he noted that the "Prueschenk company consisted of deserters and insolent rabble, whereat blood turned to water and all spirits sank in all of us of the old staff, who until now had commanded the most upright and obedient of men."[56] Such a reaction demonstrates how the introduction of inferior material can weaken the morale of a hitherto strong unit. That reaction was not confined to Ewald and Wreden, "even Colonel Donop, who was delighted with the reinforcement of the Jäger Corps because it was his idea, was startled over this riffraff."[57] The situation quickly reached a boiling point, as "The discontent of our old men was so great that they refused to serve with this rabble."[58]

The refusal of Ewald's men to serve with the new drafts demonstrates an important point concerning the Hessians troops. They considered themselves professionals. At least those who had seen some years of service saw themselves as such. To some extent, this dispels the idea that they were merely mercenaries, with low morale and motivation. The Jäger seemed, at least from the above incident, to possess a sense of esprit d'corps.

The solution to the dilemma came as Ewald and the other officers began to integrate the recruits into the existing unit. As Ewald describes his efforts, "Since I was duty officer today, I had to conduct a patrol with fifty old and fifty new men. I mixed the detachment so thoroughly that one old and one new Jäger were constantly together."[59] The approach described above was one often employed in armies of the period. New recruits were placed with veteran soldiers. This served to build unit cohesion as it gave the men a chance to become acquainted with one another. In addition, it provided the opportunity for the veteran troops to pass on the skills they had acquired to the new recruits.[60] Education of new soldiers was a matter usually handled by the sergeants and corporals of the unit. By the same token, if an officer observed a private soldier not following orders, or not learning quickly enough for their tastes, they often used corporal punishment as a corrective. The Jäger were no exception to this rule, and the new recruits were disciplined with a cane.[61]

Still, Ewald's approach of intermingling the men must have had some success, as he notes that by the end of the day, when the unit skirmished with a party of Americans, even the recruits acquitted themselves well.[62]

Soon after the above affair, the army was on the move again. The companies of Ewald and Major von Prueschenk served in advanced guard of the left flank under the command of General Howe.[63] The march was part of yet another attempt by the British commander to try and goad Washington into a major engagement. Failing in this task, the army marched back to Staten Island on June 30, with the Jäger serving as a part of the rear guard, along with the grenadiers and the light infantry.[64] All of the units then camped on Staten Island that evening. Howe's grand design for the campaign of 1777 would soon be set in motion.

Howe began developing plans for the campaign of 1777 in November 1776, when he had Washington at his mercy. These plans received significant modification following the battles of Trenton and Princeton.[65] As his designs stood in July 1777, Howe would move southwards from New York by water, utilizing the mobility brought about by his brother's ships, and strike at Philadelphia, the American capital. His goal was to take the Continental Congress, and thus destroy the rebel government, or to force Washington into an engagement to defend the city in which he could defeat, and possibly crush, the Continental Army.

Both of these outcomes held the possibility of bringing on the defeat of the Americans in 1777. The capture of Philadelphia, one recent commentator observed, fell in line with accepted European military practice.[66] If the rebel capital were captured, then the government apparatus would inevitably fall with it, and there would be no direction for the field army.

This thinking overlooked the transient ability of the Continental Congress, something the body already demonstrated the previous year when it had moved to Annapolis, Maryland when Pennsylvania lay under imminent threat of invasion by Crown forces.

As for the Continental Army, without a military establishment to defend the drive for independence, the British would be in a position to restore Crown authority with impunity. Beyond serving as the primary military force of Congress, the Continental Army provided a rallying point for other Whig military organizations, such as the militia. As numerous historians have observed, by 1777, the Continental Army had come to embody the Revolution.

At the same time, there were drawbacks. If Howe proceeded with the move to Philadelphia, he would leave only a token force of some 4,000 men in New York City, under the command of Sir Henry Clinton, far too few to coordinate with General John Burgoyne's advance down the Hudson Valley. Howe's awareness and support for this movement have long been controversial among historians.[67] Essentially, Burgoyne planned to march down from Canada and separate New England, long considered the heart of the rebellion, from the remainder of the colonies. It was believed that if this were accomplished, the rebellion would simply flicker out in the other colonies. While Howe had advocated a similar plan in 1776, he seemed less than enthused about supporting his subordinate's independent command.[68] Considering the possibilities, the Philadelphia venture made more strategic sense. Still, to exploit these possibilities, the army had to be set in motion and directed at Philadelphia.

On July 3, the troops were given orders to prepare for embarkation on transports. On that same day, a major change took place in the command of the Hessian forces. The Hessian commander, von Heister, was recalled to Hessen-Kassel. This order came as the result of the efforts of William Howe, who felt that Heister was "too unsteady and timid" for his post as overall commander of the Hessian contingent. Among the other reasons given by Howe for Heister's recall was his age. The commander arrived in America at age 69. Howe believed he needed that a younger, more aggressive officer to help him prosecute the war and so petitioned London for von Heister's removal.[69] Von Heister was replaced by Lieutenant General Wilhelm Baron von Knyphausen.

Born in November 4, 1716 in Lütetsburg, East Frisia, to the colonel of a Prussian regiment which had seen service under John Churchill, Duke of Marlborough, Wilhelm von Knyphausen received his education at Berlin. He entered the Prussian service in 1734. He thus served in the Prussian Army through both the War of the Austrian Succession and the

Seven Years' War. By 1775 he had attained the rank of general in the Prussian service, which was equal to the rank of lieutenant general in the army of Hessen-Kassel. He switched to the Hessian army in time to leave with the first division of Hessian troops sent to North America in 1776. At the time, he was sixty years of age, making him eight years William Howe's senior, but possessed some 42 years of military experience. One of his reasons for accepting the command so late in life lay in the attractive wages paid out by the English, and the possibility of further financial gain during his service North America. His experience made him an ideal leader for the Hessian contingent.[70]

While Howe initially held some reservations regarding Knyphausen as well, the latter quickly demonstrated his skill as well as his professionalism, and won over the British commander. The two generals eventually forged a solid working relationship.[71]

Soon, the men were boarding transports, and on July 23, they set sail. Lack of wind prevented them from sailing out of New York Harbor for several days and the voyage truly began on July 25. Washington received intelligence of the fleets departure the following day but had no idea as to its intended destination.[72] The fleet made its way down the coast of New Jersey and entered the Delaware Bay on July 29.[73]

Shortly thereafter, the *HMS Roebuck* a British frigate which had been on patrol in the Delaware Capes for some time and possessed ample opportunity to observe the American's river defenses, rendezvoused with Admiral Lord Richard Howe's flagship the *Eagle*. The captain of the *Roebuck*, one Andrew Snape Hammond, boarded the *Eagle* and reported to the Howe brothers on the state of the American river defenses. These were impressive, but at the time incomplete. They consisted of a series of obstacles, known as chevaux-de-frise, sunken in the Delaware River to block the approaches to Philadelphia. To prevent the British from simply removing the obstacles, they were guarded by several fortifications located at Billingsport and Red Bank in New Jersey, and Fort Island on the Pennsylvania side of the river. Finally, a fleet of small vessels including numerous gundalows and fire rafts served in the Pennsylvania Navy and could supplement these other defenses.[74]

In addition, the Howe Brothers learned that Washington was in Pennsylvania with the Continental Army, and thus might seek to oppose a landing either at Wilmington or Newcastle. Finally, as one recent historian pointed out, the Delaware River itself posed certain problems. As they observed, "It was narrow and tricky, and it possessed a fast current, hardly the place to deploy and anchor large warships, vulnerable transports, and heavily leaden victualers."[75]

Based on this intelligence, the Howe brothers determined to leave the Delaware Bay and sail up the Chesapeake, though, as Hammond later alleged, the port at Newcastle, Delaware was below the defenses and could have served as a point of debarkation for the army.[76] The result, the fleet sailed back into the Atlantic, and the wind promptly died. The ships spent the next six weeks drifting southward in the midsummer heat of the east coast. Provisions began to run short and storms were common. Life for the crews and passengers became miserable. For the horses of the army, it was positively deadly.[77]

Finally, the fleet made its way into the Chesapeake Bay on August 14. They sailed up the bay to the Head of Elk (modern Elkton), in Maryland, with the first division coming ashore on August 25. The Jäger Corps actually composed the first group to come ashore out of the first division, along with the first and second battalions of Light Infantry and the first and second battalions of British grenadiers.[78] As the troops moved out from the shore, the briefly skirmished with some American militia who fell back. Other accounts discuss the militia fleeing the beach without firing a shot. Such unsteadiness on the part of militia is understandable considering their fighting spirits would likely have been depressed as they witnessed wave after wave, five in all, of British and Hessian troops disgorge from their transports onto the shore. For untrained and inexperienced troops, the mere sight of such professionals may simply have overwhelmed their determination to stand and fight.[79]

By nightfall, the army was encamped about two miles beyond the town, with the Jäger, the British Light Infantry contingent and the Queen's Rangers serving as perimeter defense. These units camped in front of a wood where two roads split off, the one in the direction of Christiana Bridge and the other in the direction of Wilmington. Ewald noted, "In this entire region we did not find a single living creature except wild animals, hence the army needed a guide, but the inhabitants had run off, taking with them all the livestock."[80] In advance of the army, patrols were sent out to search for potential guides, and especially horses to attempt to make up for the wastage that had stricken the latter on the long sea journey. Still, the range of these activities was curtailed due to the terrain and the lack of intelligence available on the area.[81]

The first real clash with the Americas was not far off. On August 29, about nine in the morning, "The army was alarmed on all sides by enemy parties. A few foot Jäger and some infantrymen were killed and wounded, since our sentries beyond the two highways could scarcely see over twenty paces in front of themselves because of the thick wood."[82] Further skirmishing followed.

On the following day, Colonel von Knyphausen crossed the Elk River in search of cattle and horses. Knyphausen's foraging brought on further skirmishing with the Americans. One result of these activities was that a captain Uchritz of Ottendorf's Corps was captured. The captain provided some intelligence on the environment the British were operating in and the plans of Washington's army.[83]

On September 3, the army began its march in earnest. General Grant remained in Elkton with his brigade to guard the stores of ammunition and maintain communication with British fleet. During the march, Ewald led the advanced guard.[84] As the army approached Iron Hill, they began to skirmish with the advanced forces of the Americans. The troops Ewald and his men encountered actually composed the light infantry brigade under the command of General William Maxwell.

Born in Ireland, Maxwell came to American to serve in the French and Indian War. He took part in the disaster that was Braddock's march in 1755 but continued his service throughout the conflict. After the war, he resigned his commission, settling in New Jersey. He became involved in the Patriot movement and took part in the invasion of Canada in 1775. By 1777, he was a brigadier general. The light infantry brigade he commanded was assigned to slow the British advance was an organization developed by Washington to compensate for his lack of riflemen. At that time, Daniel Morgan and his Corps of Riflemen were supporting Gates against Burgoyne in New York.[85]

Maxwell ordered his men to skirmish with the van of the British army, and then fall back when the pressure became too great. They did this repeatedly over the course of seven hours of fighting. In ways, the fighting at Iron Hill resembled the Second Battle of Trenton fought earlier that year. Still, the fighting occurred at much closer range, as Ewald observed, "The majority of the Jägers came to close quarters with the enemy, and the hunting sword was used as much as the rifle."[86] The fighting at Iron Hill, which has yet to receive a full treatment, represent the type of close quarter action at the heart of *petite guerre*. It was up close and personal, with the men firing from cover, and engaging hand-to-hand. On this occasion, Ewald survived unscathed, though not without coming very close to injury. His horse was wounded in one of the engagements and died later that evening.[87]

After the days' fighting, the Army camped behind Cooch's Creek, with the Jäger Corps posted "in a wood on the highway to Newark, between Fischer's Mills, to the left of the army."[88] For the conduct of his troops in the fighting, Ewald received the personal recognition of William Howe in the orders of the day,

The courageous manner in which Lieutenant Colonel Wurmb, all the other officers, and the entire personnel of the Jäger Corps, defeated yesterday the picked troops of the enemy army on the mountain near Cooch's Mill deserves the highest praise and the fullest acknowledgement of the Commander in Chief, and has attracted the greatest admiration of the entire army.[89]

As the troops began to move out from their beach head, they continued to travel light, without much of the heavy baggage which remained stowed aboard the transports of the fleet. The result, "Everyone now clearly saw that the army would remain destitute of tents and all necessities until we were master of Philadelphia."[90]

On September 8th, the army resumed its advance, with the jägers again forming part of the advanced guard. They marched past Newark and crossed the White Clay Creek. The creek was surrounded on both sides "by steep, rocky heights that formed a most frightful defile half an hour in length."[91] For his part, Ewald could not understand why the Americans did not choose this location, "where a hundred riflemen could have held up the army a whole day and killed many men," to make a stand against the invaders.[92] His observations on the tactical advantages of this point again demonstrate his sharp eye for terrain.

This portion of the army's march clearly left a lasting effect on the Jäger captain, as even years later Ewald recalled, "My hair stood on end as we crammed in the defile, and I imagined nothing more certain than an unexpected attack at the moment when we would have barely stuck our nose out of the defile." Much of this concern stemmed from the terrain, "For the precipitous rocks on both sides of the creek and along the defile were so steep that no one could scale them."[93] For someone who practiced careful examination of terrain, the idea of leading a force through choke points such as these without first gathering intelligence on the area seemed nothing short of suicidal.

After passing through the defile, the army made their camp along the road from Newport, Delaware to Lancaster. At this point they learned through several prisoners that the Continental Army was preparing to meet them at Brandywine Creek.[94] The army prepared to attack.

Howe's plan for the battle of Brandywine encompassed another wide flanking maneuver, much the same as he followed the previous year on Long Island. In this case, one force under General von Knyphausen, would launch a direct assault on the American position at Brandywine Creek. The frontal attack was merely a demonstration in force, howev-

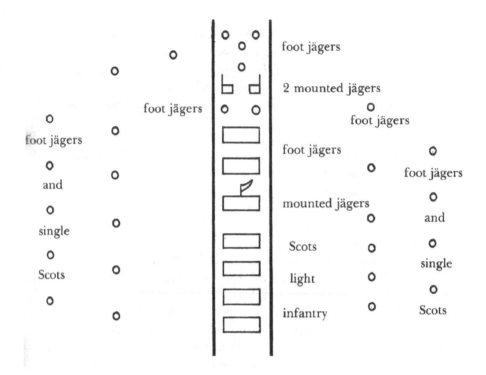

Figure 1: Diagram demonstrating how Ewald's detachment advanced during the Battle of Brandywine, September 11, 1777. From Ewald's Diary, page 83.

er, as it was designed to occupy the Americans and pin the Continental Army in place while the main British thrust, under the command William Howe himself, and with Earl Cornwallis, would move to the westward, and search for an unguarded ford. Once across, the British would fall on the American flank. On September 9, the army moved forward in two detachments. The first, under Knyphausen, made their way to New Garden and Kennett Square. The second, under Cornwallis, made its way to Hockisson Meeting House. The two forces combined to meet Washington after a well conducted night march.[95] The army was passing through an area settled predominantly by Quakers, whose farms were quite productive, as Ewald remarks, "Here, in this area, the army found an abundance of everything, through which the insatiable appetite of the soldier was satisfied to the greatest extent."[96]

As they arrived in Kennett Square on the morning of the 10th, "the army brigades rested one behind the other," in essence making their camp in the order of march.[97] The following day, September 11, the British attacked the Americans in what became known as the battle of Brandywine

Creek, following the plan already described. While Ewald seems to have some knowledge of Howe's overall plan for the battle, this most likely came after the attack, as Howe kept his intentions secret from all but his senior staff.[98]

Ewald fought in the column under Cornwallis and Howe, which successfully outflanked the Americans. As often happened, the Jäger served as the advanced guard for Cornwallis's column, which consisted of sixty foot and fifteen mounted Jäger under a Lieutenant Hagen. In addition, there was a company of Scottish Highlanders from the 42nd Regiment under a Captain McPherson, and a company of light infantry under a Captain William Scott.[99] In fanning out ahead of the main column, Ewald described how, "I had hardly marched half an hour when I ran into a warning post of the enemy five to six hundred strong, who withdrew from one favorable position to another under constant skirmishing until around noon time."[100] This was likely one of the patrols that Washington had thrown out upriver in case the British should attempt to outflank him.

The captain moved forward with his foot Jäger interspersed with the mounted troops, and the Scots Highlanders and light infantry to provide protection against any ambush the Continentals may have set. All the troops were within mutually supporting distance, as he illustrated in his diary.[101] Another important factor, which Ewald did not fail to mention in his reminiscences was the presence of a guide provided him by Cornwallis, most likely a local Loyalist. His knowledge of the surrounding area was invaluable, as Ewald noted, "I always found the enemy where he [the guide] presumed him to be."[102]

About two in the afternoon, Ewald's column crossed the Brandywine. In crossing the river, which is generally very shallow but wide, he deployed his men in the following manner,

> *I took twelve Jäger and let them pass the defile by twos, two hundred paces apart, with instructions to take post as soon as all twelve were across and had reached a point where they could see far around. But as soon as the van of the enemy was encountered, they were to retreat by twos.*[103]

By sending the men ahead in small detachments, they could gain a lodgment on the opposite side of the river, without risking his entire force. At the same time, as they fanned out, they might gain some intelligence as to the deployment of the enemy. Being very small in numbers, however, Ewald specifically enjoined them not to engage. This would prevent them

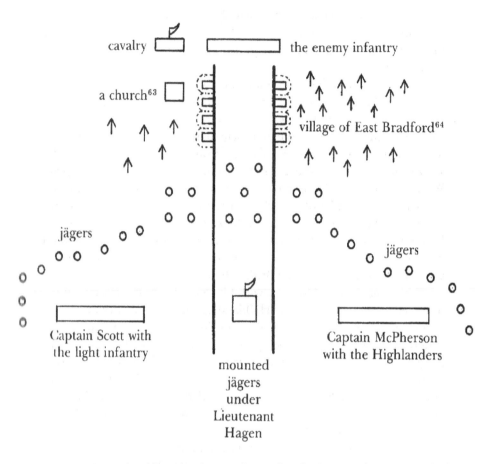

Figure 2: Diagram of Ewald's attack with supporting troops, late afternoon, September 11, 1777. Taken from Ewald's Diary, 85.

from giving away the location of the British assault column for as long as possible.

As the advanced force proceeded across the river, Ewald remarked on his astonishment that the ford was left unguarded.[104] Later historians have determined that Washington suffered from faulty intelligence on this point, believing that there were no additional fords for some twelve miles upriver, and that the roads to these were impassable.[105] By the same token, it is true that he did receive some warnings concerning Cornwallis' movements, including from James Ross of Dunlap's Partizan Regiment, and from Theodoric Bland of the Virginia cavalry.[106]

At about noon, the army halted for half an hour so that the men could refresh themselves and prepare for battle. It should be kept in mind that the troops had been on the move since before sunrise. At this point,

Adjutant General Ross gave the men some heartening disinformation, "One more good hours' marching and you will eat Welsh hens. General Knyphausen has thoroughly beaten Washington."[107]

Clearly, the above falls into the category of rumors of war. Ewald himself observed a party of Americans around three in the afternoon guarding a road. His guide informed him that these men were likely guarding one of the roads to Chester which Washington would use for his escape. That being the case, Ewald sought permission to attack them from the senior captain of his force, McPherson, who agreed with the enterprise. After their brief council of war, Ewald "drew up at once and deployed the Jäger, asking McPherson and Scott to support me on both flanks, and ordered the mounted Jäger to follow the foot jägers in the center." [108]

Ewald diagramed the dispositions he employed in his attack in his diary. Essentially, he pushed out his Jäger as a screen in front of the light infantry, mounted Jäger and Scottish Highlanders.[109] What followed developed into a very small but sharp engagement.

"I reached the first houses of the village with the flankers of the Jäger, and Lieutenant Hagen followed me with the horsemen. But unfortunately for us, the time this took favored the enemy and I received extremely heavy small arms fire from the gardens and houses, through which, however, only two Jäger were wounded."[110] The problem here was that as Ewald and Hagen advanced, they did so slowly enough to take in their surroundings. This, in turn, gave the Americans time to prepare their defense. "Everyone ran back, and I formed them again behind the fences or walls at a distance of two hundred paces from the village."[111] Thus, Ewald conducted a successful tactical withdrawal in the face of heavy enemy resistance. Rallying the troops proved a difficult endeavor as "They shouted to me that the army was far behind, and I became not a little embarrassed to find myself quite alone with the advanced guard. But now that the business had begun, I still wanted to obtain information about these people who had let me go so easily."[112] Once again, Ewald had risked getting himself cut off from the main body of the army in his desire to take advantage of a tactical opportunity. Once again, in his case, fortune favored the bold.

After the engagement, Ewald, still seeking to gain intelligence of the enemy, "took with me the mounted Jäger Hoffman, a very courageous fellow, and two Scots and tried to reach a hill which lay to the right of the village." What he found when he crested the hill left the Jäger captain in astonishment, "for I found behind it—three to four hundred paces away—an entire line in the best order, several of whom waved to me with the hats but did not shoot."[113] Had he pressed his pursuit, he would have run directly into this force. Instead, "I kept composed, examined them closely, rode back, and reported it at once to Lord Cornwallis by the Jäger Hoffman."[114] As he returned from his reconnaissance, he likewise dispatched a Scot with this intelligence to Lord Cornwallis.

The Scot found a column of Americans in retreat, at which Ewald remarked, "Had I had a battalion with me, I would have cut off his [the American] column."[115] By now, the remainder of the British force was moving into position. This body included the Jäger, the British Guards, the Light Infantry and the grenadiers, along with artillery support. A second line included the Hessian grenadiers and various other additional troops.

As the British forces came into position, Ewald remained in front. He initiated contact with the Americans, "As soon as the army had drawn near me by three or four hundred paces, and I received no orders, I attacked the village and the church on the hill, which the enemy abandoned as soon as he saw the line of the advance guard at the same hill."[116]

The British attack drove the Americans back as far as Dillworthtown, however, this occurred only after "a steady, stubborn fight from hill to hill and from wall to wall..."[117] During much of this fighting, the Jäger fought in open order dispersed along the British line and as the Americans withdrew, Ewald regrouped his men.[118]

As the Americans retreated, Lord Cornwallis moved forward, ordering Colonels Meadows and Monckton to occupy the village. At this juncture Ewald believed that the engagement was essentially over, and asked Colonel Monckton if he could accompany him into the village. Ordering his Jäger officers to form their men into the advanced guard, "We had hardly reached the village when we received intense grapeshot and musketry fire which threw the grenadiers into disorder, but they recovered themselves quickly, deployed, and attacked the village."[119] As the grenadiers moved forward, Monckton sent Ewald back for reinforcements. Clearly, there remained some additional fighting to secure the village.

With the daylight failing, both sides broke off the fighting. The Americans retreated towards Chester. They had fought hard, and though they were outflanked, they were not demoralized as they had been the previous year on Long Island. If anything, much the opposite sentiment prevailed in their camp, they looked forward to another test of arms with their British and Hessian adversaries.

Numerous contemporaries, and generations of later historians have criticized William Howe for his conduct of the Philadelphia campaign, or even going there at all. Interestingly, Ewald is one of the few who highlights the general's positive attributes in the fighting. Concerning the battle of Brandywine, he noted, "When one reviews the entire attack on the enemy, one will perceive that General Howe is not a middling man but indeed a good general, and it really is regrettable that the results of the battle fell short of the excellent and carefully prepared plans."[120] Here, Ewald is likely referring to the fact that the British failed to capture of destroy the bulk of the Continental Army, one of the hopes for the campaign overall.

At the same time, Ewald asserts that had his column moved more rapidly, the British could have successfully crushed the Americans in the battle. Further, he maintains that the slow march was performed intentionally in order to allow the Americans to escape, and facilitate further negotiations.[121] Interestingly, many British participants attribute the slow advance to the Hessians who held back their movements.[122] Finally, Ewald observed that, "My suspicions were strengthened anew when I observed the army on the battlefield overnight—perfectly quiet, without a single man sent after the enemy and without any outposts—so quiet in fact that if Washington had been such a great man as they proclaimed him to be on the other side, and had returned during the night, he would have been able to recover everything lost, double and triple."[123]

As evidenced in the above sentence, Ewald did not see Washington as the great military commander he was often depicted as in American literature on the war. Still, his assessment is interesting, that the British held back from delivering a crushing blow for political reasons. It is hard to agree with this assessment however, in that Howe was a fairly cautious general, even when he was aggressive. He practiced managed risk. That being the case, making a march through unknown territory with few local guides, whose loyalty at the time was still dubious, while searching for an enemy whose exact location he was uncertain of, would lead him to move cautiously. The idea that Washington could have restored the balance, or even obtained a victory rests on some weak pillars as well. First, it assumes that the Americans would have been capable of launching a successful night attack. Night attacks were uncommon in the eighteenth century because they were risky and very uncertain of success, even with well-trained veteran troops. Washington's army was likely not up to the challenge. Their inability to launch a night attack would be compounded by the fact that they had just fought a major engagement, and many units were still assessing the damage they had suffered. All in all, Ewald's ideas, on this occasion, demonstrate the theorist overriding the fighting soldier.

A portion of Ewald's account of the fighting is revealing, as it demonstrates the manner in which the Continentals were improving as foes. In discussing Knyphausen's attack, in which he played no part, Ewald observed how the Americans reacted once the Hessians general launched an advance at approximately two in the afternoon,

> *A part of the enemy infantry took a new position behind the first fence or wall, defending itself from wall to wall in the best way possible, but was constantly attacked from post to post by our gallant troops and finally completely driven back over the Hills towards Chester.* [124]

The preceding demonstrates one of the major changes in the nature of the conflict from the previous year. In 1776, when the Americans realized they were outflanked, many units broke and ran. In 1777, when it became apparent that Howe had found an unguarded ford, the Continental army pivoted to meet the new threat, with Nathanael Greene's brigade covering four miles in roughly twenty minutes. The Americans were improving, though Ewald did not recognize the fact, either at the time, or later when he composed his diary.

In the days following the battle of Brandywine, the British and Americans maneuvered about the Delaware Valley outside of Philadelphia. This movement led to several additional clashes. For example, Ewald notes how on September 15, "the Jäger Corps sent out constant patrols toward Turk's Head, which usually encountered enemy patrols." When these patrols came into contact with one another, "They skirmished with them and brought in several prisoners, through whom we obtained information that Washington would not move his army to Philadelphia but toward Lancaster to keep his rear open." In addition, they learned that "he would abandon Philadelphia to us without striking a blow." [125] With the two forces in near constant contact, the chances for a second major battle were high. These nearly came to fruition on the following day.

On September 16, elements of the two armies came into contact, and it appeared that another major engagement was in the offing. For his part, Ewald was ordered by Knyphausen, to clear a wood containing some American riflemen. In order to perform the task, "I had to cross open ground for several hundred paces before I reached the wood in which the enemy was hiding." His advance was no simple movement considering "During this time I was exposed to enemy fire, which did not seem to be very heavy..." He attributed this to the fact that most of the rifles did not fire owing to heavy rain. He then ordered his own troops to fire, "and discovered at the second shot that the rifles misfired." This complicated matters, "But since the attack had to be carried out, I ordered the hunting swords drawn." Continuing his advance at top speed, Ewald and his men "came to close quarters with the enemy, who during the furious attack forgot that he had bayonets and quit the field." As a result, the "Jäger captured four officers and some thirty men." For the Jäger, the loss in the clash was five killed, seven wounded and three missing.[126]

This was only an opening skirmish as the two armies came into position to fight. As noted there had already been some heavy rain. Just as the two main armies were about to come into contact, a cloudburst erupted over the men, soaking all of the ammunition. "This terrible rain caused the roads to become so bottomless that not one wagon, much less a gun, could get through, and it continued until toward afternoon on the 17th, which gave the enemy time to cross the Schuylkill River with bag and baggage."[127] Since the only alternative would have been to close with the bayonet, both sides broke off. This near clash earned the amusing title of Battle of the Clouds.[128] Concerning the battle that almost occurred, Ewald noted, "Indeed, the enemy corps under General Maxwell held up our march somewhat, but it would not have provided much advantage for Washington's army had not the severe downpour occurred."[129]

Again, the Americans managed to break of the engagement and march away, much to Ewald's disappointment, "I firmly believe that we still could have caught up to with the greater part of the enemy army, at least the baggage, somewhere near the right bank of the Schuylkill River, if it had been the will of General Howe."[130] Instead of a rapid pursuit, however, the British army remained camped in the vicinity for the succeeding three days, giving up the quarry.

On the 18th, Ewald's force was met by additional troops under Cornwallis and General James Grant and camped on some high ground in Tredyffrin Township. "The Jäger received their post where the two roads from Yellow Spring converge near Swedes Ford." That same night, a force composed of British light infantry attacked the American depot at Valley Forge and captured or destroyed much of their supplies.[131]

The Americans, for their part, maintained pressure on the British, Brigadier General Anthony Wayne of Pennsylvania kept his men close to the British rear, hoping to capitalize on any opportunity that presented itself.[132] Instead the British, under General Charles "No Flint" Grey turned and launched a daring attack on Wayne on the night of September 20, 1777 at Paoli. In the fighting, the British inflicted fifty-three killed and 113 wounded on the Americans, while reporting only four and seven of their own in the respective categories.[133] The Journal of the Jäger Corps reported simply on September 21st, "The past night, Major General [Charles] Gray with the Light Infantry, the 42nd and 44th Regiments were detached in order to surprise an enemy corps of 1,500 men under General [Anthony] Wayne, which stood alone in the woods."[134] While the Jäger Corps Journal stated the objective facts of the engagement, public opinion was much more concerned with perception than reality. Rumors quickly spread on the American side that soldiers had been killed in their sleep, while unarmed or while trying to surrender, and the event quickly earned the title of the 'Paoli Massacre.' For the British it remained a bold and brilliantly successful night action.[135]

Shortly after the engagement at Paoli, Ewald was on the move again. "On the 22nd, at six o'clock in the morning, I conducted a patrol with eighty jägers, fifty grenadiers, and a noncommissioned officer with twelve mounted Jäger to Pikeland Township, which lay in the rear of the army, where an enemy party was believed to be stationed."[136] As the patrol came upon the village, Ewald discovered "An enemy party had placed itself behind the houses and fences and fired several shots, to which no attention was paid, whereupon I ordered quick march to get straight at the enemy."

The charge was a tactic developed to take advantage of the chief weaknesses of American riflemen: the slow reloading time of their weapons, and their lack of bayonets. It allowed Ewald and men to close with the Americans and use their swords, and the grenadiers their bayonets before the Americans had the opportunity to reload.

In this case, it proved the breaking point for the Americans' combat motivation, "But just as I drew up within one hundred and fifty yards of the village, the enemy fled into the wood so hastily that not a single man was caught."[137] The village Ewald was now in possession of consisted of some fifty buildings and proved to be deserted. Surveying the site, "I deployed on the other side behind the hedges or walls and searched through the village, where I found a blown-up powder magazine and rifle factory." While the site was abandoned and destroyed, it still yielded "several thousand pieces of fabricated and unfinished rifles and sabers of all kinds..." While his main objective was to clear the village itself, Ewald dispatched "Lieutenant Hinrichs with twenty infantry Jäger into the wood to search it thoroughly for a short distance, but he returned without seeing or hearing anyone." His reconnaissance of the area complete, Ewald then "ordered everything smashed to pieces, set fire to the factory, and marched back."[139]

The preceding encompasses a prime example of the sort of small unit action at which the Jäger, and their captain, excelled. The reconnaissance of an area, and the seizure and destruction of enemy stores were the sort of action that Maria Theresa's Pandours and Croats were initially raised to perform.

Ewald's diary did not consist solely of his military adventures. As his time in America continued, more details of his personal experiences found their way into its pages as well. For instance, as the British army was maneuvering to gain Philadelphia, Ewald came into contact with a woman from the Palatine, who challenged the presence of the Hessians in the war. If Ewald replied to the woman's harangue, he did not include it in his diary.[140]

In the larger context of the campaign, with the Americans driven off, the British maneuvered around them, and on September 26, a column led by Cornwallis and Pennsylvania Loyalist Joseph Galloway entered Philadelphia.[141] Immediately upon entering the city "Several batteries were set up at once on the Delaware River, above and below the city."[142] These batteries were designed to protect the British garrison from attack by the small but dangerous Pennsylvania Navy. The garrison did not have long to wait for just such an instance.

The day after the British took control of Philadelphia, a number of American ships, including the Continental frigate *Delaware*, attempted to make a run up the river past the British garrison in the city. A cannonade ensued, during which the *Delaware* grounded on Windmill Island in the river and was captured by the British.[143] It seemed that the defenses of the American capital were crumbling from the inside.

Once in possession of the city, the British confronted a new dilemma, the lack of supplies. Since leaving the landing area at Head of Elk in early September, the British army relied on overland transport to bring necessary to supplies to the troops. This practice, in turn, meant very long supply lines, which Washington's Continentals or the local militia could attack and disrupt. One effect of the logistics dilemma was that prices for basic food stuffs became quite high. Ewald noted that on September 31, "a convoy with provisions arrived at Philadelphia...through which the great wants that the army had endured on the march from Turkey Point were remedied in some measure." He went on to clarify, "I speak here not of tea, coffee, sugar, and wine, but only of the necessities of salt and good bread."[144]

Given his supply dilemma General Howe determined to open the Delaware River. In order to accomplish this, he sent a force under Colonel Stirling consisting of the 42nd Highlanders to cross the River at Chester, and attack one of the American posts at Billingsport in New Jersey. This effort took place on October 1.

Washington, seeing that Howe had detached some of his forces, decided on an effort to drive the British from Philadelphia, or at least achieve a tactical victory against part of their forces. He determined to use the Continental Army to attack the British outpost at Germantown. For his part, Ewald was camped outside Philadelphia, near the site of the planned attack. On the evening of October 3, a Professor Smith came to see Ewald. The man owned a country house near the Jäger camp. Ewald had given protection to the professor from foragers. Smith asked Ewald to walk with him and led him behind the camp. Once they were away from camp, "when he thought no one would discover us, he addressed me with the following words: 'My friend, I confess to you that I am a friend of the States and no friend of the English government, but you have rendered me a friendly turn. You have shown me that humanity which each soldier should not lose sight of. You have protected my property. I will show you that I am grateful. You stand in a corps which is hourly threatened by the danger of the first attack when the enemy approaches."[145]

After giving this warning, which left its recipient in some shock, the doctor left for Philadelphia without uttering another word. For his part, Ewald "stood for a while as if turned to stone." When he recovered from the impact of the intelligence he received, Ewald "hurried into camp and reported it to Colonel Wurmb, who immediately mounted his horse to report this information to General Knyphausen and to headquarters."[146] According to Ewald, Howe reacted to the news with disbelief.[147]

Howe's subordinates did take the warning seriously, and when the Americans attacked the following morning, the British troops were prepared. Ewald was duty officer and "the colonel ordered the pickets which were posted from the Schuylkill along Wissahickon Creek doubled at midnight." This was done because the Schuylkill covered the army's front on their left flank. The colonel further ordered Ewald to "patrol steadily both roads near and the highway to Norriton [Norristown]." Ewald performed this duty, "unceasingly, and assigned each part of the picket its place, which should be taken at the first shot."[148]   Thus, at least a part of the line stood alerted and prepared for the coming attack.

The problem for the British and Hessians was that the area they were operating in was not well disposed to them. As he recalled, "We could not learn much from our patrols because they were constantly betrayed by the country people and attacked and did not venture farther than they could get support."[149] Even with this constraint, the Hessians knew an attack was imminent and took precautions accordingly.

As the Americans approached the following morning, "one of my [Ewalds's] patrols ran into the enemy a quarter of an hour away and withdrew under constant fire to the defile I had to defend." As the attack developed, he "immediately ordered the rocky heights occupied from the left bank of the Schuylkill along the ravine and bridge, which were at Vanderen's Mill, and awaited the enemy." At about 6 AM the attack materialized, by Ewald's reckoning it included some two thousand men and several artillery pieces. It was under the overall command of a general

James Potter. He held out at his post until the end of the engagement.[150] In the wider battle, Ewald actually fought against a feint attack led by Pennsylvania militia general Potter.

Still, the Americans initially gave a good account of themselves, driving in the pickets and some of the outer lines of the British. Three factors combined to deprive the Americans of victory. First was the plan itself, which involved three different columns marching by different routes to meet at the attack position. Second, the house of Benjamin Chew, Clivenden, popularly known as the Chew House. As the British fell back, elements of several units took possession of the house and took refuge there. Instead of simply leaving a cordon of troops around the house and continuing the advance, so as not to lose momentum, Washington allowed his chief of artillery, Henry Knox, to convince him to squander precious time and troops in repeated attacks on the edifice. All of these failed, but they did slow the impetus of the American attack, giving the British forces time to regroup, and allowing for reinforcements to arrive from the city.[151] Commenting on the defense of the Chew House, Ewald noted, "This example of a single brave and intelligent man, through whom the entire English army was saved, shows what courage and decision can do."[152] The final factor that broke the American assault lay in the weather conditions. The morning was quite foggy, and some of the troops became disoriented, leading several American units to fire on one another.[153]

As for the Jäger, their casualties in the fighting amounted to three killed and eleven wounded. Most of the wounded died of their injuries in the following days.[154] Ewald checked on the condition of the wounded in Philadelphia the day following the battle, and was clearly upset at what he came upon, "I found these unfortunate battle victims still lying on the straw, almost without any care." The reason for their predicament lay in the fact that the Delaware River remained closed to British shipping. As a result, "There was still a lack of necessary medicines and bandages, which were requisitioned at first from the city and now awaited from the fleet."[155] This comment further eludes to the idea that the American strategy of closing off the river was indeed succeeding as the British were unable to supply their needs through requisition from the city, and were likewise incapable of getting enough supplies through the American cordon to maintain themselves.

Ewald described the method then in practice for bringing supplies into the city, "Up to now the army had obtained its provisions with great risk and much inconvenience, for they had been transported from Chester to Philadelphia in flatboats manned by armed sailors along the banks of the Delaware..." At times, this meant passing very close to the ships of the Pennsylvania Navy in the river, so it was only done "under the cover of dark night, in spite of enemy vessels."[156] This method of supplying the city was dangerous and quite precarious as well. A fact not lost on Ewald, "Should such a convoy be taken by the enemy, the army would be exposed to the greatest privation."[157] Ewald reported an additional factor contributed to the precarious nature of the supply situation, "I once saw such a provisions flotilla arrive. All the sailors had been made completely drunk to stimulate them to fight in case of an attack."[158]

Following the battle of Germantown, and due to the supply situation described above, the attention of both army commanders shifted to the Delaware River. As Washington grew to understand the British supply predicament in the city, he reinforced the forts along the Delaware, and asked that the Pennsylvania authorities do all they could to support their small state navy. Washington's growing interest in the river defenses is evidenced in a letter to John Hancock, then President of the Continental Congress, written on September 23. Washington reported sending troops in to strengthen the garrison at Fort Mifflin. His goal, that "General Howe's Situation in Philada [sic] will not be most agreeable for if his supplies cannot be stopped by Water it may be easily done by land." He concluded by stating, "To do both shall be my greatest endeavor, and I am not yet without hope that the acquisition of Philada may, instead of his good fortune, prove his Ruin."[159] Washington was beginning to discern the role the forts on the Delaware could play in an active defense of the region.

William Howe was quite aware of the necessity of opening the Delaware to British shipping as well. As noted above, his first attempt to open the river was to dispatch the force under Colonel Thomas Stirling to take Billingsport. Stirling's force included men of the 10th and 42nd regiments as well as some troops from the 71st. These men easily overwhelmed the one hundred or so defenders who composed the fort's garrison. In fact, the defenders of Billingsport retreated and spiked the fort's guns rather than make a stand.[160] Howe now saw clearly that further efforts would be necessary if he were to open the river to his shipping and maintain his position in the city. He therefore resolved to take the American post at Red Bank in New Jersey. Operationally, this constituted a sound decision on Howe's part, as the post at Red Bank, subsequently referred to as Fort Mercer, served as the key link to maintain the garrison at Fort Mifflin on the Pennsylvania side.[161] If Fort Mercer were taken then Fort Mifflin would be left hanging in the air with no source of supplies or reinforcements. Likewise, it would be impossible to evacuate any wounded troops from the fort. Without the forts, the small vessels of the Pennsylvania

Navy would be little more than a nuisance to the larger vessels of the Royal Navy and could be driven off so that the obstructions sunken in the river could be removed and the port reopened.[162]

Howe had initially planned for a British force to march on Fort Mercer and take the post. The Hessian Colonel, Count Carl Emil von Donop, however, sought permission to make the attempt himself. Most historians ascribe his desire to lead the assault with the Hessian contingent as a matter of assuaging the colonel's hurt pride. He had been in command in the area of Trenton the preceding year at the time of Washington's attack. Thus, leading a successful assault on the American post would help to regain the corporate pride of the Hessian contingent and improve their reputation in the eyes of their British counterparts.[163]

Howe gave von Donop permission to lead the assault with his own troops. From that point onward, issues began to crop up that would undermine the mission's chances for success. For instance, when von Donop asked Howe for additional guns to batter the fort's walls, Howe responded that if he wanted heavy British siege guns, then British troops could make the attack. As a result, von Donop took only the lighter Hessian field guns with him to New Jersey.

The expedition left Philadelphia from the Arch Street Ferry on October 22. In all, the force consisted of the Hessian and Anspach Jäger Corps under the overall Colonel von Würmb, and Donop's three Hessian grenadier battalions, von Linsing, von Minnigerode, and von Lengerke, respectively, as well as the infantry regiment von Mirbach. In addition, Donop brought with him the battalion artillery which consisted of ten three-pounders. One key element the force lacked were scaling ladders to ascend the walls. These were necessary as the guns would be too light to batter through the walls of Fort Mercer.[164]

Once across the river, the Hessians proceeded towards Haddonfield, New Jersey, with the Jäger out in front, once again serving as the advanced guard. Before they had moved inland a half an hour, Ewald reported skirmishing with the New Jersey militia. Once at Haddonfield, the column camped for the night. During their bivouac, von Donop took precautions to preserve the security of his force and to prevent information on their numbers from reaching the Americans. He ordered all the young men of the town who expressed pro-Patriot views to be gathered in the center of Haddonfield and to remain there until the Hessians had departed on the following day. The Loyalists in the town aided Donop in rounding up possible rebel sympathizers. Still, quartering an army in a town in the eighteenth century meant that the perimeter would remain somewhat porous. Due to these gaps, New Jersey militia were able to inform the

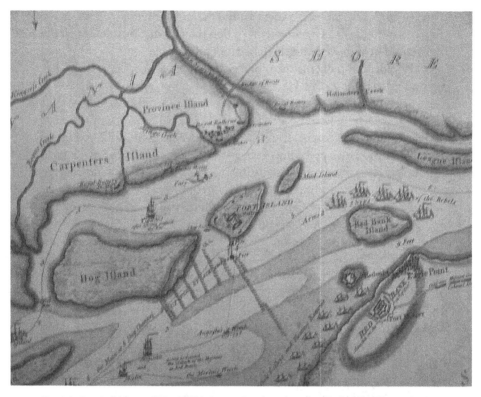

Figure 3: Detail of the siege of Fort Mifflin showing the relative location of Red Bank and Fort Island, as well as the chevaux de frise. Philadelphia Maritime Museum. Author's collection.

garrison commander at Fort Mercer, Colonel Christopher Greene, of the approach of the Hessian forces. For his part, von Donop spent the night of October 20 at the house of local Loyalist John Gill.[165]

The following morning, October 23, the Hessian column marched toward the fort at Red Bank, guided by local Tories. This fort, named Fort Mercer in honor of General Hugh Mercer who fell at the battle of Princeton, was begun in 1776 as part of the Pennsylvania Committee of Safety's efforts to provide some defenses for the city of Philadelphia from maritime assault. The initial works were laid out by one Colonel John Bull of the Pennsylvania militia, however, his knowledge of military engineering was limited to frontier fortifications. Later, some attempts at improvements were made by the French engineer Philippe Charles Trouson du Coudray. In reality, the engineer's alterations, which consisted of expanding the fort to accommodate a larger garrison, made the post more difficult to defend. The Americans had committed much the same error on their own the previous year with regards to Fort Washington in New York. However, the

Frenchman's plans called for a much more extensive work that there were troops available to garrison. As it turned out, this mistake transformed into a stroke of luck for the Americans.

As noted above, following the failed attack on Germantown. Washington seemed to gain a greater grasp of the river forts. Accordingly, he dispatched the First and Second Rhode Island regiments to garrison Fort Mercer. This move placed the post under the overall command of Colonel Christopher Greene of Rhode Island. To aid Greene in his efforts at stiffening the defenses of the fort, Washington dispatched the French engineer Captain Mauduit du Plessis.[166]

Greene and du Plessis seemed to develop a close working partnership, which was not always the case with Americans and the many foreign officers who served with the Continental Army. After a brief inspection of the fort, du Plessis informed Greene that the works were far too extensive for the garrison they possessed and suggested building an abatis that effectively reduced the size of the fort by half.[167]

In the event, the Hessian force arrived at the fort around noon on October 23. They were supposed to await a signal from the British fleet in the Delaware River before launching their attack as it formed part of a concerted attack on the American River defenses, with the ships of the Royal Navy and land batteries engaging the small Pennsylvania navy and the post across the river at Fort Mifflin respectively. Most historians charge that von Donop, in his desire to restore Hessian pride, attacked he post prematurely, without awaiting the proper support.

As they came within range of the fort, the Jäger fanned out in front of the main column to act as a screening force. As the leader of the Hessian contingent, Captain Ewald recorded, "I approached the fort up to rifle-shot range and found that it was provided with a breastwork twelve feet high, palisaded and dressed with assault stakes."[168]

The lack of scaling ladders would hamper any direct assault. Ewald positioned his men so as to provide covering fire for a direct assault on the post. The Jäger were posted around the artillery, Ewald having placed "sixteen good marksmen at the edge of the wood in the vicinity of the battery, who were to shoot at those men who showed themselves on the parapet."[169]

Before attacking the post, von Donop followed standard European practice and asked Colonel Greene to surrender the fort. Ewald discussed the demeanor of the officers after they issued the summons, which Greene rejected. He noted, "All these gentlemen regarded the affair with levity." There was one exception, a Captain Krug. Ewald approached the captain and sought his opinion of the undertaking "whereupon he answered: 'He who has seen forts or fortified placed taken with the sword in hand will not regard this affair as a small matter, if the garrison puts up a fight and has a resolute commandant." Krug further added, in an implicit criticism of von Donop's calling on the garrison to surrender, "We should not have summoned the fort, but immediately taken it by surprise on our arrival."[170] Almost prophetically, the captain continued, "But now they will make themselves ready, and if our preparations are not being made better than I hear, we will get a good beating."[171]

On hearing the news that the fort had rejected his summons to surrender, von Donop ordered his men to make fascines, bundles of sticks tied together that would be thrown into the ditch outside the fort to create a sort of ad hoc bridge for the attackers to cross when they stormed the post.[172] On hearing that the fort was to be taken by storm, Ewald commented, "This was the order which was given, and no one thought about axes or saws with which the obstructions and palisades could be cut down."[173]

The assault on Red Bank utilized three columns that were to make their attacks simultaneously, one from the north (von Minnegerode), one from the center (von Mirbach), and the other from the south (von Linsing). The Grenadier Battalion von Lengerke, and the Jäger were held back in reserve and also to provide covering fire. The infantry assault was set to go off at 5 PM.

For reasons that remain unknown, the von Linsing Battalion began to storm the outer works of the fort ahead of the other Hessian units. As the men approached the outer defenses of the fort, they slowly pushed their way through the abatis. The lack of saws and axes for such work impeded their progress. As the assailants attempted to pull themselves up the wall by hand, musketry erupted from the defenders stopping the assault dead in its tracks. At the same time, the small ships of the Pennsylvania Navy under the command of Commodore John Hazelwood added their fire to that of the fort's defenders and threw back the assault with great loss.[174]

The momentum of the attack collapsed, the survivors seeking escape from the withering fire raining down on them. With the prematurely launched assault thus driven off, Greene and Du Plessis quickly repositioned the defenders in order to meet the other threats to the post.

The defenders finished repositioning themselves just as the second attack began to clear the obstructions on the inner wall of the fort. This inner wall stood where du Plessis had reduced the size of the fort in order to more effectively defend it with the garrison available. Once they had pushed through the obstacles, the Hessians entered the outer works and found them empty. As the Hessians cleared the abatis and began scaling up the inner wall, they were greeted with a massive volley from the defenders. Von Donop went down in this assault. Lacking command and control, this attack soon fell apart as well, and the troops began to retreat, carrying off their wounded as best they could.[175]

Israel Angell of the Second Rhode Island Regiment left a gripping account of the fighting from the perspective of the defenders of Red Bank, "there begun an incessant fire of Musketery which Continued forty minutes when the hessians Retreated in the most Prescipited [precipitate] manner leaving 200 killed and wounded in the field. We spent the greatest part of the Night in bringing in the wounded."[176]

In the end, both attacks were driven off with heavy losses to the Hessians. During the retreat, the lack of wagons for the transportation of the wounded became a serious issue, and many of the men had to be abandoned to the Americans. Among the wounded taken prisoner by the Americans was von Donop, who was transported to the nearby farmhouse of Jacob Whitall.[177]

With von Donop out of action, command of the retreat devolved onto Lieutenant Colonel von Linsingen.[178] He collected the wounded as best he could and began the long march back to Philadelphia. Some assert that a determined assault by either Colonel Greene or the New Jersey militia could, at this juncture, have transformed the defeat of the Hessian attack into a complete route.[179] While the possibility exists, it is far from likely. The men in the fort had just repulsed two major assaults. Ammunition had to be tallied, and damage to the garrison assessed. At the same time, the New Jersey militia were conspicuous by their repeated absences up to this point in the campaign. Given their previous inactivity, the chances of them coming out to fight were far from clear. Finally, Greene did not know if there were any Hessian reserves lying in wait that could attack a force sent from the fort. In the end, the colonel determined to hold his position.

The Hessian retreat from Fort Mercer was both arduous and horrifying. Many of the wounded had to be abandoned on the field, for "Since we had flattered ourselves in advance with a successful surrender, no retreat was thought of, and no wagons brought to transport the wounded."[180]

It is worth noting that the assault on Fort Mercer constituted the largest setback Ewald had yet experienced during his service in America. He was not present for the American attack on Trenton, nor did he take part in the battle of Princeton. At Brandywine, he had been part of the advanced guard and not involved in the main clashes of the day, while at Germantown, due to the fog, he would only have discerned a small area of the field. In addition, most of his experience was in the small war of patrols and raids that composed the bulk of the partisan's war. As a result, the reverse at Fort Mercer exercised a particularly telling effect on the Jäger Captain that reverberates from the pages of his diary even years later. He took the time to list out the names of all of the officers killed or wounded in the attack.[181] He continued, "This day was especially sad for me. I lost five of my oldest friends among whom was a relative, and four of my best friends were severely wounded."[182]

Sentiments similar to these echoed throughout the Hessians Corps. Reading the other Hessian accounts of the battle and its aftermath, it is clear that many other soldiers empathized with Ewald's sorrow.[183] For instance, Lieutenant Colonel Ludwig Johann Adolph von Wurmb, writing to Major General Friedrich Christian Arnold Jungkenn, noted "It is painful for me to lose so many good people, I can't describe it. Your Lordship will pardon the confusion of this letter."[184] Von Wurmb noted that all the English pitied von Donop, who had suffered a wound in the hip while leading the assault.[185] Even more poignant was the diary entry from Ensign Wilhelm Johann Ernst Freyhagen Jr., a musketeer in the Regiment von Donop. As the troops regrouped after the failed assault and prepared to retreat towards Philadelphia at 7:30 that evening, he noted simply, "many brave souls were missing."[186] Finally, the attack and subsequent repulse severely diminished the effectiveness of the units involved. As noted by Captain Levin Friedrich Ernst von Münchhausen of the Leib Regiment, "The Three battalions, which had lost almost all their officers and nearly 400 men, were lodged in the barracks, for they could not possibly do service very soon."[187]

Beyond listing the killed and wounded from the action, Ewald, as was typical, noted some of the things the assault column had done wrong. He listed two principle mistakes: First, "We should not have summoned the fort, but attacked as soon as we arrived." The consequence of the summons was that, "Through this mistake the garrison was alerted, and the armed vessels gained time to draw near for the defense." Second, and more significantly, he observed, "The plan of attack was faulty." He continued, "We ought to have made the feint attack where the Linsing Battalion attacked, and the real attack in full strength there where the Minnegerode Battalion attacked, because we were covered on this side by the wood up to musket-shot range."[188]

The first part of Ewald's analysis of what went wrong with the attack on Fort Mercer is quite clear. By summoning the fort, the attackers yielded the element of surprise, and gave the defenders time to prepare to receive them. For a force that had no heavy siege guns and would have to seize its objective by storm, this was a perilous mistake. The second major flaw in the attack, having to do with the positioning of the assault troops is the more complex.

By coming on the fort from three directions simultaneously, von Donop greatly complicated the assault and enhanced the chances of things going wrong. Timing the assaults to go off synchronously, which clearly failed on this occasion, being the most obvious possibility. Added to this was the difficulty of communication between the three attack columns. Likewise, as Ewald noted, making the principal attack from cover would screen it until it was in close proximity to the works.

Ewald went on to make some additional, minor criticisms of the manner in which the attack was made. Instead of simply pointing out flaws, however, the captain described the manner in which he would have led the attack were it up to him.[189]

Ewald's final verdict on the attack on Fort Mercer was that "On the whole, this attack belongs to the quixotic variety, which occurs in wars at times. For it was impossible to capture this work without the aid of armed ships, which had to be assigned to drive away the enemy vessels. But this was impossible, because the Americans had constructed very skillful chevaux-de-frise below Mud Island in the Delaware, where the entrance was blocked with a very thick chain."[190] He goes on to acknowledge that von Donop was actually supposed to make his attack the following day, when ships from the British navy were to engage the Pennsylvania navy and the Fort Mifflin.

Commenting on von Donop's impatience, Ewald attempted to be somewhat charitable, "Colonel Donop was a man of action. He had compared the siege of Mud Island with those of Bergen op Zoop and Olmütz and had offered to capture Fort Red Bank with one grenadier battalion." He further noted that this boast "offended the pride of the English." He therefore blamed the English, whom he charged "led him [Colonel Donop] into danger and he fell, whereby so many men—indeed, so many really brave men—had to bite the dust."[191]

The British did attack on the 23rd and bombarded the fort from their land batteries in Pennsylvania as well as numerous ships form the Royal Navy that had taken up station in the Delaware below the line of the chevaux-de-frise. In the fighting, a fire broke out on the British ship-of-the-line *HMS Augusta*, and soon her powder magazine exploded in a blast that shattered glass windows in Philadelphia and was heard fifty miles away in Reading, Pennsylvania. A smaller vessel, the *HMS Merlin* attempted to retrieve some of the survivors from the *Augusta* and became grounded in the mud. Efforts to free her were unsuccessful, and the *Merlin* had to be abandoned and set on fire as well. Therefore, the British lost the *HMS*

Augusta and later *HMS Merlin* in their attempt to force the American defenses.[192] The efforts to open the Delaware River to the British Navy were becoming a very costly campaign of attrition.

For the Jäger, however, there were still some further duties to attended to. They played no further role in the efforts to reduce the river forts. Still, Ewald and his men would take part in several subsequent operations prior to going into winter quarters in Philadelphia. Supply continued to be a major problem for the men, however, as the control of the river remained contested well into November. On November 6, Ewald noted, "Thus far we are still in a bad situation. Washington is making the route by land very unsafe between Chester and Philadelphia."[193] As for the defenses along Delaware River, after the failed assault on Fort Mercer, the Howe brothers focused their efforts on Fort Mifflin. After virtually encircling the fort, and pounding it into rubble, the American garrison abandoned the post in the night of November 16, after spiking the few remaining guns and setting fire to anything that may still have been of use to the British.[194] Another Hessian soldier recorded that it was "A very dull and cold day. At noon it began to snow."[195]

Even when the river was reopened to British shipping,

Although the army could relax moderately during the lull, nevertheless the partisan war was carried on constantly in full force. Not a day passed in which the Jäger Corps, the light infantry and the Queen's Rangers were alarmed, and several people of the parties killed, wounded, or captured.[196]

With regard to the Queen's Rangers, this was a unit of loyalist raised by Colonel John Grave Simcoe. They would often serve in tandem with Ewald and his Jäger.

Born in 1752, to a Royal Navy Captain, John Graves Simcoe received his education at Exton, Eton and Oxford before enlisting in the Royal Army and purchasing a commission as ensign in the 35th Foot in 1771. This regiment was one of those deployed to Boston as the troubles with the colonies escalated, and Simcoe accompanied it as adjutant. He saw service in the fighting around Boston in 1775 and was promoted to captain in the 40th Foot that same year. After being seriously wounded at the battle of Brandywine, he was promoted again to Lieutenant Colonel and placed in command of the Queen's Rangers, a unit originally raised by Robert Rogers. This unit was a mixed force of infantry and cavalry, composed of loyalists, which served much the same purpose as Ewald's jägers, thus their regular service together.[197]

Ewald described how the Jäger, who were being pushed out as far as Vanderen's Mill and Wissahickon Creek, had thus far been fairly successful.[198] On November 13, Ewald commanded a party of one hundred foot and twenty-five mounted Jäger who went out partly in search of fresh provisions, but sought to gain some intelligence of the enemy in the region of the Falls of Schuylkill. The patrol led to a skirmish as Ewald "drove back the sentries I found on this side of Watt's Ford, whereupon a few small bodies appeared on the heights of Smith's plantation." As the American reinforcements arrived, "I exchanged several shots with them, but they let me finish my business and march back in peace."[199]

With the Delaware defenses finally breached on November 16, the British could then focus on clearing the obstacles from the river and shipping in much needed supplies. This occurred on November 24, when Ewald noted, "On the 24th, to our joy, some thirty large vessels arrived at Philadelphia laden with all kinds of merchandise and provisions, through which the army was suddenly delivered from its wants."[200]

The ships not only brought in much needed supplies, but reinforcements as well. On November 27, a ship arrived carrying two new Jäger companies as well as some "240 recruits for the Jäger Corps." Ewald was not particularly pleased with the quality of the reinforcements. Concerning the officers, he wrote, "The officers consisted of two French officers who had been ordered to this war from the regiments remaining in Hessen." Of the enlisted men, "The noncommissioned officers and jägers consisted partly of deserters from all nations, partly of ruined officers and noblemen, students from all the universities, bankrupts, merchants, and all kinds of adventurers."[201] A motley crew indeed! Clearly, the human material he had to work with in order to rebuild his company after the losses sustained in the campaign was fairly poor.

While the supplies brought into the port of Philadelphia offset the needs of the troops to some extent, they were not enough to sustain both the garrison and the civilians who remained in the city. In order to provide for everyone, communications had to be opened with the Pennsylvania countryside. Farmers had to know that they could bring their produce to the city without fear of American raiding parties. In order to accomplish this goal, the troops were stationed on the outskirts of the city. On November 28, the Jäger Corps was ordered to position itself "behind the defile of the Morris plantation, which was situated on the Schuylkill in front of the army's left flank."[202]

The officers and the bulk of the Jäger Corps took as their headquarters a house belonging to Robert Morris. There would be a particular temptation to loot this estate, since Robert Morris was a very well-known member of the Patriot movement. The house itself was fairly large, and the property included some twenty outbuildings.[203]

While much of the rest of the army settled into winter quarters in Philadelphia, the Jäger Corps remained active. For instance, on December 2 "a patrol of one corporal and eight mounted Jäger ran into an enemy patrol of equal strength." The Jäger attacked. Several of the Americans were cut down, and the Jäger pursued them as they retreated. The Jäger fell into an ambush set by the Americans, "whereby one Jäger and two horses were killed, two Jäger seriously wounded, and one captured."[204]

In these skirmishes, the Jäger often captured American supplies and equipment. This could lead to some surprising finds. In one instance, Ewald recorded the contents of an America officer's haversack, which earned his grudging but heartfelt respect, "For the lover of justice and in praise of this nation, I must admit that when we examined a haversack of the enemy, which contained only two shirts, we also found the most excellent military books translated into their language." These included, "Turpin, Jenny, Grandmaison, LaCroix, Tielke's Field Engineer, and the Instructions of the great Frederick to his generals." For Ewald, this likely a very nostalgic cache as he studies many of these works when he was recuperating from his duel back in Kassel. By way of contrast, he asserted that his own officers "consider it sinful to read a book or to think of learning anything during the war."[205]

Soon thereafter the Crown forces launched a much larger expedition against the Americans near Edge Hill. The sorties came about as a result of the heightened skirmishing between the two armies in this area. As the British marched out to the area known as the Northern Liberties, they burned a number of houses in the area which the Americans had been using them to shelter and conceal their raiding parties.[206] As their part in the mission, the Jäger Corps came up against an enemy outpost. The defenders withdrew as the Jäger grew closer. The advance troops followed the Americans and the Jäger Corps deployed for battle. They came on the flank and rear of Americans troops who consisted of New England troops and riflemen. This unit was "thrown into great disorder and shot up so severely that a colonel, ten officers, and a large number of men were killed or captured."[207] In the engagement, the Jäger lost four dead and eleven wounded.[208]

The above attack was part of a larger reconnaissance on the part of the Crown troops in an attempt to determine if they could successfully attack the American position. William Howe personally surveyed the American lines and determined that they were unassailable. Meanwhile, Colonel Grey, whom Howe positioned to make a supporting attack, grew impatient after several hours of waiting and advanced. A sharp engagement developed, and the British withdrew with some casualties.[209] In the fighting that followed, the Jäger came up against Morgan's riflemen, recently returned from New York.[210]

After the preceding expedition against the American lines, the army returned to Philadelphia. During the march, Ewald's troops skirmished with American patrols.[211]

Soon after their return to Philadelphia, Earl Charles Cornwallis sent the following missive to Ewald,

Sir,

I cannot leave this country without desiring you to accept my best tanks for your good services during the two Campaigns in which I have had the honor to command the Hessian Chasseurs. If the war should continue, I hope we shall again serve together. If we should be separated, I shall ever remember the distinguished merit and Ability's[sic] of Captain Ewald.[212]

On the December 30, the British army finally went into winter quarters in Philadelphia. The Jäger were quartered "on plantations on the neck."[213] For his part, Ewald took up residence "with an old Strassburger." Reflecting on his experiences, his thoughts echoed those of any infantryman after a stint of hard service, "I was heartily glad that I had arrives safely under cover after two very hard campaigns, and could stretch my bones peacefully in a bed again—How sweet is rest when one seldom enjoys it."[214]

CHAPTER 6

THE PARTISAN WAR: CAMPAIGNS OF 1778-79

While Johann Ewald was clearly pleased with going into winter quarters after almost two years of constant activity, his respite was not to last very long. Outside Philadelphia, Washington utilized both his regulars and drafts from local militia to interdict supplies going into the city. In essence, he recreated the skirmishing efforts of the previous winter, which had succeeded in keeping the British off balance in the aftermath of the Trenton and Princeton campaigns. These efforts were quite successful and led to a call for renewed partisan activities by the British on January 26, 1778.[1] The skirmishing, which began while the contest for control of the Delaware River played itself out, continued into the New Year. At the same time, the British were occupying a city where the population was divided, but predominantly loyalist. Thus, the British occupation of Philadelphia is often depicted as a pleasant time for the officers of the Crown forces. Still, there were some among the populace who harbored patriot sympathies, and they provided information to the Americans, who grew increasingly apprised of British interdiction efforts.

As the campaign of 1777 came to an end, the strategic aspects of the war were altering significantly. British successes in the Philadelphia campaign were limited, and certainly not enough to offset the effects of the defeat of General John Burgoyne's invasion through the Mohawk Valley. In fact, the dogged resistance shown by the defenders of the Delaware River forts demonstrated the depth of American determination to fight for their independence.[2] This proof of American determination finally influenced the court of Louis XVI to openly recognize and ally with the fledgling republic as of February 6, 1778.[3]

Through their spies in France, the British Ministry were well aware of the direction in which French policy was moving. With this awareness came the understanding that the strategic contours of the war were altering dramatically. Open war with France was soon to follow, and when it did, the conflict would be global, and the British were forced into a strategic reassessment. No longer did the suppression of the American revolt stand at the top of the list for British military commitments. In fact, it dropped down several steps coming after the defense of the Home Islands, and the protection of the Sugar Islands and the India trade. These latter two were powerful economic generators for the Empire and would not be let go easily.

While the dynamics of the war began to shift across the Atlantic in Europe, the British and Hessian garrison in Pennsylvania hunkered down to face the winter. The Crown forces in Philadelphia did not suffer too much from want during the winter of 1777-78. Ewald noted, the "Jäger received twenty English shillings monthly with his small clothes..." this leading him to comment later that, "On the whole, it is safe to say that never in this world was an army as well paid as this one during the civil war in America."[4]

Nor was all of the Jäger captain's attention focused on the martial life during winter quarters. Ewald took advantage of the time to experience some of the different cultural and intellectual opportunities offered by the largest city in the colonies. For instance, on January 30, he attended a Quaker Meeting in the city near his quarters. He did this, "partly out of curiosity and partly just to hear something good once again."[5] In this case, his investigation did not pan out, as he noted "I went back to my quarters, my curiosity satisfied, but I was little edified."[6]

In addition, Ewald engaged in some humanitarian activities while quartered in the city. Possibly he learned about the plight of the Reverend Doctor Caspar Dietrich Weyberg of the First Reformed Church. Weyberg had been imprisoned by the British when they entered the city for his staunchly Whiggish views and political activities with the Continental Congress. Ewald, who was of the Reformed faith as well, worked to gain the release of the minister from prison, his efforts meeting with success.[7]

Summing up winter quarters he observed that "Though there were bloody heads at times and everything necessary and unnecessary for bodily existence was so expensive, nevertheless every soldier lived lighthearted, merry, and in abundance in this large city where, to be sure, no resident was certain in his property among the fifteen thousand men from all classes of human society."[8]

While much of January was spent in winter quarters, training new recruits, repairing equipment, and resting from the rigors of the last campaign, it soon became evident that the Jäger were itching for action once again. By January 25th, the Jäger, or at least their captain, were unhappy that they had not been sent out on patrol for some time. They were assured by General Howe that they were being given a rest period only. Further, "He expressed his complete satisfaction concerning our sensibilities; and wished that the same esprit de corps existed in the entire army."[9] They would not have long to wait to be back in action.

The hard hand of war still held the Philadelphia area in its grip in January 1778. Possibly in response to the burning of homes outside the city in the vicinity of Edge Hill the previous year, the Americans were now burning Loyalists out of their dwellings on the outskirts of the city, and the Jäger were dispatched to put a stop to this activity.[10]

As the weather warmed and winter gave way to spring, the *petite guerre* between the two armies intensified again. Both armies stirred from their respective winter quarters and began to patrol more heavily.

Historians often comment on the harsh winter at Valley Forge in 1777-78. Certainly, there were periods of privation, and the weather conditions were exacerbated by the lack of supply. As the most thorough exploration to date demonstrates, it was not so much a breakdown in the Quartermaster's Department that led to privation as the simple impassability of the roads due to weather conditions. It is important to bear in mind that most roads in North America during this period, especially those in rural areas, were little more than dirt tracks. Thus, rain, snow and even a sudden thaw could turn them into veritable swamps, and effectively cut communications.[11]

The focus on the suffering endured by the soldiers at Valley Forge has often overshadowed the more lasting transformation that occurred there. This was the training regimen developed and implemented by the Baron Frederick Wilhelm Augustus von Steuben. Von Steuben was a noble of Prussian birth. He possessed a title, but no land, had seen his first military service in the Seven Years' War, and been a confidant of Frederick the Great, but had fallen from grace. Recruited in France and groomed by both John Adams and Benjamin Franklin, he arrived in America at a time when an overabundance of foreign officers, demanding high rank and equally high compensation and delivering little in return save arrogance and failure had soured the opinion of many both in the army and in the Continental Congress. He had to tread carefully.[12]

Two things aided von Steuben immensely. First, the previous Inspector General of the Continental Army, General Thomas Conway was clearly on the outs with Washington as a result of debatable grab for power known as the Conway Cabal.[13] Secondly, The Prussian Baron agreed to work for free.

Steuben created the model company, consisting of men draw from most of the units in the encampment, and developed a series of simplified drill movements. These were taught to the model company in the morning with the understanding that they would disseminate them to their parent units in the afternoon. As a result of these efforts, the Continental Army that emerged from Valley Forge was one that possessed something it never had before, a uniform approach to military life in general, and combat in particular.[14]

The Continentals that the British and their German allies would face for the remainder of the war were a markedly more professional force. As soon as April 2, 1778, Ewald was once again skirmishing with American units outside of Philadelphia.[15]

The Jäger captain left a detailed account of his method in these operations: "I have constantly made my patrols or reconnaissances [sic] by echelon. One thus covers his rear and if you have to withdraw before a superior enemy, you always become stronger while the enemy becomes confused." He continued, "This is the safest way of all, especially in cut-up areas; one cannot be defeated."[16] Ewald constantly practiced these same methods of patrolling throughout his active service in America.

On April 20, for instance, he left Philadelphia on patrol towards Lancaster. Since they marched too far out to return before nightfall, he camped outside of the city for the night with his force. The following day, April 21, he was attacked in broad daylight by a patrol of six American infantrymen and two cavalrymen. Ewald's response, "I ordered several Jäger to sneak up on them on the right and left, for I wanted to capture them alive." His replacement troops, however, were not as experienced as they had been previously, "But one of the Jäger fired his rifle, whereupon the enemy ran away and only one man, whose horse was killed was captured."[17] During the interrogation, Ewald's prisoner attempted to outwit the Jäger captain by resorting to a classic ruse de guerre, "This man tried to assure me that Morgan with his whole corps followed hard on his heels; But since I had made it my principle to be strengthened in opinion by sight and experience, I remained at the place and posting until nine o'clock and no one appeared."[18]

In these patrols and skirmishes, Ewald also witnessed the harsh nature of the war at the local level, and often recorded vivid descriptions. He preserved one of these episodes in his diary, presented as an *"Example of a zealous patriot, through which one perceives that no brother spares the other in a civil war, when they are of different beliefs."*[19] The tale that followed described the manner in which a loyalist man living on Gloucester Point who had received protection form the English army was assailed by his own brother, who was a captain in the Continental Army. Washington had ordered the captain to go out with a party of men and burn all the forage in the vicinity of his brother's farm. The captain followed his orders to the letter, then visited his brother to inform him that if he did not break his ties to the British, the captain would ask Washington to return with another party and burn his farm. The farmer hurriedly left "home, wife and children and came to us."[20]

Even with the return of *petite guerre* between the two armies, Ewald still managed to find time to engage in some educational fulfillment. On May 1, 1778, for instance, he "inspected the library of the Quakers, which consisted of four thousand volumes, among which were to be found the works of the best English authors of old and modern times, together with various French writers."[21] In addition he viewed the libraries coin and natural history collection, noting that "since the collection had been started only forty years ago, the whole was not of great importance." Though he did note that "a number of mathematical and astronomical instruments were found in another room."[22]

Several days later, on May 7, Ewald visited the Academy and College of Philadelphia. There he met a Dr. Smith, "who is celebrated for his moral orations and his history of North America."[23] While Ewald left no comment as to the nature of the library or the curiosities he viewed at the College, the mere fact that he took the time out of his rigorous schedule reinforces the image of him as a soldier-intellectual.

At the same time, there came an official change of commanders on North America. Coming under increasing criticism for his lack of success in the colonies, Lord George Germain believed Howe was not prosecuting the war with enough vigor. By the same token, the communication between the two men had deteriorated over time to the point where one historian described the two as simply not listening to what the other was saying.[24] William Howe tendered his resignation at the end of the 1777 campaign. Major General Sir Henry Clinton replaced Howe in overall command.

Sir Henry Clinton continues to stand as a controversial choice to succeed Howe. While he was certainly the most well-read of the three generals who had come into Boston in May 1775, he was also the most timid and difficult to work with.[25]

Clinton would lead from the distinctly disadvantageous position of having to prosecute the war in North America with a drastically reduced amount of manpower than his predecessor. With France in the war, Britain's financially important sugar islands now became a potential target, as did her mercantile interests in India. Likewise, there now existed the possibility of a cross-channel invasion which further distracted Britain's military efforts from North America. As a result, the importance of the North American colonies decreased significantly.[26]

On May 10, a ship arrived in Philadelphia bearing the new commander of British forces in North America, Sir Henry Clinton. It is somewhat ironic that Howe should be superseded by Clinton, as the relationship between these men had soured over the course of the two preceding years. Beginning in 1775, when they got along quite well, it had deteriorated over the course of the 1776 campaign to the point where the two men no longer spoke to one another.[27]

Soon thereafter, a new wave of reinforcements arrived from Hessen-Kassel. In all, they amounted to about three hundred men. After discussing one of these men, whom he knew personally, he summed up the new recruits, "The remainder consisted of nothing but foreigners of all classes and the scum of the human race."[28] In addition to the new drafts, the ship brought correspondence from Hessen-Kassel. Among these was a letter from the Landgraf awarding Ewald the *pour la virtue militaire* through General Knyphausen. Ewald's response to receiving the decoration was one more of nostalgia than joy, "it reminded me of the days gone by, when faithful service and valor were rewarded with a golden chain, on which an estate usually hung. Nowadays the award consists of a pair of cuffs but without the shirt."[29]

It would seem from the preceding that the captain was growing embittered from his long service with so little to show for it. Clearly, Ewald had hoped to earn a title to the nobility. At the same time, in considering his reaction to the new recruits and his decoration, it should be noted that he was now a veteran with almost twenty years of service to his state, and he had not received a promotion since before departing for America. Given that context, the captain's cynicism becomes more understandable.

Shortly after assuming command, Clinton ordered the Army to make a demonstration, hoping to goad Washington into a general engagement. This occurred on May 19. As part of this movement, Ewald was ordered to the Falls along the Schuylkill. He was to take 150 infantry Jäger and twenty horse and "push my patrols as close as possible to the enemy, and to make a demonstration from this side."[30] At daybreak, Clinton led a large force of British and German troops, consisting of two English brigades, the Lieb and Donop regiments, and the entire Jäger Corps. He marched through Germantown and over Chestnut Hill in an attempt to draw the Americans' attention to his front. The maneuver was intended to outflank and encircle a force under the command of the Marquis de Lafayette. While Clinton drew Lafayette's attention toward himself, a covert march by General Grant was to circle around and attempt to cut off the young Frenchman. Lafayette detected the maneuver and managed to extricate his force with minor losses.[31]

During this operation, Ewald was thrown from his horse and injured two ribs. He observed, "for a time I could neither lie, nor stand, and suffered such extreme pains that I thought I would suffocate."[32] As in 1776, Ewald would spend some time recuperating from his injuries.

Shortly after the above expedition, on May 22, Ewald and the other troops received orders to pack their heavy equipment in preparation for the return to New York. On receiving this information, Ewald recorded the reaction of many of the Loyalists in Philadelphia to the news of the British departure, "All the loyal inhabitants, who had taken our protection, put their heads together and lamented that they now had to give up all their property."[33] He went even further, noting that the people had an "absolute right" to their dislike of the British move.

In this entry, Ewald captured the see-saw nature of the civil war within the American Revolution, noting that many who had rendered important service as Loyalist militia, were to be left behind. "They grumble and swear that hey army will leave Philadelphia and would rather let them be hanged by the Congress that serve England."[34]

One ray of light did penetrate this depressing scene, at least in so far as Ewald himself was concerned. Shortly before leaving for England, William Howe issued the following thanks publicly to Ewald and his fellow jäger captain, von Wreden,

> *Please allow me to bear witness, before my departure, to the extreme satisfaction I have always had in your distinguished conduct in the two campaigns during which I have had the honor to command you. The conduct of the two premier companies of Hessian chasseurs, incited by the zeal and brave example of their chiefs—you gentlemen— has been noticed by the entire army, and made such an unforgettable impression on me that I will always have the honor to be, with the most perfect esteem*[35]

> *Gentlemen*
> *Your very humble and obedient servant*
> *W. Howe*

Still, even such high praise from the former commander of all Crown forces must have had a hollow ring as the troops watched their heavy equipment and baggage being loaded for the return to New York. The efforts of an entire campaign, with all its attendant suffering and losses, especially for the Hessians, were simply given up.

As the army prepared to abandon the city, the shipping was taken up with the baggage of many prominent Loyalists and their families. It was therefore decided that the bulk of the army would march across New Jersey back to New York City. As preparation for the evacuation continued, fewer and fewer troops remained in Philadelphia. By June 16, 1778, only the Jäger Corps, the light infantry, the English and Hessian grenadiers the Queen's Rangers along with a few provincial troops still occupied in the city, acting as something of a token holding force. That same day, all the aforementioned units received orders to be ready to march at a moment's notice.[36]

As the Crown forces withdrew from Philadelphia, Washington learned through his informants that the British were in the process of abandoning the city. He sought to take advantage of the opportunity to engage the British in an open engagement and demonstrate the abilities of his Continentals now trained up to a new level of proficiency by the Baron von Steuben.[37]

Though there was some resistance from a council of war, Washington determined to test the British. The chief opponent of attacking the British in the open was Charles Lee, the recently returned Major General who had been captured by the British in late 1776. At the time of his capture, Lee was considered the most experienced professional officer in the Continental Army. Two years in captivity with the British in New York, however, had placed him very much outside the current of developments in the Continental Army. Returning to the army just in time to take part in the spring operations, Lee gave it as his considered opinion that the Continentals were still not capable of standing up to the British in an equal confrontation.[38] After listening to the various arguments and counter-arguments, Washington's final decision was to attack.

As a result, when the Jäger left Philadelphia on June 17, they constantly skirmished with the Americans as they made their way across New Jersey as the rear guard of the army.[39] The same pattern emerged on the following day as well. This time the Jäger formed the advanced guard, followed by the Hessian grenadiers, the provisions wagons and then the main army. The rear guard consisted of the Queen's Rangers, and provincials.[40]

As soon as the troops moved out, advanced patrols of New Jersey militia began skirmishing with the rear guard of the army. This harassment continued throughout the day as the New Jersey militia not only assaulted the British column but tore up bridges and generally made the route of march difficult for their opponents.[41] This was done in order to slow the British march and allow Washington and his Continentals to get into New Jersey and launch their planned attack.

For his part, Ewald patrolled forward of the main body of the army. At one point, he came upon a bridge destroyed by the enemy. He crossed the stream, Belly-Bridge Creek, with eighty Jäger. Once across, Ewald posted his men so that the engineers could repair the bridge for the rest of the army. The bridge repaired, "I then took thirty Jäger with me to patrol the area ahead. When I had ventured one hour further on, it seemed to me from my map that the terrain in the distance indicated that must not be far from Eayrestown, where the army was headed according to my idea of the march.[42] Thus Ewald was going far out in advance of the main army in order to determine of the route of march was clear. Once he spied what he believed to Eayrestown, he "sent back a Jäger who was to guide a lieutenant and thirty men to the place I had left, and I continued on my march."[43] The Jäger therefore advanced in echelon to secure the route in the front of Clinton's main army.

The army continued their march on the 20th with both the head and flanks of the column again under attack by skirmishers. The Americans set up ambushes wherever the terrain favored such a practice. For instance, while marching on the 23rd, the British army came upon a bridge. On the opposite side, the Americans had uncovered a section and thrown up a breastwork, which they occupied with artillery and infantry. They had concealed themselves so well that they were not fully visible to the British column. When the British advanced guard came in range, the Americans unleashed a volley. The Jäger returned fire, and the skirmishing continued until nightfall. In this encounter ten Jäger were either killed or wounded.[44]

Ewald and his Jäger set out for Crosswicks and rejoined the main army just beyond the town on the morning of the 24th.[45] During the march, Ewald observed that the plantation of a Mr. Lewis near Bordentown had been burned by the Americans. This effected Ewald as he had been quartered on the Lewis family in the winter of 1776 while on outpost duty. In addition, he promised a servant of the house protection for it shortly before it was set on fire.[46]

As the retreat continued, the Jäger Corps was placed opposite the Maidenhead Pass in order to cover the left flank of the army. Once the main army passed by the Jäger were to form the rear guard.[47]

On June 25, the Jager Corps skirmished throughout the day with the enemy. During this fighting, a Captain Cramen of the Anspach Jäger commanded the rear guard.

At daybreak on June 26th, the army marched off to the right towards Monmouth Courthouse. Ewald noted, "It was an extremely warm day and I felt it doubly." His troops served as the rear guard for the army and "Before daylight the enemy riflemen began to fire at the sentries."[48] The skirmishing grew more intense as the day progressed. Once the main army had passed, "I had scarcely received orders to follow the army when they drew up on all sides." The Americans outnumbered Ewald and his Jäger to the extent that "I was so hard pressed on the flanks at different times that the Corps and the light infantry had to support me." The Americans were relentless as well, "The enemy kept hanging on me up to the new camp." All of this fighting took its toll as Ewald reported losing sixty men out of his one hundred eighty infantry Jäger and thirty horsemen, in all slightly over a third of his force.[49]

On June 28, the army left in two divisions. The van was commanded by von Knyphausen and included the Jäger Corps.[50] They soon engaged with the Americans.

As Ewald and his troops continued in their own fight with the Americans, the main forces of the opposing sides clashed at Monmouth Courthouse. Initially, the advanced guard of the Continentals, under General Charles Lee, attacked the rear of the British column as they proceeded out from Monmouth Courthouse. The British charged, and Lee's troops fell back. At that moment, Washington arrived on the field and a hot exchange of words transpired between him and Lee. The result, Lee was relieved of command and Washington assumed the overall direction of the battle. As both sides funneled in more troops, a back and forth battle developed under a blazing June sun. In the end, the armies fought a day-long engagement in which the Americans refused to break off. Instead, they stood toe to toe with their British opponents and gave as good as they got. As the sun set, it was clear that this was a drawn battle. It was likewise clear that the American discipline and esprit de corps had altered significantly, proof of the success of von Steuben's training regimen.

That night, Clinton abandoned the field along with his wounded, and continued his march to New York. Both sides claimed victory in the affair.[51] As Ewald described in his diary, "At midnight the news arrived that the enemy was repulsed with considerable loss and the army had passed Crosswicks."[52] The spin on events likely came from British officers.

The battle of Monmouth Courthouse was the last major engagement fought between the two main armies in the North and is often seen the end of active operations in that theater. While it is true that there were no more major confrontations, the small war, in which the Jäger were constant participants, continued unabated. Even as the British column marched away from the battlefield on the following day, American skirmishers hung around its rear and attacked constantly.[53]

Ewald reckoned the casualties on both sides to be about 1,100 men.
He noted the change in their esprit d'corps as well, "Today the Americans
showed much boldness and resolution on all sides during their attacks."[54]
Still, he observed some weaknesses in the American command, "Had
Generals Washington and Lee not attacked so early, but waited longer,
until our army had pushed deeper in to the very difficult defiles in this
area, it is quite possible we would have been routed, since one division
could not support the other, being separated by the great number of wagons."[55] During the subsequent retreat after the battle of Monmouth, the
Jäger were nearly cut off more than once by parties of advancing Americans. Likewise, the Americans, Continentals and regulars, maintained
their pressure on the retreating British column.

For instance, on July 1, Ewald noted that "a strong enemy corps appeared here from Middletown." The appearance of these troops brought
on "A sharp skirmish," that "occurred between the Jäger and the enemy
riflemen, in which three Jäger were killed and five wounded." Finally,
toward evening the Americans withdrew. The following day, in another
skirmish, two additional Jäger were captured.[56]

Clearly, the constant action the Jäger engaged in made the retreat
across New Jersey extremely difficult. While Ewald did not comment on
this factor in his diary, the continuous skirmishing, as well as the vigilance
required to prevent falling into an ambush surely must have exacted a
psychological toll on the captain and his men. For them, the march could
not end too soon. Still, the troops made their way back to northern New
Jersey, and were eventually ferried across the river to New York and its environs. Their transport was delayed somewhat due to fears of the possible
arrival of a French fleet.[57]

For most, the history of the northern campaigns of the American War
of Independence ends with the battle of Monmouth. When looking at the
major battles, this assessment holds merit. At the same time, the partisan
war continued. It anything, it intensified. This assessment is borne out by
the following engagements.

On July 23, Ewald led a patrol composed of sixty infantry Jäger and
twelve horse past Philipse's house, to a distance of two German miles.[58]
Concerning this patrol, he noted, "I had no guide, did not know the
country, and just had to follow my nose."[59]

As was becoming more his practice, Ewald quickly reconnoitered the
terrain and used it to his advantage, "I took my route over impossible hills
cut through with rocks and woods in order to march as concealed as possible and to arrive near the precise spot."[60] As he proceeded, "Halfway there
I found a ravine with a stone bridge over it, where to my relief I discovered

a church with a graveyard which was surrounded by a wall." This location, with its structure surround by a wall provided a natural defensive point, so Ewald "left there half of my detachment to cover my rear."[61]

On his return, passing by Philipse's house, Ewald gained some useful intelligence from the steward there. Realizing that the man could be useful in the future, "Afterward, I made an arrangement with him to let the wash hang out of the attic of the house when enemy parties were in the vicinity of his house, which could be seen halfway from our post."[62] The preceding demonstrates that Ewald was gaining an understanding of the political dimension of the war, and growing more capable at utilizing the political divide between Patriots and Loyalists to his advantage.

A further instance of the small war occurred on July 1, 1778. Colonel Wurmb agreed to launch a three-pronged assault on American troops in his vicinity that consisted of Major John Graves Simcoe's Queen's Rangers, the Chasseurs of Colonel Emmerich and the Jäger Corps.[63] "These three parties were to march very slowly and to hold in ambuscade at different times for hours at a stretch, in which every enemy party which went out must fall into the hands of one or the other."[64]

Shortly after the Jäger Corps arrived at their planned position, near Philipse's house, they encountered a party of Americans. Ewald noted that his adversaries were "well concealed behind rocks overgrown with bushes that our advanced guard, which they took for one of our patrols, had already passed them."[65] The Americans fired and withdrew as they realized they were up against the entire Jäger Corps. While clearly a win for the Crown forces, this encounter demonstrated the growing prowess of the Americans at *petite guerre* as well. During the fight, a thick fog came up, making pursuit of the retreating Americans impossible.[66]

The growing prowess of the Americans, possibly complimented by their use of Native Allies, came across clearly on a patrol a little over a week later. On the evening of August 9, Ewald made a patrol with a party of sixty Jäger. His force included twenty infantrymen and ten cavalry troopers as well. This party made their way over a mountain between the Albany and Boston highways. He did not encounter any of the enemy while on his patrol and returned to make his report. As he described, "I had scarcely rendered my report to my chief when our spy arrived. He congratulated me on having escaped by luck, because an ambuscade of twenty Indians and three hundred Americans was concealed on my right."[67]

In explaining his lucky escape, Ewald determined, "Since they had not attacked, they must have thought my patrol was stronger than they were."[68]

The three corps, the Jäger, Simcoe's Queen's Rangers, and Emmerich's Chasseurs were by now becoming quite used to working together. Their ability to be mutually supporting, and the determination of their commanders to come to one another's aide is evidenced by the following incident.

On August 20, Emmerich's corps had gone out on patrol towards East Chester and ran into a superior enemy force. As soon as the Jäger heard the firing, Ewald dispatched fifty men and ten mounted troops toward the fighting. Their purpose was to cover Emmerich's left flank. As the Jäger approached, they broke cover too soon. However, their exposing themselves worked to their advantage on this occasion, as it caused the American force to break off. The Jäger could link up with Emmerich's men and provide cover for them. The latter force lost some twenty men in the fight.[69]

These losses were significant in several ways. Training these troops to proficiency took longer than training regular troops. Each Jäger, or chasseur came to possess a valuable skill set. When they were lost, the skill set was lost as well. Even with new recruits arriving regularly to make up the losses, the units overall effectiveness declined over time. The recruit may have occupied the physical space of a fallen Jäger, but it would be some time before they were trained to the level of their veteran comrades. In the interim, their lack of skills could be of great danger to the unit overall. This was the case even if the new recruits were in good physical condition and willing to learn their duties. As the war progressed, the recruits' determination to learn their duties grew less and less evident. For instance, Ewald noted, "On the 29th three hundred Hessian recruits arrived, consisting of all classes of human beings, of which a part had rebelled against their officers on the ships."[70] These troops would be very difficult to train to a level of tactical proficiency where they would be useful to the Corps.

On August 31, a Captain Donop led a large patrol of one hundred infantry Jäger and fifteen horse in the vicinity of Philipse's house. He was scarcely a mile from the Jäger outpost when he fell into an American ambush. Four Jäger were killed, and six wounded in the first fire of the Americans. The Americans took four additional troops captive. Only a speedy flight by the remainder saved the patrol. Ewald attributed this to the fact that "he had marched with his nose without taking every precaution," meaning he had trusted too much in his instincts without following the procedures the veteran commander so often advocated.[71]

The above skirmish demonstrated the growing tactical acumen of the Americans, and Ewald understood this as well, "The Corps hurried to help as soon as it heard the firing, but the enemy who knew his business, had withdrawn immediately after his well executed stroke."[72]

The Americans would not get away unscathed, however. As word spread through the British camp of the attack, Armand's corps was seen heading towards East Chester, "through Philipse's Manor into the area where Simcoe, Cathcart and Emmerich were posted."[73] Once these three men learned of the raid, they broke camp immediately. Simcoe then moved with his troops through a wood to screen his movements, and passed the enemy party to cut off their retreat. The other two corps, Cathcart's and Emmerich's, approached the Americans from the front in order to distract them and draw their attention as Simcoe got into position. They disposed of their forces, especially the cavalry, behind hills in order to ambush the Americans.[74]

In addition to these efforts, Simcoe requested additional troops, as the American raiding party was said to number somewhere near two thousand men. Likewise, part of the American force was comprised of Indians, whom the troops feared, for as Ewald noted, "it had been described to them as more dangerous than it really was."[75] Ewald took a position in an area known as Cortland's woods with his troops.[76]

Around four in the afternoon the enemy appeared, and a skirmish began. The various Crown units withdrew and the Americans "pursued them vigorously."[77] At this point, "The cavalry of Emmerich and the Legion burst forth, charged, and drove back the enemy, who was now attacked in the rear by Simcoe between Post's and Valentine's plantations, where he had to cross a defile."[78]

The skirmish then broke up into five of six separate fights, as both sides used the terrain to their advantage. In the fighting, "The Indians as well as the Americans defended themselves like brave men against all sides where they were attacked…"[79] Still, by seven in the evening, most of the Americans were either dead or wounded. The contest was vicious and bloody. Ewald reported that "No Indians, especially, received quarter, including their chief called Nimham and his son, save for a few." He further noted, "Only two captains, one lieutenant, and some fifty men were taken prisoners."[80] Armand managed to escape the ambush with some of his men. An American general, Scott, tried to bring up reinforcements, "but he arrived on the second scene just as late as the Jäger Corps had arrived on the first one in the morning."[81]

After the fighting, Ewald walked the field. In particular, he was interested in the native foes they had engaged. He examined the bodies of the fallen Indians and left a thorough description of them. Specifically, he "was struck with astonishment over their sinewy and muscular bodies."[82]

Still, the small war of outposts between the Americans and the Crown forces continued. On September 16th, Ewald and his comrades learned that the General Scott had dispatched a Colonel Gist with 500 men up to a point known as Babcock's Hill.[83] They immediately set plans in motion for a surprise attack. Emmerich and Simcoe set their troops on the march at midnight, marching past Mile Square. Their goal was to position themselves so as to be able to catch [Colonel Nathaniel] Gist's men in the left flank and rear respectively.[84]

Later, at one in the morning, Captain Wreden moved out with one hundred of his Jäger and marched on the Richmond road to position his men to attack the enemy on his front by the time daybreak arrived.

All three of the detachments reached their marks by the preappointed time, an indicator of their acumen as partisan fighters, and their knowledge of the territory in which they were operating. At the last moment, Emmerich changed his orientation, and formed his men in an arc. This movement alerted the Americans to the presence of the enemy troops, and only some six officers and seventy men were captured. Still, the attackers did burn the American camp and all of their baggage.[85]

On the 19th, Simcoe and Emmerich set out to discover the movements of the Americans in the area. They marched down the East Chester Road in the direction of White Plains. Lieutenant Colonel Wurmb and the Jäger Corps marched down the main Albany Road. Ewald and his men formed a part of the latter force. Specifically, Ewald and his Jäger company, with fifteen horse "took the footpath across the mountains which led between the Albany Road and the road past East Chester towards White Plains."[86]

Following their different routes, the forces converged towards sunset on an abandoned American camp. "There we gathered information from the country people and several prisoners, who probably were marauders that Washington had moved toward Peekskill and Gates with the Northern army toward Boston."[87]

On September 23rd, the Jäger Corps were posted on the North (Hudson) River as the advanced post for the left wing of the army. In this position, they covered Clinton's flank as he marched into New Jersey and camped at New Bridge with the main army.[88] Soon the British forces withdrew, and the Jäger Corps was once again positioned in New York.

On the evening of September 28th, Ewald was "detached with 120 Jäger to occupy the post on Sneading Hill, because Simcoe had left it."[89] Simcoe had been temporarily reassigned to General James Grey, who was marching with a force across the Hudson, hoping to surprise the Americans stationed at Tappan.[90] The planned attack failed to materialize, as Armand, the American partisan leader in the region, refused to take the bait.

Still, there were some clashes around Sneading Hill, a section of the modern Bronx in New York, as Armand's patrols came up against the ambushes Ewald set to meet them.[91] Shortly thereafter, Ewald went on a reconnaissance. This operation serves as an excellent example of balancing risk through careful preparation, a skill the captain was learning through the hard school of experience.

On September 30, 1778, at daybreak, he went on patrol with sixty Jäger and twelve cavalrymen in the direction of Dobbs Ferry. His goal was to discover information on an American detachment rumored to be operating in the vicinity of Tarrytown, New York. Exceeding his orders, "I went still further than I was ordered, since I risked nothing and had covered my rear in echelon but could not collect the slightest news form the country people and returned safely."[92]

Setting out rear guards allowed the captain to "risk nothing." If he ran into trouble, Ewald would have the ability to fall back on his own detachments, growing in size as his enemy extended themselves. In effect, he would become stronger as his opponent's force became weaker since they would have to leave detachments to cover their line of retreat or risk being cut off. Likewise, he would be moving back in the direction of his own lines, and additional support, while at the same time, pulling his opponents further form their own lines. This combination, which Ewald's dispositions helped make possible, allowed him to risk exceeding the scope of his orders without compromising the safety of his force. Ewald's skill is further realized when contrasted with the escapades of a Captain Donop, a man junior to Ewald by some years, who led out a patrol and ran into an American ambush. In relating the incident, Ewald noted, "This misfortune was attributable to nothing other than the carelessness and weakness of Captain Donop, who in all fairness should have been punished because he had not been made wiser by the previous incident."[93]

On October 10th, the army moved back to their old camp, with the Jäger serving as the rear guard. The purpose of the move was to gather forage. In addition, the British hoped to draw Washington's attention from the region.[94]

Shortly thereafter, Ewald set out on a mission, ostensibly to set up a prisoner exchange. In reality, he was attempting to gain information concerning the strength and dispositions of Lee and Armand's corps. Ewald was taken to an outpost and questions. The troops on duty then held him for several hours. At the end of this period, "Colonel Armand arrived with six officers and an escort of twelve dragoons. I was received by him

with the utmost politeness."[95] The two men discussed the possibility of
a prisoner exchange for some time, then Ewald was released and allowed
to return to his lines under escort. While he did not gain the intelligence
he sought, Ewald managed to return form the risky enterprise, an accomplishment in and of itself.[96]

Almost as important, this provides another example of partisan tactics, the use of deception to gain intelligence of the enemy. It seems clear
that Ewald did not truly seek a prisoner exchange, nor would he have been
able to authorize one, as a captain, he was far too junior. Still, the ruse
provided him with an opportunity to try and gain some information on
his opponent's strength and dispositions.

As the weather changed and winter began to set in, operations of the
various corps slowed. However, they never completely came to an end.
As late as November 2, the Jäger Corps, the Queen's Rangers and the
British Legion along with Emmerich's Corps were all set in motion. They
marched in the direction of White Plains, in order to draw a cordon between the Bronx River and the Hudson.[97]

The purpose of the cordon, in turn, lay in the destruction of all the
structures in the region. These were used for cover by American raiding
parties and bandits and thus posed a significant security risk for the British
perimeter. As Ewald later recalled, "They were to protect several thousand workers with some hundred wagons who had orders to demolish
the houses of all the disaffected persons in the entire district of Philipse's
Manor, Cortland's Manor, and East Chester."[98] Clearly, given the numbers engaged, this constituted a significant operation.

The workers then transported the lumber from the structures they
knocked down to York Island where it was used to construct barracks for
the troops in the garrison force on the island. During the operation, "Our
antagonists constantly tried to attack our chain, but they were always driv-
en off."[99] The expedition was completed on the 5th, "when each corps
marched to its post."[100]

On the 13th, the different contingents of the army began going to
winter quarters on York, Staten and Long Islands. Those units assigned
to an area where no buildings stood to house them were "to receive the
necessary lumber to construct their own winter quarters."[101] The Jäger
Corps were assigned to Flushing on Long Island, arriving there after a
march of three days. Emmerich's Corps remained in its post at King's
Bridge on York Island. The Queen's Rangers and the British Legion took
up winter quarters in and around Oyster Bay, covering the right flank of
the Jäger Corps.[102]

Once established in their winter encampments, Ewald reported, "Except for a little duty of patrolling the shore, we enjoyed complete repose along the Sound, of which both men and horses stood in the greatest need."[103] He went on to note, showing some concern for his men, "The most displeasing part of the accommodations was that only the officers and mounted Jäger received actual quarters with the inhabitants. The foot Jäger had to construct their own quarters, for which they received the necessary wood and tools."[104] He further noted that the weather had already turned and deep snows, accompanied by a hard frost had set in and that "the poor men soon learned the necessity of working in order to get under cover."[105] Thus the experiences of the Jäger in ways paralleled those of Washington's troops as the established their encampment at Valley Force the preceding year. Washington's Continentals were experiencing much the same hardships as they moved into their own winter encampment in Morristown, New Jersey. This winter proved particularly harsh, worse still, the men in the ranks of the Continental Army began to see themselves as abandoned by the people.[106]

The winter encampment occupied by the Jäger Corps fell under the overall command of Earl Charles Cornwallis. Cornwallis was born in 1738 into an old British noble family. Educated at Eton, Cornwallis entered the military at age 17 in 1755. He saw his first military experience in the Seven Years' War, where he campaigned in the European theater in the army of Ferdinand of Brunswick. He was present at the crucial battle of Minden in 1759. He came to America in 1776, leading some 2,500 reinforcements for Howe's army. He quickly showed himself to be a competent and aggressive subordinate, hounding the beleaguered remnants of Washington's Continentals across New Jersey in November. He also took part in the second battle of Trenton and Princeton. In January of 1778, he returned to England, where he was promoted to Lieutenant General. He then returned to North America to serve as second in command to Clinton. The two men had a difficult working relationship, almost certainly exacerbated by the fact that Cornwallis carried with him a commission from the King which would allow Cornwallis to succeed Clinton on the spot should the former resign.[107] In late 1778, the friction between Clinton and Cornwallis still lay in the future. For the moment, they enjoyed a professional working relationship as then men under their command settled into winter quarters.

Over the course of the winter, the Jäger Corps, which saw a great deal of hard service the preceding year, enjoyed five months of rest. The time was not totally idle however, eighteenth century armies utilized winter quarters, and the reduction in active campaigning, as a time to train and amalgamate new recruits into their units. In addition, lost or damaged equipment was repaired or replaced. As a result, winter quarters served an important function in the preparation of the army for the subsequent campaign season.

In May 1779, Ewald visited the post of the Queen's Rangers, where his friend John Graves Simcoe held command, as well as the light infantry who were quartered on the eastern and southern parts of the island respectively. On his visit, "I found that all the officers of this corps (The Queen's Rangers) were speaking very badly about General Clinton."[108] The reason for their complaints lay in the fact that they "felt greatly offended that only the regular troops were used on occasions where they lined their pockets with money, in which case the light troops were quite forgotten."[109] Essentially, these men were upset that the regular troops were being sent on operations which held the chance of plunder, while they were not. He went on, "On that account they were disposed to send a grievance to the Commander in Chief, and they hoped that the Jägers Corps would make common cause with them."[110] While there were inequities in the system, "In all respects, there was something disgusting in the way it was managed, for during each campaign each commander in chief of a light corps or a party had to provide for his own spies and guides himself, and it was never asked whether they cost money.[111] Apparently, these issues reached a head when, "Now, during winter quarters with all the leisure, they devised such expeditions against the enemy as they knew could not fail, whereby little was risked that would enrich the officers and men."[112] In discussing the matter, Ewald demonstrated a line officers' disdain for the staff officers in rear areas, "They gave these plans to the friends of the pastry-crust eaters in headquarters to command, in order to let their names shine in the Gazette in London."[113] Finally, he noted, "However, the headquarters forgot that the light troops did not have anything to give up in the last campaign, since it was only defensive, and that they were marched into their quarters with reigned horses, worn out clothing, and empty purses." He concluded, "They should have been permitted to carry out coups in order to improve themselves."[114]

The last remark is somewhat telling, in that Ewald shows that the best thing for partisans or elite troops, was to keep them active. This allowed them to maintain and even hone their skills. Interestingly, he did not connect the fact that the men had stood idle for several months with the decline in their morale. The connection may, of course, stood as so obvious to the captain that it need not be mentioned explicitly.

In the end, the commanders of the light troops submitted their grievances to headquarters. Ewald commented on the reply. First, he stated the official reply for the reduced use of lights troops, "they explained at headquarters that since the troops of the line had seldom faced the enemy during the entire campaign, they should have the opportunity of getting to see the enemy again, whereas the light troops ought to be allowed to rest."[115] The captain did not accept this explanation, as he commented, "even in a headquarters court intrigue finds entry."[116] While there is certainly some truth to the notion that every organization, past or present, possess some internal politics, at the same time, the claim made in the reply, that the Jäger Corps required rest holds merit as well. The men had campaigned hard through much of 1778. Considering the almost continuous action described above, they were due for a period of relief from the constant stress of *petite guerre*.

Moreover, the above-mentioned friction in the British camp highlights two themes that often arose in Ewald's later writing: one being the manner in which the regular troops and officers often looked down upon the men in light forces. The second was the fact that the light troops often had to fend for themselves where supplies were concerned, as they were not always carried on the regular establishment. Ewald's solution to both of these problems was incorporating them men into the regular establishment.

Meanwhile with the change in weather, the troops prepared to take the field again. In May of 1779, Ewald noted that the troops were ordered to store their heavy baggage, a clear sign that they were moving from garrison to field operations. The light troops were especially enthusiastic, according to Ewald, "No one was more joyful than the light troops who were unaccustomed to long rest and whose purses had become empty by their own good housekeeping."[117]

The Jäger Corps returned to its area of operations from the previous year. The small war of raids between the Crown forces and the American commenced almost immediately. The troops moved out of their winter quarters on May 25, and Ewald, serving as the officer of the day, reported visiting his command post in the evening of the 30th. He had hardly reached the site "when I heard assembly blown in the Jäger Corps."[118] Hurrying on to discover the reason for the alarm, he found "Major Prueschenk, Captain Lorey, and I, each with one hundred men, were ordered to march immediately to Philipse's wharf." They were met there by additional units.[119] What he thought was an enemy incursion was in actuality the call to assemble on the wharf in order to board transports. They were embarked, "Eight hundred men were thrown on each ship, whereby everybody was stacked in such an unpleasant position that no one could either sit or lie down..."[120]

Clearly, the embarkation and the planned destination of the troops had been kept a secret. The men had no time to prepare. Ewald, usually someone in the confidence of his superiors, noted that, "We had nothing with us but what we carried on our back, not even a bite of bread."[121] Ewald was part of a 6,000-man assault force assembled by Sir Henry Clinton to take what was then described as the key to the Continent. The fleet set sail on the 31st.

The American fort at Verplancks Point (Stony Point) stood as the goal of the expedition. The Jäger took part in this assault, along with Patrick Fergusson's troops on June 1.[122] Ewald describes the difficulty incumbent on the men in the assault force, "The Jäger and Ferguson's force had to approach as close as possible on the land side in order to harass the garrison of the fort with rifle fire, but this could not help much since the whole fort was built of rocks and building stone."[123] Still, the garrison of the fort surrendered after a brief resistance.[124] On inspecting the fort after the battle, Ewald noted, "In a word, the work was too small, and since everything was of stone, each shell caused the greatest injury to the garrison."[125]

Shortly after taking the post, the Crown troops began to withdraw. On June 3, a foraging expedition set out in the direction of Peekskill. On the way, they were stopped at the Peekskill Bridge, which the Americans had partially destroyed. A group of riflemen, posted on the opposite side of the bridge, "insulted us and killed and wounded several men by good shooting."[126] At this point, General Clinton, who was with the army, ordered Ewald to cross the beams of the bridge, as the enemy had removed the planking, and drive off the Americans. Ewald took some forty of his Jäger. In addition, Ewald was ordered to go "as far as Continental Village and to burn it and to catch a few of the country people, because all the people in the entire surrounding area had been obliged to leave by order of General Washington except for several old men." Ewald accomplished his mission, setting fire to the village, and by evening, the army had returned to its former position.[127]

Ewald left a detailed description of the defenses he built up around his camp. His account warrants some attention as it exemplifies the approach to security that he would later advocate in his professional writing. "To the right and left of the bridge lay two small houses, which I ordered barricaded on the side toward the enemy. I constructed a flèche of wood between the two houses, which made our post quite secure, since it lay under the rifle fire of the detachment." Essentially, Ewald utilized the features in his area, the houses, and formed them into strongpoints which would anchor his position. He then added to this the flèche, a pointed fortification with its points facing outward, which provided additional security.[128] A few days later, on June 6, Ewald threw out an ambush party of a corporal and ten Jäger in front of his picket.[129]

The deployment of his men in ambush soon yielded results, "In the forenoon an enemy party of New England light infantry appeared, which fell into the trap, but because of the over hasty ardor of the Jäger, only three were killed and two captured..."[130] This episode demonstrates that even a well-conceived and executed plan can unravel when the troops are not up to the task. It should be kept in mind that the replacements Ewald had received for his corps, at least in his mind, were declining in quality. Likewise, they were fairly inexperienced in *petite guerre*, which would contribute to their inability to carry out plans such as the one above.

Still, the prisoners captured in the ambush were "very agreeable to the Commander in Chief, nevertheless, since [he] could collect some information about the enemy from these people."[131] Among those captured was a Native American, whose interrogation Ewald describes in some detail, concluding that "From this story of a people, one perceives that all our acts depend upon out upbringing and customs."[132]

Soon after his interview with the Native American chief, Ewald had another clash with the Americans. On June 7, an American party attacked a Hessian outpost. The Americans withdrew, so Ewald pursued them with the picket under his command. "I then went to the noncommissioned officers' picket on the right side, who had his post in a house which I put in a defensive position." On doing this, Ewald made a startling discovery, "much of the wood work had been ruined or burned." Essentially, the noncommissioned officer neglected the care of his post, and as a result, its defenses were weakened. "Thereupon I punished the noncommissioned officer with the flat of my broadsword."[133] Striking with the flat of the sword was a punishment often meted out to soldiers in the eighteenth century. It was usually done publicly. The officer would strike the man on the buttocks with the flat of his sword. It was meant more to inflict humiliation than pain. Likewise, it was usually reserved for private soldiers.[134] In this case, however, just as Ewald struck the man, "two rifle shots were fired at me from the left side."[135] Thus the Americans intervened on the noncommissioned officer's behalf.

The preceding incident demonstrates some of Ewald's character. Deeply professional, he had no tolerance for subordinates who neglected their duties. When he discovered such neglect, his first response was to punish it, even forgetting the dangerous position in which he found himself. When Ewald looked around after hearing the shots, "I saw two riflemen fleeing, who must have sneaked up and hidden behind the rocks in the area. I went at once to the nearest sentry, who had not seen these two men until they had fired and were running away."[136]

One brief incident once again reinforced the importance of security for Ewald. It occurred on June 14. "Today for the first time, we neglected to lay an ambuscade, and to our chagrin a part of enemy dragoons appeared on the highway."[137]

Ewald attempted to remedy the deficiencies of his area of operations as well. For instance, he observed that his sentries had great difficulty seeing any distance from their posts at night. This was chiefly due to the broken nature of the terrain. In order to compensate, Ewald "ordered an abatis made whose ends reached up to the creek and surrounded the houses where the pickets were stationed, behind which I withdrew the sentries at night."[138] An abatis was a fairly fast and relatively easily constructed defense composed of felled trees with the branches positioned to face the enemy. It would slow down and disorganize any attempted assault on the lines.[139] It is noteworthy as well that Ewald deployed a line of pickets, advanced guards, further out from his post, and then the sentries, creating concentric rings of security, which would make it very difficult for an enemy to gain access to his camp without discovery.

Ewald's determination to deprive the enemy cover in the night is further evidenced by the fact that he ordered large pile of wood stacked about three hundred paces before his pickets. At night, these were to be lit on fire so that "the pickets could not be approached unseen."[140] His attention to detail concerning his pickets soon paid off for Ewald, as some American prisoners were taken who revealed that a planned attack on his post was cancelled when the alertness of his sentries was observed by the American commanders.[141]

The tempo of operations once again increased, as the Jäger Corps patrolled along with some of the 17th Light Dragoons near Harlem Heights. They occupied some of the battlefield from 1776. The force encountered one enemy patrol around 4 o'clock in the afternoon, but the Americans withdrew before the British cavalry could make contact.[142]

On June 25, in the early evening, the Jäger once again on the moved out. Brigaded together with a battalion of light infantry under the command of Colonel [Robert] Abercromby, they were dispatched to Dutch Crompond.[143] Their mission involved surprising an enemy patrol. An additional battalion of light infantry as well as the British Legion, were posted on the heights of Peekskill to cover the rear of the Jäger and light infantry. Abercromby arrived before the village at daybreak and ordered Ewald forward with fifty Jäger and fifty light infantrymen "to surround the place and seize a defile formed by a dam, whereby the enemy's retreat was cut off."[144] The detachment they were attacking consisted of some four hundred infantry supported by about fifty cavalry.

Ewald scarcely arrived in his designated position when small arms fire broke out on the opposing side. On hearing the gunfire, Ewald's position came under attack from a large body of infantry and cavalry. He responded, "I fired at them on sight, and immediately ordered the fifty men of the light infantry to charge." In this initial volley, a few of the Americans fell and "Almost one hundred men threw away their arms and surrendered as prisoners."[145]

By eight o'clock the following morning, the engagement was over and in Ewald's words, "we were masters of the whole area, counted three hundred prisoners and thirty-three horses and marched back." He further noted that "The most unpleasantness during the stroke was the catching on fire of the village, the cause of which we could not discover."[146]

On June 27, the Jäger were ordered to prepare to embark for New York City on the following day. They would embark in two detachments, the first at 8 AM, and the second two hours later.[147] The following morning, at daybreak, "we set fire to the Jäger's posts and burned the bridge across Herecland's Creek."[148] The troops began their march at 5 AM, and by 11, all were aboard their designated transports. Soon, Ewald's detachment was reunited with the larger Jäger Corps.[149] It is interesting that Ewald left no comment on the abandonment of their post. Significant effort, especially on the part of his troops, had gone into securing the territory, and now it was being abandoned.

For much of July, the duty of the Jäger Corps consisted primarily in "strong and small patrolling toward Tarrytown." However, this patrolling lacked any opportunities for action for "no man of Washington's army lingered in this area."[150] On July 31st, the army moved back to York Island. Here they took up the same positions they had occupied the previous year. Concerning the move, Ewald observed, "This is now the third campaign where we have continually lost in the end what we won with the first rush at the beginning."[151] His spirits could only have sunk further when he received news of an American tactical success.

August 19, 1779 witnessed Anthony Wayne of Pennsylvania's successful raid on Paulus Hook, with the support of Lighthorse Harry Lee's partisan legion. This raid demonstrated further the growing tactical proficiency of the Continental Army.[152]

The attack on Paulus Hook constituted a further stroke in the ongoing partisan war, in this case, quite literally the war of posts. Ewald provided a stark description of the frustrations of this kind of war for the soldiers involved, noting

> For us light troops these two campaigns in one area are very dis-
> agreeable. We are troubled with party sorties and patrolling just as
> much as in an offensive campaign, I venture, because this constant
> patrolling of one kind is bound to take away one's respect with each
> step.[153]

He added further that "The endless monotony makes the whole business tiresome, since every Jäger already knows where he is supposed to go
when he starts out."[154] Basically, the repeated fighting in the same area
dulled the men's combat edge. The monotony of continuous operations
led to their growing complacency.

These constant skirmishes, patrols and ambushes exacted their own
toll. Men were killed or wounded and the equipment worn out. The arrival of a ship carrying recruits for the Hessians obviated the manpower losses
to an extent. All told, there were nine hundred recruits, of which the Jäger
Corps received one hundred and thirty-seven. In ways, these men differed
from previous reinforcements to the Hessian troops, a fact which Captain
Ewald commented on. On the voyage over, the men revolted against their
officers, some of whom sustained injuries in the process of subduing the
uprising. There were twelve ringleaders, and they were locked up, awaiting court martial in New York. Among the ringleaders were several who
were both students and nobles. Perhaps they had gained inspiration from
some of the Enlightenment discussion taking place in Europe at the time?
In any case, Ewald, the military professional concluded noting that "Generally, they are handsome people, whose ways of thinking will no doubt
be changed by good discipline."[155]

Shortly thereafter, Ewald laid in ambush on one of the roads in the
area, when "About eleven o'clock in the morning I detected a body of
horsemen in the distance which was making its way toward the ambuscade."[156] On seeing these troops, he "immediately crawled behind the
walls which surrounded the fields, in order to be in a position opposite
them and shoot down whatever should pass by the ambuscade."[157] The
enemy party, however, did not get within range.

In late October, orders arrived for Ewald and his troops to withdrawal.
This meant abandoning both Verplanck's and Stony Point as well. The
frustration of the overall stalemate shows clearly in Ewald's reaction
to the orders, "Once more, we are now no further than we were at the
beginning of the campaign." Ewald placed the blame for his predicament
on the commander of Stony Point, "How easily can the plan of an entire
campaign be upset by the negligence of an officer to whom a post is
entrusted."[158]

In a skirmish, soon after the withdrawal from Stony Point, Ewald's close friend, John Graves Simcoe was wounded and captured. Ewald described the event, turning it into an occasion to reflect on perils of irregular warfare, "From this example one can perceive how dangerous is the service of light troops in this country. One never gets true information from the enemy. Each step one takes is soon betrayed. And then one is likely surrounded by armed country people who are excellent shots without considering the regular troops of the enemy."[159] The end of the campaign season brought with it fresh hardships.

The time came for the Jäger to go into winter quarters once again. Late in 1779, they were stationed in huts at Morris House as well as a set of ruined houses in Harlem.[160] On this occasion, the Jäger again experienced a taste of the hardships experienced by Washington's Army as it went into winter quarters at Valley Forge in December of 1777. The men were assigned to very dilapidated huts, and quickly determined that these were uninhabitable, and therefore they had to build their own dwellings. As they were in the process of constructing shelters for themselves, the weather turned, and "the men suffered very much until they dug and built their hovels so well that they were protected against the frost."[161] The officers took part in the work as well. As for the captain himself, he "appeared to have a somewhat better fate, for I moved with my company into the ruined houses of Harlem, in order to support the refugees of Morrisiana in case of an attack."[162] Ewald fulfilled his purpose soon after as he and his men drove off an American attack on Morrisiana.[163]

In December, Ewald learned of a projected move to the South. This was not difficult, as the plan was far from secret in the British camp. Still, the possibility of a change of location and a warmer climate tempted the captain, "My heart bled with longing to look around in the South."[164] Such a feeling is understandable considering the war in New York had degenerated into a stalemate, with neither side capable of obtaining a clear advantage, or willing to risk its forces in a major engagement. As for posting to the southern expedition, Ewald was requested personally by both Clinton and Cornwallis. Accordingly, he sailed with his eighty Jäger on the *Pan*.[165] There were some difficulties getting the British ships together and out to sea. The Pan actually ran aground due to the ice, and Ewald's contingent was split amongst the other transports. Even with these changes, the fleet weighed anchor on December 29.[166]

The expedition on which Ewald found himself stood as one part of a major strategic shift on the part of Great Britain. While small-scale confrontations continued between Crown and American forces in the northern theater on a very regular basis, major combat operations, while on occasion planned, were no longer attempted. For the British, much of Clinton's reluctance to engage in major operations stemmed from the fact that the scope of the war had expanded drastically with the entrance of France. The French entry into the conflict forced Britain to reassess her interests and reallocate finite military resources accordingly. Once the Ministry reassessed their interests, North American shrank in importance as compared to the Sugar Islands of the Caribbean. As a result, the ministry shifted troops stationed in North America, as well as ships stationed off the coast, to the Caribbean to defend British interests there. Clinton would have to continue the fighting in North America with substantially fewer troops. This situation led to what is termed the Southern Strategy.

As one recent historian summarized, "The British Southern Strategy was based on the idea of a counterrevolution by Loyalists who, it was argued by British officers in America, comprised the majority of the population of the South."[167] In essence, it relied on southern Loyalists to provide the bulk of the manpower necessary to achieve victory in the war effort. Under the Southern Strategy, a small force of British regulars would invade and subdue a state with the aid of local Loyalists.[168] Once one state fell to British arms with Loyalist support, Crown forces would move on to the next in what historian David Wilson views as and eighteenth-century version of the domino theory.[169]

All of these factors combined with persistent rumors of major support among Loyalist communities in the South to work in favor of the development of what has come to be known as the Southern Strategy. In essence, the southern strategy constituted a means for the new British commander, as well as the ministry, to wage the war in the Americas on the cheap.

CHAPTER 7

THE SIEGE OF CHARLESTON

The British strategic shift led first to the invasion of Georgia in late 1778. Initially, the invasion yielded excellent results. The British expedition quickly took the principle seaport of Savannah on December 29, 1778. The fall of Savannah sent the Whig government of the state reeling. January witnessed an expedition to the inland town of Savannah, a crucial post for Crown control of Georgia. The expedition quickly faltered due to lack of turn out from Native allies and Loyalists. Likewise, the battle of Kettle Creek on February 14, a Patriot victory and Briar Creek on March 3, 1779, a British route of southern militia, left the future of the southern colonies uncertain at best.[1] In April 1779, Major General Augustine Prevost launched a Crown invasion of South Carolina, which, while unsuccessful, demonstrated that the British threat from Georgia was more contained.

The youngest colony, and the one with the smallest white population of all thirteen, Georgia, received a special dispensation from the Continental Congress to recruit men to fill its quota in the Continental Army from outside the state's borders.[2] Given its relative weakness, Georgia stood as the perfect place for the first test of the new Southern Strategy. On December 23, over three thousand British troops began arriving off the Tybeee River.[3] The city was quickly surrounded and fell to British arms on December 29, 1778. While the capture of Savannah seemed a great victory, many of the veteran officers viewed the success with a more jaundiced eye. Captain Heinrichs of the Hessian Crops, for instance, noted in a letter home,

> *Our expedition down south has been successful, having captured the entire Georgias. There was however but little art in this, as the enemy there consisted of nought but Militia, gathered up in a hurry, while on our side brave officers and smart regiments made up the expedition.[4]*

In autumn 1779, one of the first combined Franco-American operations under the alliance encompassed an attempt to liberate the city. A
combined force of French infantry and marines, as well as Continentals
under General Benjamin Lincoln, and South Carolina militia besieged
the city beginning on September 16. The siege efforts did not go well. In
hopes of capturing the town before the French contingent left for the Caribbean to avoid the hurricane season, a dangerous assault was launched
October 9. The key to the enterprise would be complete secrecy, however,
the movements of the French and Americans disclosed their intent. The
3,500 French, 600 Continental troops and various South Carolina militia
contingents were ordered to parade at one in the morning. Their movements alerted the commander at Savannah, General Augustine Prevost, to
the allied intentions. The assault, when it came, was driven off with heavy
casualties. For the French, this equaled 828, including the French Admiral
d'Estaing, who was wounded twice while leading the assault.[5] The Continentals suffered 250 killed and wounded out of 600 engaged.[6] Among
the fallen was Count Casimir Pulaski, a Polish noble who raised a partisan
corps as part of the Continental Army.[7] The siege of Savannah was thus
lifted on October 19, 1779. It should be noted that this failure, as well as
the inconclusive efforts by both sides in the battle of Rhode Island, exerted
significant strains on the Franco-American alliance.[8]

With Georgia now firmly in their grasp, the British leadership could
look northward to the next goal of their campaign—Charleston, South
Carolina. South Carolina held particular importance for the rice it produced fed the slaves on the sugar producing islands in the Caribbean.[9] In
this context, the significance of Charleston was readily apparent. That
city, older and more developed than Savannah, stood as the most important port south of Virginia.

Johann Ewald did not take part in these initial successes to the south.
He remained with the main force of the British army in New York City
and its environs, continuing the war of posts with the Americans. The
Hessian Jäger Corps, as well as other contingents were called to the southward in late 1779. Ewald arrived in South Carolina just in time to take
part in the second siege of Charleston in 1780. It seemed, for the moment
at least, that the Southern Strategy might indeed pay off. From the British
perspective, they seemed finally to have discovered the combination that
would lead them to victory. Even if they only retook the southern colonies,
these were, economically speaking, the more vital to the British Empire.
The lieutenant governors of Georgia and South Carolina drove home the
economic importance of the region for the rebellion in a memorial they
sent to Lord George Germain in which both men argued that without the

trade in tobacco, rice and other commodities that passed through the port, the colonies would be unable to sustain the rebellion.[10] Ewald's account of the siege is extremely detailed and shows his understanding of an aspect of warfare in which he had little experience for some time.

Ewald and his force of Jäger arrived on Simmons Island off the coast of South Carolina. Sir Henry Clinton preferred this landing area as it was south of Charleston. He ruled out the area north of the city along the coast due to the shallow waters there and the proximity to rebel fortifications.[11] Likewise, the disembarkation point at the North Edisto River ensured that the navy would have a sheltered anchorage, and the troops could therefore land unopposed. The compromise was that the men landed nearly twenty miles from their intended target, thus giving up any potential advantage of surprise.[12] Perhaps the ghosts of the 1776 attempt on Charleston haunted the general?

In any event, Ewald and his Jäger Company constituted one part of the second debarkation of additional British forces.[13] At this point, his company numbered roughly eighty men.[14] Following a brief period of recuperation from a stormy passage, Ewald and his men took to the field again. They were combined with the British 33rd Regiment under Colonel James Webster and sent to occupy a road leading to Stono Ferry. This road served as a key communications artery across the Stono River and fixated Clinton's attention at the beginning of the campaign.[15] In addition, it covered the left flank of the British grenadiers and light infantry, who camped on the mainland. The remainder of the British force remained on Simmons Island.[16]

Always casting his trained eye on the terrain in which he operated, Ewald leaves a very detailed description of Simmons Island at the time of his troops' debarkation there. As they began to make their way inland, the Jäger captured a young male slave of about eleven or twelve years of age whom they attempted to use as a guide. However, there were extreme difficulties in communications. The lack of any map exacerbated these difficulties.[17] It should be recalled that this was just the sort of blind situation Ewald cautioned against ever falling into in his *Thoughts*.

As the Jäger moved forward off the island, they came to a causeway about noon and began to cross. The advanced guard consisted of a corporal and eight Jäger. The remainder of the Jäger and the 33rd Regiment followed in the main body. The slave guides they acquired led them across the causeway, and as they approached the far side, the men observed infantry and mounted troops forming among the houses. "All of us became cautious and discovered that this post was situated on the other side of the crossing of Stono Ferry, and that this detachment was the one which covered the crossing."[18] Ewald and his party had run directly into the enemy, and their only means of escape was the narrow causeway across which they'd come!

A cursory observation revealed that the houses they observed were fortified, and that the men were the advanced guard and that the main body was deployed behind them at some distance. Describing the mood among the men, "Each of us silently wished to get out of this affair with honor, but we were in a column on a narrow causeway between impassable morasses that formed the right bank of the Stono River, which separated us from the enemy." Under these circumstances, "it depended on the enemy to shoot us to pieces."[19]

At this point, the colonel ordered the men to turn back, which meant re-crossing the narrow causeway in the open, more than likely under enemy fire. The Americans did not fire, and "we certainly did not want to fire any!" In the end, the Jäger and the men of the 33rd Regiment "reached the causeway safely, laughed heartily and were astonished over the strange behavior of the enemy."[20]

Shortly after his harrowing escape from the causeway, Ewald received a report from some of the flankers that they had observed ships in the river. Knowing that the army would cross the river in this area, Ewald resolved "to reconnoiter this post by a ruse in order to render a service to the Commander in Chief." The captain's decision in this matter demonstrates the sort of independence of action that he would later advocate in his writings when he asserted that service in detached parties encompassed the best school for generals, since the officer had to make on the small scale all the key decisions that a general had to make for his army.[22]

Deciding on his course of action, Ewald, "without saying a word to anyone, I took Lieutenant Wintzingerode with me and approached the enemy post within rifle shot. Here I took a handkerchief out of my pocket and waved to the people who appeared to be observing us, among whom I could recognize a few officers."[23] In this way, Ewald engaged the American officers in conversation and managed to gain some information from them before returning to his camp.[24]

Returning to the British camp, Ewald could not resist the urge to tell the other officers of his discovery of the preceding day. Likewise, his "daring little enterprise was amply rewarded by the approbation of the Commander in Chief."[25] Soon, the army moved to cross the Stono River, during which the Jäger provided cover for a reconnaissance by the general officers.[26]

On February 19, the Jäger were tasked with going out in three parties toward the passes of Cox Swamp. Their objective was to collect information about the enemy and secure any slaves and livestock they could. Each of the parties possessed its own guide, however, communications again proved a hindrance in utilizing the guides to their fullest. As Ewald's party, consisting of about one hundred Jäger, moved out, they were "obliged to cross three creeks with marshy banks where the inhabitants had removed all the bridges, and I was compelled to wade through water over my navel." As they proceeded the captain, "left a few behind at each creek to secure my withdrawal."[27] On this occasion, his conduct demonstrated a combination of confidence and caution, probably due to the fact that he was operating in a new area, of which he had no knowledge and his guides were essentially useless due to the language barrier.[28]

As the Crown forces moved forward, they came across numerous abandoned plantations. It seemed the majority of the residents fled on news of the invasion. Here and there a sole refugee remained, and these were often pressed into service as guides. Likewise, they could be good sources of intelligence, such as when several of Ewald's Jäger came across a slave in an abandoned plantation, "who agreed quite sensibly to tell the truth about everything."[29] The man then gave the Jäger the location of Generals Lincoln and Moultrie and the number of men in each's command. The party returned to camp in the evening with their prisoner, who "appeared to be a great treasure to General Leslie."[30]

On February 24th, the British and their Hessian auxiliaries began construction on three redoubts and several fleches with abatis surrounding them. These fortifications gave the Crown forces control of the Stono River.[31] As the British and their German auxiliaries prepared to invest Charleston, it became clear to Ewald that the local population opposed them, primarily because the soldiers carried off slaves and livestock. As a result, the locals often provided information on British movements to the Continental forces.[32]

On one occasion, this resulted in an attack by the remnants of Pulaski's legion on a British patrol sent out to collect livestock and slaves. The patrol came under fire from the Americans. As soon as they heard the firing, "every Jäger grabbed his rifle and hurried to their [the British] assistance with all speed."[33] The Jäger arrived just in time to save the British detachment from their assailants. Such incidents were common during the campaign.

As the Crown forces moved forward, Charleston prepared to defend itself. On March 3, the garrison received reinforcements in the form of 600 North Carolina Continentals under Brigadier James Hogan. These men were veteran troops.[34]

On March 4, Ewald received orders to take his turn in the redoubts across the Stono River with a detachment of Jäger. Concerning the works, Ewald observed their poor condition, "Since I had made a very thorough inspection of these miserable works, which resembled heaps of sand, I requested thirty Negroes provided with axes and shovels to repair the works and strengthen the abatis surrounding them."[35] The rapid deterioration of the works stemmed from the sandy soil used in their construction, which quickly eroded from exposure to rain as well as the current from the river.

While occupying the redoubts, "Toward evening Monsieur Vernier appeared with foot and horse and again on the 5th, about eleven in the morning. However, he withdrew after several of his men and horses were shot dead and a few wounded."[36] Major Chevalier Pierre-François Vernier commanded the remnant of Pulaski's Legion, which had been severely mauled in a frontal assault on the British lines outside of Savannah.[37] The Americans were keeping the British works under observation. Realizing what Vernier was about, Ewald determined on some counter-measures. "But since I thought he would return toward evening, I placed a corporal with six Scots, and six Jäger in two ambuscades in the outlying pine woods along the main road."[38] These men were to act as sentries against the Frenchman's return. Ewald deployed two additional Jäger out in the open as decoys.[39]

Vernier's regular reconnaissance of the British redoubts actually played into their hands, "My plan was quite correct. Toward seven o'clock in the evening a small party of about fifteen to twenty men appeared."[40] These were the expected troopers from Pulaski's Legion. "The signal for the ambuscades was the firing of a double shot which I had placed right in the open in front of the works."[41]

Ewald selected two of his Jäger to show themselves to the enemy. "The sight of these two men was so pleasing to Vernier's gentlemen that they surrounded them in such a way that they thought they had cut them off."[42] This was all a part of Ewald's plan, "Those well-chosen Jäger allowed the enemy to play with them until it became serious."[43] The men in Vernier's force circled Ewald's sentries, attempting to cut them off. As they closed in on their prey, they entered the kill zone of the ambush, never realizing they were in fact the prey. At the right moment, the sentries gave the signal for the ambush.[44] "They fired the signal, the ambuscades attacked, and the enemy was nearly all shot to death." The only thing that prevented a complete route of Vernier's force from Ewald's perspective was the fact that "Since night fell, some of them escaped."[45]

Just after Ewald's successful ambush of Vernier's Legion, the British army moved forward on Charleston. As a result, "On the morning of the

6th I received orders to abandon the post [the Matthews Ferry works] completely and destroy as much as possible." The purpose of these orders was to prevent anything of valuable falling into the hands of the enemy. Ewald complied, having the sandy redoubts pulled down, the abatis set on fire and the boats from the crossing broken up as they could not be taken with the army.[46] At this point, Clinton's entire army, save for a small rear-guard detachment, had moved over from Johns Island to James Island.[47]

On March 9th, Ewald made his own reconnaissance of Charleston harbor and Fort Sullivan, leaving a very detailed description in his diary.[48] The following day, the Jäger, along with the 33rd Regiment under Colonel Webster, established a camp at Rose's Plantation on the main road to Ashley Ferry. Later that day, supply ships were sighted in the bay where the Wappoo joins the Stono River. For Ewald and his men, this was a welcome sight as "we Jäger had almost nothing on our bodies and our feet."[49] The condition of the men's clothing stands as yet another testament to the nature of their fighting and its effects on their equipment.

On March 15th, the Crown forces undertook a major foraging operation. Beginning at daybreak, Major Dundas of the light Infantry moved forward with five hundred men of the light infantry to the vicinity of St. Andrews Church. Their target, the plantation situated on the right bank of St. Andrew's Creek. Simultaneous with the advance of the British light infantry, the Jäger and the 33rd Regiment under Colonel James Webster moved forward on Lowndes Plantation.[50] Their purpose was to cover Dundas left flank in case of attack. They were to divide any enemy forces in the vicinity and forage there as well.[51]

As they moved forward, the mixed force learned that the Americans had demolished the bridge near the church. In addition, a number of riflemen were posted along the creek. The Jäger skirmished with some of these as the advance continued. They continued in the fighting until the foraging operation was completed.[52]

On March 16th, Ewald held an outpost, and received an American trumpeter and officer, appearing to exchange letters with the Commander in Chief. The following day, the 17th Captain Hinrichs held the post, and Ewald related an example of his conduct as a cautionary tale on when to risk the men in a command, "He placed an ambuscade of one corporal and ten Jäger along the highway to the Ashley Ferry, since the enemy knew we were without cavalry." Up to this point, the positioning and deployment were sound, "But since the captain had set a bad example of sparing his men, which a young officer often follows and generally observes at the wrong time, he let the men leave the ambuscade in the morning about eleven o'clock because it was very warm." He further related that "This step was hardly taken when to his and our dismay a party of thirty horse appeared which would have been his." Heinrich's mistake was compounded by the fact that "These horses would have helped all the officers, because we still had to go on foot."[53]

Soon the British forces began to encircle the landward side of Charleston in preparation to lay formal siege to the city. The previous century witnessed the refinement of siege warfare to a virtual science, especially as practiced by the French under Louis XIV. His chief engineer, Sebastien de la Pestre de Vauban is commonly recognized as one of the greatest practitioners of this form of warfare.[54]

The siege of Charleston presented some different challenges however, in that the city was a port on the Atlantic coast, and therefore could not be surrounded solely by land forces.[55] The Royal Navy would be essential in blockading the town while it was attacked form the landward side. The British possessed a fair amount of recent experience in what are today called joint operations dating back to the siege of Havana in the Seven Years War.[56]

As the crown forces prepared to lay siege to Charleston, Ewald continued in his partisan operations. On March 21, he recorded that "Since up to now all our efforts to lay an ambuscade have been wasted, and the Commanding General wanted to take a prisoner, I tried to approach the enemy today with a small party to reconnoiter the changing of his patrols." While on this reconnaissance, he "was lucky enough to find the place where the main party stayed and the smaller ones departed toward our post. Since the ground is sandy there is no other thoroughfare in this area, I could easily detect hoof prints and distinguish the fresh tracks from the old."[57] Here, Ewald demonstrated another important skill of the partisan, the ability to track enemy movements based on the condition of the ground. Once he had located a suitable site, he "placed a corporal and five Jäger in ambuscade in a small thicket near the place where the enemy party which alarmed our post usually turned back. I gave each man a guinea and ordered each one to take a bottle of water and bread and not to stray off until I recalled him."[58] In this manner, Ewald significantly reduced the chance that the men he deployed would leave their posts and allow the Americans to pass through the ambush unscathed. The preceding demonstrates that the captain understood the power of financial inducements. The weather conditions were important for Ewald's plan as well, and he noted that the moonlight on this particular night was quite bright. With his men deployed, there was nothing left to do but wait, when, "about midnight a party appeared, which was attacked from the ambuscade after they had fired their pistols toward our sentries but only one sergeant major with his horse was wounded and captured."[59]

The captured cavalryman provided important information, such as the fact that General Benjamin Lincoln had occupied Charleston with 7,000 men. Likewise, he informed Ewald that several strong detachments had been thrown out from the city, and were holding Ashley Ferry, St. Andrew's Church and Bacon's Bridge.[60]

On March 22, the British army moved out. As usual, the Jäger were in the van. General Leslie once again commanded the advance. This time Ewald and his men were joined by the 33rd Regiment and the light infantry as well. As they moved forward, "We had scarcely arrived in the vicinity of St. Andrew's Church when we were greeted with cannon shots from the opposite bank of St. Andrew's Creek, whereupon the army halted."[61]   Leslie called on Ewald to probe a bit further up the creek and try to outflank the American position and force them to withdraw, as a frontal assault appeared too costly.[62] Ewald demonstrated, again, a facet of his personality that served as a major source of motivation, the desire to distinguish himself in the eyes of his superiors. When asked to perform the mission, he readily agreed, and selected fifty Jäger to accompany him. Along with Captain Boyd and three companies of light infantry.[63]

The party followed a circuitous route and crossed the creek where it was only three feet in depth. They made their crossing about seven in the evening. Once across the men discovered they were in a fairly large swamp, which took about a half an hour to cross. The terrain was "so deep and muddy that many of our men sank up to their chests."[64] At this point, his force was quite exposed to an enemy attack, being dispersed and occupied with making their way through the swamp. Instead, the Americans abandoned their post, and Ewald and his men only skirmished with their rear guard.[65]

Shortly thereafter, Ewald was called upon with his men to escort the British leadership from one camp to another. He described the experience "The road from our camp to the positions where the Paterson Corps was situated ran continuously through woods in which four highways fell in, all coming from Dorchester. When I noticed this, I took the liberty of telling the generals that this presented an excellent opportunity for Colonel Washington, or Monsieur Vernier, to seize all the generals, for he needed only to put twenty or thirty horsemen in ambuscade along this communication line." At this, "Lord Cornwallis joked and said, 'Let us ride on. Ewald almost frightens me.'" Reflecting on the experience, Ewald observed that they should have kept the British light infantry as a part of the escort.[66]

Ewald's observation was given credence later that day. After escorting the commanders, they ordered him to stay for dinner. "The meal was not yet finished when an officer of the Legion appeared, who announced breathlessly that Colonel Hamilton and Inspector General Schmidt of the hospital had just been seized, and that only his good horse had saved him."[67] The Jäger captain noted, concerning the prophetic nature of his earlier observation, "Now had happened what could have occurred this morning." Now the British command issued orders and a Hessian grenadier battalion posted to keep open the road between the two camps. Ewald summed up his role, with some understandable smugness, "Now the generals liked my timely idea, and I laughed up my sleeve."[68]

On March 28, the expedition force gathered on Drayton's plantation, and began to cross the Ashley River the following day. As the Jäger and light infantry climbed up a hill on the left bank of the river, they received fire from an American patrol. The Americans' fires were ineffectual, and the party "seemed to be observing rather than hindering us."[69]

As additional troops crossed the river, they fanned out and took up their standard crescent formation. "The three Jäger divisions, under their captains, had to advance to the center and select their positions at both ends of the crescent, and as the crescent expanded they had to try to gain ground."[70] As they moved forward in an expanding crescent, the Jäger captain spied some American troops off in the distance, however, these quickly moved off as more British troops crossed the river.

Ever hungry for information, Ewald decided on his own initiative to find out what he could concerning the Americans. "I greatly desired to obtain information about the enemy. Since I could not discover anyone in the countryside, I risked several Jäger volunteers, who crawled under cover to the plantation to see if one of the inhabitants could be found or caught there." Unfortunately, it proved impossible to approach the house undetected.

Ewald then tried to move forward in echelon through a ravine. Using twenty men, he "went cautiously through the ravine with four men deployed one after the other; as soon as they were through I let four more men go and gradually all twenty men."[71] When his party were all in position around the main plantation house, Ewald, "had a dozen shots fired into the windows and doors of the dwelling." This produced the desired effect, as "The occupant of the house appeared at once."[72] Ewald waved the man towards him, but he quickly disappeared back into his house. The Jäger captain ordered more shots fired, "whereupon he appeared with his better half and approached me."

So the captain succeeded in taking a prisoner to interrogate, "But since I did not consider myself safe here, I ordered the good man, whose neatly dressed spouse clung firmly to his arm and would not leave, to go back with me through the very muddy ravine."[73]

Ewald observed his captives, "both good people trembled like an aspen leaf." Fighting for several years in North America and taking numerous prisoners taught the Jäger captain how to respond to the fears of civilian captives. "I spoke kindly to them, assuring them that no harm would come to them if they would tell me the truth of what I wanted to know, and what they themselves knew."[74] In this case, the straightforward approach paid clear dividends, as the plantation owner admitted to Ewald, "that this corps, which observed us from all directions was under Washington and Vernier; that the garrison in Charleston was seven thousand strong, and that he himself had a son in the city serving as major (his name was Horry)."[75]

Ewald considered sending the man back to Cornwallis for further interrogation, but his wife begged the captain not to. He decided to let them both go, and instead made a verbal report to Cornwallis. Curiosity got the better of Ewald on one point, however, and he asked the man why he allowed his son to serve in the rebel forces. The answer he received was that it stood as a matter of simple coercion. At that, Ewald "shrugged my shoulders, assented to all this in my heart, appreciated the sincerity of this man and permitted him to return quietly home."[76]

In his interview with Horry and his wife, Ewald demonstrated several of the points he would later make concerning dealing with the civilian populace in his *Treatise*. First among these stood the quality of mercy. Throughout the fighting in North America, Ewald demonstrated himself to be a consummate military professional, and while certainly was not averse to fighting, he did not revel in an excess of bloodshed either. His restrain often paid very well, as shown in the preceding interlude. By guaranteeing the safety of his charges, the captain obtained the information he was after, the real goal of his mission. Yet he did so without resorting to unnecessary violence, a practice that would often mar subsequent actions by both sides in the Southern Department and contribute to the brutal nature of the War of Independence in that theater.[77]

As the British army continued its advance on Charleston, beginning about 5 PM, their forward units constantly skirmished with some rebel forces that observed them and retreated towards the city. The British and their German auxiliaries made camp for the night about six miles from Charleston.[78] On the following day, the army set out again, with the Jäger once again serving as the advance guard. This constant service as the tip of the spear pointed at the colony's largest city contributed the high casualty rate experienced by the unit. The casualties sustained during the advance and their subsequent replacement, in turn, helped to undermine the effectiveness of the unit as the war progressed.

Around noon, the advanced guard clashed with an American party near the Governor's house, "a good German mile from Charlestown."[79] While the skirmishing continued, General Leslie surveyed the area from the second floor of the Governor's House. He then ordered the Jäger to advance slowly, "since the generals were afraid of an ambuscade in this area, which was intersected by deep ditches and short bushes."[80] Meanwhile, the fighting continued, led by the Jäger with the British light infantry in support, pushing the Americans from ditch to ditch, until they finally came to an advanced flèche, which sat just within cannon range of the main American fortification. Here there was severe firing between the two sides.[81]

While the opposing forces engaged in a firefight, one Captain Bodungen, who led the vanguard, worked his way around the flèche, gaining their flank and thereby forcing the Americans to abandon the position. "But we had hardly mastered it, and had scarcely reformed a little, when we were attacked again with considerable violence and driven back, whereby three Jäger were stabbed with bayonets." At this point, the light infantry moved up to support the Jäger and the combined force drove the Americans back from the flèche for a second time.[82] At this point in the engagement, Sir Henry Clinton appeared and ordered the troops to press forward, as they assumed the American "merely intended to provoke us by his maneuver and lure us under the fortification into a violence cannonade."[83]

The Americans, seeing that their opponents had guessed their intentions, launched an attack on the Jäger and light infantry with a full brigade of infantry supported by six guns. The British artillery now joined the fight, and opened up on the Americans, driving them back into Charleston. The Jäger and light infantry did not pursue their retreating opponent beyond the flèche. In fact, the Jäger, who took on the lion's share of the fighting to this point, were relieved by the light infantry. Still, the men did receive recognition from Sir Henry Clinton, who "had the Jäger assembled and personally extended his warmest thanks to them, while everyone in the army, under whose eyes the action had occurred, expressed thanks and delight to us."[84]

The clash stands out as an intense fight, and a part of a hard day's campaigning. The Americans were not going to allow the British to cut off Charleston without a fight for control of the outlying areas. In the days' actions, the Jäger sustained significant casualties for the small size of their force. They had nine men killed, and another eleven wounded, with five additional men missing. In the aftermath of the fight they were assigned a post at Gibbe's plantation.[85] Ewald's troops were placed under the command of Major Moncrief of the British Engineers. Always desiring a more complete knowledge of the area in which he operated, Ewald set off on his own in the dark to reconnoiter the position, gaining intelligence firsthand of the terrain with its attendant strengths and weaknesses. Through the night, Ewald "remained under arms without a fire and relieved my sentries often to keep them awake."[86] It was only late in the night that Ewald recalled that the day was birthday, "I had thought of celebrating since I had kept all my bones intact."[87]

With sunrise on the following day, Ewald reconnoitered again and performed a much more thorough inspection of his location and discovered that it was in fact much better than he had previously supposed. Likewise, the advance resumed toward the American lines outside Charleston. Clinton and Cornwallis rendezvoused with Ewald about ten in the morning, with some pioneers. These men tore down a barn near Ewald's position and used the wood to construct a bridge across the swamp. Once they completed the bridge, Clinton ordered Ewald, with thirty men to cross over and scout as far as possible ahead of the main army, "so that he would be able to observe the works of the fortifications."[88]

With his reconnaissance of the American position completed, about three in the afternoon, Clinton gave Ewald a signal to retire by raising a white handkerchief. Ewald, in turn, communicated the order to his men by whistling, noting that "on such occasions no horn is blown but one whistles."[89] Likewise, the use of whistling stemmed from the fact that a whistle would better blend in with the background noise made by various birds as opposed to a hunting horn. Once he had returned to his camp, Ewald ordered the bridge he crossed removed. He was relieved by the company of Captain Hinrichs that evening.

His constant duty over the preceding days certainly would have contributed to fatigue among his men, and the Jäger especially were rotated fairly often as a result. Shortly after being rotated out of the vanguard, some British light infantry found the remains of the five Jäger missing after the previous engagement. All were dead, they had been bayonetted and one had his eyes cut out. Ewald interpreted the atrocity to mean that "the enemy was very angry and must have lost many men."[90] His interpretation of the atrocity is interesting, unfortunately, he did not leave any explanation of his reasons for believing as he did.

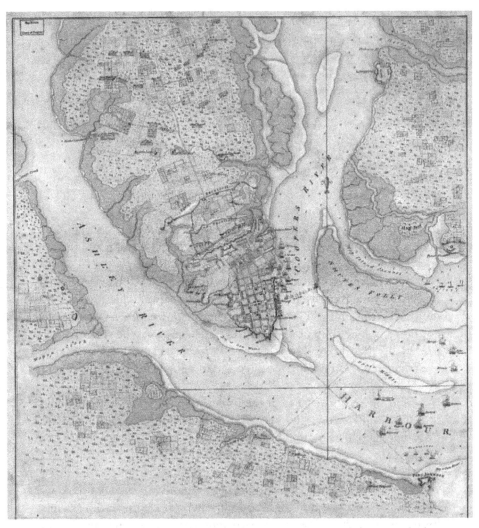

Figure 1: The Investiture of Charleston, S.C. by the English army, in 1780. With the position of each corps]. [?, 1780] Map. Retrieved from the Library of Congress, https://www.loc.gov/item/gm71000638/. (Accessed March 25, 2017.)

While the British drew their cordon around Charleston, they located the artillery park and depot for the siege at Gibbe's Plantation.[91] On April 1, Major Moncreif conducted a reconnaissance of the American fortification. Six Jäger, armed only with swords, served as his escort during the patrol.[92]

On the night of April 2, 1780, the British opened their siege lines in front of Charlestown. The following day, a deserter came into the lines from the American side. From him, Ewald learned that in the last skirmish in front of the city, the Americans sustained some forty killed and the same number wounded. This information vindicated his assessment of the reason for the treatment of the five missing Jäger. He further learned that among the dead was a captain and four other officers.[93] Finally, that day the Jäger were able to establish their own camp, which they set up in three divisions next to one another in front of the army, "and enjoyed their rest."[94] Certainly he and his men enjoyed the respite as this was the first formal encampment they had since entering the theater. Likewise, it came after much hard marching and fighting. They had earned their rest.

The transition to siege warfare from the advance on Charleston constituted only a short relief for the Jäger and light infantry, however, as their particular mode of warfare made them especially useful in sniping as well as defending siege works from enemy sallies. As the attack on the city progressed, they were often ordered to guard the lines as the fatigue units extended the trenches surrounding Charleston. For instance, on April 4, just after the British finished constructing two redoubts, both Ewald and Major Wurmb with one hundred Jäger each were ordered forward to reinforce the works on the right and left of the line.[95]

During their time defending the redoubts, there was heavy firing from both sides throughout the day. "As soon as night fell the Jäger departed."[96] When conducting siege operations, it was important to relieve the troops in the lines regularly lest they become too fatigued from the constant danger and lose their edge.

About nine that evening, General Clinton ordered the British batteries on Fenwick's and Linning's Points to fire on Charleston to quiet the American batteries. While the bombardment achieved the desired effect, "A terrible clamor arose among the inhabitants of the city, since the firing came entirely unexpectedly."[97]   These were the unfortunates who remained in Charleston. Many who could had already abandoned the city during the British advance.[98]

As the British artillery continued to pummel the defenses of the city, Ewald took advantage of the cover it created to reconnoiter "quite close to the city to discover the effect of these batteries, and in short intervals between the shooting I could often hear the loud wailing of female voices, which took all the pleasure out of my curiosity and moved me to tears."[99] In the future, Ewald would often comment in his works on the importance of gathering intelligence of both the terrain where one operated, and the enemy. What comes across on this occasion is that Ewald was not completely bereft of emotion. He could tell the effects the bombardment was having, and he grieved for the civilians being killed and terrorized in the city.[100] His reaction may hearken back to the attacks his home city of Kassel endured during the Seven Years' War as well.

In the succeeding days, the British hold around Charleston tightened. On April 6, Ewald noted the British movement of boats from the Ashley to the Cooper Rivers. As the British marched up the line of the Ashely, they gained control of that river. Once they secured control of the Ashley, the besiegers sought to cut off another line of supply or escape from the interior of the state.[101]

As the Crown efforts to cut off Charleston coalesced, the troops began to be rotated through the works. All the elite units in particular were assigned rotations in the redoubts.

That same day, Ewald advanced with his division up to the sandhills on the banks of Ashley River. Here he set up his command post in an old Indian fort which lay on a hill, and thus afforded him a good view of the surrounding territory. The breastwork of the fort was constructed of oyster shells.[102] Here, as so many times previously, Ewald chose a site based on consideration of the surrounding area. Likewise, the site provided Ewald with some cover, which he would need sooner than he thought.

The defenders in Charleston launched a violent bombardment of the siege lines in the evening, which continued until about midnight. During the cannonade, the British had two killed and two wounded.[103]

On April 7, as soon as night fell, Ewald and his command "began moving the heavy pieces to the left-wing redoubt." Placing these artillery pieces proved difficult, however, due to the swampy ground.[104] Reinforcements for the British arrived on the following day, sailing down the Ashley on schooners.

It is clear that Ewald understood the gravity of the event in which he was taking part. This was his first formal siege since the Seven Years' War, and it differed from his experiences at Kassel due to the topography of Charleston. These facts likely motivated him to record the progress of the siege in great detail. He essentially provides a running account of the operation.   For instance, he notes that for the night of April 9, "the besieged kept up their fire throughout the post all night." He relates, as well, that for all the violence of the fire, it was not very effectual, "Thus far, one English officer and one man have been killed and five wounded."[105] Likewise, he noted on April 10 how, "During the past night we erected a battery of six 12-pounders between redoubts Numbers 4 and 5, three hundred paces in front of the first parallel. As we expected an enemy attack on this outlying battery, I was ordered to occupy this unfinished work with forty Jäger and fifty grenadiers one hour before daybreak."[106] While Ewald and his men were serving another rotation in the siege lines, the British fleet entered Charleston harbor, cutting off any hope of support or escape from that direction as well.[107]

Ewald and his men were in position well before dawn. "When day broke I was bombarded extraordinarily hard, during which one Jäger and five grenadiers were killed and four wounded." This bombardment lasted for some time, during which the besieged "fired nearly three hundred canon shots at this work alone, so that pieces of the breastwork flew up in the air."[108]

On April 10, Clinton summoned General Benjamin Lincoln, the commander of the Charlestown garrison, to surrender. Lincoln, under pressure from the civic leadership, refused. Responding to Lincoln's rejection, the besiegers intensified their efforts. On April 11, Ewald recorded that "During the night we worked on all the batteries."[109]

Through his descriptions of the siege, Ewald showed a keen understanding of military engineering, a topic he had no doubt read thoroughly on during his convalescence and during his stint at the Collegium. He demonstrated this knowledge in accounts such as the following:

> *Last night several hundred paces of approaches were prepared between the redoubt on the right and the sailor's battery. The engineer laid out a demiparallel from the advanced battery up to an inundated area which the enemy had on the right in front of his outer works, during which the besieged did their utmost to disturb this work.*[110]

On April 13, work commenced on the second parallel. This would, if carried out properly, bring the heavy English siege guns close enough to the American works to make a practicable breach in them. The fourteenth witnessed further extension of the works and more intense artillery exchanges. On this night, for the first time, Ewald reported that "our batteries were louder than those of the enemy."[111] About an hour before daylight, Ewald was ordered to take possession of the head of the new work with sixty Jäger.

As noted above, serving in siege trenches was nerve-wracking work, and it could quickly wear on the morale of soldiers. Ewald discerned this effect on his own men, "Since the besieged diligently pounded us with gunfire and shells, I noticed the Jäger were not cheerful and that time hung heavy on their hands." Ewald worked to alleviate the boredom and attempt to lift the men's spirits, "I tried firing rifle shots with one and a half loads at a communication consisting of palisades which connected a detached work on the right with the fortifications."[112] These shots, fired at a communication trench with additional powder to give more range, elicited a telling effect, "I observed with astonishment the effect of the rifle shots, for I was certainly five hundred paces away, whereupon I decided to shoot at the embrasure, as not yet expected."[113]

Firing at the embrasure could potentially wound or kill some of the artillerists on the American side. When the lines of besiegers were closer, such small arms fire would be expected, and at the very least would make the artillerymen on the opposing side reluctant to serve their guns. At the range Ewald and his men occupied, however, it would not be expected for them to fire, as their shots would not likely reach the American works. Since the captain stumbled upon a means to affect such fire, he was trying something out of the ordinary. Ewald's actions were not innovative in the true sense, it is likely that many understood that increasing the charge could increase the range of a weapon. At the same time, they were not without risk. The heavier charge placed greater stress on the barrel of his rifle, and could have caused it to burst, which would quite likely have killed the captain. Still, it likely made his men feel empowered as they could see they were actually having an effect on their foes.

During much of the fighting described above, Ewald and his men were under the command of the British engineer Major James Moncrieff. For his part, Ewald held a decidedly low opinion of the engineer.[114]

April 16 saw the British besiegers well advanced in the construction of their approaches. Still, the defenders managed to throw out a heavy fire from their works. On this day, Ewald and his men were not at the head of the works. A Captain Franz Christian von Bodungen and his company occupied the position instead. In his diary, Ewald noted how the captain "exchanged fire the whole day with the sharpshooters of the besieged, who were protected by a counter approach which they had constructed from their right up against the advanced trench."[115] He continued, "Since we have now advanced up to rifle range, the enemy fired mostly grapeshot to-day."[116] The besiegers responded with shot from coehorns, small mortars, "which we had placed at the head of the approaches to the right and left, which fired most effectively."[117]

The following night, April 17 the captain recorded, "We extended the approaches considerably, and during the night we constructed a demi-parallel on each side. During this activity, the besieged fired continuously with grapeshot and musketry…"[118] That same day, Ewald occupied an unfinished section of the siege lines with sixty of his Jäger. The section of the lines they now occupied constituted a particularly dangerous post. There were no safe places to take refuge from enemy fire "Since we had not constructed traverses in the bayou and were now working into the crescent which forms the fortification, this work was enfiladed in such a way that the balls passed the entire length of the communication trench and the bayou."[119]

As this work progressed, the fire of the garrison with Charleston increased. Ewald described the fire as "extraordinary," and noted that the defenders "fired scrap iron and broken glass."[120] This sort of ammunition sounds as if it could be quite dangerous for the targets, however, Ewald dismissed its lethality, and instead focused on its morale dampening effects, "Although this fire is not very dangerous, and the fragments usually fly up in the air, my men lost their composure and thought of nothing else but to conceal themselves, despite the fact that they could not hide"[121] Ever cool under fire, Ewald responded to the threat to his command almost nonchalantly, "Since I was tired of the firing, which had cost the legs of nine men, I sent for entrenching tools and constructed five traverses within one hour, which protected us and spared many people." A traverse consisted in a bank or a wall, usually set at a right angle to the alignment of the main work in order to protect its defenders form enfilade fire.[122] From Ewald's description, it would appear that the Americans were firing low, and thus wounding his men in the legs. The traverse he constructed would offer them some level of protection from the enemy fire.

On the night of April 18, Ewald's men worked to complete the entrenchment they were assigned to, "while the besieged kept up a constant grapeshot and small-arms fire," as a result of which "the Jäger were kept extremely warm."[123]

Even in the intense combat Ewald and his men endured, the captain took advantage of the opportunities to observe the vast differences he encountered in the new area where he served. Another instance of the captain's innate curiosity occurred during the siege, a Native American chieftain, known as Ravening Wolf came to visit the British siege lines. The British hoped to impress the leader with their operations around Charleston as a part of British strategy included spiriting up the Indians to attack the frontier and thus divide the Patriot military efforts.[124]

Amidst the tumults of war, Ewald took time describe the chieftain, "He was copper-colored and of average size. His eyes sparkled like fire…" Not only did Ewald note the chieftain's physical traits, but his dress as well.[125] Such attention to detail concerning the chief's appearance, especially under the conditions of intense combat Ewald engaged in well illustrates the captain's interest in a broad spectrum of topics.

On April 20, Ewald and his men occupied a new post with his usual compliment of sixty Jäger. This new post was close enough to the American lines that "we were lucky enough to fire several well-placed rifle shots into the embrasures which flanked us on the right, so that this part of the enemy guns was very badly served the whole day."[126] Essentially, the shots fired by the Jäger drove the artillery crews away from their guns, and thus gave Ewald and his men a respite even while stationed in the forward part of the trench. Concerning the accuracy of their fire, Henry "Lighthorse Harry" Lee noted in his early history of the war, "For two days, the fire from the third parallel continued without intermission, and with great execution…" He further observed, "the sharpshooters were placed so close to our lines as to single out every man who exposed himself to view."[127]

The following day there was a parley between the British and the Americans. The purpose of the negotiation was to attempt to find some means of ending the siege and allowing the American forces to withdraw. It was unsuccessful.

By the same token, the fact that the Americans were willing to negotiate at all signaled their weakness to the British who promptly stepped up their efforts in the siege lines. The following day, April 22, "We pushed a parallel forward from all three approaches. Captain Bodungen occupied it with sixty Jäger." The British move generated a response on the part of the Americans, whom, Ewald observed, "Today the enemy riflemen used all their power to silence the fire of the Jäger, one of whom was killed."[128]

The next day, Ewald reported that "Last night we began to push forward with the double sap from all three heads." This meant that the Crown forces were moving their trenches forward to breach the enemy lines from all three of their access points. As the Hessians extended their lines forward, he observed "We have now approached so close that one could easily throw a stone into the advanced ditch on the other side, which is dressed with pointed trees."[129]

As the British forces extended their lines forward, it grew clear that the besieged were running out of ammunition. On the 23rd, Ewald was at the head of the trench with his usual detachment, "and was kept very warm with stone missiles and scrap iron."[130] Their proximity to the Americans came with a price, as one Jäger and two light infantrymen were killed and an officer severely wounded the same day.[131]

In a desperate attempt to break through the siege lines, the Americans launched a sortie on the night of April 24. Since it was night, Ewald ordered his men to defend the trench with their hunting swords only. This was so that the flash of their rifles would not alert the enemy to their position. Fighting in this manner, they drove off the sortie.

The night attack constituted one of the few sorties the Americans made during the siege, a fact that perplexed Ewald: "On the whole, I cannot understand why General Lincoln makes hardly any sorties, since he has with him the skillful engineer du Portail, who will surely assist him with very good advice, although he is not very experienced in siege warfare."[132] The preceding is interesting for several reasons, as it shows Ewald had some knowledge of the men in the American garrison, as well as their background. It is unclear whether he possessed this knowledge during the actual siege or if it was added in as a later reflections. In any case, it demonstrates that Ewald made it his business to know something of the other practitioners of his profession with whom he come into contact, both friend and foe. In this way he practiced the dictum of Sun Tzu, who said "know your enemy and know yourself."[133]

On April 27th, the Jäger captain reported that the Americans kept pitch fires burning in front of their works through the night. He added that they did this "since they expected to be taken with sword in hand, which really was the unanimous wish of the besieger, so that the disagreeable task might come to an end."[134] After days and nights spent in anxious waiting with brief spurts of combat, the men, including Ewald, were fatigued and understandably so. Still, for Ewald, it was not the combat so much as "the intolerable heat, the lack of good water, and the billions of sunflies and mosquitoes" which combined to make up the "worst nuisance" during the siege.[135]

On April 28th, the British and German forces extended their lines further and worked diligently to add new artillery batteries to the works. Their efforts were constant, with fatigue parties laboring through night. On the 29th, Ewald recorded how "Last night we advanced from the left head to destroy the lock and let the water out of the canal which protected the front of the enemy's fortifications on the right."[136] In draining the moat before the siege works, the Crown forces removed an important obstacle to breaching the American fortification. This fact was clear to both sides, the Jäger captain observing that "I occupied the new sap today and since it seemed to be very important to the besieged they threw small shells and stones at this approach all day long."[137]

Later that same day, Ewald and his men learned that the Americans had "abandoned" their works on Lempiere's Point. Lempire's Point and Mount Pleasant were two key American redoubts which kept open a line of communication to Charleston from the mainland. Two days previous, the American Volunteers, the 23rd Regiment, and the Volunteers of Ireland marched from the bivouac at Wappetaw Bridge some seventeen miles to Mount Pleasant. The garrison fled this post, and the British were able take it, thus sealing off one side of the conduit. However, Cornwallis felt that the redoubt at Lempiere's Point was too strong to attack, so he ordered his forces to withdrawal back the way they had come. Upon receiving information on Cornwallis's move and fearing an attack, the

French commander of the garrison at Lempiere's Point, Colonel Marquis Francis de Malmedy, abandoned his post.[138]

The garrison then withdrew into Charleston in a most disorderly fashion, essentially every man for themselves, compounding their disgrace. As a result of their departure, the defenders were now surrounded on all sides, with no open escape route, and no way for supplies and reinforcements to get into the city. It was only a matter of time for the British batteries to do their work and create a practicable breach on the fortifications surrounding the city on the landward side.

This news certainly gave heart to the besiegers, and that night they continued work on their new approach, "with good results in places." Likewise, they "advanced the sap so far toward the dam that the water from the flooding started to drain off."[139] On the same day, Captain Johann Heinrichs took his turn at the front of the new approach, with fifty Jäger. Since the British were getting close to the American lines, the fire was intense, "All kinds of fire from both sides was very severe."[140] As a result, two men were killed and eight wounded in the works.

The following day, May 1, the men "worked diligently on repairing the batteries and cutting through the dam."[141] Meanwhile, the Americans maintained a staunch defense of their works. For instance, on May 2, "Through their fire the besieged destroyed the lodgement [sic] of the advanced ditch and held up the work opposite the dam so much that little was accomplished."[142] Reflecting on the intensity of the combat that day, and perhaps allowing some of his own fatigue to show through, Ewald remarked, "I was on duty today and the fire was as always."[143] Strictly speaking, there were no easy posts for the Jäger during this fight, as their particular talents, especially for sniping, were in Stood demand. The constant exposure to combat certainly reduced the effectiveness of the Jäger over the course of the operation. At the same time, while the work was intense, it did show results. On May 4, the besiegers pierced the dam almost completely causing much of the water to run off. That day "The fire of the besieged was violent, while ours was silent."[144] Still, such intense fighting was not without its costs, about twenty men died that day in all.

As the attackers closed the net around Charleston, the defenders reacted with concentrated fire. On the night of May 5, for example, "In the evening, at ten o'clock the cannon and musket fire of the besieged was so violent and directed with such good effect that the workers could do little."[145] During this same night, the Americans began a counter-approach from their bastion on the right of the British lines in an attempt to block the move on the dam. Ewald noted that this attempt hindered the work of the besiegers.[146] Clearly, the contest for the counter-work went to extremes, as Ewald, not one prone to exaggeration, stated, "I tried to protect the workers as much as possible, but there were at least one hundred sharpshooters in the hole, whose fire was so superior to mine that the jägers no longer dared to fire a shot."[147]

By May 6, the work of the British saps had finally succeeded in draining the canal before the American works, even though it placed the besiegers under constant heavy fire. The constant danger and monotonous nature of the work caused some frustration on Ewald's part. He vented this frustration in his diary, "I cannot understand our work. We excavate the earth toward the entire front, we shoot at the entire front, and nowhere do much damage."[148] In more formal siege operations such as those he would have experienced and studied in Europe, a weak portion of the enemy's defense would be selected, and the artillery targeted on that area as opposed to a general bombardment of their lines. This deviation from the standard practice upset Ewald, and he took his complaint to Moncrieff. The British engineer responded, "You and your Jäger shall still force them to surrender, for you and your good men stop the enemy gunners more than once—that they can't fire a shot." Moncrieff continued, "We took Pondicherry from the French by the same method."[149]

For his part, the Jäger captain seemed only partially assuaged by the above response, "Thus spoke this man always." He went on, "It is true I have never met a braver and more energetic man, for what he lacks in scientific knowledge, he makes up by his courage."[150] Ewald continued in his assessment Moncrieff to some of the great French engineers, and determined that the Scot "could hardly serve as an errand-boy for an engineer during a siege in a European war..." He called Moncrieff's works before Charleston "confused nonsense."[151] From the preceding, it is clear that Ewald did not believe the Scot possessed a solid understanding of his craft. As previously noted, however, Moncrieff attended Woolwich and graduated with a commission as an engineer, so he did have professional training. In this sense, Ewald seems to have played the part of the novice criticizing the expert.

Though Ewald showed frustration at the lack of progress in the siege, the lines did move closer on Charlestown. As they did so, new directives came to the troops in the trenches, "Orders were given to use small arms constantly, for which purpose double-barreled guns were distributed at the lodgment, in the trenches and at the dam."[152] In addition, boxes filled with cartridges were placed along the parapet, so that the firing could be sustained continually."[153] While placing open ammunition crates in the trenches allowed the troops to keep the American defenders under constant small arms fire, it came with attended risks. If an incendiary should land in one of the boxes, the results could be devastating.

On May 10, Ewald reported that "Last night we advanced the sap up to the canal and built a new lodgment." He further noted that "The fire was murderous, and two officers and ten men either killed or wounded."[154] That night, the British and Hessians managed to construct a gallery, essentially a very large tunnel, over the canal and break through the abatis on the American side. However, they only accomplished the breakthrough "under the most terrible fire."[155] The attackers then constructed a lodgment "about thirty paces from the main fortifications, another one was constructed through the advanced ditch."[156] Ewald was on duty and occupied both works. He was supported in this action both by his own Jäger and by some grenadiers. The fire continued to be so heavy that "almost every minute lost the lives of several men."[157] During the exchange of fire, the Americans managed to dismount all of the breaching batteries constructed by the British.

The heavy exchange of fire led to another call for negotiations. The talks between Clinton and Lincoln continued through the remainder of the day, until 4 PM on May 12, when the garrison surrendered, at which point the garrison formally marched out, and stacked their arms.

The fall Charleston stood as a tremendous bow to the American cause. Virtually the entire Continental Army in the southern department laid down their arms, to the tune of some four thousand troops. In addition, roughly a thousand militia surrendered with the town as well. If the losses in manpower were not devastating enough, the fall of the city yielded up large quantities of weapons and equipment to the British.

After the fall of the city, Ewald seized on the rare the opportunity of speaking with some of his former opponents. He noted with some professional satisfaction that "The besieged concealed their losses, but one officer told me that the largest number had been killed by rifle bullets." He likewise added that he often altered the casualty figures he recorded in his diary in case it should fall into enemy hands, since he kept it constantly upon his person.[158]

Shortly after this event, Ewald was nearly killed when, on May 14, while storing the weapons captured from the Americans, a musket went off in the magazine in Charlestown. The discharge ignited a massive blast obliterating the magazine. He vividly described the aftermath of the blast, "Never in my life, as long as I have been a soldier, have I witnessed a more deplorable sight."[159] This is sobering testimony as to the magnitude of the destruction and the injuries considering that not only had Ewald participated in many of the major battles in North America, but previously served in the Seven Years' War as well. Toward evening, Ewald learned that the death toll had been placed at about 300, with numerous others, civilian and military, injured as well. He did observe "the entire disaster had occurred through carelessness."[160]

Ewald took advantage of the lull in operations following the city's capitulation to investigate the city and its defenses. In his diary, he complimented the work of the French engineer Louis LeBeuge Duportail on his work on the city's defenses, "Had this man arrived in Charlestown sooner, I believe we would not have obtained such a cheap bargain."[161]

The prisoners taken at Charlestown would be treated in very different ways. The Continentals were placed on prison hulks in Charleston harbor, where many eventually died. The militia were allowed to return to their home as long as they accepted parole, essentially, a pledge not to take up arms for the remainder of the conflict, something Ewald described as ridiculous. He added that while he understood this move derived from a desire to avoid sustaining the militia prisoners, "this economy will cost the English dear, because I am convinced that most of these people will have guns in their hands within a short time."[162] It is worth noting that before he left to return to New York City, Sir Henry Clinton altered the conditions of the parole to what amounted to a pledge of loyalty to the king. This change in conditions, along with the reports of British mistreatment of surrendering Americans at the battle of the Waxhaws contributed in no small way to the rising of irregular forces in the South Carolina backcountry.[163] By this time, however, Ewald was back in New York fighting on the same ground he had fought over in previous years. Ewald, therefore, was spared from participating in the bitter struggle that raged in the South Carolina backcountry through the summer and fall of 1780. Likewise, he was not present to witness such actions as the American defeat at Camden, and the reverse of Loyalist forces at the battle of King's Mountain.

While the hour was dark for the Patriot cause in South Carolina, not all was lost with the fall of Charleston. During the siege of Charleston, the governor of South Carolina, John Rutledge, abandoned the city in order to maintain a government in exile should it be taken. He set up his office in the region known as the High Hills of the Santee, where the Wateree River becomes the Santee. This was an area in the interior where residents would withdrawal to so as to escape the worst heat of the summer. On receiving news of the capitulation of the city, he withdrew westward down the Camden Road with General Huger and a small escort composed of the Third Continental Dragoons.[164] Not only would there be a resistance led by local partisans. There would still be a government in South Carolina to challenge the legitimacy of British rule.

CHAPTER 8

RETURN TO STALEMATE

As the Union Jack once again flew over the city, on May 30th and 31st, 1780, the Jäger Detachment, as well and the English and Hessian grenadiers, embarked on transports in the Cooper River above the city of Charlestown destined to return to New York. The southern foray proved, at least for the moment, a great success for British arms, Sir Henry Clinton had to return to his headquarters in New York to oversee the overall conduct of the war in North America. With success seemingly insured in the Southern Department, it only made sense for the commander to take with him his elite troops. These men would find more pressing employment to the northward.

Ewald boarded his transport towards evening on June 2. Shortly after he came aboard, the ship's captain notified him that there was a fire burning in the galley, which was strictly forbidden at night. In trying to inform the corporal of the deck watch in the fading light, Ewald fell through an open deck hatch, plummeting to the bowels of the ship a depth he gauged as some twenty feet. Remarkably, he emerged unhurt, save for some stiffness in the limbs, which subsided after a few days. Ewald interpreted his experience as proof that "what God will protect will be saved."[1]

The voyage took from June 3 to the 17th, when the ships passed Sandy Hook at the entrance to New York harbor. The period spent at sea stands out as one of the few true respites for Ewald and his men through their entire service in the war. The captain noted, "We were supplied with an abundance of all necessities and spent these eleven days in real rest with good food, wine and sport."[2] This lull undoubtedly rejuvenated the spirits of Ewald and his men, who had recently taken part in some incredibly brutal fighting outside of Charlestown.

On their return to New York, Ewald and his company were again placed under the overall command of the British General Alexander Leslie. The men disembarked at Cole's Ferry on Staten Island. They then dispersed to cantonments at Richmond, Rosebank and Newtown.[3] Not long after their return, General Knyphausen led an expedition composed of five thousand men from New York by water to Elizabeth Point in New Jersey. Knyphausen had developed this approach to fighting the war in the environs of New York while Clinton was south capturing Charlestown. Essentially, it involved countering American raids on the British and Loyalist held areas around New York with raids of his own. These raids focused on specific targets. Knyphausen saw the Continentals, for instance, as a worthy target for raiding activity, while the various rebel militia groups in New Jersey were not deemed important enough to warrant the effort.[4]

The overall goal of this expedition was to surprise and attack American corps under the command of General William Maxwell (Scotch Willie), based between Elizabeth and Springfield.[5] The greater objective stood as launching a quick swipe at Washington's forces and perhaps drawing them into battle when they were not prepared. If they refused to engage, they would be forced to abandon their supplies and artillery to hasten their retreat. The plan counted on the element surprise for its successful execution. It was based on information Knyphausen received from informants that the morale in the American camp, especially among the militia, stood fairly low. Knyphausen did not expect them to put up anything resembling a spirited resistance, thus the plan for a quick thrust seemed workable. To execute the assault, Knyphausen brought along 6,000 troops, all that he could spare form the New York garrison.[6] Clearly, he meant this as a major incursion into rebel controlled territory.

Ewald considered Maxwell a mediocre general, but the latter was on his guard, and received prompt word of the expedition's landing. Maxwell positioned himself at Connecticut Farms Meeting House with a strong force of New Jersey militia. His front "was covered by a marshy brook which cut through a range of hills and by marshy woodlands."[7] Narrow flank approaches, well-guarded by American troops complimented the general's position. These flank positions tended to be defended by the militia, whom Washington directed.[8] As Knyphausen worked his way inland from the landing area, he encountered American skirmishers, who successfully delayed his advance. In Ewald's opinion, this was when Knyphausen realized the assault held little chance for success. Rather than attempt a retreat in full view of the enemy, however, the Hessian general sought to achieve some check on the Americans. As part of implementing this contingency, "The Jäger Corps under Lieutenant Colonel Wurmb, reinforced by the English Guards and Hessian Leib Regiment, made the attack on the pass at Connecticut Farms Meeting House."[9]

The ensuing battle, fought on June 7, 1780, stood as one of the last major clashes in the northern theater during the war. It is not given the same attention as Monmouth Courthouse two years previous as it involved American militia rather than Continentals After putting up a stiff resistance, the American militia retreated. Still, Ewald realized that even with the Americans withdrawing, "it would cost many men to dislodge him."[10] Although they were eventually forced to fall back, the Americans managed to hold up Knyphausen's advance for the better part of the day. The fighting reached such a pitch that the Jäger expended almost all of it cartridges, and "no rifle fired any longer."[11] When the Jäger ran out of ammunition, the English Guards and the Lieb Regiment relieved them and continued the fight until nightfall. In doing so they deprived the Hessian general of the key element of his plan, surprise. After spending the night in the region of the battlefield, Knyphausen withdrew the following day.[12] Ewald attributes the withdrawal to Knyphausen's receiving intelligence that the Americans had been reinforced. Knyphausen fell back behind the Elizabeth River with the main army while the Jäger Corps occupied the town of Elizabeth itself.[13]

Ewald estimated the losses on both sides as roughly a thousand men. The toll on the Jäger Corps stood as a heavy one. The dead included one Lieutenant Ebenauer of the Anspachers and twenty-two non-commissioned officers and privates. Captain Donop, Lieutenants Cornelius and Bohlen and fifty-nine non-commissioned officers and soldiers made up the wounded. To a small unit such as the Jäger Corps, this was indeed a heavy price. These men would be difficult if not impossible to replace.[14]

The Jäger Corps remained in their position for much of the month of June, and regularly skirmished with American forces. In order to maintain an open line of communications with reinforcements on Staten Island, Knyphausen ordered a bridge of boats constructed across the Sound. On June 20, Ewald crossed the bridge to check on his men. On his arrival, he found generals Clinton and Leslie. He asked General Leslie for permission to remain at the post with his men, since, due to lack of officers, his company was then under command of a sergeant. Instead, Leslie ordered him to return at once to Staten Island with his detachment.[15]

The following day, Leslie's troops were ordered to be in readiness to march at a moment's notice as it appeared Washington was on the move with the goal of attacking Knyphausen. The attack, however, failed to materialize, and on the 22nd, Leslie's Corps were placed on transports. The next day, the flotilla moved up the North River to Philipse's House. It should be recalled that Ewald spent much of the campaign season of 1779 operating in the same area This maneuver forced Washington to withdraw to a place known as the Clove or risk letting the British get between the Continental Army and West Point.[16]

When Knyphausen learned of Washington's withdrawal to the Clove, he determined to attack the American advanced units in order to gain some maneuver room and secure a safe retreat for his own forces.[17] The British assault drove the Americans back behind Springfield, during which, according to Ewald, over seven hundred men on both sides remained engaged.[18]

The Jäger Corps launched this attack as well, and sustained fourteen killed, as well as several officers and thirty-five men wounded. In the evening, General Knyphausen withdrew his forces past Elizabethtown to Elizabeth Point. The Americans did not harass his retreat. Once his force was at Elizabeth Point, they dismantled the bridge behind them as they retreated across the Sound to slow any American pursuit. The troops then embarked on sloops and moved up the North River, and in the evening joined Leslie's Corps at Philipsburgh.[19]

The preceding episode demonstrates the type of combat Ewald faced on his return to the New York theater. Due to the expansion of the war, and the opening of the new front in the southern colonies, Clinton and his subordinate Knyphausen lacked the material strength to launch a full-on offensive against the Americans. By the same token, Washington, always numerically inferior to his British foes, refused to hazard his meager forces on an offensive either. There ensued a war of maneuver in which both sides jockeyed for superior position or to lure a portion of the enemy force into a compromising position and inflict a crippling defeat on them. In all essentials, it was a game of cat and mouse.

On June 25, Knyphausen's troops disembarked at Philipsburgh. Ewald expressed some frustration with the entire operation in his diary, stating, "Thus I was back safely in this area where we had roamed about on the defensive for the past two years."[20] The war of posts, with the two armies essentially stationary and staring at one another was clearly not to the captain's liking, he continued, "Had I been able to follow my own desire, I would have gladly remained in Carolina with Lord Cornwallis."[21]

In the South Ewald experienced a war of maneuver, with the armies actually accomplishing things of note. There was a chance to earn distinction, something Ewald always craved, and to enhance one's military reputation in the eyes of their peers. Alternately, in the North, there seemed little opportunity to accomplish anything, or to earn any fresh military honors. His desire to remain in the South came as no new whim. Prior to returning to the North, he had even asked the British commander, Sir Henry Clinton, if he could remain in the southern theater. The commander of British forces in North America denied the request, telling Ewald that he needed the services of the Jäger Corps and their leader to the north, a compliment to be sure.[22]

The recognition by the commander of his talents likely came as little consolation to Ewald, who reported in July 1780 that he and his troops were once again assigned to Philipse's woods, between the Hudson and Saw Mill Rivers, a post they had held repeatedly over the preceding two years.[23]

Due to the expansion of the war, Sir Henry Clinton had to conduct operations with fewer troops than his predecessor, Sir William Howe.[24] Likewise, instead of calling for reinforcements, as Howe repeatedly did, Clinton worried about losing what troops he did have to operations in the West Indies. These were considered more important to the economy of the Empire, and thus demanded a higher priority than the northern colonies.[25] Given these strategic constraints on his conduct, it comes as little surprise that the commander of British forces in North America attempted operations that were limited in both scope and objectives. The great hope was to lure Washington into the field to give battle on conditions advantageous to the British. Numerous attempts were made to accomplish this goal. One of these occurred beginning July 9, 1780.

Colonel Wurmb marched out with the entire Jäger Corps toward Tarrytown, New York. During the march, Ewald, serving with the foot Jäger, covered the passes by Odell's House and Dobb's Ferry. During the operation, Ewald enjoyed a brevet command of sorts, as he held overall command of the foot Jäger. He exercised this command since Lieutenant Colonel Prueschenck was recovering from wounds and Major Wurmb was sick.[26] Still, the march did not yield any engagements with the Americans, and the men returned to their starting point.

While the efforts to bring Washington to battle only came on several occasions, the small war at which Ewald and his Jäger were by now consummate professionals returned as well. Once again, the war of posts would provide constant employment for the captain and his Jäger. On July 14, for example, the Jäger received information that a party of Americans were lying in wait near Tarrytown to ambush a party of men from DeLancey's Refugees, a Loyalist unit.[27] Ewald set out at nine in the evening with twenty horse and one hundred foot Jäger but could not discover the Americans and so returned to his post.[28]

Soon after this mission, a French force was sighted off Rhode Island and it was feared that they might make an attack on New York.[29] Nothing, however, came of the French presence. As usual, however, Ewald kept a detailed account of the number and type of ships that arrived off Rhode Island.[30]

Little worth recording took place in the following weeks in New York, as the next incident Ewald recorded in his finished diary came in late July. On July 22, the Jäger Corps were ordered to move out, along with other regiments. The troops marched to Frog's Neck, where they boarded transports the following day. Ewald and his men boarded a ship named the *The Two Brothers*.[31]

Sir Henry Clinton arrived with the expedition on July 27 aboard the armed ship *Grand Duke*. The purpose of the force, according to Ewald, was to attack the French who had recently landed in Rhode Island. The captain set down a note of pride at finally facing a European foe, "the honor of fighting the French excited me very much."[32] At the same time, he held temporary command over three hundred Jäger, a privilege he might not enjoy again for the remainder of the war.[33] By the same token, if he distinguished himself in this post, his temporary assignment may be made permanent at some later date.

Once again, however, the best laid plans of Ewald's superiors came to naught, as the fleet received information on the 31st that the French had left Rhode Island destined for Massachusetts. Having no target, the fleet weighed anchor and returned from whence it came. All of the troops disembarked over the course of August 2nd and 3rd at Whitestone. After disembarking, Ewald was sent to the woods overlooking Flushing, with a Colonel Robert Abercromby and the light infantry stationed in the town below.[34]

Ewald continued to exercise his expanded command for several more weeks, when, on August 17, he was relieved by Lieutenant Colonel Prueschenk. The captain returned to his command at Morris Hill on York Island, confiding to his diary "I do not deny that I would have liked to enjoy this repose more, at least to have had time to equip myself with the necessities."[35] His higher status brought with it greater pay, and Ewald could have used the additional income to purchase equipment and so forth.

Once back at his old unit, Ewald returned to the routine duties and patrols and the conduct of small operations against his counterparts on the American side. The night of August 20th stood as typical in the type of mission the captain performed. He was ordered out with one hundred and fifty infantry jägers to Philipse's Church. Once there, he occupied the post until Lieutenant Colonel Wurmb arrived with the mounted Jäger.

As he arrived at the designated location. "I had scarcely taken my precautions when I ran into an enemy party which attacked me so swiftly that I could hardly reach the bridge."[36] The clash was brief but sharp, with the Americans withdrawing after exchanging only a few shots with Ewald and his troops.

When morning came, Lieutenant Colonel Wurmb arrived on the scene and ordered Ewald to hold his position, while he reconnoitered towards Dobbs Ferry with the mounted Jäger in order to gain further information on the enemy. He returned around noon with two prisoners and the entire unit marched back to Morris Hill.[37]

Shortly after this, Ewald fell ill with a severe fever. By his own account, he was one of many who were ill in camp at the time. His illness prevented him from further duty for some time.

The situation changed dramatically in early October. For the past few weeks, Ewald and his company, as well as all of the grenadiers and men from five other units were kept under arms, prepared to embark at a moment's notice. The reason for this heightened alert turned out to be the treason of one of the top American officers, Benedict Arnold.[38]

It remains unclear just when Arnold determined to sell his services to the British, but it is certain that on assuming his new command, he quickly set about reducing the effectiveness of the West Point defenses.

The defenses at West Point were laid out by the Polish engineer Thaddeus Kosciuszko. Working under difficult conditions, which included not only the physical environment, manpower, supplies and tool, but jealous French rivals who took any opportunity to try and discredit the Pole. Despite these obstacles, Kosciuszko constructed a very strong post that served to guard the Hudson Highlands from sudden British assault. As a part of his treason, Arnold attempted to weaken these same defenses preparatory to a British attack.[39]

Arnold narrowly escaped capture on the discovery of the plot and made his way to the HMS Vulture at anchor in the Hudson, then on to British headquarters in New York City. His plan had come within a hair's breadth of success.

Arnold's treason sent a shockwave through the Patriot ranks. While often quarrelsome and difficult to get along with, no one ever doubted Arnold's devotion to the cause. If he were capable of such an act, then who else?

Ewald understood very well the damage caused to the Americans by Arnold's defection, noting his diary "He was truly a great loss for the united provinces."[40]

Arnold went on to become a brigadier general in the British Army and would lead an incursion into Virginia later in the war, in which Ewald would serve. His treason created additional problems at the moment how-ever, in regard to the fate of Major John André.[41]

André was a very ambitious and respected young officer in the British army. He purchased his first commission in 1771 and went to America in 1774 as a Lieutenant in the 7th Regiment. He demonstrated throughout the war both competence and a desire to attain higher rank. He served as an adjutant to General Grey during the Philadelphia campaign and took part in the surprise attack on Wayne at Paoli. His service under Grey led to the latter's recommendation that he join Sir Henry Clinton's staff. An-dré became Clinton's Aide de Camp and was entrusted with handling the commander's intelligence network. It was in this capacity that he became enmeshed in the Arnold plot.

On his capture, André wore civilian clothing and was therefore tried and convicted as a spy. The penalty was death by hanging. André protest-ed that he had his uniform on underneath and therefore deserved to be executed as an officer, by firing squad. Washington refused to acquiesce in his plea, and André was hung on October 2, 1780.

Ewald actually met André two years before the war, when the young man was traveling through Kassel. Likewise, they had served together during the Philadelphia campaign. He joined many of the British officers in lamenting the Major's death, noting "He was my friend and had shown much friendship for me and the Jäger Corps."[42] The effect of André's death was felt for some time among the troops. Several weeks later, Ewald would note that "From this time on the army occupied its winter quarters, and it seemed as if all the courage was gone with Major Andre's death."[43]

Even as mourning for André circulated through the British forces oc-cupying New York City, the rhythm of military life continued. On Octo-ber 18, a much-delayed provisions fleet arrived in the city. These convoys were vital to the British force's ability to operate in North America as they transported not only recruits for the various units but supplies as well.[44]

The convoy then entering New York harbor constituted a fairly large one, in that it brought 2,300 recruits in total, 900 of which were Hessians, with one hundred forty-six being assigned specifically to the Jäger Corps.[45] Commenting on the troops sent to replace losses among the Jägers, Ewald noted that "Most of them were Imperial and Prussian deserters."[46] Once again, the partisan captain was not impressed with the new human ma-terial he was being sent. He further observed that the fleet arrived at just the right moment, since there were only about fourteen days supplies re-maining in the depots, and for the past six days, the men had been issued rice instead of bread.[47]

Shortly after the arrival of the supply convoy, Ewald and his men received a new assignment. They were dispatched along the cost of Long Island, in order to interdict the raids on the island by American forces coming south from Connecticut. In particular, Ewald assumed command of an area that included Cow Bay, Cow Neck, Searingtown, and Hempstead Harbor.[48] Behind him were located the mounted Jäger, stationed at Norwich. The Lieutenant Colonel of the Jäger Corps had his headquarters at Westbury, which was the center of the zone entrusted to their supervision. Ewald described the region as encompassing about two good German miles, and being occupied by roughly one thousand men. The men themselves were billeted in houses, each of which held between ten and twelve troops, though detachments could run as high as sixteen.[49]

The main purpose of this deployment stood as an attempt to suppress the raiding activity of some American militia out of Connecticut. The men used whale boats to land on different portions of the coast, conduct brief inland forays into British controlled areas and move out again before the general alarm was sounded. Both Patriot and Loyalist militia took part in this raiding activity which has come to be known as the whale boat wars.[50] In keeping with this objective, the men of the Jäger Corps were often deployed in pickets along the main roads leading to the bays and landing places. To maintain themselves in these positions, the soldiers constructed straw huts for the winter and built up large watch fires to keep themselves warm.[51] Even under these conditions, Ewald reported that "everyone was glad he was under a roof."[52] By the same token, this was far from a peaceful winter posting. Ewald noted that "every officer could only rest with is saber in his hand." Likewise, it was not until November 15 that he could note in his diary that "twenty-four hours have passed without an alarm sounding at one of the other parts of the cordon." The foregoing makes clear that by this point in the war, the American's had become quite adept at partisan war themselves. They knew to keep the British posts under constant pressure in order to wear down the men's morale. At the same time, this tactic allowed them to probe for weaknesses in the Crown defenses.[53]

Under the same date, Ewald noted the particulars of a raid by one of the American units. At noon he received word that about a hundred men had landed at Cow Bay, which lay under his jurisdiction. He proceeded to the site and the Wurmb Company followed. When he arrived on the scene, he found that "after having plundered a few houses, they had cast off in their boats and were already beyond rifle range."[54]

Raids of this sort could be quite unsettling for the local inhabitants, people whom the Crown forces needed on their side, both as a means of support and as sources of intelligence. Ewald grasped the importance of providing security to these people, as he noted "Now since the people there believed the enemy would return during the night, I remained in the vicinity until an hour before daybreak on the following day." On this particular occasion, the raiders did not return.[55]

Shortly after this incursion, Ewald was called to headquarters and informed that he and his Jäger were to compose a part of a secret expedition to Virginia under Benedict Arnold. The goal of the expedition was to take some of the pressure off of Lord Cornwallis, operating further south in the Carolinas. While the prospect of serving under Arnold was not one that excited Ewald, Lieutenant Colonel John Graces Simcoe and his Queen's Rangers were taking part in the expedition as well. He noted, curtly, "My friend Simcoe also was in the party. I accepted with joy."[56]

Another major participant in the campaign would be Major General Alexander Leslie. By this point in the war Leslie stood as an experienced combat veteran. Shortly before the outbreak of hostilities, he served as the lieutenant colonel of the 64th Regiment. Stationed at Boston under General Thomas Gage, he received orders to lead an expedition into the Massachusetts countryside on February 26, 1775. This march almost caused the outbreak of open fighting several months early. The following year, he commanded the light infantry at Long Island and Kip's Bay and took part in the pursuit of the remnants of Washington's army across New Jersey. At the end of the 1776 campaign, Leslie and his men went into winter quarters. On the news of the surprise at Trenton, he was dispatched to New Jersey in an attempt to salvage the situation there. He served in several other capacities in the following years, demonstrating an aptitude for independent command.[57]

CHAPTER 9

THE RETURN SOUTHWARD

Since Ewald left the South following the successful conclusion of the siege of Charleston, what had seemed a bright start for Crown arms in South Carolina had dimmed considerably. Much of the diminishing British prospects in the region derived from their own mishandling of the political dimension of the conflict. The two main factors, changes in the conditions of paroles proclaimed by Clinton shortly before his departure, and the rumors of a massacre following the battle of the Waxhaws, May 29, 1780, brought about a considerable insurgency that erupted throughout the South Carolina backcountry.[1]

Numerous local leaders, such as Thomas Sumter, Francis Marion, and Andrew Pickens gathered men and took to the field against the British regulars, as well as Loyalist units the Crown attempted to raise in the state. These men raided communications, attacked small detachments, and generally disrupted the British control of the area. While they quite effectively kept the British occupiers off balance, and at times terrorized Loyalists away from open support, they lacked the power to drive the British from South Carolina completely.[2]

The Continental Congress, for its part, dispatched the self-aggrandizing Horatio Gates to take command of the remains of the Continental Army in the Southern Department. Gates northern laurels quickly transformed into southern willows, however, as he led his troops against the British forces around Camden, South Carolina. Many of the troops in Gates' Army were untrained. Some likely never fired a shot in anger, and they were literally thrown against the hardened veterans of Cornwallis's army.

The result, predictably enough, came in the form of another Patriot defeat at the battle of Camden, August 16, 1780. One reason for the defeat stemmed from the American general's deployments. Gates, a former British Army officer, followed the European practice of placing the best troops in his army on the right, the position of honor, and his most inexperienced troops on the left. Cornwallis followed the same pattern of deployment. Consequently, the best troops on the British side faced the most inexperienced men on the American, and vice versa. In the fighting, the Baron Johann de Kalb, a foreign officer of German ancestry who had done much to aid the American cause was severely wounded and captured. He died of his wounds several days later. For his part, Gates ran ignominiously from the field, galloping by many of his retreating soldiers on horseback.[3]

The same day, another British force surprised and defeated the partisan band of Thomas Sumter at Fishing Creek.[4] The prospects of the rebellion in the south appeared bleaker than ever. Several days later, a bright spot came when the partisan of Francis Marion managed to defeat a British column marching back some of the prisoners taken at Camden. Marion and his men managed to liberate some of the soldiers from the Maryland/Delaware brigade, among the top units on the Continental establishment.[5] Still, many of these men chose to desert or turn themselves in to the British in Charleston rather than serve further.[6]

When Congress received word of the defeat at Camden, they consulted George Washington on whom he would select to take command in the Southern Department in an effort to save the situation in the south. Washington selected his most able lieutenant, Major General Nathanael Greene.[7] Greene was, at that time, moving from the Quartermaster Department, which Washington had previously urged him to take over, to the command of West Point, left leaderless since Arnold's treason. Some of Greene's actions while heading up the Quartermaster's Department had run afoul of the Congress, and currently there were calls for an inquiry concerning his actions while holding the post.[8]

Nonetheless, with the current crisis on the South, the members of the Continental Congress had little choice but to accept Washington's recommendation, especially since they had previously chosen Gates without consultation. Given the result of their previous action, the Congressmen were in a poor position to do anything but accept the Continental Army commander's recommendation without question.[9]

Greene set out to take command over the remnants of the Continental Army of the Southern Department. As he traveled south, Greene stopped at the Continental Congress, meeting in Philadelphia, as well as visiting the governors of all the states along his way and literally begged support for his army.[10] It is worth noting that Washington did not send Greene alone to the southern department. The Continental Army Commander dispatched the Baron von Steuben southward with Greene in order to help train troops in Virginia and move them southward to aid in the defense of the region against the British. These plans would be thrown off by Arnold's invasion of Virginia. In having von Steuben along however, Greene possessed a talented organizer and trainer. While the Prussian soldier ached for a field command of his own, he was willing to subordinate his personal desires to the needs of the greater cause on this occasion. While the results of his efforts in Virginia are more difficult to discern, it is necessary to keep in mind that von Steuben simultaneously helped shore up the Virginia defenses, and attempted to forward troops and supplies to Greene.[11]

While Greene was making his way southward, the partisans in South Carolina continued to keep the Patriot cause alive. They scored a number of small victories and continued to interdict British efforts at control of the region. Probably the most significant of their successes occurred on October 30, 1780 at Kings Mountain in South Carolina. Here a composite Patriot militia force defeated a Loyalist militia force under the command of Major Patrick Ferguson.[12] The defeat at King's Mountain curtailed Crown efforts to raise Loyalist militia units in the South Carolina backcountry.

Finally, Major General Nathanael Greene assumed command of the Continental Army of the Southern Department at Hillsborough, North Carolina on December 3, 1780. The force was meager even by American standards, a mere 900 Continentals, destitute of even the most basic necessities, and their morale at rock bottom.[13] Some of the men even resorted to plundering the local populace. In fact, on assuming his command, one Greene's first acts was to sign the warrant for the execution of two Continentals who had been caught plundering. This action went some way to restoring the discipline of his fighting force.[14]

When Greene assumed command at Hillsborough, North Carolina, a slow resurgence of Patriot fortunes began in the Southern Department. Daniel Morgan, who resigned his commission over what he perceived as unfair treatment by Congress after the victory at Saratoga and Washington's choice of Anthony Wayne to command the Corps of Light Infantry over him, came out of retirement and joined Greene.[15] Greene dispatched Morgan into the western part of South Carolina in order to garner supplies and show that the state was still considered important to the Continental forces. It should be borne in mind that the people had not seen any Continental troops since Gates ignominious defeat at Camden the preceding August, and as a result many in the region felt abandoned by the Continental Congress.[16] If Greene were to succeed in rekindling the embers of the revolutionary fire in the Carolinas, he would need the fuel provided by Virginia. The preceding constituted the operational environment into which Johann Ewald and his Jäger would soon deploy.

By late 1780, the significance of Virginia to the American war effort had become clear to the British as well. The state constituted a source of manpower for the Continental forces operating further southward, as well as a source of supply. There were numerous industries in the state that produced goods necessary for the Continental troops. Most importantly, it held a vibrant agricultural economy that provided crops such as tobacco that could be traded for war material on the international market. Thus, Arnold's raid was designed in part as a form of economic warfare.[17]

On December 7, 1780, Ewald received orders to be ready to embark with 125 infantry Jäger. The Hessian Jägers as well as the Anspach contingent were to take part in Arnold's expedition. Both groups were specifically enjoined to "take no more equipment than what each could carry himself."[18] The expedition left camp on December 9, and embarked, along with the Althouse sharpshooters the following day.[19] By Ewald's reckoning, the full expedition contained some 2,200 men.

As the force made its way south along the Atlantic coast, the ships were scattered by storms. Previously, instructions had been provided to the various ship masters that if such an event should occur, the vessels of the fleet were to rendezvous at Cape Henry at the mouth of the Chesapeake Bay.[20] The bulk of the ships, save those carrying the artillery and the horse for the mounted rangers, made it to the rendezvous point by December 31. The men then disembarked from their transports and boarded open sloops and smaller boats for the trip up the James River. They were escorted up the river by several smaller armed vessels.[21]

The purpose of the British raid was to destroy Virginia's ability to support the Patriot war effort further south, and in doing so, relieve General Earl Charles Cornwallis as he attempted to maintain and expand British control in that area. Cornwallis himself had come to believe that the key to winning the southern campaign was to stop the flow of men and supplies form Virginia.[22] Historians of the American War of Independence have tended to overlook Arnold's raid into Virginia, however, it was a crucial step on the road that led to Yorktown.[23] Through his participation in the raid, and subsequent campaigning in Virginia, Ewald would witness some of the bitter fighting that seemed to mark the southern campaigns in the American War of Independence. He would also participate in another siege, this time from the perspective of the besieged, at Yorktown. His discussion of these events is valuable in the first instance as it issues from the pen of an objective observer with a professional background, and secondly for the lessons Ewald would cull from them as he wrote his subsequent military treatises after his return to Europe. His experiences began as he led a group Jäger landing on the banks of the James River.

Toward evening the expedition had its first encounter with local troops when a "small body of Americans appeared on the left bank of the James River at Warwick."[24] Many of the local residents along the James and its tributaries had fled in the face of the British invasion.[25] The ships in the flotilla anchored, and Arnold dispatched Ewald and his men along with the Althouse sharpshooters, "to approach these people and reconnoiter them." Specifically, Arnold enjoined Ewald to "land at my discretion and attack them, and in particular I should try to capture several prisoners and catch a few natives." The rangers would in turn provide support to Ewald's command.[26]

The attack Ewald launched stands as a classic example of partisan reconnaissance. As he came onshore, Ewald "approached within rifle shot, the shore was high. I ordered several shots fired at them, which they answered with small-arms fire, whereupon I concluded that they did not have any cannon with them."[27] His probing attack succeeded in gaining intelligence of the enemy while engaging them, which distracted his foes from the movements of the main force under Arnold as well.

Discovering that the Americans had posted themselves behind a fence, Ewald tested the depth of the water and found it to be only waist deep. He then ordered his men to fire another volley, draw their hunting sabers and jump into the water. They were to swim ashore and attack the Americans. His men did as ordered; three being wounded as they jumped from the boats. Still, the unexpected move on the part of the Jäger surprised the American militiamen and they withdrew. Once his men were safely ashore, Ewald pursued the Americans for a short distance, hoping to capture a prisoner and gain additional information as to the enemy's numbers and deployments.[28]

While he did not take any prisoners, he did drive the Americans from the shore. At the same time, Ewald confided to his diary that "this little trick left me with no great opinion of General Arnold's judgement, ordering men without bayonets to land and attack an enemy equipped with bayonets, especially since the light infantry was just as close to them as I was."[29] In keeping with his regular practice, Ewald analyzed the situation, and decided his success in the attack was borne more out of luck than any other attribute. At the same time, he noted that there had not been any time to challenge the order from Arnold, and that he was fearful "that the man, on his false principles, would hold me on for insubordination or cowardice."[30] Clearly, Ewald perceived Arnold as a man without honor which, for Ewald, stood as a core virtue. Even when the general came ashore and tried to compliment Ewald on the performance of his men, the Jäger captain chafed at the kind words and left as soon as he could.

Ewald's discomfort soon developed into resentment at serving under Arnold, whom he perceived as a man without honor.

Soon after this landing, on January 1, 1781, Ewald again skirmished with the Americans, then, "Towards nine o'clock orders arrived for the troops to leave the land and board the boats, which took place at once."[31] As they waded their way back to the waiting boats in water that was navel-deep, Ewald recalled his gratitude for the warmer southern climate.[32]

About the middle of the day, the Hessian Jäger and the Althouse sharpshooters were placed on smaller vessels, since there was no room for them on the larger ships containing the main army. The small fleet then anchored off of Hog Island.[33] Much of the maneuvering up until this point concerned finding a way into the Chesapeake and locating the best targets for the raiding force to focus on. At the same time, the invaders sought to ascertain some idea of the strength and caliber of the local defenders. While most of these defenders would be militia, by this point in the war, many had previous experience as Continentals, and were therefore trained to a higher standard than that commonly expected of the local troops. Some may have possessed considerable combat experience as well. For older men who had established farms and businesses as well as families, the militia stood as a way for them to balance patriotism and economic responsibilities.[34]

Soon, the British invasion force encountered a band of American militia. On January 2, Arnold's flotilla came across a party of Americans posted on the shore. Arnold dispatched a boat carrying an English officer to secure the surrender of the American troops. The commander of the American force asked the Englishman if it was Colonel Arnold the traitor who had sent him, and if it were, was there another officer to whom he could surrender. For if it were Arnold the traitor, he could not possibly surrender to him, but would try to hang him up by his heels as called for by Congress. Ewald noted with a certain relish, "The English officer delivered the message word for word, and Arnold was obliged to make a wry face."[35]

The day following the encounter with the American militia, orders were issued for the men to disembark. Then came a second set of orders countermanding the first. The reason for the about face was that in the interim, Arnold received news of a strong American unit operating in the vicinity.[36] Later in the day, the Jäger and the Althouse sharpshooters along with Simcoe's Queen's Rangers attacked an American position and drove off the defenders.[37]

The actual landing by Arnold's force occurred on January 4. Between eight hundred and a thousand men came ashore on the north bank of the

James River at Westover. The first habitation they came across was a plantation owned by the Byrd family that even then was nearly a century old.[38] As was often the case, Ewald and his Jäger formed the tip of the spear and therefore stood among the first to come ashore. They encountered and drove off a small party of Virginia militia.

After they drove off the Americans, Ewald inspected their works and came to the following conclusions: "The fault of these works lay in the fact that they were not closed at the gorge, for had they been in a better state of defense, and the garrison commanded by an enterprising officer, they could have easily delayed us until the militia had assembled and strengthened the position." He went on to note that "Since the channel in the river lay within small-arms range, this could very easily have prevented us from further undertakings."[39] Once again, in the preceding description, Ewald exhibited his trained eye for seizing up a set of defenses and noting both their strengths and weaknesses. For the captain, a quick, critical examination of one's surroundings stood as a key attribute of a successful partisan. Ewald would encounter ample opportunity to further hone his skills as the column marched out.

Arnold and his men began to march in the direction of Richmond. To this point, the expedition had encountered only limited and uncoordinated resistance. The most recent historian of Arnold's raid notes "Inadequate resources, too few troops and a lack of organization doomed Virginia's defensive efforts."[40] He goes on to observe that the Virginia authorities, most notably then governor Thomas Jefferson, were surprised by Arnold's sudden descent upon the state, a fact which served to exacerbate their lack of preparedness.[41] While the preceding may serve to explain some of the initial lukewarm response of Virginia to Arnold's expedition, it fails to justify it, especially when it is considered that the state had been the target of various British enterprises going back to the efforts of its last royal governor, Lord Dunmore, in 1775.[42]

In response to Arnold's incursion, Virginia raised about 4,000 militia, however, they were not concentrated in one location; nor were their activities coordinated.[43] The defense Virginia mounted was no match for the concentrated assault unleashed by Arnold. Since his Jäger served as the advanced guard Ewald recorded the dispositions he assigned his men on the march to Richmond: First, there were "four Jäger, two of whom marched along the fences on the right and two on the left." Next came, "At a distance of twenty-five paces behind I had six Jäger follow in the same manner, where I was myself." Third, "an officer and twenty Jäger at a distance of fifty paces." This group was followed by "An officer with thirty horse of the Queen's Rangers at a distance of fifty paces." Next came "The Jäger and Althouse sharpshooters in six platoons at a distance of one hundred paces." Finally, there were "The light infantry of the rangers."[44]

Thorough, detailed descriptions of the tactical dispositions of his troops are one of the reasons why Ewald's diary stands as such a valuable source on the war of Independence. Here is a description of precisely how an advanced guard was arranged, something vital to understanding precisely how the war was fought, at least by one unit during the American War of Independence. By the same token, such a thorough description provided Ewald a reference to look back on once he began to set his ideas on irregular warfare down on his return to Europe.

Ewald not only detailed his arrangement of the troops under his command, but included his justifications for their dispositions as well:

> *Since we had to be fearful of ambuscades, especially since the night was very dark, with this formation I could never get into disorder if the outermost point fell into an ambuscade, for each group had room to help the other if it was alarmed.*[45]

In order to preserve silence while on the march during the night, Ewald further directed "first for men to let everyone pass through that they met, and in case of emergency to use only their hunting swords."[46] Such orders could drastically reduce the chances of minor scuffles with civilians, thus preserving silence and secrecy. Likewise, the injunction to use only swords if they got into a confrontation would reduce the chance of guns being fired in the night, and thus giving away the position and illuminating the advanced guard.

Moving forward with these dispositions, Ewald was supported by Colonel John Simcoe, who commanded the grenadier company of the 80th Regiment, followed by the remainder of the unit with four light six-pounders. In addition, there was Robinson's Corps, followed by the light infantry of the 80th, and finally an officer with ten horsemen of the Queen's Rangers.[47]

As these forces moved out into the Virginia countryside, Ewald quickly became involved with his usual method of fighting. He noted how about midnight, he took a major of the Virginia volunteers, the man's orderly, and two captains prisoner, along with their horses. The latter were distributed to some of the Jäger.[48]

The troops continued on their march to Richmond. The following day, January 5, 1781, at about two in the afternoon the men reached the heights above Richmond. Simcoe was on a mission to destroy an American cannon foundry in the area, which they did. Here they ran into an

American force which had posted itself on the left of the town with several cannons. Arnold sent in the Jäger to take the position, during which Ewald lost one soldier wounded and three captured in driving off the Americans. Once they had reached the crest of the hill, "I formed my men as quickly as possible in order to come up with the enemy, who had withdrawn to a wood behind a steep ravine, where he made a new stand."[50]

Quickly analyzing the situation, Ewald realized that he would have to cross the ravine under fire from the Americans, so he determined to hold them in position by skirmishing in order to buy time until more reinforcements could come up to support him. He noted:

> *On the whole, it was a crucial moment for me. I was on barren, level ground and the enemy could count my men. I discovered he had not riflemen, but infantry equipped with bayonets. My men appeared so tired and worn out that I no longer dared to rely on their legs for a hurried flight.*[51]

At this point, Simcoe rendezvoused with Ewald, who asked the latter if his men were still capable of marching, as he planned to attack an American cannon foundry and powder magazine at Buckingham. Ewald, in turn, called for volunteers from the men under his command. A composite force was quickly assembled consisting of troops from the Jäger, Althouse sharpshooters, some of the Queen's Rangers, and some of the 80th Regiment. The cavalry of the Rangers volunteered for the raid as well.[52] At this point, Simcoe took a part of the composite force and headed to Westham in order to provide cover for Ewald, who was to march on the foundry and destroy as much of it as possible before the former returned.

Ewald successfully surprised the Americans, capturing the workers as well as the Inspector of Ordnance, Lieutenant Colonel Baron Werneck. Ewald reported that this Hanoverian noble had served as an artillery officer in the Seven Years' War. Ewald and his men worked quickly to render as much of the machinery at the site inoperable as possible. In addition, they blew up the powder magazine, which contained some seven hundred barrels of gun powder, as well as two powder mills. Ewald's attack therefore encompassed a heavy blow to American logistics.[53]

After completing his work of destruction as best he could at the site, Ewald received a message from Simcoe about ten in the evening. The colonel called on Ewald to fall back on Richmond as quickly as he could. Simcoe reported that he could no longer hold out, as he had information that a strong American force was headed in his direction.[54]

As he assembled his men and prepared to move out, Ewald confronted one of the challenges that often arose during these sorts of actions. Two-thirds of his men were drunk, having located large quantities of wine and beer stored in the houses near the canon foundry. This created problems for the march as "They were now so noisy that one could hear them two hours away."[55] The preceding demonstrated a certain lack of discipline among the troops, likely due to the thinning of experienced Jäger from years of attrition. Breaking ranks and getting drunk while on the march were endemic problems among undisciplined troops. Luckily, Ewald ran into Simcoe's force about halfway back to Richmond and the two forces marched back together. On their return to Richmond, they found "General Arnold and his men were cantoned in sweet repose."[56] Ewald was commenting on the idea that Arnold sent out subordinates to conduct operations and hazard themselves while he waited in the rear. Ewald's dislike for Arnold would soon become quite clear.

The force next set fire to the magazines and workshops for shipbuilding in Richmond before moving out on January 6. The destruction included all of the ships under construction on the blocks. In addition, some forty-two vessels laden with cargo were captured and became part of the expedition's booty.[57] They destroyed numerous small arms, four thousand French-made musket locks, hemp rope, shot, fuses and tobacco as well.[58] Arnold and the various contingents under his command succeeded in wreaking a great deal of havoc on Virginia' ability to support Continental efforts in the Southern Department in a very short amount of time.

After spending the morning engaged in their work destruction at the docks in Richmond, the force began to move towards Westover around noon. They camped for the night on the left bank of Four Mile Creek. The next day, they were in motion again. After marching about half an hour, a rumor spread that an American force had moved into their rear to cut off the retreat of Arnold's raiders. The report later proved to be false, but the anecdote does, in some measure, describe the state of the British army at this time.

They were a relatively small, isolated force, operating deep in enemy-controlled territory. Consequently, great uncertainty pervaded in the ranks as to the exact strength of the Americans. If they possessed superior numbers, and could concentrate their forces, that could spell the end of the expedition all together. Likewise, their leader was a hated traitor to the enemy cause, and one that many Americans would love to have the opportunity to capture and bring to justice. These concerns manifested in the fact that as the expedition moved out on the seventh, roughly sixty men who dropped out of the march due to fatigue were captured by the Americans. As Ewald noted, "the swiftness of the marches, which amounted to fourteen German miles in all, led to the successful outcome, for we had really caused very great damage to the enemy's magazines."[59] He further noted, "we met with very little resistance, since the enemy did not expect such an audacious stroke and divided his forces."[60] One of the reasons for this lack of resistance stemmed from the Virginia militia's sluggishness in mustering.

The expedition targeted more than simply the military supplies of the state. For instance, on the march out of Richmond, Arnold detoured in the direction of the Berkeley Plantation where he freed some slaves in order to undermine the economy of the region.[61] Summarizing the exploits of the operation to date, Ewald made an interesting observation, "On the whole, this expedition greatly resembled those of the freebooters who sometimes at sea, sometimes ashore, ravaged and laid waste everything. Terrible things happened on this excursion; churches and holy places were plundered."[62] His description draws out the notion that Arnold's raid was very much a form of economic warfare against Virginia. Simultaneously, it exhibits Ewald's low opinion of this form of warfare. It would seem that the Hessian captain considered this campaign less than honorable. His opinion mattered little, however, as Arnold pressed his offensive against his former county's logistics.

On the morning of January 10, the entire expeditionary force re-embarked on ships and set sail at once. Toward the evening Arnold received word that General von Steuben was advancing on him with a corps from Petersburg. Steuben was attempting to interdict the movement of the raiders by occupying Hood's Point and thereby making their passage very difficult.[63]

While the men were on ships, a violent thunderstorm broke out, accompanied by gale force winds. Shortly after the storm, while the waters remained choppy, Arnold ordered a sizeable force into the boats to go onshore and investigate the intelligence concerning Steuben's presence in the area. The force consisted of Ewald with fifty Jäger, Simcoe with two hundred of his rangers, and Colonel Dundas with two hundred men for the 80th Regiment, along with Major Robinson with two hundred men from his corps. The men landed on Hood's Point at ten in the evening and saw no signs of the enemy.[64]

Ewald was the first to go ashore, and ever the professional soldier, he refused to let an opportunity to gain solid intelligence of the enemy slip away. Thus, "Since the thunderstorm had subsided and a beautiful, clear evening with moonlight followed, by which one could see far around, I took four men, a horn blower, and Captain Murray of the rangers to reconnoiter and patrol a short distance into the country." They moved forward, with Ewald sending two men ahead by about fifty paces and following with the remainder of his party.[65] Even with this very small force, the men were divided in order to prevent the entire groups from falling into an enemy ambush.

The party did not go very far before making contact. As Ewald reported in his diary, "I had hardly gone four to five hundred paces when I heard horses trotting through the water. I bent down to the ground and could detect something approaching me."[66] On the approach of the enemy party, Ewald opted to conceal himself and the four men accompanying him behind a fence as "I had no desire to run back, since I thought that it would be several men I could seize."[67] At this point, Ewald's miscalculation was exposed as a party of twenty men approached. Even when it became clear that he was heavily outnumbered, however, the intrepid partisan thought of firing on the enemy party from the rear but was discovered before he could act on the impulse. He ordered his men to fire, and they unleashed a volley at the enemy party, causing them to retreat into the darkness. This constituted a great stroke of luck for the partisan captain,

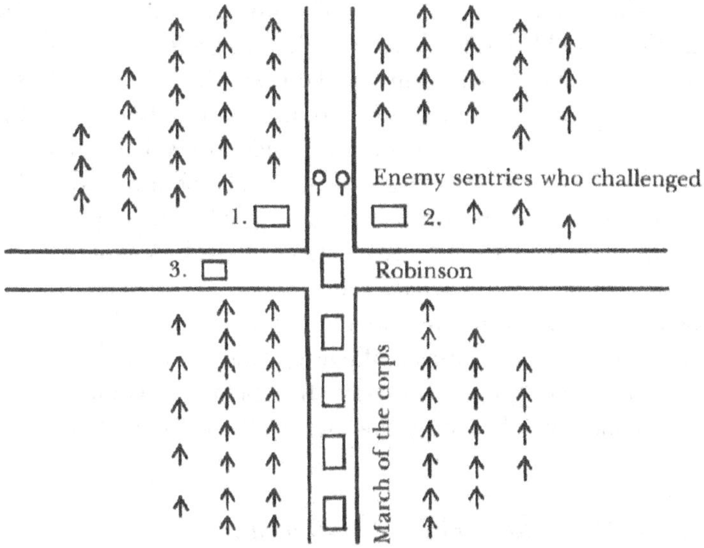

1. 2. 3. The ambuscades. From here, they could see by the bright moonlight how we came up the road.[37]

Figure 1: Ewald's diagram of the march from Diary of the American War, 271

his fifth of the war thus far, or he likely would not have lived to compile his diary afterwards. By the same token, Ewald was a soldier who lived by his wits, balancing the risks and rewards of every operation he undertook. These stood as the characteristics of the successful partisan. In this case, he missed some important variables and almost paid with his life.[68]

After the clash with the American party, Ewald and his men retreated back to the British lines. Ewald reported on the affair to Arnold directly. The general's only reply was disappointment that Ewald had not taken a prisoner.[69] The exchange between the two men could easily be read as another example of Ewald's growing dislike for his superior. The relationship, at least on Ewald's side, was strained. The following day, when the order of march was handed out, Major Robinson's provincials were given the advanced guard. Simcoe personally went to Ewald and begged his comrade not to take the slight personally. In his diary, Ewald presents the affair in the light of Arnold doing a favor for Robinson's father, General Robinson, who was friends with Arnold. While such behavior among senior officers was certainly not uncommon in militaries of the eighteenth century, and continues to occur on military organizations today, it very likely rankled Ewald's sense of professionalism. Simultaneously, it likely reminded him of his common origins and lack of family ties. Ewald was a soldier who worked diligently for every promotion he earned. The irony being that Arnold possessed some of the same foibles as Ewald, coming from very common origins himself. To then witness distinctions handed out purely on the basis of familial connection clearly infuriated him on some level. Still, the only mention he made in his diary concerning the matter was to note that "His father, General Robinson, was a friend of General Arnold, who probably wanted to give him an opportunity to get his name in the Gazette. I smiled, for I knew the honorable man."[70]

Still, the choice did effect the conduct of the subsequent march. Roughly a half an hour after moving out, the advanced guard came under fire. Ewald noted, "Instead of halting and searching this wooded area with reconnoitering patrols, everybody kept on marching."[71] After another half an hour, there came another attack on the head of the column, this time

> *a terrible fire fell out of the woods from the front and left among Robinson's honorable Americans. Weeping, wailing and gnashing to teeth arose, and one captain, two officers and some forty men were either killed or seriously wounded.*[72]

At this point, Ewald ran to the head of the column, where he found "a deplorable situation: the honorable fellows were so disconcerted by their bad luck that if the enemy party had suddenly attacked them with the bayonet, the entire column certainly would have been thrown back to Hood's Point."[73] Arnold himself soon arrived on the scene, and Ewald could not restrain himself, but burst out with "So it goes when a person wants to do something that he doesn't understand!"[74] Arnold's only reaction to the captain's outburst was to courteously ask Ewald if he would assume command of the advanced guard. The brigadier general seemed duly chastised by the results of his own favoritism. At the same time, Arnold understood Ewald's value as an officer and leader, especially in the important position of commanding the advanced guard.

Now with Ewald leading the advance, the column moved forward once again. The march was conducted in small, separate parties. They implemented this deployment, pictured above, to prevent the entire column being surprised. The parties were spaced far enough apart to prevent the group from being attacked all at once, yet close enough for the dispersed sections to be mutually supporting if any were ambushed. They moved forward for about half an hour in this configuration when Arnold called a halt.[75]

Ewald took advantage of the break in the march to perform an additional personal reconnaissance. "I posted a few men around me here and crept forward. As I lay on the ground, I could perceive a slight rustle coming from dry branches lightly touching in a wood." Staring intently, he noted, "Although the wood was very dark, I could detect a defile right in front of me."[76] It seems that Ewald may have discovered another group of Americans waiting in ambush for Arnold's column. The captain could not confirm his observation, however, as the column marched back, returning to their ships at daybreak.

What is impressive about his personal reconnaissance is Ewald's use of his senses to observe for any indications that could give away a possible enemy position. His practice of irregular warfare, on this occasion, had much in common with the tactics imputed to Native Americans in the raiding parties.[77] At the same time, his practice relates back to the roots of the Jäger as well. They were, after all, initially recruited from among the game wardens of the various European states. In that capacity, much of their role involved protecting game on royal preserves from poachers.

Arnold's operations in Virginia continued, with the men moving by water, and then landing to attack various American towns. The use of water transport certainly facilitated operations, as it allowed the men to arrive physically refreshed, as opposed to tired from the march.

On January 14th, the fleet continued up the James River, and cast anchor in the Isle of Wight County.[78] The troops prepared to disembark at Hardy's Ferry, commencing their landing at dusk. During this operation, Simcoe with his rangers, and the Jäger were posted at a plantation about halfway to the landing place in order to cover the disembarkation of the other troops. As they covered the landing, they "captured an American major and a preacher of extraordinary size, one of the greatest of the partisans of the rebels, who was armed with a pair of pistols."[79] As a tribute to his stature, his captors dubbed him the "High Priest."[80]

The landing of troops continued on the following day, so that the cavalry and artillery, as well as their horses could be disembarked. Once ashore, the entire force received three days cooked rations. This sent a message to the men in the ranks that they were in for some extended operations away from their shipping.

As they moved out from the beachhead, Ewald and his men "marched over a range of hills where the road ran like a corkscrew, and where a handful of men could have performed wonders."[81] As they moved further inland, at the last defile the Jäger captured a Major Pierce from the American side who had ridden out to reconnoiter the movements of the invaders. In the evening, Ewald established his post at the captured major's plantation.

The following day, a composite force of thirty Jäger, thirty horse and one hundred men of the 80th Regiment under a Major Gordon attacked an American force of superior numbers and put them to flight.[82] A few hours after that skirmish, Lieutenant-Colonel Simcoe went out to reconnoiter in front of the army at a pass by Mackie's Mill, which the army would have to use when it moved out. Simcoe sent back word that an American force composed of infantry with two field pieces in support occupied the pass. On receiving this news, Arnold dispatched Ewald with his Jäger and three companies of rangers to support Simcoe and do everything in their power "to dislodge the enemy."[83]

Since Ewald arrived with the confrontation already in progress, he deployed his troops on the fly, without fully reconnoitering the terrain. He did notice that the fighting was around a bridge, which the Americans had wrecked, over a stream with high banks, and that the Americans were deployed so as to be able to "enfilade the bridge and a great distance on our side."[84] Ewald quickly positioned his men along the one side of the stream, where a rise in the bank placed them above the Americans on the opposing side of the stream, "Here I took post at once with a one officer and thirty Jäger, of whom I ordered fifteen men to shoot at the people in the gardens, and directed another fifteen should keep up a constant fire on the guns."[85] Once this was accomplished, Ewald "distributed the remaining Jäger along the creek and ordered them to fire continuously at anyone who showed himself."[86] The American artillery did unleash several rounds on the British force, but then moved back as the fire of Ewald's men on the gunners proved too intense. Accurate fire from Jäger, or riflemen, could prove a real nuisance to artillerymen, as demonstrated in the siege operations outside Charleston.

At this point in the engagement, a Jäger informed Ewald that he had noticed a footbridge across the stream on the left, roughly a thousand paces from the mill. Acting on this information, Ewald distributed his men among the rangers under Simcoe, and quickly hurried to the bridge to determine its potential for himself. Moving to the left of the main engagement, "I found it [the footbridge] and immediately ordered ten or twelve men to cross over. This had the effect of causing the enemy to abandon the gardens and hedges, and it looked as though he intended to withdraw to the wood lying behind them."[87]

Things quickly devolved out of the captain's control, however, as "To my astonishment, however, all the Jäger and rangers left their posts, rushed to the footbridge and crossed it, without my being able to prevent it."[88] Ewald was thus challenged by one of the most potentially dangerous situations for a successful partisan officer, losing control of his men during an engagement. There was little else for Ewald to do but follow his men and attempt to restore in them some semblance of order,

> *In this I succeeded. Now there was nothing else to do but to attack the enemy, who, however, was so surprised by the spirit of the men that he ran head over heels to the woods. My men pursued him for over half a league. - Thus, chance often has the greatest share in the outcome of events in war.*[89]

In ascribing the success to chance, Ewald presaged one of the great military thinkers of the next century, Carl von Clausewitz.[90] The Prussian would elevate the idea of "chance" as a major element in war to the level of dogma. Still, Ewald's observation should not be taken too far, his was merely an off-hand quip.

In the aftermath of the contest for the stream, Ewald and his men located eleven American dead and took an additional eight prisoners. They sustained losses of two Jäger and one ranger killed and five wounded.

Once the fighting ended and the wounded were attended to, Ewald set about repairing the main bridge over the stream as best he could to allow Simcoe to pass over it with his cavalry. In addition, Ewald reported his action to Arnold. The latter sent forward some engineers who made additional repairs to the bridge so that the entire army could cross over it.[91]

The Jäger and Queen's Rangers did not restrict their efforts to daytime enterprises during Arnold's raid. They fought at night as well. For instance, on the night of January 19, the Jäger, along with Simcoe's rangers and the Althouse sharpshooters crossed the Nansemond River in flatboats.[92]

On the same evening, just after midnight, Simcoe set out toward Portsmouth, with a mixed force consisting of the rangers, part of the Jäger detachment, and the Althouse sharpshooters. The expedition moved out toward Portsmouth, which stood as their objective. At daybreak, Arnold ordered Ewald to follow with the remainder of the Jäger. Ewald's eight-hours march was generally uneventful. He reached Portsmouth in the evening and took post. Arnold followed these two advanced forces with the remainder of his corps, arriving in Portsmouth on the 20th.[93]

Three days prior to these maneuvers, the Americans scored their most complete tactical victory of the American War of Independence at Hannah's Cowpens in western South Carolina. There, on January 17, Daniel Morgan in command of a mixed force of Continentals and militia and with the aid of William Washington's cavalry, shattered the British Legion of Banastre Tarleton.[94] Many members of the Legion, who were among the elite troops of Cornwallis's army, were killed or captured that day. These men represented a vital manpower asset to the British commander, and he sought to regain them. Thus, he launched a pursuit of Morgan, who proceeded to fall back with his prisoners toward General Nathanael Greene in North Carolina. Cornwallis's pursuit of Morgan, and later Greene, led to the race to the Dan River.

In order to maintain pressure on Greene's retreating Continentals, Cornwallis essentially turned his entire army into a rapid striking force, burning all of their heavy baggage at Ramsours's Mills in North Carolina.[95] These actions would eventually have profound effects on the British expedition to Virginia and start Cornwallis down the road that led him to Yorktown.

As had become his habit when posted in a new location, Ewald set out to describe the layout of the town, and its terrain. This description was likely intended as reference should he have to fight in the town at a future date. By the same token, it has come down to the present offering a valuable objective insight into the physical conditions prevalent in Portsmouth at the time of the American War of Independence. He made similar notes concerning Norfolk.[96]

Once in Portsmouth, the army went into cantonments, with thinly spread pickets, since all the information they had been able to gather indicated that the Americans were not in the vicinity.[97] On the 22nd, the reason for the move to Portsmouth became clear, as the soldiers began work on constructing a series of six redoubts to defend the town. The redoubts were connected by an abatis. Arnold's actions in the raid to date had raised the ire of the Virginians, and he was now taking defensive measures should a major uprising break out.[98] Ewald observed that Portsmouth "was designated as the fortified post for this province."[99] The Crown forces were establishing a semi-permanent base of operations in Virginia.

With the expeditionary corps in cantonment, Ewald received the rare opportunity for some relaxation, as his duties were much reduced from the standard of patrolling and conducting the advanced guard. Ever the professional soldier, however, Ewald did not remain idle in camp. After resting for a day and a half, he "used the opportunity to roam through the entire area to orient myself."[100]

During his walks, Ewald discovered a causeway through a wood, which seemed an important location to prevent an enemy surprise. "On my return, I proposed that I should lie in this wood at the causeway, since otherwise Portsmouth could easily be reconnoitered and attacked from here through the aid of the woods." This proposition seemed logical enough, but yet again, the upper levels of command, most likely Arnold, did not see the situation from Ewald's perspective, "But since no enemy was to be feared, no attention was paid to my idea."[101] Ewald further discovered that from his current post he could easily be bombarded on his right.

By this point, Arnold, who had been known for his audacity earlier in the war seemed uncertain of himself as well as those around him. Perhaps this was due the fact that he now commanded men he once fought against. Arnold may also have heard some of the murmuring in camp by British officers and known of their dislike for him.

The following day, at around three in the morning, the Jäger and rangers crossed the Elizabeth River and landed on Powder Point above Norfolk. They immediately continued their march towards Great Bridge to reconnoiter in that area.[102] Soon, they came upon a civilian, "We had hardly arrived when we found a loyal-minded subject, which was regarded as a miracle, although General Arnold had asserted when he made an appearance the people would change their minds in droves."[103]

As was often the case throughout the war, the Loyalist proved to be an important source of information, "the man gave us news that six hundred Americans were advancing toward us." Based on this information, "It was

decided immediately not to wait for them but to proceed toward them."
Taking this approach would at least give the composite force of Jäger and
rangers the advantage of surprise, which could, in turn, throw their opponents off balance. "We set out at once on the road toward Suffolk, and we
were scarcely a quarter of an hour away when I, with the advanced guard,
ran into an enemy party which withdrew hastily after a few rifle shots."[104]

After the above exchange, Ewald and his men captured a captain
and three dragoons, through whom they gained further intelligence.
They learned that the American General Gregory, with a corps of about
three thousand troops had established himself in a position behind some
swamps about one and a half German miles behind Great Bridge.[105] Since
they now realized that they were attacking an opponent with much greater
numbers than previously thought, the force of Jäger and rangers immediately retired on Great Bridge.[106]

Once the rangers and Jäger posted themselves at Great Bridge, they
sent out an additional detachment towards the evening. This force moved
out towards Kemp's Landing to reconnoiter in that area.[107] On the following day, January 24th, toward ten in the morning, the force moved out
from Kemp's Landing, leaving behind a captain and sixty rangers. The remainder of the corps marched back by way of New Town and Norfolk.[108]

On the 28th, the Jäger and rangers marched to Great Bridge and took
up a position there. They were tasked with protecting a number of workers assigned to throw up a redoubt large enough to accommodate roughly
one hundred men and two guns. Several hundred slaves were taken who
arrived at about the same time as the British led force. These people were
likely put to work on completing the redoubt, as it was finished in just
three days. Once the redoubt was finished, the troops took up a part of
the Great Bridge and replaced it with a foot bridge for communication
with the mainland. The British signaled a switch from the offensive to
the defensive.

While Great Bridge was being transformed into a British bastion of
sorts, Simcoe remained with the workmen. For his part, Ewald and fifty
of his Jäger took station at Edmunds Bridge toward Suffolk. They were
joined there by two companies of the Queen's Rangers.[109]

After holding their position for two days, Ewald and his men returned
to Great Bridge and found the redoubt complete. It was now garrisoned
by one captain and a hundred men of the 80th Regiment.[110] The rangers
and Jäger remained at Great Bridge for several days.

On February 9, the British received reports that Virginia militia
General Lawson was in the region with a force of roughly one thousand
troops.[111] The intelligence further indicated that this force had taken

position at the planation of a Doctor Hall. Arnold resolved to attack this force.[112]

The men began to move out at eight o'clock in the evening in what Ewald described as "very rainy, dark and stormy weather." According to his recollections, the force included "the Jäger, one hundred rangers and one hundred men of Robinson's under Colonel Simcoe."[113] These men silently boarded their boats and set off from Portsmouth, entering the Western Branch of the Elizabeth River.[114]

The force landed at midnight, and made their way alongside the river, "through pathless woods and marches until we fell into the highway from Suffolk, about a half an hour from Hall's plantation."[115] There the men halted and formed into what Ewald described as "close platoons, one behind the other."[116] The Jäger were under orders to shoot and thus provide covering fire for the remainder of the force who were to attack with the bayonet.[117]

As the force moved closer, they came upon a bridge which the Americans had occupied to cover their own rear. Lieutenant-Colonel Simcoe ordered Ewald to select twenty men and "make myself master of the Bridge by trick or by force."[118] Ewald quickly devised a plan, "I asked my men to remain silent and follow me. He "Took two brave fellows and made up my mind to say nothing like a 'Good friend!', but to attack the enemy sharply and follow him swiftly."[119] The Americans, it seems, had other ideas.

When Ewald and his detachment attacked, the found the bridge unguarded. The Jäger captain observed, "The bird had flown the nest an hour before."[120] At the campsite, where the fires were still burning brightly, they met Colonel Dundas and his force of cavalry and infantry from the 80th Regiment. The following morning, the raiders returned to Portsmouth empty handed. This tactical grab at thin air demonstrates that the Americans were themselves becoming more adept at the war of posts. Now they were capable of avoiding the sorts of night attacks that had cost them dearly in the early years of the war, especially at Paoli in Pennsylvania.[121]

Throughout the night march, Ewald suffered from the effects of a fever, and the medicine he had taken to combat it. As usual, he commented only in passing on his physical condition, and then only to demonstrate his high sense of professionalism, "I mention this only to show that one must do everything one can to perform one's duty scrupulously; and that a man, if he will, can do very much."[122]

The day after they returned to camp at Portsmouth, the British learned that Major Amos Weeks was harassing the Loyalists in Princess

Anne County. Weeks's activities were making communications between Great Bridge and Portsmouth unsafe. Arnold, therefore, determined to send two forces to drive off Weeks, one under the command of Simcoe, and the other under Ewald. For this action, Ewald's detachment consisted of two hundred infantrymen and thirty horse. They landed at Powder Point. Simcoe, for his part, began moving on Kemp's Landing. The plan was for Ewald to attack the enemy in the rear, while Simcoe remained stationary, or to trap the Americans between the two forces. Towards evening, Ewald arrived at Great Bridge, and took the opportunity to gather some information from the commanding officer there.[123]

From Great Bridge, Ewald arranged his march with the goal of arriving at Brick's Bridge on the morning of the 13th.[124] Ewald did not get the opportunity to put his plan into practice, however, as he received orders to return to Portsmouth. The reason for his recall lay in the fact that three French ships had been sighted at the mouth of the James River. Arnold believed the ships to be part of the fleet under the command of Admiral de Ternay and it was assumed in camp that they formed part of some planned operation against his raiding force.[125]

As he retraced his route of march, Ewald linked up with Simcoe and his detachment at Powder Point. There the orders were countermanded yet again. This time, they received orders to follow the original plan.[126] Clearly, this constituted a rapidly evolving operational situation. Still, it is possible to discern in Ewald's diary a certain amount of frustration as orders constantly changed the mission and objectives.

At the same time as these developments were unfolding in Virginia, Washington reacted to the disheartening reports he received from the South and decided to send additional regular troops to Virginia in order to halt the British depredations.[127] Likewise, the Continental Congress ordered Pennsylvania troops under the command of General Lafayette south on February 9.[128] These would later be joined by those under General Anthony Wayne of Pennsylvania.

Lafayette, though lacking in military experience when he first arrived, offered his services to the Continental Congress in 1777. Repeatedly, over the following years, the young Frenchman demonstrated his profound commitment to the cause of American Independence. His close connections to the French court, and the aid these translated into certainly did not hurt his assent in Patriot circles. He quickly became one of Washington's most trusted subordinates. Such a close relationship developed between the two that one recent biographer of both men summarized "that Washington saw in Lafayette the son he never had..."[129]

The troops under Lafayette encountered difficulties before they even entered the theater of operations, such as when they arrived at the Chesapeake, no boats were available to ferry them across.[130] The general further noted, "Contrary Winds, Heavy Rains, Disappointments of vessels And every Inconvenience to which we Had No Remedy Have Been from the day of My Arrival Combined Against our Embarkation."[131]

While additional American forces began to make their way southward, Ewald and his Jäger continued to prosecute the war of posts at which they excelled. At the same time, the exertions of this type of campaigning exacted their toll on both men and horses. In one instance, Ewald described leading a night march in which the men crossed a swamp, up to their knees in water, in two hours. Night marches were considered very risky, as the men had to find their way, often through foreign territory, in the dark. The chances of troops becoming lost, separated, and wandering into enemy ambushes increased sharply. The chance of them setting off some disturbance as they foundered into an enemy sentinel rose greatly as well. By the time they reached the other side of the swamp, "Men and horses were so worn out that they could hardly go on when I happily left this abominable region behind."[132]

Once he reached a Loyalist's plantation, Ewald found a message left for him by Simcoe, in cipher, directing him to place his troops in some woods close to where the highway intersected with the foot path leading from the swamp. As he implemented these orders, Ewald grew concerned when he did not receive further communication from Simcoe. Still, the captain posted sentries, and looked to the needs of his men. A particular concern for the captain on this occasion arose from the lack of bread for his troops.

Ewald was uneasy lest his men should sneak off to forage for food in the night. In order to prevent such a response, he "resorted to a short talk in which I exhorted my men to maintain good conduct. I promised them that they would have very good subsistence after accomplishing this task."[133] Essentially, he gave his men a pep talk! Again, his response to the situation exemplifies the ideal Ewald developed in his *Thoughts*, that the commander should have a close rapport for his men and look to their needs personally. Such a close professional working relationship formed a pillar of the respect and trust necessary to conduct successful partisan operations.

Soon the Jäger captain received word from Lt. Colonel Simcoe that he should proceed at his own discretion. Ewald retuned out of the swamp, with the second crossing more arduous than the first due to heightened water levels, which placed his men in water above their knees and had them scrambling over fallen and rotted trees. Making his way back to camp, Ewald seemed surprised that he still had all the men he set out with the previous night.[134]

As he and his men made their way out of the swamp for a second time, Ewald did take one prisoner, a local man he found in a house on the periphery of the swamp. Ewald's interrogation of the man demonstrates both the captain's willingness to threaten extreme measures, and his understanding of the human nature, "I threatened the man with the noose if he did not disclose to me what he knew, and at the same time I showed him several guineas he could earn if he spoke the truth."[135]   The stark alternative Ewald presented convinced the local to provide what information he had in response to the captain's interrogation," The threat of the gallows and the love of gold softened the heart of this man."[136]   In comparison to the methods often used by both sides to gain information on their enemies in the southern campaigns, the means Ewald resorted to on this occasion seem quite moderate. While it is unclear if he would actually have hung the man in order to gain the information he sought, it does not fit with the manner in which Ewald conducted himself or his men up to this point, nor does it agree with his practices thereafter.

Based on the information he gained from the farmer, Ewald determined to make his way through the American camp. As a means of insurance to prevent their movements from being reported, the captain kept his prisoner with him.[137]

> As the march progressed, holding on to the prisoner turned out to be invaluable, I made my way through the wood with the 180 Jäger and rangers, but I had marched scarcely eight hundred to a thousand paces when I heard strong rifle fire. The man from the small house informed me that the enemy must be situated at James's, rather than Jamison's plantation, which was close to out left, since there was a crossroad from London Bridge and Northwest Landing at this plantation.[138]

The changes in the tactical situation required a rapid change in his plans. Ewald, not to be thrown off by the new challenge, acted accordingly. He reformed his men on the flank closest to the sounds of the firing and ordered them to fire a volley as soon as they caught sight of the enemy. After discharging their pieces, the men were to "boldly attack the foe with the bayonet and hunting sword." In keeping with this new disposition, Ewald "ordered the Jäger to disperse on both flanks and kept the rangers in close formation."[139]   Recall that Ewald had utilized this approach with great success when he first entered the theater. The sudden assault, combining the firepower of the Jäger's rifles followed up by the shock of the charge with their heavy hunting swords could wreak havoc on the determination of even the most steadfast and experienced opponents. In this case it certainly succeeded.

After leading the successful attack, "I let my men enjoy the luxuries of the American planter, who was a very rich man."[140] This appears to be one of the few instances in which Ewald condoned some amount of plundering by his men. It remains unclear, from the captain's brief account of his activities, whether his men engaged in out and out plunder, or were simply taking provisions from the plantation they occupied. If it was the latter, while such behavior would definitely not be considered a best practice in warfare at the time, however it was generally accepted as necessary, especially when it meant feeding hungry troops. Recall as well, that his men had not had a bread ration. Now their supply situation was answered, for the moment at least. In addition, the presence of Ewald and his subordinate officers and non-commissioned officers made a difference as well. With officers' supervision, the men were less likely to take their scavenging for resources to the excesses they would otherwise be prone to engage in. Their activities would therefore be considered more foraging than out and out plunder.[141]

Following his stint at the plantation, Ewald moved his troops to the Dungo Church. It is worth noting that churches were often utilized as strongpoints in European wars due to their stone walls. The steeple, likewise, served as an excellent vantage point to support an observation post.[142] The Dungo Church possessed many of these attributes. It was constructed of brick and enclosed by a wall. In Ewald's opinion, these features "made it a very good post, since it was surrounded on both sides by swamps for a great distance."[143]

At the church, Ewald rejoined Colonel Simcoe, who ordered him to set up an ambush in the churchyard. Simcoe further advised him to forage in the direction of their left flank, as the Americans in this area seemed fairly scattered, and a plantation stood close by.[144] They parted company, with Simcoe riding off towards another nearby plantation in order to gather any additional information he could. Still, before they parted, the two officers conferred and planned a rendezvous point to reunite their forces.

Following their conference, Ewald implemented the orders from Simcoe. After first placing an ambush of ten Jäger and ten rangers in the churchyard, he then moved off in the direction of Tale's plantation. After moving off to the left for roughly an hour, one of Ewald's men reported seeing sentries dressed in blue coats a few hundred paces distant.

Sizing up the situation, Ewald quickly decided that the usual approach for moving against alerted sentries would not work. He determined to divide his force, sending some troops from the right, and others from the left. Their purpose was to locate and attack the Americans. Ewald, for his part, would lead a party of rangers directly up the middle towards the planation.[145]

The first party to make contact with the Americans were Ewald's right flankers. The flankers on the left, in accordance with their orders, moved to the sound of the gunfire. When he reached the scene, Ewald found the Americans "in full flight through a marshy meadow to a wood."[146] In the skirmish, two Americans were killed, and five, including a lieutenant, captured. The attack nearly succeeded in capturing Major Weeks as well.[147]

Due to his constant activity in skirmishing with many American partisan leaders, Ewald seemed to develop a sort of professional respect for the more capable ones. Reflecting on the above attack, Ewald complimented his foe,

This man, whom I had the good luck to chase all around, knew the countryside better than I could ever know it. That was evident from the positions he took, for a retreat always remained open to him in the impassable woods which he alone knew.[148]

On this occasion, Ewald evinced respect for a fellow practitioner of his form of warfare. At the same time, he noted that in this particular instance, "my spies were better than his," and further, that "luck, on which everything depends in war, was on my side."[149] In regard to the last point especially, Ewald demonstrated his growing understanding of the role of chance in war.

Philosophical ruminations on the art of war aside, Ewald pursued the fleeing Americans for some distance. In order to capture as many as possible, he divided his own troops into eight smaller parties. The tactic succeeded in that he took eleven additional prisoners, from whom he learned the American rendezvous point to be at Great Dismal Swamp. Ewald's pursuit of the Americans took him past Tale's plantation to Akiss's plantation. Toward evening, Ewald reunited with Simcoe at the latter location, and the two marched on Cornick's plantation. There they made camp briefly and rested for a few hours.[150] Considering the exertions the men underwent in the preceding day, the rest was certainly well-deserved.

The following morning, Ewald breakfasted with a prominent local Loyalist. The man, likely Thomas Reynolds Walker, was not engaged in the struggle and Ewald questioned why he would not raise a battalion and join the fight.[151] The man's reply demonstrated the complexity of a long and bitter civil war. Walker stated, "I must first see if it is true that your people really intend to remain with us. You have already been in this area twice." Walker continued, with a keen assessment of the strategic situation in the south, "Who knows where you will be this autumn? And should the French unite with the Americans, everything would surely be lost to you here. What would we loyally disposed subjects have then? Nothing but misfortune from the Opposition Party, if you leave us again."[152]

Ewald's rejoinder revealed the frustrations likely felt by many Crown troops at this point in the conflict, "We are supposed to break our bones for you, in place of yours, to accomplish your purpose. We attempt everything and sacrifice our own blood for your assumed cause."[153]

Their discussion ended abruptly when one of Ewald's Jäger arrived and informed the captain that the troops were on the move. He took his leave of the loyalist and rejoined his command. Still, the above exchange possesses a timeless quality in that it could just as easily have occurred between an American soldier and a South Vietnamese national nearly two centuries later. More recently, it could have occurred between an American soldier and an Afghan or Iraqi national. Their conversation shows the difficulty that anyone from an external force thrust into an insurgency surely faces. The internal dynamics and politics of these types of conflicts are well known for their complexity. Shortly after their exchange ended, these realities began to dawn on Ewald, "When my blood had cooled down again, I realized that this man who did not want to be a soldier would have been a fool if he had acted as I had advised him. For he possessed a fortune in property of 50,000 sterling and had for a wife one of the most charming blondes that I have ever seen in my life."[154]

When they reached their next location, Ewald wanted to build a fixed post. The constant marches through enemy territory, and the conscious destruction of property were taking their toll on the discipline of his men. He therefore wanted to construct the post as a means of keeping them under control. Ewald's approach to raising the field fortification underscores the captain's own grasp of military engineering, and his use of the materials at hand in order to achieve his goal. In arranging the post, he "had a number of trees along the creek felled crosswise into the water, in order to block the passable places, and had three apple trees cut down and pointed to a barricade in the causeway, but without hindering free access."[155]

The post Ewald ordered constructed proved an asset as the Americans continued to probe his force over the next few days. Ewald reported on March 5th, that in their incursions the enemy had managed to seize and burn one armed boat and two carronades. The line of march stood as a concern for the force as well.

On March 10, they received word that an American corps under a General Gregory had taken a position on the heights above Edmunds Bridge and threatened the post at Great Bridge.[157] Further jeopardizing the security of Great Bridge, Major Weeks placed his force in a position to cut off the communication between Great Bridge and Portsmouth. In responding to the situation, Colonel Simcoe received orders to march with his Corps to Great Bridge and guard the post against American attack. Since he was then serving alongside Simcoe, Ewald and his troops served as a part of this guard.[158]

The two men worked well together for the most part, and grew to become close friends as well as colleagues, and would continue to exchange letters after the war.[159] Through the month of March 1781, Ewald and Simcoe were almost constantly active, shifting position, setting up ambushes and patrolling for enemy activity. Arnold, still in overall command of Ewald and Simcoe, seemed to grow more concerned for his personal safety as the raid continued. Ewald asserted the commander lost his calm when he received a report of a French fleet moving into the Chesapeake. Arnold reacted to the news by ordering the construction of strong defenses, including earthworks. Unfortunately, Arnold's force possessed insufficient entrenching tools to construct very solid defenses, and even the British engineer who constructed them was uncertain of their utility.[160] The lack of entrenching tools likely stemmed from the fact that Arnold's force was designed for rapid movement rather than static defense. Therefore, it would not have carried such implements which would prove more cumbersome than useful overall.

The stress of the campaign also seemed to wear more deeply on Ewald, as he used the threat of hanging more liberally in order to gain intelligence of American movements and dispositions. For instance, on the night March 11-12, as Ewald was checking up on his pickets, one of his patrols returned with a prisoner. Ewald related, "When I threatened to hang him he confessed that a corps of five thousand men under the Marquis de Lafayette, Baron Steuben, and General Muhlenberg was on the march toward Portsmouth to join the French troops which were on board the French fleet in the Chesapeake, and then to take Portsmouth by storm."[161] Ewald further learned that the man was an inhabitant of Suffolk who had been instructed to watch for any British movements on the highway.[162] Based on the information gained form the prisoner, Ewald ordered his patrols to crisscross one another in order to prevent observers from the other side watching their movements along the highway.[163]

Later that morning, Ewald was invited to dine with Arnold. He had not finished changing when he heard shots from the direction of his own pickets. He ordered reinforcements and went to see for himself what was going on. When he reached the scene of the disturbance, he found the entire opposite shore occupied by American forces who laid down a heavy fire on him and his troops. He rushed back into the woods, where he found his own Jäger. "With sword in hand I drove them toward the causeway again, where they fought like heroes in spite of the most frightful fire."[164] Ewald called for reinforcements as well and fed them into the battle as it developed. The Americans moved forward, attempting to cross the causeway that separated them from Ewald's position. Each time they moved forward, however, the Jäger captain's troops laid down sufficient fire to drive the back, to the extent that not even the American officers could drive their men forward again. This diligent defense exacted its own cost. During the fighting, Ewald was wounded in the knee.

Ascertaining the seriousness of his own wound, "Since I felt that the bone and the large tendon must have been injured, I sat down and asked these eight brave men, of whom three already were wounded, not to leave their post, since the enemy could not come further as long as they stood firm."[165] Soon Ewald was relieved when a Captain Murray arrived. He checked in with Ewald, who showed the captain his wound. Murray left and returned with a Lieutenant Bickwell. The Lieutenant and Captain Murray helped the wounded Ewald to mount a horse and led him back through the woods. As they made their way through the woods, the party came across a British officer with some fifty men. Ewald ordered him forward to the causeway to help shore up the other defenders.[166] The *Journal of the Hesse-Kassel Jäger Corps* reported laconically on April that on March, Ewald led a reconnaissance force that had been in a heavy engagement with some five hundred militia.[167]

Ewald's removal from the battlefield ended his active role in the fighting, but his real ordeal was just beginning. Medical science stood barely past its infancy in the eighteenth century. There was nothing in the way of anesthetics along today's lines. Likewise, antiseptics were virtually unknown. In addition to these obvious technological limitations, the plain fact was that the best doctors usually did not beat a path to the local recruiting sergeants. Many of the regimental surgeons were little better than quacks or dragooned medical students.[168]

As he made his way back from the fighting, Ewald ran into Arnold, who asked him if the enemy could take his post. As Ewald recorded in his diary, "The question annoyed me, for he could see it all for himself. - I said' No! As long as one Jäger lives, no damned Americans will come across the causeway.'"[169] After this encounter with Arnold, Ewald continued back to his lodgings. Later that say he received news that his men drove off the Americans, "I rejoiced over the magnificent behavior of my brave Jäger, who with all éclat had thus distinguished themselves before the eyes of the English. For surely one Jäger had fought against thirty Americans today."[170]

Ewald's joy soon turned bitter however, as on the following day, the orders for the day contained no mention of the performance of the Jäger in the encounter, "I did not learn of one word of compliment in it concerning the excellent conduct of my men, which displeased me no end."[171] Ewald passed along his displeasure at the omission to Arnold's adjutant, and later that day, Arnold himself visited Ewald to express his satisfaction at the conduct of the Jäger. Arnold assured Ewald that he would commend the Jäger at the issuing of the evening password, which he did. It seems likely that on this occasion Arnold would have been particularly sensitive and understanding regarding Ewald's perceived slight. Arnold himself endured many slights and had seen others claim credit for his exploits while in the service of the American cause, to the extent that it is often argued that this constituted one of his motivations for changing sides.[172] Still, beyond the injuries to the honor of his troops, Ewald faced the daunting prospect of his own physical injury.

The basic procedure for wound treatment involved the doctor probing the wound until he found the bullet, a process that could excruciating in and of itself. Once they located the projectile, they would remove it, and any other foreign matter from the wound with forceps, leading to further agony. Finally, the doctor dressed the wound. Then the long period of convalescence began. Ewald's greatest concern would no doubt be that the injury to his leg would be so severe as to lead to amputation. Ironically, this procedure had a greater chance of survival than surgery, as the limb would be placed in a tourniquet, and after the section was removed, the remaining flaps of skin would be sewn together and bandaged. Torso wounds carried with them a much greater chance of injury to bodily organs leading to sepsis and slow, agonizing death through infection.[173]

The bullet that struck Ewald remained in his leg for some time. As can be imagined, while it did the captain endured great pain that prevented him from sleeping. On March 29, the surgeon made an incision in his calf to draw out pus from the wound, and Ewald reported "I have slept several hours for the first time."[174] He continued, describing the specifics of his wound and the treatment suggested,

> *Up to now I ran the risk of losing my leg, since the upper part of the bone, directly under the bend in the left knee hung only by a thread. Meanwhile, the skillful English surgeon General Smith assured me that if I kept quiet the muscle would grow strong, then stretch again, and I would not have a stiff leg.*[175]

As a result of following the course of treatment outlined above by the British surgeon, Ewald could report on the 30th that "Since yesterday I have become so well that I can write in my diary in my room, aided by a noncommissioned officer, and have been able to dictate this myself."[176]

Ewald's injuries were serious enough for him to be out of commission for some time. While he recovered, the partisan commander enjoyed some time to reflect on his situation, and his surroundings. One aspect of his situation that Ewald clearly did not care for was his commanding officer, Benedict Arnold. Concerning Arnold's treason, he confided in his diary, "His dishonorable undertaking, which, had it succeeded, could have actually turned the war more favorably for England, nevertheless cannot be justified, for surely self-gain had guided him, and not remorse for having taken the other side." Ewald continued, expressing what he conceived of as the more honorable course of action, "If he really felt in his conscience that he had done wrong in siding against his mother country, he should have sheathed his sword and served no more, and then made known in writing his opinions and reasons." He concluded that such an approach "would have gained more proselytes than his shameful enterprise, which every man of honor and fine feelings—whether he be friend or foe of the common cause—must loathe."[177] In setting down his views on Arnold, Ewald again discloses some of his personal conception of honor. It seems from the above that for Ewald, realizing one's loyalty had been misplaced and redressing the matter was permissible, but only within certain limitations. It was acceptable to leave the fighting if one realized they had chosen the wrong side, but not to change sides. This was going too far, especially when it appeared personal gain motivated the change. Perhaps the best account of Ewald's feelings concerning Arnold, as well as his conception of honor, derives from his own pen, "Gladly as I would have paid with my life for England's success in this war, this man remained so detestable to me that I had to use every effort not to let him perceive, or even feel the indignation of my soul."[178] It is worth stating that Ewald was not alone in his dislike for Arnold, many British officers held a low opinion of him as well.[179]

Ewald continued including descriptions of the area he was operating in as well. His descriptions of Portsmouth and Richmond and their respective environs are very thorough. It seems likely that Ewald used his time in recovery to polish his descriptions while he was still in the region.

While Ewald continued his convalescence, and expounded on his views, the war in the Southern Department continued without relent. After the battle of Cowpens on January 17, 1780, Cornwallis turned to pursue Morgan. Morgan, in turn, fell back on Greene who was still in North Carolina. Their forces reunited at Guilford Courthouse.[180] Cornwallis then burned his baggage at Ramsour's Mill in North Carolina. In destroying his heavy baggage, including his own personal equipment, the early turned his army into a rapid reaction force. At the same time, he exposed his men to the extremes of winter.[181]

Still, Cornwallis soldiered on, launching a relentless pursuit of General Nathanael Greene and his Continentals. This pursuit came to be known as the race to the Dan, as the Dan River formed part of the boundary between North Carolina and Virginia. Greene won the race and entered Virginia on February 14 taking all the boats necessary for moving an army across the river with him.[182] Cornwallis, arriving the next day and realizing he had failed in his attempt to corner Greene, turned back southward to search for supplies for his foot-sore men. Sensing an opportunity, Greene then turned about and attacked his British opponent, bringing on the battle of Guilford Courthouse on March 11, 1781.[183]

Here, Greene attempted to mimic the tactic employed so successfully by Morgan at Cowpens. Greene's troops, however, did not hold, and on the rough broken terrain of Guilford, North Carolina, some elements of his army became separated, essentially fighting their own battles against the British. Even under the circumstances, the Americans nearly won the day, but when the issue seemed in doubt, however, Greene opted to leave the field rather than risk his entire army. Cornwallis did not pursue.[184]

Cornwallis remained on the field that night, tending to his wounded. He then fell back on the Scottish settlement at Cross Creek, with Greene's light troops nipping at his heels. The British lieutenant general quickly proclaimed his victory in the battle and called on the rebels in the area to take an oath of allegiance. He further called on the Loyalists to take up arms. Most residents, however, failed to see why the victor would be in retreat, with the troops of the vanquished on his tail and opted to stay at home. Shortly after arriving at Cross Creek, Cornwallis pushed on to

Wilmington, North Carolina, from which he could secure aid from the Royal Navy.[185]

In a striking and audacious move that contradicted received military wisdom, Greene broke off contact with Cornwallis's Army, and instead turned south, marching his army into South Carolina. Greene's decision possessed both political and military overtones. No organized Continental Forces had taken the field in South Carolina since the battle of Camden on August 16. While the partisan bands of Marion, Pickens and Sumter did much to keep the flame of rebellion burning, they could not, on their own, drive the British out, and many in the state believed that the Continental Congress had turned their backs on South Carolina. By marching into the state, Greene could use his army, such as it was, to demonstrate in a very physical way the continued commitment of the Congress to the defense of South Carolina.

Militarily, there remained a number of small British garrisons to clear out of the state. Combining his forces with those of the partisans on occasion, Greene could hope to reduce these, and drive the British forces out of much of South Carolina. After all, Marion had already informed the Rhode Islander that with Continental support much more could be achieved in the state than he was able to accomplish with his partisans.[186]

For his part, in the aftermath of Guilford Courthouse, Cornwallis came to the conclusion that to truly control the southern colonies, he had to cut the flow of supplies and reinforcements from Virginia. He withdrew from the battlefield without pursuing Greene, and made his way to Wilmington, North Carolina. Here the earl received supplies and reinforcement via the Royal Navy. Cornwallis could gain naval support for what he now perceived to be his next logical step—the invasion of Virginia.

As these events transpired to the southward, Ewald's convalescence continued. In early April, he received word from his sometime commander and close friend, Colonel John Graves Simcoe that the British General Philips had arrived from New York with reinforcements.

Major General William Philips (1713?-1781) was a respected officer of the British artillery. Educated at Woolwich, he first served in Europe during the Seven Years' War and commanded the British artillery at Minden. In that engagement, he brought his guns into action at the gallop, which at the time was believed to be impossible. This action made him somewhat of a hero in the British artillery. In the War of Independence, he served in Burgoyne's campaign in northern New York. On March 27, Philips arrived in Virginia at the head of a two thousand man detachment, which included two battalions of light infantry, the 43rd Regiment of Foot, 76th Regiment, part of the17th Regiment of Foot, the Hessian

Fusilier Regiment Erbprinz, Hessian artillery, and the 1st and 2nd An-
spach-Bayreuth regiments.[187] Philips orders from Clinton were to aid in
the raids in Virginia by destroying rebels supplies along the James and
Appomattox Rivers, and offer such aid to Cornwallis as he could.[188]

Ewald hoped that Philips would assume command over the entire
force from Arnold. Ewald noted in his diary on April 6th how Philips had
landed on the first and quickly set about placing the defenses in better
order. Philips placed Colonel Fuchs, of the Erbprinz Regiment, in command of Portsmouth. Concerning this change in command, the Jäger captain observed, "The general drove everyone zealously to his duty, which
the majority of the men who had served under Arnold up to now did not
feel, because everything had been done in the American fashion."[189] Ap-
praising Fuchs himself, Ewald recorded simply, "He was a man just as a
man should be."[190] Not very high praise, but certainly far above the Jäger
captain's views on Arnold.

Philip's arrival signaled other developments as well. Cornwallis moving into Virginia, and additional troops moving in to supplement Arnold's raiding force, all indicated clearly to Ewald that a major British
effort against the Old Dominion stood in the offing.

At the same time, Ewald did not like the idea of Cornwallis corps
moving into Virginia, "as long as Greene still had an army in Carolina, for
it meant an acre of land won here and fifty lost there." By this point, the
Jäger captain had clearly grown quite frustrated with what he perceived as
English strategy as well, "once again, it is the favorite plan of England to
have something in every corner and much nowhere."[191] Clearly, the partisan commander saw the British efforts as a dispersion of force when concentration was necessary to achieve their ends. At the same time, it could
be argued that the invasion of Virginia constituted a concentration of
force against the most powerful center of rebellion in the southern states.
If Virginia's industry were crushed, it could no longer support the war
efforts further south. Armies, no matter how professional and determined,
cannot remain long in the field without supplies. In any event, Virginia
now stood as the focus of British military operations in the South.

The war of posts continued, with the tempo of operations growing
more aggressive. Once Cornwallis and the other British commanders arrived in Virginia, their goal manifested in the heightened conduct of economic warfare. With their marked abilities in irregular warfare, the Jäger
played an important role in these operations. For instance, on April 18,
they embarked on boats at Portsmouth, then moved up the James River
to the Chickahominy. The troops landed on the right of the latter and
"laid waste the enemy works and magazines at York and Williamsburg."[192]

After spending several days wreaking havoc in Jamestown and its environs, the raiders next moved up the James River to City Point, landed and marched for Petersburgh on April 26th. Here, they came up on an American force, which they attacked and drove across the right branch of the river.[193]

Ewald did not take part in the above raids, as it was only on May 2nd that he recorded being able to leave his bed. Even then, he had to support himself by the use of two canes in order to walk around Portsmouth. On May 10, he noted "My knee is actually still crooked and stiff, but I feel that if I don't follow the advice of the surgeon and exercise vigorously, which I have done since yesterday, I shall not be able to leave for the army soon."[194] He further described how two fragments of bone came out with the changing of the dressing on his wound, an event Ewald attributed to moving his leg.[195]

His recovery was no doubt aided by the receipt of a letter from General Knyphausen dated April 30, 1781. The letter expressed condolences on the captain's wounding and hopes for a quick and complete recovery. In addition, the general informed Ewald how he had recommended the captain to the Landgraf for his good conduct.[196] As noted elsewhere, recognitions of this sort held great importance for Ewald, both professionally and personally.

Ewald returned to some level of duty when the American partisan Major Weeks returned to the area. He threatened to burn the English hospital at Norfolk, and the Hessian Colonel Fuchs requested that Ewald assume command of the post. While Ewald accepted the command as a means to enhance his reputation, it soon proved more than he could handle with his continued convalescence. In taking command of the hospital, Ewald suffered from a distinct lack of manpower. In the circumstance, he resorted to training a unit of some twelve free blacks to act as cavalry. Concerning his approach to training these men, the captain observed, "I trained them as well as possible and they gave me thoroughly good service for I sought to win them by good treatment, to which they were not accustomed."[197] This remark demonstrates, if taken at face value, Ewald's capacity as a leader, in that he understood how to motivate a group from a very different background.

Ewald's return to duty was marred by the death of General Philips, who succumbed to typhoid fever, which he contracted shortly after arriving in Virginia. Not only did this deprive Ewald of a commander whom he respected but it once again placed Arnold in command over his force. By the same token, he began to demonstrate more frustration with the war effort overall. Noting in his diary on May 23, "What use to us are the victories and defeats of the enemy at Camden and Guilford? We now occupy nothing more in the two Carolina provinces than Charleston, Wilmington and Ninety-Six."[198] Clearly, Ewald was growing more and more exasperated with the entire conduct of the war. He further vented his sentiments, stating, "In these areas, we hold not more ground than our cannon can reach."[199]

In typical style, Ewald did not stop at merely criticizing the strategy he believed to be ineffective, he suggested an alternative as well. He argued for a concentration of forces in order to become masters of at least one colony. He continued, challenging the current diffusion of efforts asserting, "What good are our victories which have been so dearly bought with our blood?"[200] Ewald's conception of the proper way to conduct the southern campaign fit well with the ideas that would later be developed more fully by both Clausewitz and the Prussian theorist's great rival, Baron Antoine Henri de Jomini. It is tempting to place Ewald's view on a concentration of efforts in order to seize and maintain control of a single colony as more closely resembling the ideas of Clausewitz as opposed to Jomini. Still, Ewald does not develop his reasoning enough for any solid judgments to be made.[201] Instead, he quickly turns to the effects of the war on the local inhabitants, especially those loyal to the Crown.

Concerning the conduct of the troops in Virginia during Arnold's raid, he noted, "We have made people here miserable by our presence." In their movements, the Crown forces had subsisted, to a large degree, off the countryside, causing great depravations for the local populace. Ewald further noted. "So too, have we constantly deceived the loyally-disposed subjects by our freebooting expeditions, and yet we still want to find friends in this country."[202] The effects of the British invasion on the civilian populace were becoming all too clear.

Soon thereafter, General Leslie arrived at Portsmouth, bringing with him the Anspach brigade and the 17th Regiment. He disembarked and assumed command of the city.[203] By this time, Ewald felt his leg recovered enough for him to return to duty. He therefore requested Leslie's permission to return to the army, which the general granted. The Jäger captain sailed on a privateer that night, on the way to return to his troops. Soon the monotony of foraging and destruction of property with its attendant war of posts and the stress it brought began to set in for the captain once again.

On June 8, 1781, he opined in in his diary "Up to now I have led the most unpleasant life in this world. One cannot go far from the shore because of uncertainty." The uncertainly Ewald mentions likely stemmed from two sources, a lack of clear intelligence concerning the region the army operated in, and the danger from partisan units harassing the fringes of the British forces. These factors combined to deny the Jäger one of his favorite activities, the exploration of the region around him. Such reconnaissance served Ewald well whenever he conducted it. Exacerbating the situation further was the fact that, as Ewald continued, "I have no books with me. I have arranged my diary in fairly good order, hence, there is nothing to do."[204]

The captain's boredom may have been disturbed by the fact that his quarters were above the privateer's powder magazine, and the regular thunderstorms they encountered on their voyage threatened to blow him up.[205] Ewald transferred to a different ship on June 9. On the 16th, he spied Simcoe's cavalry on the banks of the James River. Simcoe gave Ewald some of his horses so that the captain could return to duty. While the Jäger captain's leg wound was healing well, it no doubt enabled him a better view to be mounted and not have to walk constantly. For a time, the Queen's Rangers and the Jäger served together in the area and helped to reopen communications between the supply ships and the British army which the activities of various American partisans operating in the area had previously disrupted. During these operations, Ewald held the responsibility of protecting the boats from attacks launched from the land side.[206]

When Ewald rejoined his command, he found that his men had sewn pieces of cowhide around their feet in place of shoes, since they had worn through their boots while campaigning. The men displayed their new footwear to their commander with laughter. In recording his reunion with is men Ewald ascribed their laughter to the hardiness of the German soldier.[207]

Back with his men, Ewald was soon engaging in the actions of the partisan once again. He missed much in his time of convalescence. Once Cornwallis arrived in Virginia, there occurred a decided increase in the tempo of British operations. Raids were carried out on a near daily basis that destroyed crops, liberated slaves, or at least allowed them to run to British lines, and generally wrought havoc on the internal stability of Virginia. Ewald thus returned to take part in a campaign already at a high tempo.

For example, on June 17, Colonel Simcoe ordered him to reconnoiter the banks on both sides of Four Mile Creek, in search of a landing spot so that troops could embark for easy movements up and down the river. Ewald quickly located a suitable spot for embarkation and crossed the James on the following day.[208] Shortly thereafter, Ewald made his way to Richmond, which at the time served as the British headquarters. There he paid his respects to his commander and patron, Lord Cornwallis, who had succeeded Arnold on May 20, while the partisan captain was still doing light duty.[209]

On June 21, the British army evacuated Richmond and crossed the Chickahominy River over Bottom's Bridge. When they established their new camp, they did so in such a way as to utilize the natural terrain to cover their flanks. The swamps from the springs of the Black Creek covered the army's right and the Chickahominy their left. At this camp, Ewald's Jäger detachment rejoined the main army. Simcoe received orders to place himself, with the Hessian jägers at Wilson's Plantation, in front of the army's right, in order to protect the highway to Newcastle. At the same time, Banastre Tarleton and his British Legion covered Bottom's Bridge over the Chickahominy River.[210]

As the British army made its way across Virginia, its tail, or the number of civilians that followed in its wake, began to grow significantly. One major group encompassed slaves taken from Patriot planters, or liberated, to an extent.[211] While Cornwallis attempted to curb this behavior, his arrangements were not enforced on the troops, and therefore not followed. While the earl did support the execution of a sergeant and a private of dragoons for robbery and rape shortly after entering the Old Dominion, this did not stop the excesses of his men, especially with regards to 'liberating' slaves. Nor did it prove to the civilian populace that the British general respected their rights.[212] Concerning the seizure of slaves by Crown forces, Ewald observed the practice with clear disdain, "Yes, indeed, I can testify that every soldier had his Negro, who carried his provisions and bundles."[213]

Upon returning to his unit, Ewald learned that his men had acquired the bad habit of taking on freed slaves, "In my Jäger detachment alone, I found over twenty horses on my arrival, and almost every Jäger had his Negro." The use of servants bred dereliction of duty and indiscipline. Knowing this, Ewald's response to the situation was brief and to the point, "within twenty-four hours, I brought everything back on track again."[214] Ewald drove out many of the captured slaves and restored the tight discipline to his unit. Such actions were essential to maintaining the high combat efficiency of elite troops such as the Jäger.

The next day, the army changed location, to New Kent Courthouse, where it camped in the afternoon. Again, the Crown forces used the natural geography of the site to cover their flanks. While the new camp was being established, Cornwallis ordered Simcoe, with the Jäger, to move off in the direction of New Castle so as to screen the retreat of the British army away from the forces of the Marquis de Lafayette.

On learning of the British actions along the James River in April, Lafayette stripped his column of much of its heavy baggage and artillery to expedite their march to Virginia's relief. His force possessed high morale, though forced to resort to impressment to secure necessary wagons later in the march.[215] One important area in which the Frenchman was deficient was that of the cavalry. Lafayette recognized his weakness and resolved to do the best he could in the situation.[216] Recognizing his overall feebleness in comparison to his British adversary, Lafayette resolved to skirmish with Cornwallis, but avoid being drawn into a general engagement.[217] The French marquis would nip at the British earl's flanks. He could only hope that promised reinforcements, in the form of Wayne's division, would reach him sooner rather than later.

By late May, the situation had reached a crisis point in Virginia. "Too weak to offer battle to Cornwallis, he [Lafayette] nevertheless had to protect American supplies in Virginia and keep up the flagging spirits of the people by maintaining his detachment in the field."[218] Essentially, the French nobleman come American general adopted an army in being strategy.

As part of covering the retreat, Ewald posted his Jäger on the right side of the Matadequin Creek and ordered to lie in ambush should any of Lafayette's patrols try to establish contact with the retreating British.[219]

On June 23rd, Earl Charles Cornwallis summoned Simcoe and Ewald to a meeting. The general ordered the two men to depart from the army in two detachments as soon as night fell. Their mission: to march through the surrounding neighborhood, and secure as much in the manner of supplies as they could. The preceding demonstrates that Cornwallis assumption of command over the operations in Virginia brought with it a return of the earl's preference for employing Ewald's Jäger as well as Simcoe's Rangers on these types of missions.

Accordingly, the two units left the army at nightfall. As they passed through the countryside, Ewald reported "I had reconnoitering patrols rummage through the terrain around me." As a result of their activities, "We had rounded up many cattle, laid waste to various tobacco storehouses, and burned several vessels in both rivers."[220]

As the Rangers and Jäger made their back to rejoin the main army, Ewald received orders from Simcoe to have his men serve as the rear guard. They had rebuilt a bridge, and Ewald was to burn it as soon as his men were across.[221] Ewald took special care in organizing his men for the withdrawal, "Since I had a constant presentiment of nothing good…"[222] He deployed his force with the grenadier company in the front, followed by the light infantry, then a brief interval, and an officer with thirty horse.

The Jäger formed the flank guard for the entire party. Additionally, ten Jäger served as the rear guard for the small column.[223]

Upon reaching the bridge, Ewald halted his column some three hundred paces away from it. He ordered the Jäger to cross first and deploy on both flanks "to protect the crossing in case of necessity."[224] Next, he ordered the cavalry across, then the light infantry. Finally, Ewald with the grenadiers formed the rear guard of the column. Once on the other side of the creek, he ordered the bridge fired and waited until it was thoroughly burned, then set out for Cooper's Hill.

The following morning, Ewald learned through Banastre Tarleton that Cornwallis had moved off in the direction of Williamsburg. An hour before dawn, the Green Dragoon ordered Ewald to follow Cornwallis with his command. He had just arrived at Spencer's Planation and attempted to get some rest for himself and his men when, "I had hardly closed my eyes, when several shots were fired in front on the left. I jumped up and asked where the shooting was, whereupon several officers shouted that the farmers had fired on the refugees who were driving the cattle."[225] The captain tried to get rest after this disturbance, but sleep proved elusive, as the American partisans continued to snipe at his forces.

The refugees mentioned above were Loyalists, who came forward and offered aid to the British as they moved through Virginia. Now that their homes were in areas that had fallen under Patriot control, necessity forced them to follow the British army in order stay alive. The American partisans in the area were successful at harassing the British column.

Trying to gain some intelligence of the enemy on his flanks, Ewald rode out from his camp through an apple orchard on Spencer's planation. In the orchard, he discovered a soldier of Armand's legion, and captured the man.[226] After a brief interrogation in which Ewald learned that the American army was very close by, Ewald determined to make a further personal reconnaissance. He turned his prisoner over to an orderly and marched forward with the rest of his party when, "to my astonishment, when I was barely across the orchard I found a long line deployed behind a fence, two or three hundred paces away, just on the point of moving forward."[227] The Jäger captain had stumbled upon an American force deployed for battle! Reflecting on the situation in later years, he observed, "God be praised that did not lose my head!"

In addressing his immediate tactical predicament, Ewald's training and experience quickly reasserted themselves, "At this moment I discovered that the enemy line extended on his right, but that the line which I had brought up on my right was longer than the enemy's left."[228]

Ewald called on his subordinate, Lieutenant Alexander Wilhelm Bickell, to halt on the right so that he could reach a small hill. From there, Bickell was to attack the enemy's left flank and rear with the entire Jäger force. For his part, Ewald mounted his horse in the center of the force of grenadiers and light infantry, ordering them to hold their fire and attack only with the bayonet. Ewald ordered the attack in this manner, for, as he noted, "the enemy would certainly be startled by our resolution."[229] The Jäger captain gambled on the idea that a determined attack carried forward with firm discipline would shake the fortitude of his opponents, and cause them to abandon the field, even though they possessed superior numbers.[230] To an extent, the ploy succeeded, as "The enemy, who had moved forward, was taken aback by our advance." Still, the Americans did not abandon the field quite as he had hoped. Instead, they "waited for us up to forty paces, fired a volley, killed two-thirds of the grenadiers, and withdrew from the position."[231] Ewald continued his advance and engaged a group of Americans in hand-to-hand combat. He continued his advance, driving the Americans back, until the latter broke off the contact. At this point, Ewald had advanced several hundred paces into a wooded area. Here he halted and reformed the remnants of the three ranger companies, who at this point numbered less than sixty men.[232]

Lieutenant Bickell urged Ewald to recall all the remaining troops, since in the attack, they had become very widely dispersed, and he feared that they would be easy targets to fall into enemy hands. There occurred a brief running fire as the Crown forces reorganized and the Americans broke contact, then all grew quiet.

At this juncture Ewald recorded, "I now observed that it was time to fall back and signaled to the Jäger and rangers. I left the wood during the lull and took post on both small hills in the plain, which Bickell and the Jäger had gone around at the beginning of the action. Here I could look around, and here I had assembly sounded so as to give the Jäger in the wood the signal to withdrawal."[233] Having disengaged his forces after driving the Americans back, Ewald passed word to Simcoe that he believed it would be best to withdrawal their entire force, to which the latter agreed.

In the engagement, Ewald's force suffered three officers killed or wounded, with additional casualties of fifty-four non-commissioned officers and privates, and eight Jäger.[234] It is clear from the preceding that the tempo of operations was intense at this time, as Ewald failed to keep a careful record of his precise losses in killed versus wounded. He did examine the area of the engagement and determined that the enemy losses were higher. He also noted, specifically, that a Jäger corporal named Meister, whom he described as a "bold and brave man," had been captured by the Americans.[235]

Ewald, reflecting on the engagement, asserted that on this occasion the lack of thought actually benefitted the Jäger, "For the enemy, who was certain of his prey, was startled because he was attacked quite unexpectedly."[236] He went on to observe, "But had we taken one backward step, the courage of the enemy would have redoubled, while that of the soldiers on our side would have forsaken them."[237] Ewald concluded, "It is a principle in war that the party which attacks when the issue is doubtful has already won half of the battle."[238]

On the evening of June 27, Ewald and his detachment rejoined the main army under Lord Cornwallis behind Queen's Creek in order to provide the detached troops with the opportunity for some rest. On his return, Ewald received the following mark of favor from the army commander concerning his conduct in the previous day's skirmish,

> *Lord Cornwallis desires that Lieutenant Colonel Simcoe will accept of his warmest Acknowledgements for his judicious and spirited Conduct in the action of the 26th instant, when he repulsed and defeated so superior a force of the Enemy. He likewise desires that Lieutenant Colonel Simcoe will communicate his best thanks to Captain Ewald, to the Detachment of the Yagers [sic] and to the Officers and Soldiers of the Queen's Rangers.*[239]

Again, for a professional soldier such as Ewald, such marks of approbation from a superior stood as sought after prizes, as well as reinforcement of their bravery under fire. Certainly, it raised the captain's spirits after so many months of constant small-scale fighting, and so little recognition for his efforts from his previous commander. Such a boost may help to explain his intervention in the following case.

At about the same time that Ewald received formal recognition from Cornwallis, he received a letter from a French captain named Griffaud. Griffaud was a prisoner and he solicited Ewald's aid in securing his parole to Petersburg with Lord Cornwallis. Ewald left for headquarters on receiving the note, secured the French officer's parole, and on his return presented the news to him personally.[240] Actions such as these were not uncommon among the officers of European states during this period, as these men often considered themselves members of a separate caste that transcended national borders.[241]

On presenting the parole to Griffaud, Ewald enjoyed the opportunity to fraternize with some of the American officers captured in the previous day's skirmish. From the interchange with these fellow officers he learned that "their design had been to bring about a skirmish with the rear guard of the army." At least, that constituted their initial goal. Once he discovered that the rear guard was detached from the main column, Lafayette "had aimed at us in order to cut us off and defeat us."[242] Ewald reflected on this newly acquired intelligence concerning the recent encounter, finally concluding that "Luck decided everything."[243]

Now that Ewald joined with the main army at Williamsburg, he took the opportunity to investigate the city, as he had so many others over the course of his campaign in North America and dutifully entered his observations in his omnipresent diary. As was his habit, he studied the position of the town from a military perspective, noting its placement, the natural obstacles that afforded the location some measure of security, or that could be altered to do so with relative ease, and the main routes to and from the city as well.[244] All this material would undoubtedly be useful should he have to attack or defend the town at some future point.

Shortly after Ewald's arrival in Williamsburg, on June 30th, he marched out of the town with a detachment that consisted of his Jäger as well as three companies of rangers at three o'clock in the morning. The force marched towards York, its mission to provide cover for Cornwallis who sought to reconnoiter towards the other town.[245]

At the strategic level, the reason for the scout encompassed the search for a deep-water port which could serve as a base for continued British efforts in the region. The British needed a major port if they wished to continue the subjugation of Virginia, which Cornwallis now believed crucial both to maintaining the gains already made in the southern colonies, and to advancing the cause of British arms in the region.

The overall strategic problem, as Cornwallis had grown to appreciate it, revolved around the fact that Virginia served as the key source of supplies and manpower for the Patriot war effort in North Carolina as well as their attempts to regain control of South Carolina and Georgia. It followed, logically, that if Virginia could be taken, efforts to the south would wither and die for lack of nourishment. This, then, encompassed the latest permutation of the British southern strategy.[246]

On his arrival in York, Ewald drove out a small force of Americans. Cornwallis then entered the town about ten in the morning and remained there until one in the afternoon.[247] On leaving, the British general gave Ewald the choice either to march back with him, or wait until the evening, when the worst heat of the day had subsided. Ewald left the town with Cornwallis but placed his men in an ambush just outside of the town. He hoped to capture some Americans when they reentered the town and gain some additional intelligence as to their numbers and intentions.

After an hour or so, Ewald dispatched Lieutenant Bickell with thirty men back to York by a roundabout route. As they prepared to march back to York, the detachment under Bickell "pulled their shirts over their coats, the leather straps and belts over that, and wore their hats pulled down like Americans, in order to look like the American militia, who were dressed in linen in this warm region." It is unclear whether it was Ewald or Bickell himself who first hit on the idea of having the men disguise themselves in this manner. In either case, it worked. On their march, the detachment "discovered a party of thirty to forty men, welcomed them from a distance, killed and wounded the greater part, and brought back the officer and nine men as prisoners."[248]

In many respects, this engagement mirrors one fought in North Carolina between a composite force of cavalry from Lee's Legion, and some North Carolina patriot military on one side and some local Loyalists under a Dr. John Pyle on the other. The engagement was known as "Pyle's Hacking Match". On this occasion, Lee had his men disguised themselves as members Tarleton's Legion. As Lee stated, his goal was to ride past the Loyalist and make his way back to the American lines. In the event, one of the local patriots disclosed the true identity of the force to one of the Loyalists. With their secret revealed, the Americans drew their swords and began to cut down the unsuspecting Loyalists.[249]

About six in the evening, Ewald left the outskirts of York, and made his way back to his post at Williamsburg. Shortly after this excursion, on July 2nd, the Americans attacked the British pickets along the road to Richmond, but were driven off.[250] Two days later, on the 4th, the army broke camp at Williamsburg in the morning and marched to Jamestown where they established a new camp at midday. Ewald gave the reason for this shift in location as comprising a response to the movements of the American and British forces then gathering outside of New York City.

At this point, Sir Henry Clinton worried that Washington, with the French troops under Rochambeau, was planning an attack on the British held city. Such an attack was actually in the planning stages, and a reconnaissance of the British positions was carried out. Eventually, the plan would be set aside as the opportunity to trap Cornwallis in Virginia began to materialize.[251]

Likewise, Ewald discerned in the movement a switch from an offensive to a defensive posture by the British force in Virginia. As a contributing factor, he noted that General Henry Clinton, in New York City, had asked for the return of the light infantry, the Queen's Rangers, the

Anspach brigade and the 43rd and 76th regiments to provide additional reinforcements should Washington and Rochambeau decide to attack him. In addition, Ewald noted that it was the superiority of the American forces, which forced Cornwallis into a defensive posture at Portsmouth.[252]

It is worth noting that while Ewald's interpretation of events has often been accepted at face value, not all later historians have subscribed to it. One recent author asserted that the move to Yorktown consisted in a choice derived from the desire to possess a deep-water port so as to continue operations in the Virginia theater.[253]

Reconsidering on the dilemma facing British forces in Virginia years later, Ewald considered the strategic options that remained open to them. He observed that Cornwallis still possessed the option of retreating into North Carolina over the pass from Northwest Landing. Should this eventuality arise, Ewald saw the proper course as loading the horses of the army with all their necessary supplies, and burning the ships at docked Portsmouth, as well as blowing up any guns that could not be carried with the army. If it were still possible to travel by a water route, he considered taking the army to Wilmington. Concerning this option, Ewald noted that with a north or easterly wind, it would be possible to reach the destination in a few days. Given the direction of the wind he cited, Ewald most likely meant Wilmington, Delaware.[254]

The preceding presents a prime example of Ewald's military mind at work. He considered the options that remained open to the British and their forces. Not only was the Jäger captain adept at devising and implementing plans for small unit actions, by now he possessed enough experiences to consider options open for the entire army. His skills as a tactical operator had matured significantly over his years of fighting in North America.

Shortly after the reduction of forces at Cornwallis disposal, and his subsequent move of the British army, Colonel Simcoe and a mixed force, which included Ewald's Jäger, as well as the Queen's Rangers, and the Althouse sharpshooters were sent across the James River to James City Island. They occupied a position on the heights in the form of a crescent to cover the crossing of the remainder of the British army.

On July 5, Ewald was sent out with a small party in the direction of Smithfield and Southampton to gather intelligence on the enemy in that area. On his scout, Ewald learned that a general John Baker stood at Smithfield with 2,000 men. Baker's mission was to observe the British.

Never one to shy away from the opportunity for combat, Ewald determined to try and surprise the American force, which he located at

Wilson's Plantation. On this occasion, the Americans managed to retreat before he could engage.[255]

Ewald took the opportunity in his diary to expound on the growing friendship then developing between him and Colonel Simcoe. He referred to the latter as "a worthy man," and declared "that he is truly my friend, that he strives to make me happy and that at all times he gladly gives me the opportunity at hand to distinguish myself."[256] At some time during this period, Simcoe offered Ewald the opportunity to become a major in the Queen's Rangers. In some ways, this was generous offer. It meant higher rank, and therefore greater pay. However, it came with numerous risks. Since Ewald possessed no connection in England beyond the officers he had become acquainted with during his American service, he stood a good chance of being reduced with the end of hostilities. Likewise, it would mean gaining release from his oaths to his own prince. Given his strong sense of honor, the latter action stood as a step not easily taken. Finally, there was remained the fact that Ewald was a commoner, another mark against him in the aristocratic world of eighteenth century officers.

In the end, it was loyalty to his sovereign that won the day. He replied to Simcoe's offer, "But I am Hessian, body and soul, and it seems to me that I could not be happy outside this splendid corps in which I serve." He continued, "It is impossible that any evil can await me in my native land, for I can say in all conscience that I have served an upright man." Finally, he declared, "If I have not been given preference by my sovereign, neither has he done me any wrong; and after all, he has awarded me the order of the *pour le merite.*—I but serve my master until he does me an injustice."[257] As will be seen, Ewald's remarks in this instance were extremely telling. He was, at this time, extremely loyal to his state and his Landgraf. He served as a dedicated professional. At the same time, he left himself an opening, if he were treated unjustly by the Langraf, he would consider his alternatives.[258] In any case, Ewald's friendship with Simcoe would outlast the American war.[259]

The game of cat and mouse between Cornwallis and Lafayette continued through the summer. The latter was not strong enough to challenge Cornwallis in open combat, even after he received reinforcements under Pennsylvania General Anthony Wayne. At the same time, the two were cunning enough to avoid being lured into combat by Cornwallis, with the notable exception of the battle of Green Springs fought on July 6, 1781.[260]

It is worth bearing in mind that Cornwallis conducted much of his campaign through the summer of 1781 under the constant threat of losing troops under his command to Clinton in New York City as there remained the very real possibility of an American attack in that theater. For instance, on July 14, the Queen's Rangers were ordered to take ship back to the British headquarters. The British general would thus be deprived of one of his better commanders of light troops. Likewise, Ewald not only lost the companionship of his friend Colonel Simcoe, but the partnership of a commander with whom he could work to mutual advantage. In discussing this change in plans, Ewald noted that it seemed to come from an assumption by Clinton concerning Washington's intentions with the combined Franco-American force under his command, "Since the Allied army had left its camp near King's Bridge and had crossed the Hudson River, General Clinton supposed that the army had something in mind against Virginia..." He further noted that Clinton now believed "That the advance toward New York had been nothing more than a demonstration, either to force him to recall the troops from Virginia or to prevent him from detaching more troops for this place."[261] In this sense, it could be said that Washington's goal of attacking New York contributed materially to pushing Cornwallis down the road to Yorktown.

On July 22nd, the British returned to Portsmouth again. This time Ewald selected his ground, and according to his account, did a much better job than the British Quartermaster General. Through the summer the men were often tormented by the variety of insects that inhabited the swampy territory along the Virginia coast.[262] The day after they had established the new camp, orders arrived from New York countermanding the previous ones, and ordering the troops who had boarded ships already to remain with Cornwallis. Simcoe and Ewald would continue their operations together.

Ewald, writing with the virtue of hindsight, noted that having come to the proper conclusion concerning Washington and Rochambeau's intentions, Clinton should have attempted to interdict the combined force as it was crossing the Hudson. Tellingly, he observed, "Consequently, our fate depends on the success of the English fleet, for as long as the English remain rulers of the sea, a door stays open for us."[263] On the one hand, Ewald here engaged in one of the pastimes of many soldiers in wartime - critiquing their commanders. This could be an especially alluring hobby when the criticisms could be made from afar. At the same time, he quite perceptively grasped of the significance of sea power for the British success in the war effort. As summer wore on, however, his own campaigning in Virginia occupied more of the captain's attention.

On the 29th, Ewald and his Jäger were ordered to return to Portsmouth. He was joined by the Althouse sharpshooters, and some men of the 80th Regiment under Brigadier Dundas. The group boarded boats and sailed that afternoon to Hampton Roads where they anchored for the night, next to the troops who had been ordered to New York several days prior.[264]

On July 31, the flotilla of transports continued up the York River. At daybreak, they heard the alarm guns of the local militia sounding as they continued on their way. The Americans were aware of their presence. While the Americans could track the movements of the British force, they could not determine their intended landing site. This, again, constituted one of the assets of sea power.

The following day, the ships moved into the York River again, and made their way to the mouth of the Severn River, where they anchored at eight o'clock that evening. That night, as a violent thunderstorm raged around them, Ewald's corps, the sharpshooters, the 80th Regiment and the twenty horsemen came ashore on the right bank of Sarah Creek. They were about a half hour's walking distance from Gloucester.[265]

Once all the men were ashore, the units split up, with Colonel Dundas taking the 80th Regiment to the town, while Ewald and his men marched around it in order to enter Gloucester from the direction of the headlands. They accomplished their goal, even though they were operating in somewhat unfamiliar territory, at night, and without guides. On entering the town, Ewald's contingent took possession of a battery of two eighteen-pounders which the Americans had abandoned.[266]

Shortly after entering Gloucester, Ewald came across a Colonel Whiting, whom Ewald came to believe was a relative to George Washington. The captain provided the Colonel with a safe passage back to his lines.[267]

Now that the British forces had established a base of operations at Gloucester, Ewald wasted no time in beginning to reconnoiter the surrounding area. The following morning he set out again with his men, moving eight to ten miles into the countryside "to collect information about the enemy, to look around for forage in the vicinity, and if possible to bring back slaughter cattle for the army."[268]

Ewald's patrol took him as far as Abingdon Church where the locals had assembled their cattle to hide them from the British. On discovering the cattle, while Ewald felt some pity for the people, he continued with his orders, and ordered the beasts driven off to the army. He next moved off in the direction of Gloucester Courthouse. Along the way, he gained some information from some Patriot militia he captured, "I learned from these men that the militia had orders to assemble at King and Queen Courthouse."[269]

CHAPTER 10

THE SIEGE OF YORKTOWN

As Ewald scoured the countryside for supplies and intelligence, additional British forces, including the light infantry, the 43rd and 76th Regiments, as well as Simcoe's Corps and the Anspach Brigade, all under the command of Lord Cornwallis, landed at York and proceeded to establish a camp on the heights around the town. Ewald asserts, "It was on this day that the plan for the fortification of York and Gloucester was settled by Lord Cornwallis."[1]

The plan grew out of the need, on the part of the British, for a deep-water port to facilitate the support of the Royal Navy. The support of the navy was crucial to continued operations in the region, not only for the landing of replacements, but for the provision of supplies as well.[2] For some time, Virginia served as the supply base for the American forces fighting in the Carolinas. As a result, much of their excess food supply had already been siphoned off to feed the American army. In this situation, the British could not risk seizing more food and supplies from the Americans and thus taking the chance of alienating those still loyal to the crown. By the same token, finding additional food stuffs was proving more and more difficult. Ewald's success in this venture can be attributed to the speed with which he moved out. Leaving on his reconnaissance the next day brought with it the vital element of surprise. Simply put, the locals did not have the time to hide their animals on that occasion. Surprise, however, is a difficult element to achieve on repeated occasions. It is worth noting, as well, that Ewald and his men could sustain such exertions for only so long before they exercised some deleterious effect.

Thus, their existed the vital need for a base of operations to provide logistical support to the army in the field. York was destined serve that purpose, or at least that was the British intention. As Ewald records, towards evening on August 2, the British began erecting three redoubts at Gloucester on the side of the town facing inland. In addition, they began

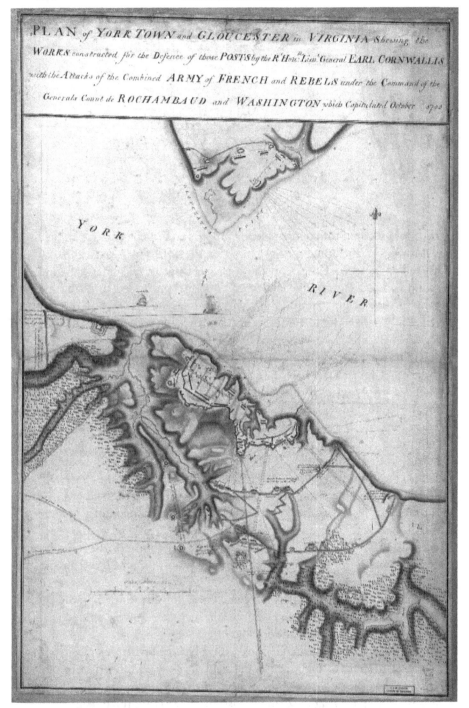

Figure 1: John. Hills, Plan of York Town and Gloucester in Virginia, shewing the works constructed for the defence of those posts by the Rt. Honble: Lieut. General Earl Cornwallis, with the attacks of the combined army of French and rebels under the command of the Generals Count de Rochambaud and Washington which capitulated October 1781. [1781] Map. Retrieved from the Library of Congress, https://www.loc.gov/item/gm71000688/. (Accessed March 25, 2017.)

construction of a battery facing in the direction of the river. In addition, Cornwallis appointed Colonel Dundas commandant of Gloucester.[3]

Soon, additional troops began to arrive at the post. For instance, on August 6, the Erb Prinz Regiment and the remainder of the 71st arrived at Gloucester from Portsmouth. The latter post was ordered abandoned by Cornwallis. In recording this move, Ewald asked his diary, "How will this look to the loyal subjects there? Have we not made enough people unhappy already?"[4] More proof of his growing appreciation of importance of public perceptions in a civil war. The following day, Ewald patrolled once again, gathering intelligence on American movements, and protecting British foraging expeditions. He was about six English miles from Gloucester, at a place called Seawell's Ordinary when he ran into an American force on the plain at Seawell's plantation. The Americans, however, withdrew after exchanging only a few shots with Ewald's force. About a week later, Ewald returned to the same area once again. On this occasion, "I had barely reached the vicinity of Seawell's plantation when a loyal negro informed me that one thousand Americans were lying in ambuscade, not far from this planation."[5]

On receiving this information, Ewald determined to turn the tables in the situation. "I withdrew to Whiting's plantation and ambuscaded myself, since it was to be expected that the enemy would pursue me."[6] Once he had set the trap, "I sent back Lieutenant Bickell with ten men to probe the area of the ambuscade, who were welcomed with shots from all directions as soon as the enemy perceived that he was betrayed."[7] Bickell, as planned, retreated on Ewald's position, but in this instance the Americans did not pursue very far.[8] The plan implemented on the above occasion encompassed just the sort of thing Ewald had developed years earlier in his first treatise.[9]

Shortly after this affair, hundreds of miles away, a momentous meeting was taking place. On August 14, Rochambeau presented Washington with a letter from the French Admiral, the Comte de Grasse. In the communiqué, de Grasse informed the two commanders that in August he would sail from Haiti to the Chesapeake in an attempt to avoid the worst of the stormy season in the Caribbean. Along with his twenty-eight warships, the French Admiral would bring roughly 3,100 troops, inclusive of infantry and cavalry. In addition, he offered the marines attached to his warships. These he would make available for operations in the northern theater, but only for a limited time, as the troops with him included men from the Hattian establishment. He warned that he would only remain in northern waters until October 15.[10]

This one communication changed the entire course of the campaign, and consequently, the war. Up to this point, all efforts had been directed at New York City. From this time forward, they would be focused clearly on Virginia. Still, there stood the problem of moving the combined French and American forces to Virginia without the British detecting them or gaining intelligence of their movements through the Loyalists.[11] To buy time, Washington ordered his subordinate William Heath to remain outside New York with his 2,500 men as a covering force. Orders were also sent out to begin the construction of bread ovens in order to deceive the British into thinking that the planned assault on New York remained in the offing.[12] As historians since often emphasized, Washington's move constituted a monumental gamble.

If Clinton did receive intelligence on Washington's movements, his forces in New York were more than capable of brushing aside the American covering force. Likewise, he could redeploy British land and naval strength and attack Washington on the march, reinforce or evacuate Yorktown, or possibly catch him between two forces during the siege.

For their part, the British showed themselves to be willing opponents, as their Admiral Rodney determined that only a part of De Grasse's force would move into northern waters and failed to even entertain the idea that the whole of his squadron would do so. By this point, moreover, the British Admiral had headed home, and sent the remainder of his force, under Samuel Hood, to New York. The most recent historian of the maritime dimension of the conflict described Vice -Admiral Samuel Graves as simply "useless."[13]

By August 16, the British had evacuated Portsmouth completely and concentrated their forces at York. On that same day, Simcoe took his post at Gloucester on the left of the town. Meanwhile, the Americans began to move in around the British camp. Many of these were militia troops. As in the past, slaves in the region proved a valuable source of information for the British on American movements. On at least one occasion during this period, Ewald successfully surprised an American camp using information gained through the interrogation of local slaves.[14]

Several days after Simcoe's arrival, on August 23, Ewald and his Jäger provided support for the former as he went on a foraging mission near Abingdon Church. While they did sight some American troops during the operation, the latter kept their distance, and Ewald could not close to attack before they fell back.[15]

All of the foraging conducted by the British in Virginia led Ewald to consider once again the issue of pillaging in his diary. While the troops certainly needed supplies, and it was always more economical for the army to live off the land, it often led to out and out plunder, which, in turn, served to drastically undermine the army's discipline. This could lead to many unwanted outcomes, as Ewald mused in his diary,

> *One perceives from this that a leader of light infantry cannot be se-vere enough in establishing a strict discipline, since otherwise the best planned stroke will miscarry. - For how many well-devised strokes have been spoiled by a marauder? And yet, I have never seen such a bad mistake punished severely.* [16]

Clearly, plunder stood as something anathema to the Ewald's sense of military professionalism. Moreover, in his estimation, the best way to pre-vent the indiscipline that arose due to plundering involved maintaining strict discipline and thus preventing it from the outset. Essentially, stop the problem from arising at all. Ewald concluded his thoughts on the con-tribution of plunder to indiscipline with the notion that "There are situ-ations in war where indulgence, indeed sympathy itself, is an offense." [17] Still, the captain's thoughts on the subject remained very much his own. During the period between August 26th and 29th, the British foraged the plantations on both sides of the Severn River continuously. This usually resulted in small skirmishes erupting between the foraging parties and their covering forces and local militia. To concentrate their supplies, the British established a magazine of forage at Gloucester. [18]

By the beginning of September, the British removed all their sup-plies and equipment from the transports that brought them to York and Gloucester. Accordingly, they set about constructing defenses for their new base of operations. While work proceeded on these defenses, rumors of an impending attack circulated in the British camp. One which Ewald preserved in his diary ran "We ...had news that the Allied army under Washington and Rochambeau was advancing toward Virginia." At the same time, he describes how these rumors were discounted as a matter of course at the time. [19] Soon, however, this camp talk took on more omi-nous tones.

On the morning of August 30, Ewald heard the sounds of cannon in the distance, and from his post, he could see smoke in the Chesapeake Bay. Out in the distance, he began to discern the shapes of several vessels. As they drew nearer to his position, he identified them as French ships, three in number, entering the York River and dropping anchor. The Jäger captain identified them as a seventy-four, a sixty-four, and a frigate. These were the vanguard of De Grasse's squadron, which disgorged their troops before taking up position once again at the mouth of the bay. For his part, Ewald believed that they would soon continue upriver and bombard Gloucester and York.[20]

These were, in fact, part of De Grasse's force, which anchored that day in three lines at Lynnhaven Bay. Soon, a representative from Lafayette's staff came aboard to brief the Admiral. That same day, Washington's Army arrived at Princeton, New Jersey. British commander Samuel Hood had brought his ships into the Chesapeake Bay five days previous, on August 25, but sighting no French ships, simply continued on his course to New York.[21] By September 2, the combined Franco-American army marched through Philadelphia, continuing on their way southward.[22]

It is worth considering that for Washington and Rochambeau to seize the opportunity presented them by Cornwallis move into York, they had to move their combined forces a distance of 450 miles, most of it overland, without being detected. At the same time success required the preservation local naval superiority to prevent Cornwallis from either being reinforced with additional troops, or simply evacuated.[23] Still, seize it they did, and while Ewald remained busy with the consolidation of the new post along the York River, he seemed vaguely aware that a noose was tightening around the entire garrison.

On September 3, Ewald reported how "news arrived that the Americans under Lafayette were advancing to Williamsburg, and that a French corps under General Saint-Simon had landed at James City Island and joined the Americans under Lafayette."[24]

The captain noted how "Now head banged against head in York and Gloucester. Now they hastily began to unload all the magazines and guns which had been brought from Portsmouth, but which—through negligence and laziness—were still on board the ships lying at anchor in the York River between the two towns." Essentially, the British camps would have been defenseless against a naval bombardment, a fact that Ewald understood, noting "Now if the French had been in better readiness or perhaps had better intelligence, the ships could be shot to pieces."[25]

That same evening, the lines for defenses were laid out around York. Ewald noted wryly, "Half the army was put to work, and now for the first time it was found that tools were lacking, just as they had been at Portsmouth under Arnold, which no one had thought about again until this time."[26] Such lackadaisical behavior on the part of the British clearly chagrined the Jäger captain. Ewald, a consummate professional, saw the manner in which the British approached the campaign at this point, and it galled him to no end.

The following night, September 4, Ewald joined Simcoe as the colonel conducted a foraging mission on the left back of the Severn. It makes one wonder whether or not the Jäger vented some of his growing frustration to his friend and comrade in arms, and if Simcoe would have shared some of the same concerns. On this point his diary is mute, as is Simcoe's narrative. Both men were true professionals and kept any conversation on this point out of their published wirings.

During the forage, Ewald took up a covering position in the "churchyard of Abingdon Church with 150 men to cover the left and rear of the foragers."[27] Ewald included a description of the Church, which he described as lying about ten miles from Gloucester on the road to Baltimore. He noted that the structure was built of brick in the form of a cross.[28]

Occupying the churchyard with his troops, Ewald deployed his infantrymen with thirty horsemen along the near side, where there was a defile. They were positioned "along the second road which ran past this church to the left beyond Burwell's and Lewis's sawmills, in order to fall upon any part of which should pass between this road and the Abingdon Church."[29] In this sort of operation, defensive precautions could be just as important, if not more so, than offensive ones. Certainly, Ewald would not neglect these, and he continued, "For my own security, since the Church was surrounded by thick woods for a distance of five or six hundred paces towards Baltimore, I placed sixty Jäger in six parties in a circle to intercept enemy parties."[30]

With his forces thus positioned, Ewald settled down and waited through the night. His precautions were not in vein, as "Several parties appeared...," however, "luckily for them all turned around at the right spot."[31] In other words, the Americans turned around before they fell into the ambush Ewald had set.

These forays out of the camps at Gloucester and York were to supply needed materials for the British army, which was now quite stationary. The construction of fortifications finalized the shift from offensive to defensive operations. Ewald was highly critical of the design and implementation of these works, much like those outside Charleston. The captain was especially critical of the Royal Corps of Engineers, noting "Indeed, we just now become fully aware that it [their position] lacked everything necessary for a good defense."[32] He further asserted that "Not a single thought had been given to where the planks and boards for the platforms were to come from."[33]

This last point directly influenced Ewald's duties, as once the lack of boards became apparent, "Colonel Simcoe with a detachment of two hundred men and I with just as strong a body were sent out on this same day to search for lumber on the plantations."[34] The two men were able to carry out their mission successfully, locating the necessary lumber at plantations along the Timber Creek, and transporting it back to their camp without disruptions from the American forces in the area.[35] Those remained too weak, and lacked the necessary horses to react to the fast-moving raids of the Jäger and rangers.

The following day, September 5, the frigate Aigrette, on patrol at the mouth of the Chesapeake between Capes Henry and Charles, reported ships coming in from the northeast, informing De Grasse that they had sighted ten sails. Initially, the French sailors believed that this was a reinforcement under Admiral de Barras coming to join them. They later determined that the approaching ships were in fact a British squadron and De Grasse ordered his commanders to prepare for battle. Many of the French vessels, however, had men out in their boats, and most of these sailors did not see the signals hoisted ordering them to return. The result was mixed in that while the ships of De Grasse's squadron went into battle undermanned, they were also less encumbered on the decks than their British counterparts.[36]

The battle of the Chesapeake Capes, fought on the same day, constituted one of the decisive actions of the Yorktown campaign. De Grasse, with his ships outnumbered, and placed in the position of taking the lee-gauge, or defensive stance, maneuvered out of the Virginia Capes. His reason for doing this was to allow de Barras to enter the Capes if he should arrive while the two fleets were engaged. Initially, it would have appeared that the French would have held the advantage, as they would have been able to catch the British in an enfilade fire as they approached. This possibility did not manifest, however, because they were at the mercy of the wind, and not all of De Grasse's ships could join in the initial battle.[37]

On the British side, Admiral Graves came within sight of the French fleet early on the fifth. He at first mistook it for a British squadron. When the truth of the matter became clear, he assembled his ships into a line of battle some five miles long. For Graves to attempt to maintain command and control over such a lengthy battle line, he separated his force into three divisions.[38] The French organized their forces along similar lines. Both commanders initially underestimated the size of their foe.[39] Still, the French held a superiority in number of guns, sporting some 1,794 to the British 1,410.[40]

For about an hour, the two fleets converged on one another, the French headed out to sea, and the British headed towards land. By about one in the afternoon, both fleets were roughly facing one another. At this point, Graves ordered his fleet to wear, a maneuver that essentially reversed his line of battle. This placed his most aggressive commander, Admiral Hood, in command of the rear division, with Admiral Drake in command of the van.[41] It also meant that both fleets were now sailing eastward, and away from Virginia. Eventually, after over six hours of maneuvering, the fleets were approaching at an angle, so that the vans of both were approaching more closely, thus coming in range sooner, than the remainder of the forces.[42]

In the resulting clash, the British were soundly beaten by the French. Five British ships were crippled, and one, the *Terrible*, was later abandoned and burned.[43] Concerning the battle of the Chesapeake, the most recent historian of the naval dimension of the War of Independence asserts that "Graves was out-thought and out-fought at the battle of the Chesapeake; he was soundly beaten."[44] It is often stated that control of the Capes spelled the doom for the British forces in Yorktown. On some level, Ewald seemed conscious of the implications of the French victory for the troops in Yorktown.

Two days after the battle, on September 7, for instance, Ewald was once again out foraging along the Severn River. This time, his mission allowed him to gain some information on the movements of the American general Weedon.[45] By this time he found it unfathomable "why the enemy lets us constantly forage so peacefully, since we would have had to slaughter our horses long ago for want of forage, or buy every bundle of forage with blood."[46] He further speculated that "The reason for this poorly designed policy of the enemy can only be that he does not want to dispirit his soldiers by a few small defeats."[47] Still, it occurred to him that the Americans could resort to attritional tactics under which they would "not need to risk much, he can disrupt our foraging by using ambuscades, which would cost us several men each time." He further noted the effect on morale of such an approach, "this surely would result in heavy desertion among us for our soldiers must realize by now that everyone will be captured with bag and baggage in the end."[48] A grim assessment of the army's operational situation, and one made before the first elements of the besieging force even arrived.

Returning to the construction of the British defenses outside York, Ewald sarcastically referred to the British Engineer, Captain Sutherland, as the English Vauban. Soon, the defenders ran into the problem of water seeping into the works. Only then did the English begin to add palisades to the defenses. Ewald observed that Sutherland "laid more stress upon repairing the works afterwards than on constructing it well in the beginning or following all the rules of fortification for laying out works."[49]

Following Ewald's line of thought, which he further elaborates upon in his diary, there were clear flaws in the British defenses from the outset. These would, in turn, contribute to the British defeat in the coming siege.

The Jäger captain criticized the entire British approach to fortification, noting that "any sensible engineer thinks in advance of palisades, assault stakes, fascines, pilings, and saucisons before he starts to break ground, but here, one thinks about these things for the first time only after the works are constructed."[50] In addressing the question of why the English engineers would approach their work in this way, he observed, "The engineer gets a daily allowance of one pound sterling as long as his works lasts, hence it is to his advantage if it drags on."[51]

On September 12, Ewald reported hearing the sounds of cannon fire, and assumed it to be another clash between the two fleets. He went so far as to say, "we flattered ourselves with thoughts of the fortunate result of a naval engagement."[52] Two days later, the troops learned the truth, that Graves and Hood had been driven out to sea.

The men in Yorktown continued to hear reports of the Allied Franco-American Army closing in on them. In response, they hastened to complete their defenses. On September 16, for instance, Ewald reported that the defenders began sinking ten transports between York and Gloucester in order to obstruct the entrance to their anchorage. He further noted that they placed a fire ship, the *HMS Vulcan*, at anchor below the town positioned to move against the enemy fleet should it approach.[53]

That same day, the 16th, Ewald took part in a foraging mission with the Jäger and rangers. While in search of supplies, the troops learned from a slave that one hundred horse and just as many infantry awaited them in an ambush at Seawell's Ordinary. Responding to this intelligence, Simcoe ordered Ewald to proceed to the spot of the planned ambush with fifty horse and fifty Jägers and search it out. Simcoe followed him up with the same number of troops to provide support. Ewald divided his force into five groups of ten infantrymen and ten horsemen each. He deployed his men in a circular formation about two thousand paces wide, which would enable him to attack the enemy post from all directions simultaneously.[54]

At the appropriate point, they sprung their attack. After a brief skirmish, the enemy withdrew through some woods to Burwell's Mill. On the 17th, toward the evening, the outposts were alarmed by the approach of several parties of the enemy, but these withdrew rapidly. Clearly, the net was closing around Yorktown.[55]

The following day, Ewald grew sick with an ailment he described as "the southern land fever." According to his account, he suffered extremely from the heat prevalent in the region between ten in the morning and two in the afternoon daily. He noted that it was a struggle for him to remain on his horse during the day, but he managed to do so. The captain attributed the ailment to the "great heat, which has decomposed our blood too much, and from the continued and frequent drinking of bad water."⁵⁶ Ewald added that there was a general lack of medicines necessary for the treatment of such ailments. He noted "that we have already resorted to using earth mixed with sugar to deceive the poor invalids, which is given to them as an emetic." Finally, he observed that "When they are bled, the blood of everyone is vermillion..."⁵⁷ He perceived the color of the soldiers' blood to be an additional sign of their poor health.

Another problem Ewald faced as the ring around Yorktown began to tighten was the lack of troops. By his own account, his detachment was down to twenty-nine men who were "still half well" as of September 18, 1781. He further noted that Simcoe's Rangers mustered less than one hundred effectives. Ewald attributed much of the manpower shortage to disease, "Simcoe and most of the officers of the Jäger detachment are dangerously ill. I consider it fortunate that I have the fever only once a day and can still do my duty."⁵⁸

On September 22nd, Ewald learned from a British naval officer that three fire ships were to be sent downstream to attack the three French ships which blocked the York River and burn them. On learning of the plan, Ewald immediately boarded a boat with the officer "to follow the fire ships and to observe this business, which I had never seen in my life."⁵⁹ Even in the midst of the siege, and suffering with a physical ailment, Ewald grasped any opportunities to add to his military experiences.

On observing the attack, he described how the "ships were set on fire and illuminated the area so brightly that we could easily detect the French ships at anchor in the very dark night."⁶⁰ However, the ships were ignited too early and as a result, "the enemy ships cut their cables and sailed away."⁶¹ If this were not bad enough, the fire ships ran aground, and thus the planned attack failed.

Early on the morning of September 28th, Washington led his combined army out from Williamsburg and began to surround the British position in York. The French took up positions on the left of the siege line, conceding the right, the post of honor, to the Americans. Later that same day, a group of French officers decided to reconnoiter the works by York. During their reconnaissance, a sharp skirmish occurred between their forces and the defenders.⁶²

Eighteenth century sieges were essentially a game of odds. The garrison hoped for a relief force before the besiegers either starved them into submission or created a workable breech in their defenses. At the same time, the besiegers hedged their bets on forcing the garrison to surrender before relief forces arrived. Working in Washington's favor on this occasion stood the fact that he enjoyed the assistance of the army commonly

seen as having written the book on siege craft. The French were widely
recognized at this time as being the best military engineers in Europe.

On September 29, the day following the formal opening of the siege,
Washington moved his army closer to Yorktown, and the British gunners
opened up on his infantry. There were few casualties on the American
side. Soon thereafter, Cornwallis abandoned his outer defenses. He did
this as he hoped to consolidate his lines and put up a stauncher defense.
Cornwallis' determination to hold out stemmed, at least in part, from a
recent communique he received from Sir Henry Clinton in New York
promising a relief force of some 5,000 troops.[63]

On the following day, Cornwallis abandoned and burned three of his
four redoubts, his troops falling back and occupying his inner defenses.
Later that day, the Franco-American forces formally invested the town
of York.[64] Concerning the remaining redoubt, Ewald observed that the
French presumed that they "would get possession of the redoubt on the
right cheaply because it could not be supported by the main works and
appeared to be left by itself." He further indicated that "For this reason
the French did not pay any compliments but attacked the redoubt right
before our eyes with a detachment of Lauzun's dismounted hussars and
grenadiers with sword in hand."[65]

By this time, Cornwallis had been able to construct some defenses for
Yorktown. These included a series of seven redoubts, which were joined
by various earthworks. As Washington inched his way closer to the British
lines on September 29, the British artillery opened up a heavy fire causing
some casualties among the Americans. Some additional skirmishing occurred between the Virginia militia, or volunteers as Ewald called them,
and the Jäger.[66]

Reacting to these movements, Cornwallis fell back from his outworks,
save for the Fusiliers redoubt on the east side, so named for the men who
constructed it, and redoubts 9 and 10 on the west side of his line. The
British commander conceded the other positions to the Americans without a fight, a fact which the increasingly frustrated Ewald criticized in
his journal.[67]

October 1st saw the Franco-American forces beginning to throw up
their own redoubts in the ravines that encircled York, beginning to establish their own strongpoints for the coming attack on the besieged. As a
part of their approach, the allies made use of two of the abandoned British
redoubts as part of their own system of trenches. The following day, an
American galley blew up in the York River.[68] October 2nd saw the arrival
of a guard boat from New York which brought communiques assuring the

defenders that General Clinton and Admiral Graves would do all in their power to send support their way.[69]

On the night of October 2, the British unleashed a furious cannonade of the American lines. The goal of this bombardment was not to create a gap in the besiegers' lines, rather, its purpose lay in deception. It covered the movement of much of the British cavalry to Gloucester. From there, the mounted troops were to provide the infantry cover for a major foraging expedition.[70]

On October 3rd, Ewald took part in one of the few operations designed to secure much needed forage for the cavalry. This stood as a necessity if they were to continue to conduct operations. As he recorded, "At daybreak I was sent out with one hundred horse of Simcoe's and the remainder of the Jäger and rangers, which amounted to only sixty men, in order to take a position between Seawell's plantation and Seawell's Ordinary."[71]

As noted, the purpose of this move was to provide security for foraging operations. Ewald reported, "I was to form a chain there to protect a foraging of Indian corn between Seawell's and Whiting's plantations, which was to be undertaken for the benefit of the cavalry to support me in case of an attack."[72] It is obvious from the preceding that the food situation, at least for the horses, in Yorktown was becoming precarious at best. The men and horses were suffering terribly for want of supplies as the Franco-American net closed ever more tightly around them.

The effort to secure supplies brought about a clash with the French cavalry under the Duc de Lauzun. Ewald's men had initially run into some Virginia militia, and begun to fall back on the British Legion. As he fell back, the Jäger captain noted, "I had scarcely reached the Legion, during which only six Virginia volunteers followed my rear guard, when the ambuscade fell out and pursued these few people into the woods of Seawell's plantation."[73]

Before probing forward, Ewald had deployed some of his troops in an ambush, just in case he ran into an American force. The clash did not end there, however, as when his men pursued the now retreating Americans,

Here, all of a sudden the scene changed. This small body of horsemen which was in the greatest disorder, suddenly ran into the entire corps under General Choisy. The Duc de Lauzun, who at this instant should have fallen on the head of these disorganized horsemen with a single troop, formed himself into two lines with eight troops of his lancers and hussars, which amounted to three hundred horsemen without the Virginia cavalry.[74]

From Ewald's rather confused relation of the event, the British Legion troops, in pursuit of the Americans, had run directly into the superior force of French cavalry under Lauzun. The situation could have been devastating for Tarleton's command. However, Lauzun paused to deploy his troops as described above. This action, in turn, "gave Dundas and Tarleton enough time to bring off their cavalry in orderly fashion to resist and withdrawal toward Gloucester."[75] As one historian described the encounter, "It was the last engagement in the American war [for the British Legion], a somewhat ironic ending to a bloody and dashing battle record."[76]

By the night of October 5, the Americans were ready to open their first parallel. Sappers and miners laid out the path for the first parallel using strips of pine. The following night, the Allied troops initiated work on the first parallel in earnest. George Washington himself took several swings with a pick axe in order to ceremoniously begin the parallel.[77] Cloud cover and rain made work on the trench unpleasant for the fatigue parties, but it served to mask their efforts from the British sentries in Yorktown.[78] The first trench was planned to be some 2,000 yards long, stretching from Yorktown proper to the head of the York River. In order to emphasize cooperation between the allied forces, the French were to command one half of the trench and the Americans the other.[79] On the northern end of the trench line, the French dug an additional trench so they could bombard British shipping in the York River. The following morning, the British awoke to see the new trench just outside of musket range.

The British defenders bombarded the allied positions while the Americans worked to mount their artillery in the trenches. This bombardment continued through the nights of October 4th, 5th, and 6th.[80] The French and Americans completed their gun emplacements over the course of October 8-9. On the morning of the 9th, Ewald reported that "it was discovered that the enemy had extended his trenches on both sides toward the York River in the form of a full crescent." He further noted how "Two batteries had been set up at both extremities of the crescent."[81] The American siege train included three twenty-four pounder and three eighteen pounder cannon, as well as two eight inch howitzers, and six mortars. The French began the bombardment at 3PM on October 9th, with the Americans joining in at 5PM. The shelling drove the British frigate *Guadeloupe* across the York River to Gloucester.[82]

Even during the siege, Ewald remained very active in the war of posts. On the night of October 9th, he described setting an ambush for enemy parties probing the British defenses, and the resulting friendly fire incident,

Since one could expect nothing else from the enemy's side at Glouces-
ter but that they would attempt a coup de main to take these works
which were occupied only by light troops, we continually laid ambus-
cades each night to the left of the York River. In the confusion they
must have fired upon each other. At daybreak I found seven hats and
five grenadier caps, as well as traces of much blood.[83]

The bombardment quickly began to tell on the British defenses, as the more British guns in the town began to fall silent. Washington ordered the firing to continue through the night to prevent the British from re-pairing what the Americans had damaged during the day.[84] In addition, some of the British ships riding at anchor in the York River sustained hits from shells that overshot their mark.[85]

The Americans located a large house in Yorktown, which they be-lieved to be Cornwallis headquarters, and proceeded to concentrate their bombardment on it.[86] The house was quickly destroyed. Ewald described a portion of the incident in his dairy. He noted, "Everyone was seated at the table." Then, "By the first cannon shot of the besiegers, Commissary Perkins was killed at the table and Lieutenant Robertson of the 76th reg-iment lost his left leg."[87]

The same day, October 10, Cornwallis received word from Clinton that a relief force would depart from New York on October 12. He replied that he would not be able to hold out for long under the intense bombard-ment. One the same day, Ewald recorded in his diary "Towards evening the three batteries were opened on the besieger's front, and the firing was sustained on both sides during the entire night."[89]

Conditions for the common soldiers within Yorktown were misera-ble. They were running low on food. Many of the horses had been slaugh-tered, and slaves who ran to the British in search of freedom now died in Yorktown from disease, injuries and starvation. The stench was un-imaginable. Many pitched their tents in the trenches in order to secure of modicum of protection from the rain of solid shot pummeling the town. As could be expected under these circumstances, many began to desert.[90]

The following night, October 11, Washington ordered his forces to begin the construction of a second parallel, some 300 yards closer to the British defenses. Ewald reckoned that the French and Americans had some seventy-six pieces active in the bombardment.[91] The noose was definitely tightening around Cornwallis. The chief obstacle for the Americans stood in the fact that they could not complete their trench by extending it to the river. They were blocked by the British redoubts 9 and 10. For their part, the British continued to fire on the original allied line, Cornwallis did not suspect that his opponents had begun a second. His lack of intelligence on his assailants was exposed on the morning of October 12, as the British looked out to find a second parallel, constructed and manned by French and Americans troops.[92]

The Allies quickly took advantage of their new position. The violence of the bombardment increased significantly. Ewald reported in his diary for October 12,

> *Since yesterday the besiegers have fired bombshells incessantly, so that the entire assault resembles a bombardment. The greater part of the town lies in ashes, and two batteries of the besieged have already been completely dismantled.*[93]

Now the time came to remove the obstacles, redoubts 9 and 10. Washington ordered the batteries to concentrate their fire on these strongpoints throughout October 14. His purpose stood in reducing them in preparation for a storming attack to be carried out that night. As predicted, the night was moonless, which afforded the assault parties some cover. In order to enhance this element, Washington ordered that the men make their attack with unloaded muskets, relying solely on the bayonet. Making the attack in this manner helped preserve the element of surprise and mitigate against soldiers firing their weapons prematurely. At the same time, launching the assault in this fashion demonstrated the general's confidence in his men's growing prowess with the bayonet.[94]

To some extent, the besiegers betrayed their intent when on the evening of October 15, they "redoubled their fire, and at seven o'clock in the evening a false attack was made on the redoubt on the right."[95] This would have been the Fusiliers Redoubt.

Redoubt nine stood closest to the river. It was held by a garrison of 70 men. Redoubt 10 stood about a quarter of a mile inland and contained a garrison of 120 British and German troops. In order to disguise their true purpose, the French were to launch a diversionary assault on the Fusiliers Redoubt. Likewise, the French were to attack Redoubt 9 with 400 troops under the command of Colonel Wilhelm von Zweibrücken. Redoubt 10 was to be the responsibility of 400 American light infantry. These were originally slated to be commanded by Lafayette's aide, Colonel Jean-Joseph Sourbader de Gimat, however, Alexander Hamilton protested that he was in fact the senior officer and should therefore claim the honor. Washington concurred with his long-time aide, and Hamilton led the assault.[96]

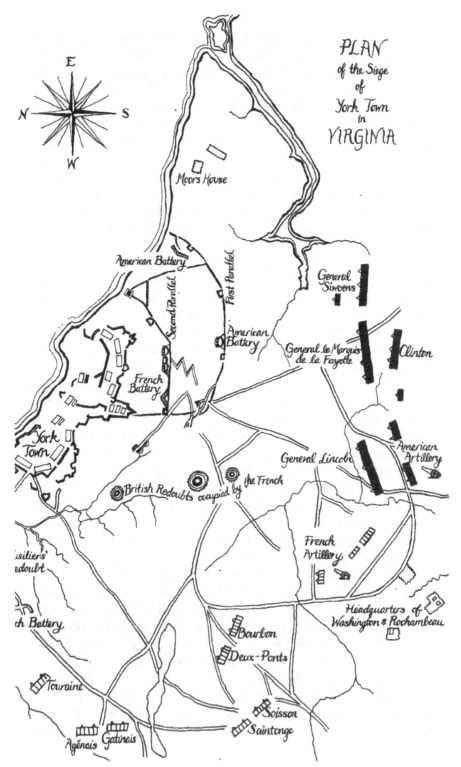

Figure 2: Ewald's map of the siege of Yorktown from his Diary of the American War

At 6:30 in the evening, the French launched their diversionary attack on the Fusilier's Redoubt. Ewald recorded the attack as taking place at seven in the evening. All along the American line, preparations were made, as if a general assault on Yorktown were in the offing. The Americans' actions placed the British on alert. Hamilton marched his force towards Redoubt 10, with fixed bayonets. He detached Lieutenant Colonel John Laurens with a small force to move around behind the redoubt and prevent and British troops from escaping.[97]

The British previously placed obstructions in front of the redoubt. As the Americans cleared these, their efforts alerted a British sentry who challenged the Americans, and then fired on them. Once the Americans cleared the wooded obstructions, they charged up the redoubt and through the abatis with fixed bayonets.[98]

Once inside the redoubt, the Americans came under heavy fire from the British defenders. Still, they managed to overwhelm them with sheer weight of numbers. The Americans managed to kill or capture almost the entire garrison of the redoubt, including the commander, Major Campbell, at the cost of nine dead and twenty-five wounded.[99]

The French assault, led by Count William Duex-Ponts, began simultaneously with that of the Americans. As the French hacked their way through the obstructions on Redoubt 9, they were challenged by a Hessian sentry. When no response was forthcoming, the sentry fired. He was soon joined by other members of the garrison. The French responded with fire of their own and charged the redoubt. The Hessians tried to drive them back with small arms fire, but the French responded with a volley of their own forcing the Hessians to retreat. They then took up a defensive position within the work but were surrounded. Then the French prepared the charge them with the bayonet, which drove the defenders to lay down their arms.[100]

The capture of the two redoubts allowed the Allies to place Yorktown itself under direct bombardment from three different angles. Life for the besieged within the town quickly grew unbearable. While he was not directly involved in the defense of either redoubt, Ewald did comment on their seizure in his diary, observing, both the "The Hessian Lieutenant Anderson of the Erb Prinz Regiment and the English captain Tailor were seized with swords in hand by the enemy." He continued, "Both officers were wounded by bayonets or swords and won the praise of the enemy." The manner in which the two officers were taken held significance for Ewald. Both had given up after being wounded and putting up a stout defense. Such conduct accorded well with the captain's sense of honor. His account concluded on a bitter note, however, "Most of the garrison

is said to have saved itself too soon."[101] Contrasting with the conduct of
their officers, the men had given up without offering enough resistance to
maintain their honor.

One incident Ewald noted occurred after the loss of the redoubts.
A footnote in the overall narrative of the siege, concerned the slaves the
Crown forces acquired during their campaigning in Virginia. With obvi-
ous distaste, Ewald observed,

> *I would just as soon forget to record a cruel happening. On the same
> day of the enemy assault, we drove back to the enemy all of our black
> friends, whom we had taken along to despoil the countryside. We had
> used them to good advantage and set them free, and now, with fear
> and trembling, they had to face the reward of their cruel masters.*[102]

Cornwallis, ever the aggressive officer, fought back. On October 15,
he concentrated his artillery on the nearest portion of the allied line. In addition, he ordered a storming party of some 350 British troops of the 80th
Regiment under the command of a Lieutenant Colonel Lake and a Major
Thomas Armstrong to storm the junction of the French and American
lines. They were to attack the as yet uncompleted allied trenches and spike
their guns. The first group they came upon were members of the French
Agenois Regiment. The storming party initially surprised the French defenders and the British gained the trench. The attackers managed to spike
some six guns in the allied trench and an unfinished redoubt as well. As
the British came up on the American sector of the line, they encountered
an alert sentry who set up the alarm. In addition, French troops under the
viscount de Noailles reinforced the Americans and drove off the British
attackers. The ssault left seventeen allied casualties, and six guns temporarily disabled. For their part, the British sustained seven casualties, five
of whom were made prisoners. By the following morning, all of the guns
the British had spiked were repaired and back in action.[103] One reason
it was so easy for the Americans to return their guns to active service lay
in the fact that, as Ewald noted, "the English artillerists, who had been
ordered to spike the guns, had brought along wheel nails to serve for spiking, which were too large, instead of the proper steel spikes."[104] Still he
noted that many officers in Yorktown believed that the sally would serve
as a turning point. The Jäger captain reacted to such confidence, "I had
listened to this foolish talk with annoyance, for everything irritated me
now, since I had to endure daily the most severe attacks of fever, during
which my nerves suffered extremely."[105]

By October 16, the allies had not only repaired their losses from the British sally, but added additional guns, intensifying the bombardment of Yorktown. Realizing his position was fast growing untenable, Cornwallis settled on a desperate gamble. He resolved to attempt to evacuate his garrison over the river to Gloucester that night. If he could move his troops without the allied forces ringing Yorktown realizing what he was doing, he stood a good chance of being able to break through their lines. The allied troops covering Gloucester were fewer in number. Once through the lines, he hoped to be able to march towards New York, and possibly be reinforced by Clinton along the way. Clearly, it was a plan fraught with danger, but if it worked, it would save both Cornwallis' army and his military reputation.[106]

As the first wave of boats made its way across the York River, the weather turned. Soon, a violent storm raged, forcing, the British general to abort his plans. The weather grew so severe the boats could not even make their back to Yorktown.[107] Ewald described Cornwallis' predicament, "this worthy man was indeed in the greatest predicament, for the majority of his troops floated on the water, or had reached Gloucester and could not get back to the York shore because of the terrible weather." He further recorded, "To our great luck, the weather was so frightful that the

Figure 3: French naval guns used during the siege of Yorktown from the Yorktown battlefield historic site. Author's photograph.

enemy could not discover anything of all this; and when the high wind died down, everyone was brought back to this place about nine o'clock in the morning."[108]

Concerning his own situation during the attempted breakout, Ewald leaves an account poignant in its description of the fatigue he felt by this point in the siege. It is therefore worth quoting at some length,

> *I will not forget this past night in all my life...I had to command two redoubts and a battery for which I was responsible. It was as dark as a sack and one could neither see nor hear anything because of the awful downpour and heavy gale. Moreover, there was a most severe thunderstorm, but the violent flashes of lightning benefited us, since we could at least see around us for an instant. And to make me really feel the harshness of my wretched life, the fever suddenly attacked me at midnight in the most horrible manner.*[109]

The allied fire on the British positions intensified on the following day, October 17. That morning, Cornwallis summoned his officers together for a council of war. It was determined that the garrison could no longer hold out. Shortly thereafter, a lone drummer was observed atop the British trenches, beating the parlay.[110]

Figure 4: The Moore House, where the terms of the British surrender were negotiated and signed. Author's photograph.

As Ewald recovered from his illness, he assessed the Cornwallis' attempted breakout from Yorktown, as was his habit with any action in which he served. He began by complimenting a superior whom he truly respected, "As much as this plan to do all that is possible and to save something when everything is at stake does honor to Lord Cornwallis…" Then he observed, "this attempt was the greatest impossibility, although worthy of admiration by posterity." Warming to his subject, Ewald hypothesized,

> *I venture to say that if Lord Cornwallis had had the luck to make an unexpected attack on the part of the army under General Choisy, the enemy would nevertheless have had an opportunity to defend himself again, because the defiles of Burwell's and Hudibres mills could not be outflanked, and would have delayed Lord Cornwallis until the main army had crossed the York River and hung on his neck while Choisy opposed his vanguard.*[111]

Negotiations began in earnest on October 18, with Colonel Thomas Dundas and Major Alexander Ross representing the British, Colonel Henry Laurens the Americans, and the Marquis de Noailles speaking for the French. The negotiations occurred at the Moore House. The final terms agreed to were "harsh but honorable and correct," given the concepts of siege warfare prevalent at the time.[112] Essentially, the longer the besieged resisted after it was clear they had no hope of relief, the less amicable the terms they could expect. The officers and seamen of the Royal Navy were to become prisoners of the French, while those of the British army would become captives of the Americans.[113] In addition, the officers of both services would be allowed to retain their side arms and personal belongings. Likewise, they would be permitted to go, on parole, either to Britain or to any area in America still under British control. Finally, a sloop was provided to carry Cornwallis' dispatches to New York under flag of truce.[114]

The articles of capitulation were signed on the following day. As Ewald recalled the actual surrender, "On the afternoon of the 19th toward two o'clock the Allies cleared away a barrier at each post, and at four o'clock the melancholy parade took place, and the arms were grounded."[115] The siege was over, and Ewald joined the numerous prisoners of war taken.[116]

These men slowly filed out of the battered city, and between the lines of French and Americans. The British were led by General Charles O'Hara.[117] The general first attempted to give his sword to Rochambeau. The Frenchman gestured to Washington, who directed the him on to Benjamin Lincoln, the former commander of Charleston.[118] As the men of the

Crown forces stacked their arms, many intentionally tried to break the locks on their guns, or otherwise render them unserviceable.

The prisoners were numerous indeed. They amounted to some 7,157 soldiers, 840 sailors and 80 camp followers. In addition there were some 2,000 sick and wounded in British hospitals.[119] Ewald placed the number of killed and wounded in siege at 653.[120] As the for the prisoners, Ewald described how, "a staff officer from each nation and a captain or an officer each with fifty men were to march to the designated place of captivity."[121] Finally, Ewald totaled up the casualties from the fighting over the previous two years, "Reckoning the entire loss we have suffered in the armies since the beginning of the year 1780 up to this moment, one can easily figure twenty thousand men."[122] It would be interesting to know how Ewald arrived at such a figure, as it seems almost impossibly high.

Following his description of the surrender, Ewald commented on the allied armies. Of the French he wrote simply, "...I do not think it necessary to write much, for everyone knows that when these soldiers are properly led, everything goes well with them." He continued, "The regiments have fine men, in very good order, clean, and well uniformed." All of the preceding constituted marks of a professional European army. He concluded his observations of the French by stating, "The men look healthy, and this climate affects them about as it does us."[123]

Concerning the Americans, however, the Jäger captain presented a markedly different assessment,

> *But I can assert with much truth that the American officer, like his soldier, hates his foes more than we do. They admit this openly, and claim as the reason that they want more freedom than we, on our side, wish to give them.*[124]

Here, Ewald stumbled over one of the reasons for the American victory in the war, though if he realized this, he did not comment on it. Instead, after some further discussion of the Americans, Ewald turned to his voyage back to New York. He, like many other officers, had accepted the offer of parole.

CHAPTER 11

DYING EMBERS

The end of active hostilities provided Ewald the time to engage in a number of other activities. First and foremost, he had the chance to get to know his former enemies. In the weeks following the surrender at Yorktown, the American and French officers took turns playing host to their former foes at a number of diners. Ewald attended some of these and recorded his impressions of the Americans in his diary. Following the pleasantries, a number of the officers from the British camp were sent on to New York, where they would be under parole as the negotiations, which eventually led to the Treaty of Paris, began in France.

Ewald took advantage of the opportunity to return to New York, however, there arose a serious lack of provisions, as well as discipline, among the officers on the voyage to New York. Still, the Jäger captain quickly found some advantages to making the sea voyage. He noted that "to my good fortune, what cheered me up was that my fever left me, and I was fresh and lively after I had been several days at sea." Ewald reached New York, and reported to his superior, General von Knyphausen on November 26.[2]

Shortly after returning to New York, Ewald left the city to check on his troops. On December 1, he traveled to the Jäger Corps, cantoned on Long Island. They were assigned the position in order to protect the shore against the incursions of New England militia who would attack in whale boats.[3]

On his return to his men, Ewald "was welcomed by my good friends with courtesy and friendship, and here I took up my quarters as a prisoner of war, and lived in peace."[4] He continued, with palpable relief, "Now I drank from the River of forgetfulness, banished all grief and sorrow, and looked forward with longing toward my exchange."[5]

The manner in which Ewald expressed his joy at returning to his men mirrored the way he felt when he returned to the Regiment von Gilsa following his initial wounding in the Seven Years' War.[6] His sense of relief

at being once more among his comrades in arms was only compounded when General Knyphausen passed along a letter he received form the
Landgraf in which the Jäger were singled out for special praise.

Most histories of the American War of Independence skip over the
period between the surrender at Yorktown and the final peace of Paris
in 1783. At most, they tend to give the impression that after Yorktown,
active combat operations came to an end.[7] Such a description is far from
accurate, however, the ubiquitous war of posts around the main armies
continued through the months following Yorktown. Similarly, the armies
on both sides, while reducing their strength in the hopes of an end to
active operations, continued to maintain some level of alert, guarding
against a resumption of hostilities. Ewald's diary provides a particularly
valuable source on this period, as he vividly captured the effects of nearly
six years of civil war and the hatred it engendered between the two sides.

With the reduction in combat operations, the Jäger captain now had
time to contemplate on his experiences over the past five years of combat.
His reflections on the war, and the reasons for the British loss were

> *This is the result of the absurd rules established during a war in
> which no plan was followed. The enemy was only pulled in all direc-
> tions and nowhere driven by force, whereby all was lost, when it was
> desired to preserve all.*[8]

Ewald's comments in this instance, while they express his bitterness
at the outcome of the conflict, are quite profound in that he attributes
the British loss to the dispersal of force as opposed to concentration, with
an eye towards the defeat of the American army. He notes the lack of a
clear British plan for victory as the underlying cause of their diffusion of
effort. Ewald's disgust at the situation is palpable, "It is terrible, when one
considers that the finest and most valiant army - after six campaigns - was
brought completely back to the point from which it started with the most
auspicious prospects six years ago." He continued, his bitterness dripping
off the page, "And this, indeed, against a people who were no soldiers, and
who could have been stamped to the ground in the first year."[9]

When it came to attributing blame for the British defeat in North
America, Ewald placed it clearly on the British ministry, "Such a calam-
ity must be incurred by every state in which there are no soldiers among
the ministers who draw up the plans for campaigns."[10] In this respect,
he either did not know of George Germain's previous military experience, or, as is more likely, was taking a jab at his record from the Seven
Years' War.[11] Ewald's bitterness in defeat grew more understandable as

he revealed that he believed if the British had won the war, many of the foreign officers would be offered continued duty on North America by the Crown, and would receive substantial material rewards in the restored colonies for their service.[12]

Now, however, there was nothing for the troops stationed in New York to do but await the decisions of the policymakers in London. Inaction was most likely a prudent course, considering that the army under Clinton, weakened by the loss of the troops under Cornwallis, was now barely capable of maintaining control over its possessions.[13] The ultimate fate of North America, however, remained unclear. On February 14, an express arrived from England carrying the King's speech to Parliament in which he said that the troops in North America were to be reinforced by ten thousand fresh troops, and the war pursued with vigor. According to Ewald, the news "gave every honest soldier fresh courage."[14]

While the king's speech may have stoked the passions of the troops serving in North America, it exerted little influence on the direction of British policy. Soon, representatives of the Crown began meeting with American negotiators in Paris to hammer out an agreement that would bring about an end to hostilities. With peace talks ongoing, the war in North America entered a state of limbo. Neither side planned any major campaigns. At the same time, they were still at war, and skirmishes continued to occur in both the north and south. As a result of these ongoing small-scale operations, Ewald and the Jäger Corps were transferred to Flushing on April 19, 1782.[15]

The transfer to Flushing brought about no significant change in the level of combat the Jäger faced. As a result, Ewald had little of interest to record in his diary, and single pages account for months, as opposed to days, when he was engaged in more active operations.

The next significant development in the captain's life occurred on July 22, 1782, he was again stricken by a severe fever. He noted the symptoms of the illness, which he described as "the most severe nerve, putrid, and bilious fevers...", observing that within twenty four hours, "I knew nothing more, and lay out of my mind, without hope."[16] Due to his location, on Long Island Sound, and the fact that he had not yet been exchanged, Ewald at first set out to treat the illness on his own, "At the first attack, I believed that it was putrid fever and I resorted to perspiring, which I thought to bring about with a half a quart of milk."[17] The captain's treatment did not bring about any relief, and as he described, "I lay in bed as if dead for two days..."[18] As the Captain lay suffering, the regimental surgeon of the Jäger Corps arrived. Ewald does not mention the surgeon's ministrations, and it seems that they had little to no effect. By his own account, he lay sick for five months with this illness, and then at the end of the year, caught something he referred to as the country fever, which he had until the spring of 1783. He noted that this subsequent illness was actually a benefit, "because my constitution was cleansed by it."[19] During this illness, Ewald was officially exchanged. Still, he noted, "it had caused too great a gap in my diary."[20]

As Ewald recovered his health, many of the German contingents who served the Crown through the conflict began to return to their various homelands. The captain observed these departures with some anxiety, hoping his own would follow soon.[21]

The new United States slowly recovered from the effects of the long war. The *journal of the Jäger Corps* recorded for January 6, 1782,

> *The Hessian Jäger were in the city, beside a detachment from the Ansbach Regiment. The Ansbach Jäger Corps was at Norwich, and the Hesse-Hanau Corps at Oyster Bay. This district, as far as the east end of the island, was under the command of Colonel von Wurmb, and from which he allowed the collection of forage for the subsistence of the Cavalry and at the same time, as all civilian government had been superseded, he had to settle all arguments between the inhabitants.*[22]

In April of 1783, the war officially ended with the ratification of the Treaty of Paris. The Journal of the Hessen-Kassel Jäger Corps noted that on April 7, "the packet boat arrived in New York and brought the armistice and the Articles of Parliament."[23] It went on to observe that the armistice was proclaimed publicly in New York on the following day.[24]

The news still did not spell a complete end to the fighting, as Ewald reported, "the New Englanders often appear on Long Island since the peace, many atrocities are perpetrated on the inhabitants, who have lived there under English protection during the war."[25] In an attempt to stem these incursions, or as Ewald put it, "to drive out these evil guests," the Jäger Corps with a detachment of British infantry totaling seven hundred men were dispatched to the eastern end of the island.[26] There they served as a deterrent against the incursions of the local patriots.

Conditions did not improve following on the peace, as Ewald noted in September "Since the peace is concluded and everyone on both sides has free passage, robberies and murders are committed so frequently that one is compelled to ride on the open highway with bare saber or with drawn pistols as soon as night falls."[27] Ewald was describing a society inured to violence by eight years of bitter civil conflict. He went on to note,

"Indeed, one has reason to remain constantly in his quarters at night, because quarters at all places are robbed and looted."[28] This was not the sort of situation Ewald recognized or understood. The economic turmoil and damage to social convention brought about by eight years of civil war constituted something new to the Jäger captain and he sought for a means with which to categorize it. While there had certainly been depredations and destruction in Hessen-Kassel during the Seven Years' War, his experience in American encompassed something entirely different. The war in and around New York City seemed to undermine the very bonds of civilization.[29] Finally, he observed, "This is another kind of war to wage."[30]

Soon after recording these observations, Ewald witnessed the execution of two Loyalists who were charged with plundering and the murder of a rebel. They refused any council from the clergyman the state provided them, bluntly stating that "they would like to die in the belief that it was no sin at all to plunder and kill any rebel opposed to the King."[31] They went on to meet their execution calmly, even placing the nooses around one another's necks, pulling the hoods over their own eyes, and pushing off from the wagon on which they stood on their own. Watching these men meet their deaths in such resolute manner, Ewald observed, "Thus this civil war can change one's mind about mankind."[32] Ewald's intent in the preceding passage is difficult to determine. Was he praising these men for their resolution in meeting their destiny or was he criticizing their executioners for implementing the punishment? Were both views intertwined in his observation? This stands as one of the few occasions in Ewald's diary where his meaning remains obscure. Still, the execution did not long divert Ewald from his usual interests.

Ever the military professional, Ewald determined to take advantage of the end of hostilities and enhance his knowledge of the war. He decided to visit West Point, "Since this post, because of its natural position, is one of the most important that the Americans held during the war, I decided to travel there..."[33] He took along a Lieutenant von Gersheim as a companion. The journey was not easy for the two Hessians, the war was newly ended, and the wounds caused by the violence and brutality of the conflict remained fresh in the minds of many of the residents of the areas through which they traveled. These scars were clearly evident when Ewald and Gersheim stopped in Tarrytown to buy fodder for their horses. Tarrytown was in the area contested between the two sides during the war and had been possessed by both at different times.[34] Most of the inhabitants were Patriots. As a result, when the two Hessian officers arrived, they received a distinctly cool welcome. As Ewald described,

The first fellow I met in town, in front of the door of the tavern where I desired to stop for lunch, was one of the most fiery ringleaders, whom I had caught on a patrol and who had been put in chains and fetters. As soon as I recognized him, I asked him in quite friendly fashion how he felt, whereupon he replied indifferently with a look distorted by spite. I asked him if I could have something to eat and fodder for my horses for money. He answered with a short "Yes!" but his face brightened somewhat, since he expected to gain some money from me.[35]

However, the prospect of financial gain did not succeed in altering the disposition of all the inhabitants. The Jäger captain noted that as he dismounted and proceeded into the tavern, a number of residents began to assemble in the street, "At the mention of my name they whispered a 'God damn!' in each other's ears, whereby I noticed that they had not forgotten the punches in the ribs they had received from the Jäger during their imprisonment."[36] The atmosphere grew more tense as the captain ate his lunch, so he finished quickly and paid "seven piasters into the woman's hand for a poor meal..."[37] Ewald's payment without complaint or argument seemed to brighten some of the faces in the room. Still, he and his companion departed quickly and went on their way.

Ewald and Gersheim stopped for the night at an inn in Peekskill. Here they enjoyed a friendlier reception. In part, the welcome they received stemmed from the fact that they were not recognized. As a result, they were mistaken as French officers. For his part, Ewald assumed the mistaken identity, "and took great care not to show that I had ever been here before, and had burned the barracks and several magazines two miles away."[38] As he continued on his journey to West Point, Ewald recorded his observations of the terrain in the Hudson Highlands, noting their fine defensive qualities.[39]

The Polish engineer officer, Thaddeus Kosciuszko had laid out a defensive complex around the American camp at West Point. One of the main functions of the post was to guard a massive iron chain set across the Hudson River to prevent British ships from gaining access to the Highlands. In devising his defense, Kosciuszko planned and ordered constructed no less than sixteen enclosed positions and ten major battery sites in three concentric rings. Essentially, he had built a defense in depth around the American camp.[40] One recent historian concluded that the Pole's efforts created a "remarkable and typically American fortification."[41] Remarkable for its strength, yet distinctly American in its use of the exiting terrain to form the basis of the defensive network.

On their arrival at West Point, Ewald and Gersheim were met by General Alexander McDougall.[42] He offered them the hospitality of his house, even though they had clearly identified themselves of Hessian officers. "But since we could not accept this, out of courtesy, we asked him for a pass to cross the North River." McDougall not only honored their request, but "He accompanied us to the plantation where we were to descend, furnished us with a pass, ordered his boat, and himself accompanied us to the opposite shore."[43] McDougall further extended an invitation for the two men to join him at his table the following day.[44]

As soon as the two men arrived at West Point, they began to observe the layout of the defenses. At that time, General Henry Knox held command of the post at West Point. A Boston bookseller prior to the war, Knox actually possessed no military experience. All of his knowledge on military affairs up to 1775 derived from his reading of the books which passed through his shop.

Despite this, or perhaps due to it, Knox quickly demonstrated his skills and understanding of the artillery. He rose to become Washington's chief of that arm, a position which he held throughout the remainder of the war.[45]

Knox received his two visitors with great courtesy. Ewald describes him as "quite distinguished and venerable." He further noted how Knox "consented at once to our request to inspect the fortifications."[46] While it may seem odd that Knox would so readily consent to an inspection of one of the key American defenses to a recent enemy, the war was in fact over at this point. In addition, following the concept of military professionalism as it existed at the time, the officer class considered themselves, in many regards, to be a separate fraternity. At the same time, Ewald was not above the use of flattery, "Since I strengthened his conviction that it was a formidable and impregnable position, he …provided us with his escort, Captain Lillie."[47] Ewald further observed regarding Captain Lillie that the officer "probably was instructed to what extent he should show us the fortifications."[48] Ewald's description of the defenses was fairly compact and lacked detail, save for his observations concerning Fort Clinton. What seemed to impress him most was the artillery park, which consisted of some eighty pieces, most of which were captured from the British, and bore the inscription of where they were taken.[49]

Seeing these pieces, especially three that were cast in Philadelphia and supposedly were the extent of the American artillery at the beginning of the war prompted Ewald to recollect that in the campaign of 1776, the ragged Americans had been chased from one spot to the next by one of the finest armies ever sent out, but that the Crown forces "had been put to

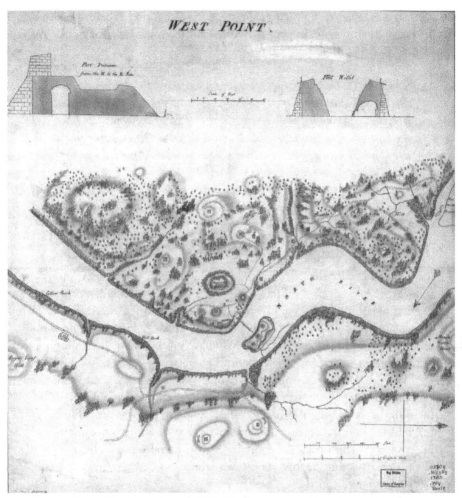

Figure 1: Map of West Point and vicinity, 1783. The area as it appeared when Ewald visited in after the war. Scale ca. 1:20,000. Source: Manuscript, pen-and-ink and watercolor. Oriented with north to the right. Has watermarks. Relief shown by shading. Shows fortifications. Includes profiles of "Fort Putnam" and "Fort Willit." Based on John Hinncks' West Point. 1783. LC Maps of North America, 1750-1789, 1208 Available also through the Library of Congress Web site as a raster image. Vault AACR2

such poor use that eight campaigns were lost, followed by the loss of thirteen provinces, which, in a word, had torn down the Crown of England from its loftiest peak."[50] Ewald blamed mismanagement of the military forces on the British side for their defeat. He later saw, but could not seem to grasp, an alternative answer.

After their tour, the Hessians were escorted to a diner with General Knox and his officers. By Ewald's report, the conversation over the meal seemed amicable enough. After the meal, Ewald and Gersheim were given the opportunity to inspect the American troops. Ewald was duly impressed by what he saw,

> *The men looked haggard and pallid, and were poorly dressed. Indeed, very many stood quite proudly under arms without shoes and stockings. Although I shuddered at the distress of these men, it filled me with awe for them, for I did not think there was an army in the world which could be maintained as cheaply as the American army.*[51]

The Hessian captain had another part of his answer, but he did not see it. It is interesting that Ewald chose to focus on the economy of the American troops. Since they did not require the supplies of other European forces in the field, they would be cheaper to maintain. It did not occur to him that the men he inspected were motivated by a goal beyond short-term material gain; that ideology played a significant role in their motivations as well.[52] Soon, the French Revolution, and its attendant conflicts would unleash these drives, only barely perceived in the American War of Independence, to a level hitherto not contemplated. His subsequent interactions with his former enemies may have given Ewald the beginnings of some new insights into the American character.

After inspecting part of the garrison at West Point, Ewald spent the evening with some American officers in a makeshift coffee house. Among the officers was Captain Lillie, his guide. The captain was probably keeping tabs on the movements and interactions of the Hessian captain and his companion in order to report back to General Knox. The war may have been over, but as long as foreign troops resided on American soil, suspicions would remain.

The men spent the evening discussing the issues of officer's pay and maintenance. They assured Ewald that they had five years of pay coming to them, in reference to the half-pay voted by Congress in late 1777.[53] Likewise, they told the Hessian captain how they had experienced extreme want during the war, and now hoped for just recompense. As the night wore on, they confided to their guest that "once the English army leaves our soil, we will try to get by force what they will not give us amicably." Thus, Ewald likely overheard some of the dying embers of what is known as the Newburg Conspiracy.

The Newburgh Conspiracy was a possible attempt by a group of Continental Army officers to launch a military coup against the Continental Congress aimed at securing their promised benefits from the body. In 1777, in order to staunch a hemorrhage of trained and experienced leaders from the army, the Congress agreed to provide these men with half-pay for life after the war. With the hostilities at an end, the body debated whether or not to renege on the plan.

Word of these discussion made its way to the Continental Army camp in Newburg, New York. On March 10, an anonymous letter circulated in the camp. The letter is often attributed to Horatio Gates via his aid, a Major John Armstrong. The letter essentially stated that Continental solders, disgruntled at their arrears in pay, should march on Congress and demand what was due them. Learning of the plot, George Washington assembled his officers five days later and gave an impassioned plea for them not to sacrifice the republic they had fought so hard to secure for their own, short-sighted ends. Through force of rhetoric, the commander-in-chief defused a potentially catastrophic situation. It seems, however, from the above remarks, that while Washington had resolved the crisis, not everyone was fully pleased with the outcome.

The following day, Ewald and his party toured several additional fortifications, including Forts Putnam and Clinton. Ewald noted their shape and location, but provided little additional information, likely indicating that to him there was nothing remarkable in the engineering of either post.[55] He did note, seemingly with some admiration, the chain that stretched across the Hudson to prevent shipping from passing up the river during the war.[56]

Analyzing the layout of the defenses, he observed that "Since the right bank of the river is perpendicularly steep and several hundred rods high at some places, the forts cannot be bombarded by warships, although they would have enough deep water."[57] He proposed an answer to this dilemma might be to use "mortar galliots brought to bear could do much damage to Fort Wyllys..." Even then, however, "they would not gain a foot of ground."[58] Clearly, out of all the American works at West Point, this impressed the Hessian captain as a strong defensive position.

After inspecting the defenses, Ewald returned across the river to General McDougall's residence for dinner. He noted during his passage that "The fortress appeared like a three-story amphitheater, and the many waterfalls tumbling down from the steep and rocky bank provided a majestic sight to the eye."[59] The captain thus disclosed not only an appreciation for military works, but the grandeur of nature as well. The preceding may belie some relief on Ewald's part of his normal professional attitude, now that the hostilities were ended. It may indicate that the falls impressed the captain significantly enough for him to comment on this occasion, when he passed over many other natural phenomena in silence.

After dining with the General and various members of his staff, as well as the general's wife, the two men retired for more private conversation. As Ewald described, "As soon as the ladies had withdrawn, and the glasses were more frequently filled, the general came closer to me." As is often the case in such situations, "Heart and mouth were unbuttoned, and I began to speak English very fluently."[60] Ewald noted how McDougall was respected even in the crown forces. Summing up their conversation, the Jäger captain paid a very uncommon tribute to an American, "In a word, I was so impressed by this man during this short acquaintance that I was very glad to have made it."[61] This fast friendship is not hard to explain. In McDougall, Ewald met a man who, like himself, had risen over various adversities and in facing them, become a military professional of sorts.

The party left from West Point about noon the following day and began their return journey to New York City. The return trip was generally uneventful, as the two men had learned by now that specie tended to serve as an antidote for lingering resentment from the war.

On their return to the city, Ewald and Gersheim became acquainted with a repositioning of the troops which occurred during their absence. The *Journal of the Jäger Corps* records that on May 29, "At the request of colonel von Wurmb, both the Jäger Corps and the Hessen-Hanauers marched today to York Island, and entered the barracks at McGowans' Pass..." The reason for the fact that since the announcement of the peace, a marked increase occurred in the number of desertions from the respective corps.[62] The answer from high command was simply to draw the troops in to keep them under greater observation. Likewise, it was hoped that soon the men would be embarked and headed for home. On June 2, "the embarkation lists for all the troops were published and all possible preparations made for leaving America."[63]

Ewald enjoyed the dubious distinction of being among the last of the German troops to leave New York. He described how on November 9, 1783, the Jäger Corps, as well as the grenadier battalion Lengerke, and the von Donop and Lossberg Regiments received orders to prepare for embarkation. Still, the actual move did not occur until the morning of the 21st. At that point, "The American General Knox and one thousand men took possession of York Island..." whereupon, the above-mentioned units, as well as the 80th Regiment abandoned the area.[64] As the two sides prepared to transfer control of the city, the Jäger Corps Journal noted on November 23, how "Everywhere in New York today, people have begun to show the American flags, which, however, are being torn down, and this is causing various small disturbances."[65] It further observed that

"A commission was established to make arrangements to receive General Washington in triumph, with all pomp and ceremony."[66]

As for the soldiers, once they removed from their positions, the troops immediately embarked on ships. This process took several days to complete. Still, by November 25,

> *On all corners one saw the flag of thirteen stripes flying, cannon salutes were fired, and all the bells rang. The shores were crowded with people who threw their hats in the air, screaming and boisterous with joy, and wished a pleasant voyage with white handkerchiefs. While on the ships, which lay at anchor with the troops, a deep stillness prevailed as if everyone were mourning the loss of the thirteen beautiful provinces.*[67]

That same day the flotilla, which Ewald placed at about sixty ships, set sail with a favorable wind.[68] The British and their allies were sailing out of New York City for the last time.

It took until January 15, 1784 for the ship bearing Ewald to reach Deal in the Downs off the British coast as numerous storms scattered the fleet during their passage.[69] The destinations for all the Hessian troops were Portsmouth and Chatham. Even this had to wait, however, as at Deal it was revealed that the transport tat carried Ewald and his Jäger could not continue further due to damage sustained in the passage. While they waited for a new ship to complete return their journey, Ewald and the two Jäger companies were assigned quarters at Sheerness on the west coast of England.

It was not until April 4, 1784, that the Jägers Corps once again embarked for Germany.[70] Thus, even the Hessian captain's return transformed into an odyssey of sorts. Unfortunately, Ewald did not write down any of his impressions of England during his brief stint in the country. His observations of his allies' homeland would certainly make for interesting reading. Perhaps he found nothing worthy of comment, or his stay there was so short that he really did not have time to engage in the sort of explorations that were so common to him while in North America. This latter explanation seems plausible since Ewald resided in England for roughly two and one-half months and it remains unclear when he and his men were taken off the transports. It is unclear, as well, when the new transport that would bear them the remainder of the way back to the continent arrived. All of his time, therefore, could have been occupied by the mundane jobs of unloading one ship, marching to and settling into barracks, and then loading troops and equipment on a new one.

In any case, the last leg of their return journey was underway by in early April. By 16 May 1784, the Jäger arrived at Münden, some two miles from Kassel. Two days later, the unit entered Kassel, where Ewald reported, with obvious distaste, "The Jäger Corps was reduced at once, despite its faithful and well-performed service."[71]

Interestingly, the *Journal of the Hesse-Kassel Jäger Corps* records the event in the following manner,

> *May 17-The Jager Corps arrived in Kassel, passed in review along with the Grenadier Battalion Linsinger, and a portion of the Donop Regiment, at His Serene Highness' riding school, and were then mustered during the afternoon.*[72]

There are some obvious reasons for the difference in depictions between the two accounts. As the official record, the Journal of the Corps was a document of the government, and certainly would not be critical of the conduct of the Landgraf. For his part, Ewald hoped for some reward for his long years of loyal service to his monarch. When this was not forthcoming, he expressed his bitterness in the pages of his then-private diary.

Several reasons existed for this seemingly abrupt dismissal. Economy definitely stood in the forefront. Despite the infusion of capital from the subsidy contract with Great Britain, the state still had not recovered from the depredations of the Seven Years' War. As for the final disposition of the Jäger Corps, the unit's journal records that "The entire Jäger Corps however, was reassigned, part in regiments, and those who wished to return to their profession as hunters, received half pay, until they could obtain employment as such."[74] Again, the description of the units return in the official record, and what may actually have occurred at the riding school could be very different indeed.

No doubt more galling to Ewald stood the fact that "His serene Highness the Landgraf and his entire suite did not bestow a single special, gracious glance on any officer."[75] To a large extent this coolness on the part of the Landgraf and his retinue likely stemmed from the change in political climate in Europe concerning the soldier-trade.

The Europe Ewald returned to was a very different one from the one he left to fight in America some eight years before. One of the changes that would effect the Jäger captain personally lay in the change in attitudes concerning the hiring of troops through subsidy treaties. As H.D. Schmidt observed, their deployment in America stood as the first time that the use of subsidy troops became a political issue within the German States themselves. He further notes that a major figure in the opposition was Frederick II (the Great) of Prussia. In part, Frederick's opposition derived from his rivalry with the other north German state of Hanover. Both coveted the leadership of the north German states, and therefore took opposing sides on many political issues in order to garner the support of the smaller states. Hanover, connected to Great Britain personally through their royal house, supported the use of mercenaries, while Prussia opposed. The debate manifested in numerous ways, including articles in the journal *Briefwechsel,* a play, and numerous pamphlets justifying the policy of the Landgraf of Hessen-Kassel. Politically, then, the subsidy troops had become a contested issue, and the new Landgraf sought to distance himself from it.[76] One additional factor that altered popular perceptions of the subsidy troops encompassed their deployment far from home, which decreased the likelihood of their ever being seen in Europe again.[77]

Not only did the political climate differ, economically, Hessen-Kassel remained poor. Once a major textile center, Hessen-Kassel never recovered from the depredations of the Thirty Years' War, let alone the more recent upheavals of the Seven Years' War. Hilly and with generally infertile soil to begin with, the country's dense population, given as about four hundred thousand in 1781, amounted to a concentration of about one hundred twenty people per square mile. Such a heavy concentration of people only exacerbated the economic problems. As noted by Charles Ingrao, "Contemporary travelers passing through Hessen-Kassel usually commented on the wretchedness of its provincial towns and cities."[79]

The subsidy treaty with Great Britain had not achieved the desired effect of helping the country to rebuild for the damage sustained in the Seven Years' War. As previously noted, these treaties had been popular in Europe in the earlier years of the century. They were still used, but the political view of them changed significantly. In large part, this transformation came as a direct result of Britain's employment of mercenaries in North America. Through no fault of their own, Ewald and his Jäger felt the brunt of changed political climate.

CHAPTER 12

RETURN TO THE OLD WORLD
AND OLD BARRIERS

Back in Hessen-Kassel, Captain Ewald now possessed a wealth of military experience to draw upon. At the same time, he faced the very real prospect of his career coming to a dead stop, or even losing his post entirely for reasons discussed in the previous chapter. In addition, the nobility of Ancien Regime Europe considered the officer corps of the armies as their own preserve.[1] Ewald's lack of a noble lineage placed him in precarious straits, as when conflicts ended, states tended to reduce their militaries as a means of reducing costs.

His service record in North America helped to preserve a place for him in the peacetime establishment. Since his pen had previously helped to secure his notice and promotion by the Landgraf, he set to work once again, distilling his experiences from the conflict in North America. His experiences spawned a number of works, the most significant of which was his *Belehrunger uber den Kreig, besonders uber den kleinen Krieg, durch Beispiele grosser Helden und kluger und tapferer Manner,* first published Schleswig in 1798. Later, this work was translated at a *Treatise on Partisan Warfare.* The translators note that Ewald noted four characteristics which set the fighting he witnessed in North America apart from his previous military experience. These were: "1) aimed fire: 2) the use of surprise attacks and ambushes: 3) speed, as the rebels perfected the use of hit and run tactics; and 4) improvisation and deception."[2] Clearly, the Jäger captain witnessed ample examples of all of these tactics during his service in North America. Likewise, Ewald's categorization of the American War of Independence makes it readily apparent that he grasped the essentials at work. The conflict he participated in possessed fundamentally different qualities than those previous seen in Europe. While the tactics he witnessed were quite familiar to Ewald from various experiences over his long career, strategically, it was a new kind of warfare.

This new form of war embraced the political dimension and brought the common people into the conflict as never before. Still, the Jäger captain seemed to understand that even within this new type of conflict, certain fundamentals of human struggle still applied.

At the same time, much of the fighting occurred within a tactical scenario to which he and his men were especially well suited. Throughout the body of his *Treatise*, Ewald drew upon real examples from his service in the American war to illustrate key points or support assertions.

Routinely in this *Treatise*, Ewald stressed the importance of maintaining a cadre of experienced light infantry soldiers and officers in peacetime. In the preface, for example, he notes,

> *One sees with surprise, once a war breaks out, how many officers try to serve with the light troops. However, they do not consider how much skill is demanded from an officer who wants to do his part with the light troops.*[3]

This was more than mere bravado on Ewald's part. Nor was it merely an attempt to insure a place for himself in the military establishment. As always, he included practical reasons for his claim, "In this part of the war an officer is often left to himself, has to do on a small scale what a general does on a large scale."[4] On this point, Ewald's *Treatise* echoes the works of other commanders of light troops who participated in the war. John Graves Simcoe of the Queens Rangers wrote in the beginning of his history of the unit's efforts that

> *The Command of a light corps, or, as it is termed, the service of a partisan, is generally esteemed the best mode of instruction for those who aim at higher stations; as it gives an opportunity of exemplifying professional acquisitions, fixes the habit of self-dependence for resources, and obliges to that prompt decisions which in the common rotation of duty subordinate officers can seldom exhibit, yet without which none can be qualified for any trust of importance.*[5]

In comparing these two accounts, it is clear that Ewald was once again notable for his brevity. At the same time, it is fair to ask if others had reached the same conclusion, what new ideas did Ewald have to offer? The Jäger captain was aware that he was not contributing anything new to the experience leader of light troops. Later on the same page he reflected,

Even though I know I am not writing anything new, I nevertheless believe that my comrades will not be displeased if I briefly present to them those rules which the leader of a light corps or a detachment, composed of cavalry and infantry, has to consider during the major events of a campaign. I have collected those rules during twenty-four years of service, and not without effort and reflection.[6]

Ewald's purpose, then, was to distill the main concepts of partisan warfare as he had learned them over the course of his career. His book would then serve as a means of training young officers who sought service leading light units. It would therefore fill an important gap in the literature, as there was little that dealt specifically with the command of light forces, and those works that did exist were growing dated by this point.[7]

The first topic Ewald addresses, logically enough, is the recruiting of a light corps. He begins by condemning the contemporary practice of providing an officer with a commission to raise a light unit at the outset of a conflict, observing that it rarely leads to the creation of a very effective body of troops. Building on this point, Ewald asserts, "The necessity of light troops in war is completely understood; one knows that they are necessary for the safety of the armies, that an army without them cannot survive against an army which is well equipped with light troops..."[8] In supporting this contention, Ewald proceeded to list a number of partisan commanders from the Seven Years' War, contending that "Every army officer who shows interest in this part of the war, and who has prepared himself through the reading of good books for it, should be allowed to serve with light corps during a war."[9] Here Ewald is returning once again to a familiar grievance, the fact that the officer corps of European armies of this time stood as the preserve of the nobility, and that officer were appointed to commands due to their social standing and their esteem in the mind of the monarch rather than their professional ability or aptitude. It should come as no surprise that the Jäger captain would decry such practices. This prejudice had stymied Ewald's own career advancement in the past and seemed to be operating against him once again.

Moving on, Ewald described some of the physical characteristics that were necessary for good light troops.

When my most gracious prince and lord entrusted me with one of the two Jäger companies which were designated for America, I followed the custom of looking for experienced soldiers. But how quickly did I become conscious of my mistake in the first campaign. The young people of sixteen to eighteen years of age were those who best withstood the climate and the strain, while the older ones, who had already been worn out during the previous campaigns had to report to the hospital.[10]

In the above, Ewald provides some idea of the physical demands inherent in the duties of light troops. Beyond the challenges of the campaign, the Jäger captain observed another reason for selecting younger men to fill out his corps: "In addition the young people, since they did not yet know the dangers of war, were the ones who attacked best, and upon whom one could rely in critical circumstances."[11] Thus Ewald counted youthful bravado and the desire to make one's reputation as important qualities in a successful leader of partisans. These qualities, however, only possessed value if they were tempered with discipline, both of the officer over himself, and the leaders over their soldiers.

Like many of his contemporaries, Ewald stressed the importance of stern discipline, especially for light troops, as they often operated away from the main army. This is especially true of soldiers who harmed civilians, "Above all one cannot deal harshly enough with those villains who mercilessly torment the peasants who are innocent of the war." For these men, he suggested "The best thing to do is to chase such rabble away, since those who once stooped to plundering can never be trusted again, and they spoil the good soldiers as well."[12] Clearly, Ewald saw these soldiers as a danger to the entire unit, though he does not expand upon his reasons. Still, his experiences in the North America, in the environs of New York City, and especially in the Virginia campaign clearly left their imprint on his position on the issue of plunder. Consider Ewald's reaction when he returned to his men in Virginia after being wounded only to see that each a freed slave as servant, and that he quickly drove these people from the unit.[13]

Considering the importance of discipline in light troops, Ewald further observed "Do not believe that you can gain the love of a soldier through an unpermissable kindness and indulgence at the expense of the poor peasant and by a policy contrary to nature."[14] In making his case, Ewald cites the partisan author Monsieur de La Croix, and provides examples gleaned from the Seven Years' War. Here again, as in his first work, Ewald supported his ideas by a combination of materials from recognized authorities, as well as his own experiences. In this context, it seems odd that he did not include any direct references to his experiences in America. It may be that for many of his potential readers, these events were too far removed to serve as useful illustrations.

While Ewald was certainly a supporter of maintaining the discipline of the troops in relation to the civilian population, he was by no means an advocate of harsh discipline for its own sake. In fact, he advised that in their dealings with private soldiers officers would be best served if they followed the dictum "Everything that you can bestow upon him legally you have to grant him, especially toward your soldiers you have to show yourself to be unselfish."[15] At the same time, Ewald recognized the importance of the soldier's attitude, concluding "Yet most important one must not let the grumbling of the soldier go unpunished, no matter how hard the inconveniences of the war may be."[16]

Ewald next analyzed the strength of his proposed light corps, as well as the arms that it should carry. He began the section by noting, "It is most important that such a corps be composed of cavalry and infantry since the strength of these arms consists in the mutual support of one through the other."[17] In this manner, he seems to support the legion concept which was then gaining in popularity in Europe. Certainly, he had recently witnessed various forms of this unit in action in North America.[18]

Following his introduction, Ewald established the size of his ideal corps, which he set at one thousand at minimum. The reason being that "if it is weaker he who is entrusted with such a corps will not be able to perform any great and brilliant enterprises."[19] He recognized at the outset that at least a third of the entire force were to be cavalry. The first group he dealt with in depth however, were his beloved Jäger. Ewald's ideal light infantry corps was to possess two corps of these troops, with each company totaling 171 officers and men. The most important qualities for these troops were that try were "hunters by trade, good shots, and young people." In addition, he specified that their weapons were to consist of "a rifle, a short hunting knife, and a good ammunition pouch with a metal lining which holds forty rounds."[20]

This may seem a small quantity of ammunition, especially if measured by modern standards, but it is important to recall that the rifles these troops were issued could, under ideal circumstances, fire roughly one shot per minute. Thus, forty rounds provided them with enough ammunition for about an hours' worth of combat. When it came to partisan operations, a clash of that duration stood as the exception rather than the rule. Jäger specialized at the quick raid and the ambush, as did most light troops.

Finally, Ewald established the parameters for his light cavalry. These were to consist of 173 officers and men each in two companies. He wanted them armed and mounted as light hussars. Cavalry such as these had essentially reintroduced light troops to Western Europe at the opening of the War of the Austrian Succession.[21]

In his third chapter, Ewald addressed the training of his light troops. He paid particular attention to the skills incumbent upon the infantry and the Jäger as these were the types of troops with which he possessed the most familiarity. With regards to the Jäger, he noted that they "have to be well trained to fight dispersed, since in most cases they will cover the front and flanks."[22] In this chapter, as well, he addressed the issue of the long re-loading time for Jäger rifles. His answer was "Since the loading of the rifles goes slowly, the Jäger in particular must be well taught that always one of two, or two of four, have loaded guns, so that they can support those who have fired already."[23] In addition, he stressed the use of aimed fire both for the Jäger and for the men of the regular infantry in his light corps.[24] As noted above, the emphasis on aimed fire constituted an innovation that Ewald had picked up while fighting in North America.

With regards to giving aimed fired, Ewald noted how this could be done during a retreat in particular.

> *If this maneuver has to be performed during a retreat, one of the two, two of the four, or three of the six, retreat 50 to 100 paces after they have given fire, while the others save their fire until the retreated party has reloaded. This is the way how to retreat alternately.*[24]

Essentially, Ewald advocated a retreat in echelon with separate sections giving fire in succession. Not only did he advocate for aimed fire among his infantry, Ewald wanted a proportion of his cavalry armed with rifles as well. In addition, he asserted that "The riflemen of each squadron need to be taught to give good and well-aimed fire from horseback." He further indicated that "Because of this they have to be given the calmest horses."[26] It would not do for the horse to bolt when its own rider discharged their weapon.

Having outlined how the corps he proposed should be raised, led and trained, Ewald turned, in his fourth chapter, to the conduct of such a force while on campaign. Ewald began by addressing some of the many contingencies the commander of such a detachment may face while on the march. Next, he emphasized that "Only general rules can be given for a multitude of reasons for the march of such a corps and for the number of incidents which may happen at any moment."[27]

However, Ewald was quick to point out, there were rewards for this form of service:

An officer who has been entrusted with the leadership of such a corps or detachment can gain fame and honor through such undertakings if they are well planned and executed with the necessary skill. On the other hand he can also sacrifice his honor and his whole corps if he loses sight of the necessary caution.[28]

Thus, along with the potential for significant reward, there existed the risk of great dishonor. The answer, implicit throughout his work, as with his earlier *Thoughts*, was balanced assessment of risks and opportunities, what modern militaries refer to as risk management.

The role of the light troops, as Ewald saw it was to conduct raids on the enemy. One factor Ewald singled out for attention encompassed the need for reliable guides while conducting a raid. To some extent, his concern on this point likely derived from his experiences in America, especially the in the south, where many of his guides were slaves, and substantial communications difficulties arose.[29] Likewise, while describing the conduct of the march on a raid, he returned to a theme addressed at the outset of the work, the treatment of civilians, "On such marches one also has to show humanitarian behavior toward all peasants." At this point, however, his observations derived more from practical concerns, "If you do that you will find in all countries people who will help you and you will not be betrayed easily."[30]

In addition, Ewald discusses how to overcome various natural and manmade obstacles while on the march. Here, his close observation of terrain in North America paid handsome dividends. For instance, he contended that "If one encounters a gorge or a bridge which has to be crossed, the detachment of *Jäger* on foot which follows the advance guard deploys on our side, occupies in the case of the gorge the surrounding heights or in the case of the bridge divides into two parts and remains on either side of it."[31]

Ewald discussed intelligence gathering as well. Here again, his experiences in America were clearly evident when he wrote,

Through spies, which one can always find when one is not stingy, one will try to collect sound information concerning the strength of the enemy and also whether some of his detachment should linger in the vicinity which could quickly come to the aid of the one found, and on the basis of this information the decision concerning attack or retreat will be made.[32]

For the attack, Ewald recommended a spirited advance, relying on the bayonet.[33] Interesting here is the manner in which Ewald utilizes the device of a scenario, which he then follows through in order to describe his approach in detail,

> *If the decision is made for an attack, one must not ponder long but immediately cross the bridge with the fusiliers and attack the enemy with the bayonet. At the same time the Jäger deploy along the river on either side of the bridge to support the attack of the infantry and to bring the enemy to disarray with well-aimed fire. The cavalry follows the infantry at a distance of 300 paces and tries to beat up the enemy. If the enemy should have more infantry than the cavalry and thus be superior, one can let half of the cavalry, especially the riflemen, dismount in order to support with them the attack of the infantry.[34]*

Here is an extended plan for an assault, with some possible variables addressed as well. While Ewald did not deal with all of the potentialities that could occur, he provided a firm basis for the reader to grasp his intent. By the same token, Ewald extended his scenario to cover some of the alternatives for the attacking commander should the enemy be forced to retreat.[35]

In discussing the march, Ewald advised that it was better to camp under cover than to take up quarters in any habitations. In doing so, the location and numbers of the corps could be kept secret more effectively. Ewald dealt with the issue of rations as well. He advocated for the use of zwieback for the troops as opposed to bread, citing the example of his experience in America: "During the American war we received zwieback for years instead of bread, and when our soldiers finally got used to it they preferred it to bread, because they realized themselves that if they carried zwieback with them they would rarely ever lack bread."[36]

When going over to the attack, especially on a plain, Ewald advocated for a system which utilized each of the formations in his corps to the greatest effect. While the cavalry and infantry attacked with the sabre and bayonet, the Jäger were to keep the enemy troops under constant aimed fire.[37] Following up on this idea, Ewald noted that the best time to attack an enemy detachment was when they had just taken a post, for, as he described "After a long march men and horses are tired, a part of them is usually sent out for food and forage, everyone tries to make it as comfortable as possible for himself."[38] In sum, this presented an opportunity to attack the foe when he was least vigilant.

In addition, Ewald showed himself a staunch advocate of ambushes,

Sometimes it happens during a march that one finds out through good and trustworthy scouts that a hostile detachment is approaching and at a certain point has to pass a defile or a long dam. If one is free to do as one pleases and is not bound by any orders. One has to approach the area under as much cover as possible, and if the enemy should lack the necessary precaution in passing the ravine, gorge or dam, as many as are convenient are allowed to pass and then they are gallantly attacked.[39]

In the above, Ewald set out a perfectly staged and executed ambush. Further, he noted that assets gained with such a daring stroke. One of these advantages lay in the force multiplier of surprise, "Under such circumstances the enemy may be twice or more superior in number, yet he is nevertheless lost since those who are beaten throw themselves upon those who are behind them and carry everything with them into disarray."[40]

Ewald further noted that in some cases, the best troops to use in such a situation were cavalry "because of the speed with which the raid has to be made."[41] In support of this point, Ewald related a raid on Tarrytown, conducted by Colonels von Wurmb, Simcoe and Emmerich, in which they used only their mounted troops, and left the Jäger behind. In addition, Ewald warned it was best to have more than one return route for the troops when they go on a raid so that they are less likely to be cut off on their return march. In support of this idea he provided the example of Colonel von Wintzgerode and the Hessian Feldjäger Corps in the Seven Years War.[42] Thus, in both cases he supported his notions with references to past campaigns, some of which he possessed first-hand experience. The preceding constitutes an important facet of Ewald's writings on the subject of light infantry. His book was not one of theory or ideals as many of the other highly regarded works of the period were. In his case, all the knowledge disseminated was gained in the school of war itself, a school which can be a most unforgiving teacher.

The fifth chapter of Ewald's treatise examines the manner in which an outpost should be selected for a detachment as well as the defense of a post once it is established. The selection and defense of posts stood as a topic with which the author held a great deal of experience. It should be recalled that such actions figured prominently in his first book as well.[43] Since then, Ewald had had numerous opportunities to refine the ideas he earlier stated in practice in America. Concerning those ideas, the author states, "The ultimate purpose for occupying a post consists in observing an enemy facing you or who is roaming the area and in watching all his undertakings so that he cannot approach or retreat without your knowledge."[44] Ewald was most concerned with keeping the enemy under observation. Thus, maintaining contact with the opposing forces was a key factor in the way he selected his posts.

Concerning the selection of a post, he urged on his readers the importance of information gained from enemy deserters and prisoners. Here he alluded to various times in America when officers discounted intelligence, with damaging results. Here Ewald refrained from providing further details, stating, "I am determined not to insult anyone, otherwise I could list various examples where this negligence and laxity have cost the Crown of England the best posts and whole corps during the American War."[45] Certainly, his own experiences before the battle of Germantown could be cited as a supporting example.[46] Likewise, there would be the surprise at Trenton, though Ewald was not directly engaged in that action.

The best way to guard against such an eventuality, according to Ewald, was to maintain one's vigilance. He recommends,

> *Patrols have to be constantly sent in the direction of the enemy so that its approach is learned of in time; especially at night they have to be continually on the road and always overlap. At night and during the daytime too, if the terrain is divided, small ambushes of one non-commissioned officer and four to six men can be laid at a certain distance before the outpost according to one's own decision.*[47]

Continuing in this line, Ewald asserts that "During the daytime or when the moon is bright the Jäger on foot can be used for this and they can make prisoners of small parties of the enemy."[48] In a rare nod of approbation to his former foes, Ewald even observed how "The Americans are very skillful in placing such small ambushes for their own safety in front of their outposts, which has cost many an Englishman or German his life or freedom."[49]

Clearly from the preceding, most of the activity between outposts occurred at night. As a result, the day stood as the time of rest. Again, Ewald provides his wisdom on how to handle the troops in an outpost, "During the daytime the corps is allowed to enjoy some rest as much as that is possible." Still security and safety remain paramount, thus "one has to forbid the officers as well as the privates to wander even one step away from their companies."[50] In supporting his caution on this point, Ewald again drew on personal experiences from the fighting in America.

Further, he maintained that it was best to place the outpost as close to the enemy as possible, observing "A soldier who can see the enemy will be twice as much on his guard and does everything willingly, and if the enemy be careless at any given moment, one can quickly deal him a blow."[51] Concern with security pervades Ewald's discussion on outpost duty. It is evident in his justification for taking up a post close to the enemy as well as in his instructions for what to do when occupying a post at night. In this case, he directed that "If one reaches his post during the nighttime one deploys in a little distance, remains under arms, and waits for daybreak."[52] He further recommended that patrols of infantry be sent out both to gain a knowledge of the local terrain, and to search for suitable billets for the men.[53]

Caution constituted an element of primary importance for Ewald when taking part in this sort of duty. He admonished his readers, "One must also remember different places in the rear of one's posts where one can retreat to in case a superior enemy should attack and force us to retreat."[54] Going even further, the Jäger captain enjoined his readers to remember "No matter how far away the enemy may be, one must never relax in vigilance and precaution, something that frequently happens on fortified posts and winter quarters."[55] In support of the preceding point, he cites the examples of the French during the Hanoverian campaign of the Seven Years' War who "had to pay dearly for their indolence."[56] The same principles set out above became even more pointed when it came to seeking shelter during inclement weather. Likewise, Ewald emphasized the importance of alarm posts when operating near a town or village.[57]

When it comes to interpreting the actions of the enemy, Ewald's years of experience are clearly in evidence. For instance, he declares "It does not mean much if the enemy should appear during the daytime, since in this case one can survey the strength and deployment of the enemy." His assessment, logical as it appears, also stands as the sort of view that can only be reached having taken part in numerous campaigns.

From how to deploy the troops under the officers' command when occupying a post, Ewald turns to the defense of the post from attack,

> *If the enemy is beaten back, a detachment of cavalry will be sent after it to tease him on his retreat, to capture stragglers, and to follow the enemy, however slowly and carefully, until it is known whether he has really retreated and where to, so that a correct report can be given to the general.*[59]

The preceding stands as a fine example of Ewald's approach to leadership in general. He advises aggression, but within limits. Pursue the foe on their retreat, but maintain some level of vigilance and caution, in case the apparent withdraw is in fact a ruse to lure one's troops into an ambush. In addition, he maintains focused on advantages to be gained by a pursuit, prisoners who can provide intelligence on the strength and attitude of the enemy force, as well as general information on their numbers and where-abouts. Glory, for Ewald, seemed more something derived from the effi-cient performance of one's duty than from taking wildly dangerous risks. It seems that the commander of a detachment should always be bold, in Ewald's estimation, but should temper their boldness by considering the possible moves of the enemy. In short, plan boldly, but never underesti-mate your opponent's capacity to do the same.

Certainly, he touched on this theme when summing up his discussion of the command of troops on detached service,

> *In general, an officer who is on charge of such a post will constantly have to be active and work on how to ensure his safety from all at-tacks of the enemy and he will be able to bring to naught even the best plans of the enemy. An officer who is concerned about his honor will do everything not to experience the shame of having been raided. Such an officer does not deserve any compassion and only a woman will feel sorry for him.* [60]

Ewald supports the preceding with a long quote from the ancient Roman Vegetius to the effect that the general who is defeated in battle may attribute his loss to chance, whereas one who allows himself to be surprised by the enemy has no excuse for it as he could have saved himself through taking the various measures discussed in the chapter.

The sixth chapter addresses how to occupy and defend a fortified town. It echoes many of the points of the preceding chapter, with only minor additions. For instance, Ewald notes that on taking the town, the commander should make a thorough inspection of the town's defenses, both inside and out, in the company of the leading officials. [61] The concern over civil-military relations, already present in the work, returns once again, when he directs his readers, "If you are in enemy country you also have to confiscate the guns and ammunition from the inhabitants, which however can be secured in a safe place, so that everyone will get his property back." [62] Here the treatment of the civilian inhabitants mixes with the concern for security, Ewald further addresses security when occupying such a location, stating "The best means to defend oneself against raids and to discover the arrival of the enemy in time is to maintain, during the night, scouts and small parties on foot and mounted in the field at about one hour's distance from the town, who continually patrol all the roads and paths in the whole area, and who do not return until broad daylight."[63] He further enjoins that if a patrol is lost, or overdue for reporting in, another has to be dispatched in order to determine the fate of the first. Moreover, the second patrol must practice even more vigilance in order to avoid falling into the same difficulties as the first. Finally, Ewald observes that "if small parties or the dispatched patrols should meet the enemy at night, they have to retreat to the town with lots of firing so that one can hear in time that the enemy is coming."[64] Their action serving, in turn to alert the garrison in the town so that it can prepare for the approaching attack.

As in previous chapters, Ewald includes suggestions that seem clearly derived from his own military experience. For instance, he advised "During market days and important holidays the men have to stand to their arms, and it is best if the former are prohibited altogether." He further recommended, "During the latter the inhabitants have to be ordered by the magistrate of the town to keep things very quiet."[65] Implicit in his reasoning here is the idea that the noise of the markets day or the holiday celebrations could serve to distract the garrison and thus aid an enemy surprise attack.

Ewald even offered counsel concerning the weather, "If it should be the season of thick fogs, the gates must not be opened until they have completely dispersed."[66] The last point was offered so that an enemy could not use to the cover of the fog to gain entrance into the town.

Summing up his guidance on the defense of occupied towns, Ewald stated,

> *If these rules are obeyed one hardly runs the risk of having the enemy at one's throat unexpectedly. However, if he appears one has to consult one's orders, and if those specify that the post be defended as long as possible or until help arrives, then one has to be firmly determined to rather die with honor than to grow old covered with shame, because the desire for true honor diminishes the love of life.*[67]

Ewald then proceeds to offer historical examples both from the Seven Years' War and the American War of Independence to support his observations. Returning to his notions of honor, Ewald enjoined his readers, "Let us prefer death to a disgraceful captivity, because here is the place to die honorably for one's king."[68]

Next, Ewald turned to "Rules to be Observed in Reconnaissance." Reconnaissance constituted a major part of the work of light troops and comprised an important chapter of his work. He describes three objectives for the officer sent on reconnaissance duty, he "either is supposed to reconnoiter the approaches to the enemy camp, or the position and strength of the enemy, or to protect a general officer in the vicinity."[69] In all the preceding cases, Ewald advises caution, and that the officer gain as much information concerning the terrain he will be operating in prior to his mission. When on the actual reconnaissance, "The most important point is not to approach the enemy with the whole detachment, which can cause the whole enterprise to fail..."[70] There are two reasons for this prediction. If the entire force moves forward, the enemy can ascertain its strength and intentions, and react accordingly. Since he will most likely possess superior numbers, the patrol will be placed on the defensive, and must make a fighting retreat, difficult proposition. On the other hand, Ewald observes, "if you have divided your detachment into two or three groups and made your disposition *en echelon* formation, you can easily retreat with that part with which you approach the enemy, since you still have a reserve force."[71] He advises that the force not waste time in enemy controlled territory, "Once you have seen what you want to see and as soon as the enemy approaches, you retreat with the greatest order."[72] This is done because, "Once the enemy finds out that you still have troops in reserve, and since he cannot know how strong you are, he will let you go in peace and only pursue you from a distance."[73] Again, Ewald reinforces his own observations with supporting historical examples. This stands as one of the shortest chapters in his treatise, as well as one of the most practical and to the point. Likely, this was due to the fact that he had enjoyed so much experience in this sort of activity throughout his career to this time. As a result, he was able to reduce his advice to the bare essentials.

In the following chapter Ewald discusses raids. It is clear that for him, these stand as one of the most important actions for a light corps: "Raids are among those actions of war which, if successful, will dishearten the enemy, cause him lots of trouble, and gradually wear him down."[74] Interestingly, the preceding passage demonstrates the manner in which Ewald connects raids to their morale effect as well as the material damage they can cause. At the same time, he notes that for the attacking side, "They also demand lots of cleverness and speed in their execution though, great prudence and knowledge of the country and a safe retreat, in a word, a thorough acquaintance with war."[75]

As he turned to practical advice on the conduct of raids, Ewald noted that "The best time for their execution is the night, since then the enemy can neither observe our movements nor our strength."[76] Likewise, it is much easier to throw an opponent off balance. He also comments on the fear engendered by a night attack.

A key factor in the successful execution of raids for Ewald are good scouts and guides. This is so because they "can lead you to the enemy via circuitous routes so that you can attack from more than one direction."[77]

Deception stood as a major factor in the conduct of successful raids as well. Ewald advised, "If you are not far away from an enemy post you can also alarm it daily, by which you can lull him into a false sense of security, and then attack him unexpectedly, which is usually most successful around noontime."[78] Ewald does not specify why noon is the best time for such action. It could be that the early morning, when twilight and fog could obscure an enemy advance had passed. Soldiers would therefore be less vigilant. Likewise, the preparations for the midday meal would likely distract many of the troops. When discussing raids, Ewald does not immediately support his ideas with historical examples.

Interesting in this regard is the manner in which Ewald instead develops a hypothetical situation. In this particular case, a river crossing,

> *If you have to cross a pass or a river in order to carry out such an attack, and if you are forced to return via the same wyt, you occupy it with a party of infantry until your return. Let us suppose you want to attack the enemy in Oberkaufungen or Helsa from Zwergen, and you cross the Fulda River near the new mill. In this case, in order to secure the retreat of your cavalry, you have to occupy the new mill and the adjacent houses with infantry, from where you can easily cover the retreat of the cavalry through small arms fire, especially rifles fire.*[79]

In this instance, Ewald drew on regions that were familiar to his intended readers, a site in central Europe, in order to reify his example. Not only that, but he followed up with a historical example. In this case, he picked an obscure, but highly illustrative example from the Seven Years' War in which a Brunswickian Major von Speth crossed the Weser with a party of 200 mounted jägers on the day following the battle of Wilhelmsthal, fought on 24 June 1762. In full view of a French corps camped nearby, they raided the escort of a Saxon hospital, captured some 150 prisoners, and sizeable amounts of supplies, and then returned across the river to safety.[80]

Ewald further stated that successful raids by infantry against cavalry could be carried out at night, even if the cavalry force was numerically superior. At the same time, he noted that the successful conduct of such operations required "especially good spies and scouts who inform you of everything and who can lead you through the most covered terrain."[81] Once again, Ewald supplements his observations with historical examples, many of which were drawn from the American War of Independence. Not all of these were actions in which the Jäger captain took part, which demonstrates that he had avidly kept up with reports of the fighting in other theaters. Of particular interest in this regard is his use of the example of a French raid against the English occupied island of St. Eustatius.[82]

When launching raids, Ewald recommended that all precautions be taken to preserve the secrecy of men on the march. Likewise, he enjoined that the men's weapons should remain unloaded, "In such cases you also have to completely prohibit all firing to your men and attack with an unloaded gun." He explained, "the less noise you make the more you can check the order and the soldiers will not get too agitated."[83] The first supporting example Ewald turned to on this point was that of British General Grey's raid against General Anthony Wayne's Continentals at Paoli during the 1777 campaign.[84] From the Crown perspective, Grey's attack constituted a well conducted, and extremely successful assault. In part because it took advantage of the opponent's lack of vigilance.

For more extended raids, Ewald recommended

In order to carry out the raid you divide your corps into groups of fifty or sixty men. They set out in all directions from the town that serves as your base. These small groups are given an assembly point which is not far away from the enemy post which is to be attacked. Concurrently you spread the rumor that each of these small parties to levy forage and food. Each of these small parties, however, have to be accompanied by an officer who can be secretly let in on the plan.[85]

Ewald explains his reasoning in sending out the raiding party in detachments, noting that it causes confusion in the enemy camp makes them think that the attacker has no great purpose in mind in launching the assault. It could further be stated that sending out numerous small detachments also compounds the lack of a clear sense of your moves to the enemy if they all proceed along different routes to the rendezvous, this would serve to keep them in the dark as to your true intentions. His advocacy of the use of deception at the end of the paragraph would make the Chinese military thinker Sun Tzu proud as the latter once declared, "All warfare is based on deception."[86]

While it is clear that this section, perhaps to a greater degree than others, owes its thinking to Ewald's extensive experience with irregular war, he does not claim all the credit for himself. As he is closing the chapter, he notes especially the writing of de la Croix, whom he asserts often used the method of sending out a raiding party in detachments, which he has just described. Ewald continues, "And he proves in his writings through examples that they often contributed to the success of his very many tricky ventures."[88]

Not only does he single out de la Croix for praise in his methods, Ewald tells his readers where copies of the Frenchman's treatise can be found.[89] Clearly it exerted a significant impact on Ewald's manner of conceiving raids.

The subsequent chapter, the ninth in the work, addresses how a commander should respond when his opponent is retreating. Ewald begins by describing the conditions under which an opponent may retreat,

> *The retreat of the enemy may occur either after a lost battle or other misfortunes which may force the enemy to it. In this case it is the duty of the leaders of a light corps to pursue the enemy closely, to harass him on all sides without endangering his corps too much, and to take advantage of the slightest disarray which can be detected during these movements of the enemy.*[90]

Here is the mix of boldness and caution that defined Ewald's style as a commander in the field. At the same time, it is apparent that should an opportunity present itself to inflict some damage on the foe, the capable commander should be willing to take advantage of it. He expanded on this concept shortly thereafter, stating "If you should notice any confusion in the retreat of the enemy, however, or if you see that the enemy in a mountainous terrain neglects the heights towering over the valleys and roads through which he is marching, this is when you can carry out the best raids."[91]

Otherwise, the Jäger captain had little to say on the subject of harassing a retreating enemy. He summed up this relatively short chapter, again mixing boldness and caution, "When the enemy retreats it is most important that you are not hasty when you pursue him." It is clear Ewald is trying to guard against the enemy employing a false retreat as a *ruse de guerre*. A point he addressed shortly before, describing how just such a trap was sprung on the Marquis de Lafayette during the Yorktown campaign of 1781.[92] Likewise, he counsels gaining good intelligence concerning the enemy, "As soon as he settles down you simply keep him under observation." Intelligence once again stood as a key factor in developing operations. Finally, he observes "But as soon as he marches off again you have to hang on to him."[93]

In the following chapter, Ewald returned to a subject in which he now possessed much greater experience from his service in the American War, ambushes. At the outset of the chapter, Ewald notes the irony of this tactic, "However much has to be censured he who falls into an ambush, it adds just that much to the reputation of an officer if he knows how to lay them with skill and to lure his enemy into them."[94] The ambush can therefore lead to disgrace or approbation, depending on which side of it an officer stands.

> *In selecting the men and horses for an ambush, Ewald gives*
> *very specific guidance. Nobody must be allowed to smoke and*
> *no one must be selected who has a cough or a cold, and among*
> *the horses there must be no stallions, since the least noise may*
> *betray the ambush to the enemy. Bread, forage and water for*
> *the people also have to taken along if none should be close by so*
> *that no one can complain about daily necessities.*[95]

Ewald takes the time to describe the reasons for laying an ambush, "Partly they are laid to attack, destroy, or seize an enemy in his foraging, partly to capture couriers with important information or distinguished personages from the enemy army, to beat a party of the enemy, and to keep the area free of such detachments."[96] He proceeds to describe how best to set an ambush in each of these specific situations.

In the first case, when the goal is to disrupt enemy foraging, he advises that the ambuscade be deployed in three different locations "so that you can attack the enemy unexpectedly from the front, the center, and the rear at the same time."[97] As in past instances in the treatise, where maintaining the element of surprise is important, Ewald councils that it is best to attack with the bayonet. Likewise, sentinels are important to the success of this type of attack as "They give notice of everything they see through pre-arranged signs, and it is best if officers or very good non-commissioned officers are used for this."[98] Information on the terrain in the area in which an enemy plans to forage is vital as well as it allows the attacking force to enter the prescribed area at night and conceal themselves as well as they can.

It is only during the attack itself that Ewald councils making as much noise as possible. His reasoning on this point is that it will cause further confusion among the enemy and lead some to run rather than fight. Additionally, Ewald advises frequent sorties against nearby enemy outposts, "from where small parties are sent as frequently as possible against the outposts of the enemy, which have to alarm them until they get tired of it and attempt to chase one away."[99] Then is the time, according to the author, to draw them further away and even through the ambush you have set for them, in order that it may attack their rear.

Concerning towns or farms which lay between two opposing forces, Ewald advises, "you have to lay small ambushes in their vicinity to catch the marauders, especially during the time when the fruits are ripe."[100]   In this instance, it is clear Ewald sought to capitalize on the desire of some soldiers to supplement their rations through pillaging. Marauders thus became easy targets for ambushes, and once prisoners they could provide information on the size and composition, as well as the intentions of the enemy. Ewald added that attacking looters paid dividends in the realm of relations with the civilian populace as well, "And since you protect the locals from the marauders through these ambushes, you will make them your friends, and they will give you a hint when a good catch can be made."[101]

Ewald's views on the subject of raids and protecting civilians in the area in which the detachment is operating are part of what sets his work apart from many of the others published by his contemporaries. More will be discussed on this point below. For the moment, suffice it to say that he seemed to be working beyond a simple manual on the conduct of irregular warfare to discussing some of the fundamental principles which governed its conduct. At the same time, it struck the balance between theory and practical advice gleaned from hard experience.

Ewald continued his discussion of ambushes with some suggestions on how to deal with aggressive opponents. "If the enemy should try to constantly alarm you through strong detachments, you can easily get him off your back through a well-planned ambush."[102]   He goes on to provide specifics on the deployments to make on such an occasion.

The Jäger captain closed his chapter on ambushes with a cautionary note, "You have to be very careful, however, not to lay too many ambushes in vain, or, even worse, that the first ambush might miscarry so that you do not annoy the soldier and lose his trust."[103]   In this instance, Ewald demonstrates an understanding of the morale of the common soldiers gained out of years of experience serving in the field. He further added, "But if you are fortunate at times you will find out that the soldiers enjoy this kind of action."[104]

Interestingly in this case, Ewald closes the chapter not with a reference to a classical military writer, but with his reflection on his own experience during the Charleston campaign of 1780, "During our march to Charleston through South Carolina in the year 1780 every day some of our *Jäger* volunteered for ambushing, and by these ambushes we were so successful that the American cavalry man no longer dared to show himself before our posts."[105] This remark demonstrates just how effective successful ambushes could be at breaking the morale of an opponent. Perhaps Ewald chose to end his chapter on ambushes with this observation for just that reason.

By the same token, he may have been unable to locate a suitable classical reference. In any case his reflection is telling.

The chapter on ambushes is one of the shortest in Ewald's *Treatise*, encompassing a mere four pages. At the same time, it stands as one of the most complete. In it, the author distills his considerable experience leading troops in irregular warfare over roughly seven years down to its key components.

Ewald's final chapter covers how to lead troops during a retreat. He opens by discussing the qualities necessary for a leader under these circumstances. In Ewald's estimation, "The leader of a corps which has to retreat has to have great knowledge of the art of war."[106]   In this case, it may be correct to equate knowledge with experience, for a commander to lead a successful retreat, they would need to possess both the knowledge of how to conduct the operation, the mechanics, as well as possess a strong sense of how to operate in their situation, with its attendant strengths and liabilities. Ewald seemed aware of this important combination, writing in the next line, "Not only does he have to try to avoid a superior enemy, but he also has to know how to encourage his despondent soldiers who become scared because of their small numbers."[107]

He then turns to the types of terrain that may be encountered during a retreat and how best to utilize them to gain some advantage. One of the most daunting geographic obstacles a commander may encounter during a retreat, according to the author, is a river. Ewald addresses this challenge noting that the crossing will be made using either a bridge or a ford. He describes, in brief, how to conduct either as well as what to do should an enemy attack while the troops are making the crossing. For Ewald, the mounted riflemen of a detachment should be the first to cross. If this advanced guard comes under attack from the enemy, "the commanding officer has to try everything to avoid being driven back by the enemy, since the well-being of the whole corps depends on his steadfastness."[108]

He continues, detailing the order in which the troops should make the crossing, "As soon as the leader of the corps arrives at the crossing, the cavalry passes the bridge or the ford, after which the *Jäger* on foot follow. They quickly disperse on the opposite bank to cover with their fire the fusiliers which form the rear."[109]   Notice, it is the light troops who assume the vanguard during the retreat, followed by the heavy infantry. The mounted troops assume the overall lead, which stood as a sensible procedure, considering they possessed the most mobility and could scout ahead in order to search out potential dangers and report back to the commander.

Drawing on his long experience, Ewald describes how daunting terrain could be turned to one's advantage during a retreat,

> *As dangerous as the mountainous and forested areas may seem, as many advantages can be drawn from them, if you know how to use them. If the enemy pursues too hotly, you can lay an ambush for him and lure him into it through a fake retreat.*[110]

Here, Ewald is advocating in favor of the very maneuver he cautioned his readers against falling into in the previous chapter! Still, it would be legitimate to set an ambush against an opponent, or at the very least make an attempt.

Finally, the author discusses what to do when caught on an open plain by a superior force of enemy cavalry. He suggests a retreat in what he refers to as quarree, essentially in the form of a large square.[111] Here, the riflemen and the fusiliers would be mixed. The riflemen would take the attacking cavalry under long distance fire, in order to try and dissuade them from pressing the attack. If the foe seemed determined, however, the regular infantry should form lines and give fire. He goes so far as to describe the manner in which to aim at a mounted opponent in order to hit the rider and not waste the shot. Further, he notes, "I myself am certain that it would be very good if, once the cavalry is close enough to strike, you go down on one knee and fire one last time, since a man can more easily fend off in this position a horse with his gun than if he were standing." Likewise, he observes, "And the cavalryman who is forced to strike his blow downward loses his balance and can easily wound his own horse."[112] Ewald makes it clear that this is only a theory on his part, "During the American War I often wanted to get in such a situation to test this idea…"[113]

The notable factor in terms of the present discussion is how Ewald's idea is based in keen observation of the different types of troops of his day in actual combat. At the same time, the author has the humility to confide in his readers that this is not something he has tried or observed personally. Instead, it stood merely a possible tactical solution.

The chapter on retreats is the last formal chapter of the work. There follows an appendix, *On the Three Most Important Tasks That an Officer of Light Cavalry Has to Perform in the Field*. It is broken down into three sections: (1) On the Outposts of the Cavalry, (2) On the Advance- and Rearguard, or of Lateral Patrols, Which an Officer of the Cavalry of a Light Corps or Detachment Has to Lead, and (3) Of the Patrols against the Enemy.

In the first subsection, Ewald makes the point that "the officer of the outpost has to be on his horse most of the time and ride about in the vicinity of his advanced posts."[114] He states that this is for security, to insure the men at the outposts are staying alert. At the same time, it again reveals his style of command. Throughout his career, Ewald demonstrated himself to be the type of officer who led from the front. While Ewald often delegated authority to subordinates, he tended to take on the most challenging parts of the mission himself.

In addition, with regards to his command style, Ewald demonstrated concern for his troops, but this came with clear limitations. For instance, in the same section he prescribes that as soon as night falls, the troops are to mount their horses and remain mounted through the night save only for "greatest emergency." He continues in this regard, "In this instance the officer must never mind the complaints of the soldier, which are rarely missing during the hardships of war." Instead, the officer, "must harshly punish the least grumbling and threaten to shoot in the head with his pistol the one who complains the most."[115] Clearly, there were limits to Ewald's empathy for the sufferings of his men. These limits were well-defined, however, anything that could compromise the success of the mission, be it a raid or standing picket duty, would not be tolerated.

At the same time, he noted "even if the common soldier should complain about the strictness of the officer you can nevertheless be certain that the majority of them prefer the officer who is too strict to the one who is too lenient, and that the soldier would rather attack the enemy with the former, if he is convinced of his courage and understanding than the latter."[116] Essentially, strictness engenders respect from the men, and their confidence in the commander. Ewald further defended this position, "If you want to throw in the weak objection here that the soldier could also do a lot out of love for his officer, I will laugh at that and assure you that the love of a German soldier is nothing but a shadow and worth nothing if he is not kept in the strictest discipline..."[117] In this, Ewald touches on one of the fundamental qualities military leadership. Its basis should be in respect rather than any feeling of fraternity. Numerous authors, both historians and military professionals have commented on this same theme.

The next section of the appendix, on advanced and rear-guards as well as patrols, despite the long heading, is fairly short. Again, the advice gained from years of active combat experience is readily apparent. He cautions the reader, "If an officer has to lead an advance guard during the night he has to be twice as careful. Since he cannot use his flankers, he has to use his ears."[118] Ewald follows up this injunction with some specific guidance on how to deploy troops under such circumstances. He then goes on to provide a lengthy example derived from his experiences serving under Arnold in Virginia in 1781.[119]

In the instance, he describes how an inferior force, on patrol in the night, can, if alert, throw back a superior one despite the numeric disadvantage. He closes the illustration with the conclusion "Therefore, it is of the utmost importance not to entrust just any officer with the command of an advance guard during a night time march against the enemy."[120]

The third part of the appendix is devoted to the conduct of patrols against the enemy. In this section, again, he passes along his years of practical experience. For instance, he notes that if an officer on patrol should "discover a detachment of the enemy which starts to flee as soon as they discover him, he has great cause to follow it step for step with the utmost precautions..."[121] His reason for exhorting caution on this occasion is "because such a detachment has most certainly been sent into an area to lure another party into an ambush."[122] Should the commander fall into an ambush, especially one that contains a superior enemy force, the author enjoins them to go over to the attack, as it will disconcert the enemy. He then supports his case with reference to an event in New York in the American War wherein a captain Merz, a lieutenant at the time, fought his way through two squadrons of Americans with only twelve mounted Jäger.[123]

Failing such an aggressive approach to responding to a superior opponent, Ewald recommends dividing up your force into smaller detachments of two men each and having all of them break off and run in separate directions, with the injunction that when they reach the main force, they report what has happened.[124]

He closes the section on patrols and ambushes with the general observation: "Everything is possible in war as long as you do not lose your head and if the officer informs his men beforehand of what can happen and if he familiarizes them in advance with all dangers."[125] Trained and informed soldiers who understand they have the commander's confidence have an advantage.

Once the commander has reached the boundary of his patrol area, Ewald advises that he send some of his men to the nearest village, where they will collect the principle inhabitants and return them to camp for questioning. Continuing his concern for the safety of the inhabitants, Ewald remarks, "It is well to remember here that such an officer keeps his men under arms and in no way considers going into the village for his men to refresh themselves, because this impermissible mistake has already cost many a man his honor, liberty or life."[126] Ewald here seems concerned should the troops break ranks to refresh themselves, or to plunder the people of the town, they make themselves easy targets for any enemy force in the vicinity to surprise. These tasks accomplished, "As soon as he knows all that is necessary he begins his retreat."[127]

Again, Ewald provides specific instructions for thy types of troops to be used, and their possible deployments while on the retreat. Likewise, he provides a hypothetical example, set in central Europe in order to illustrate how his system would work in practice. Ewald follows up his imaginary scenario with several historical examples from the Seven Years' War and the American War of Independence.

At the end of his appendix, Ewald returns to his injunction from the outset of the work, "Thus I repeat one more time at the end that an officer will do very well if he learns in peacetime so much that he can be used for any kind of service in the field."[128]

While it is true, as Ewald himself noted, that his observations are not new, they speak instead to one of the fundamentals of warfare. Consider that throughout his *Treatise*, Ewald not only provided examples from his recent experience fighting in America but reaches back to the Seven Years' War as well. In some instances, he goes so far as to include classical examples gleaned from his extensive reading of military history and the theories of his contemporaries. All of these factors combine to demonstrate an awareness in his writing of certain fundamentals that governed the prosecution of irregular warfare.

Having examined Ewald's ideas concerning partisan or irregular warfare as set out in his *Treatise*, the question remains, how was the work received by contemporaries? The initial reception of his Treatise was mixed. Reviewing the work in the contemporary publication *Orbus*, the Prussian officer Gerhard von Scharnhorst declared that there was not much new in its pages. The translators of Ewald's *Treatise* attribute this "either to a superficial reading or a failure to grasp the new kind of warfare that emerges out of Ewald's writing."[129] While Scharnhorst dismissed Ewald's work, Frederick the Great gave it his approbation.[130]

A little more than a decade after its publication, an English translation of the book appeared. The translation of the *Treatise* was the work of a Lieutenant A. Maimburg and appeared in London in 1803. This version of Ewald's treatise served as a manual for Sir John Moore's troops in the Peninsular War.[131] Likewise, is seems to be this translation that brought Ewald to the attention of the English-speaking world, his influence on which will be addressed below.

In its native German, Ewald's *Treatise* found a more receptive audience in no less a military thinker than Carl von Clausewitz. During his time as a lecturer at the Kriegsakademie Clausewitz utilized Ewald's

Treatise for his lectures on *kleinen krieg.*[132] Clausewitz appreciated Ewald's work and singled it out for notice in his second lecture on the subject due to its numerous examples drawn from the author's own experiences. Specifically, Clausewitz observed, "General Ewald's analyses of the services of light troops distinguish themselves through a number of examples taken from personal experience, which the author places next to his rules thereby making them very practical and instructive."[133]

As noted above, the English translation of Ewald led to his ideas exerting a profound influence on the development of the British light infantry in the Peninsular War. Thus, it exercised some effect beyond the borders of Hessen-Kassel. Likewise, this English translation is the version most likely consulted by J.F.C. Fuller in the early twentieth century.

Fuller, while writing on the revival and training of the British light infantry during the Napoleonic Wars, is positively ebullient in his praise for Ewald's work. In comparing his *Treatise* with the writings of a contemporary, Colonel Rothemburg, Fuller states "Where Colonel Rothemburg is the good soldier, Colonel Ehwald [sic] is the genius; where the former writes an exercise, the latter produces a classical work on war."[134]

Fuller goes on to stress, following Clausewitz, that the importance of Ewald's *Treatise* lies in the fact that it is based in the author's experiences. Fuller tends to stress Ewald's experiences in the American War of Independence over those he attained in the Seven Years' War.[135] He further indicates whom he perceives as the best audience for Ewald's work: "To the leader of an army von Ehwald may be of little use, but to the regimental officer, who has to act on the spur of the moment, in place of pondering over maps …we have yet to discover his equal as an instructor, in spite of the fact that his treatise was written well over a hundred years ago."[136]

Fuller proceeds to summarize the salient points of Ewald's *Treatise*. His reading of Ewald is decidedly aggressive; however, he does not omit the Hessian's consideration of security and defense. Still, Fuller, a man of his time, was a follower of the cult of the offensive, and that aspect of Ewald's works clearly assumes precedence in his reading. For instance,

> *The offensive is the very spirit of von Ehwald's[sic] tactics, and though he deals lengthily with the protective services which formed such an important part of the duties of the light troops in his day, he never forgets that to hit out is to fight. Do not waste your time evolving plans of operations in your head, make your dispositions immediately, and charge the enemy resolutely, even if he be superior.*[137]

After the Great War, Ewald, as well as his *Treatise*, lapsed into semi-obscurity, known mainly to experts on eighteenth century warfare. Ewald's disappearance into the oblivion of the past ended with the publication of his diaries from the American War of Independence in 1979. All this was in the distant future however, back in the eighteenth-century Ewald hoped that his pen would once again gain the notice of his superiors and open doors to higher rank.

For the author, the publication of his book did not generate the consequences he intended. While generally well-received, Scharnhorst's review aside, the publication of his *Treatise* did not alter Ewald's standing in the Hessian army. Much of its failure to exert an impact on his career stemmed from the internal politics of Hessen-Kassel. In October of 1785, the old Landgraf, Frederick II, died. He was succeeded by William IX. William had previously ruled the state of Hessen-Hanau, and it seemed his allegiance still lay more with that state. He relieved Ewald of his command in the army of Hessen-Kassel and ordered him to undertake a reorganization of the Hanau Jäger Corps. Ever the dutiful soldier, Ewald obeyed the command of his new sovereign.[138]

Still, Ewald remained a captain, he had not received a promotion in eleven years. This despite an impressive wartime record and outstanding peacetime service. His common ancestry stood as a major obstacle in Ewald's path to higher command. Across Europe, at this time, the nobility in many countries were retrenching themselves and using the military as a bastion of power. While this trend appeared most clearly in France, the states of the Holy Roman Empire were far from immune.[139] For some time, Ewald accepted his lack of advancement with forbearance. In 1787, however, he was passed over for promotion once again. On this occasion, two junior officers who lacked any understanding of the use of light troops, but came from noble stock, were promoted over him.[140] Finally, Ewald could stand no more, the advancement of these men stood as the ultimate slight. He asked to be released from the Hessian service, requesting that the Landgraf and the Prince of Hessen recommend him to the King of Prussia.[141]

At least a portion of Ewald's growing discontent with his position stemmed from the fact that he now had greater responsibilities. On February 3, 1788, he married Susanne Ungewitter of Kassel. Now he had a wife to support with the possibility of a family soon to follow. It seems likely that this drove, at least in some measure, Ewald's decision to request a release from service.[142]

Initially, Prince Charles attempted to dissuade Ewald from leaving the service of Hessen-Kassel and Hessen-Hanau. It quickly became apparent, however, that the captain stood resolute in his decision. Realizing there lingered no hope of keeping Ewald in the Hessian service, Prince Charles instead brought the possibility of service in Denmark to his attention. Here, the prince's brother in law, Frederick VI was crowned prince. The fact that Denmark was rumored to be preparing to enter a war then raging between Sweden and Russia further fueled Ewald's shift in thinking. War opened the possibility of winning new martial laurels, which could in turn further his career ambitions. On August 23, Ewald set out for Denmark, leaving behind the state he had served faithfully for twenty-eight years.[143]

Unfortunately, no papers in Ewald's hand came to light during the research that give any insight into his mental or emotional state on making this change. Certainly, they must have been profoundly effected as he had served Hessen-Kassel with such loyalty and forbearance for his entire adult life. Still, new challenges and opportunities were in offing. With his recent courtship and introduction to married life, it may also have seemed that this change constituted an opportunity to begin anew.

Further military laurels eluded Ewald in the short term, as the conflict between Denmark and Sweden ended before he could engage in any field operations. Still, shortly after his arrival in Schleswig, the king directed Ewald to organize the Jäger in that province. Ewald was able to levy the corps and rose to the rank of lieutenant colonel.[144] Clearly these were busy years for Ewald, with establishing married life, and raising and organizing a new unit. This fact makes it all the more impressive that military works continued to flow from his pen. These included: *Gesprache eines Husarencorporals, eines Jäger und liechten Infanteristen uber die Pflichten und den Dienst der liechten Soldaten,* published in Altona in 1794 and *Belehrunger uber den Kreig, besonders uber den kleinen Krieg, durch Beispiele grosser Helden und kluger und tapferer Manner,* published in Schleswig in 1798. The latter standing as another work quoted by Clausewitz at length in his lectures on kleinen Krieg.[145] In addition, there was a second edition of his *Abhandlung von dem Deinst der Leichten Truppen* published in 1796.[146]

In addition, Ewald supervised the transcription of his Diary of the American War from the notebooks he had kept while on service in North America.[147] At the same time, his work with the Schleswig Jäger Corps kept him occupied. He encountered some initial resistance from the local nobility who perceived him as somewhat of a common interloper, challenging their traditional preserve in the officer corps. Ewald's professionalism and strong work ethic quickly won them over however, and they began to accept him as he was.

By the same token, Ewald's career finally began to move forward from the seeming static state it had fallen into on his return from America. In

1790, Ewald was elevated the Danish nobility, allowing him to add "von" to his surname. On a more practical level, the king appointed him chief of the Schleswig-Holstein Light Infantry Battalion stationed at Kiel.[148]

In 1795, Ewald was promoted to colonel. Clearly, his decision to enter the Danish service had broken through the ceiling that prevented his further advancement. Even as colonel, Ewald continued to work diligently at honing the skills of his troops. He founded a corps library and established a school for non-commissioned officers. The latter taught the practical skills necessary for military administration including writing, basic math, how to compose written reports, and map reading.[149]

This period was not spent entirely in garrison, however. With nearby France disintegrating into revolution upheaval, civil war and a new continental conflict brewing out of the attempts by the other great powers to squelch the French Revolution, it would be foolish to assume that Denmark would pass placidly through such upheavals. The country experienced some internal upheavals during this time, and the army was called out to restore order. Ewald's handling of these upheavals demonstrates some of the lessons he learned while taking part of the fighting in America.[150]

On October 4, 1794, for instance, Field Marshal Charles dispatched Ewald with a detachment of troops to suppress riots taking place among the peasants in the town of Kaltenkirch.[151] The riots were the result of the inefficient measures of a minor government official. Ewald was empowered to take whatever measures were necessary to restore order to the community as quickly as possible.[152]

Upon his arrival at the town of Brumstead, he observed two angry crowds in the town. He ordered his men to remain under arms, but at a distance, while he rode into town alone to speak with the mob. Ewald made his way into the middle of the two factions and addressed them in a loud clear voice. He listened to and addressed their grievances. Ewald then implored the crowd to disperse and return to their homes, which they did. Remarkably, the colonel managed to quell the disturbance without resort to force, something that surely endeared him both to the court and to the people of Brumstead.[153]

In 1801, Denmark occupied the towns of Hamburg and Lübeck, and Ewald received the appointment to serve as military governor of the former. The citizens were so pleased with his fairness as military governor, that a committee of them asked if Ewald would consider assuming the post permanently. He declined, citing loyalty to his adopted country.[154]

CHAPTER 13

THE FRENCH REVOLUTION
AND NAPOLEONIC WARS

While Ewald's life had changed significantly in the 1780s, in addition to his switch to the Danish service, and his marriage, the continent of Europe was about to experience a watershed moment. France, whose support of the American cause made independence possible, now faced a monumental national debt. Attempts to pay down this debt met with resistance from the entrenched social elites of the country - the clergy and nobility. In an effort to break the impasse, Louis XVI called together the Estates General, the medieval representative institution of his realm, which had not met since 1614.

The opening the Estates General on May 5, 1789 touched off a political maelstrom. Calls for reform rapidly expanded into demands to create a constitutional monarchy. The concentration of troops outside Paris in the summer of 1789, exacerbated by a grain shortage and drought, convinced many of the working class in Paris that the king was bent on suppressing the Revolution by force. The fear of the people, that the chance for real, positive change would be nipped in the bud, brought about the first of the revolutionary *journees* with the July 14 storming of the Bastille, a medieval fortress then in use as a prison in central Paris. While popularly seen as a symbol of royal oppression, at the time of the storming, the Bastille held only a small number of actual criminals.

Driven by a similar paranoia stemming from rumors of a conspiracy to suppress the gains achieved already, peasants across France attacked the chateaux of their landlords. Fearing further attacks, the nobles renounced their privileges on the night of August 10, 1789.

Additional reforms followed in rapid succession with the overall result culminating in the fact that the king's power was radically curtailed, especially after the royal family's attempted flight to Varennes. By 1791, France teetered on the brink of all-out war with much of Europe. Both the king and the revolutionary government welcomed the test of arms, but for very different reasons. By this time, the Royal Army was in many ways reaching a nadir of effectiveness, as many of the officers had resigned their commissions and left the country. Louis XVI sought the conflict in the hopes that the great powers of Europe, especially Austria, would defeat the husk of the royal army and restore him to full power. The revolutionaries, meanwhile, sought the conflict in the hopes that it would unite the country behind them and provide them with the necessary support for further reforms, such as the elimination of the monarchy once and for all. Meanwhile, the established monarchies of Europe sought to contain the revolutionary virus and prevent it from infecting their own realms. With the two most powerful groups in the country pushing for war, it came as no surprise that war broke out in 1792.[1]

The War of the First Coalition, as it was known, started out with France taking on a combination Prussia, Austria, and Great Britain. The first two of these powers fought the war half-heartedly, as they were more concerned with keeping an eye on Russia, and seizing sections of Poland than in putting an end to the revolution in France.[2]

Still, the French Army was only a shadow of its former self. Many of the nobles who composed the officer corps had previously fled the country. Some were conspiring, along with the king, to gain the support of the other crowned heads of Europe and put down the Revolution.[3] The result, the French Army lacked trained and experienced officers at all levels. The enlisted ranks, however, possessed a solid core of long-service professionals.[4] Many of these men, having spent years in the ranks with little chance for promotion, were plagued by low morale. By the same token, the passionate zeal to defend the Revolution motivated a crop of young men to volunteer in the parallel organization first founded by the Marquis de Lafayette, the National Guard. These national guardsmen flocked to defend *la patrie* from foreign invasion. What they possessed in patriotic fervor, however, could not make up for solid training in basic military drill, and more often than not, these troops broke and ran when confronted by the more professional forces of their opponents.

Over the course of the next few years, a winnowing process took place that reached its fullest extent in the amalgam of 1794. This directive supplemented one battalion of line infantry with two of national guardsmen, creating a heavy unit known as the demi-brigade. At the same time, it brought together the strengths of both. The men of the old royal line regiments brought the training in military discipline, while the national guardsmen provided the zeal.[5] This combination of patriotic passion and solid training, combined with the massive manpower of the *levée en masse* provided France with the winning combination to defeat their opponents.[6]

During this period, a young officer of Corsican descent, Napoleon Bonaparte, embarked on his rise to fame and power.[7] His quick victories in Italy in 1796 made him the talk of Paris. At the same time, his independence in negotiating the Treaty of Campo Formio with the Austrians gave the members of the contemporary French government, the Directory, some pause. An attempt to sideline Napoleon by making him commander of the Army of the Interior failed.[8] When the young and very ambitious general requested permission to lead an invasion of Egypt in order to threaten Great Britain's trade with India, the political leaders were more than happy to oblige.

While initially successful, the Egyptian campaign quickly bogged down, especially once the French troops were cut off from reinforcements due to British naval superiority. Furthermore, plague began to ravage the ranks of his army. Thus, when Napoleon learned that France was once again threatened by a coalition of European Powers, he deserted his army and returned secretly to France.

Back in his adopted homeland, Napoleon's brother introduced him to a group of conspirators led by the veteran revolutionary, the Abbe Sieyès. Sieyès was then in the process of engineering a coup to seize control of the government from the Directory, which he perceived as possessing too weak of an executive. In order to accomplish his goal, Sieyès needed a military leader who could guarantee the support of the army. While there were other contenders, Napoleon appeared the most willing to play along, and Sieyès believed he could control the general. Together, these men formed two-thirds of the triumvirate that seized power in the coup of 18 Brumaire.[9]

From the outset, Napoleon had to defend his newly acquired power against the threat of a resurgent Austria. This he managed to accomplish through a remarkable crossing of the Alps that culminated in the battle of Marengo fought on June 14, 1800. Thus, he defeated the Second Coalition.[10]

For a short time, under the Peace of Amiens of 1802, Europe enjoyed peace for the first time in a decade.[11] Napoleon took advantage of this time to consolidate his hold on power. Soon, he had himself made First Consul for life, and shortly thereafter, he was elected Emperor of the French by plebiscite.[12] It was during this period as well that work began on the fundamental restructuring of the French legal system, known as the Civil Code or Code Napoleon.[13]

It was apparent from the outset, however, that the peace that encompassed Europe would be a fleeting one. Napoleon held designs on England. Seeking to bring what he referred to as "perfidious Albion" under his sway once and for all, he sent his troops to the north coast of France to a series of camps, the largest of which was located at Boulogne. Here the men trained and honed their skills, with additional recruits being incorporated into the ranks. He would eventually christen this force, some 400,000 strong, the Grand Armée. He also sought to expand French naval power so that it could support his goal of a cross-channel invasion.[14]

A key reform Napoleon enacted at this time stood in what is known as the corps de Armée. Essentially, the corps de Armée emerged a precursor of the modern combat division.[15] The French had experimented with the division as far back as the Seven Years' War.[16] These efforts, however, were contrived by field commanders and enacted on an ad hoc basis. They were never previously implemented in anything resembling a systematic fashion. In many ways the military bureaucracy of the Old Regime mitigated against such a broad effort.[17] With one single supreme commander of the military forces, capable of enforcing reform from the top down, it was now possible to implement such a broad reform.[18]

In practice, this meant that the French armies were now divided into corps of varying sizes. Each of these included infantry, cavalry and artillery as part of its composition. As a result, they essentially formed smaller self-contained armies capable of fighting a battle on their own. Thus, the famous Napoleonic dictum of having his marshals "march to the sound of the guns."

Europe's brief respite from the vicissitudes of war ended in 1804, when Napoleon had the Bourbon duke of Enghien executed on suspicion of espionage.[19] Shortly thereafter, an assassination attempt provided the Corsican usurper with the opportunity to seize power, one which he readily grasped.[20]

As with his previous ascendancy to the Consulate, Napoleon soon had to defend his seizure of power. This led to the 1804 campaign, or War of the Third Coalition.

While the reforms Napoleon set in motion already succeeded in making the army a vastly more efficient organization, he could not accomplish the same for the French Navy. The crushing French naval defeat suffered at the battle of Trafalgar, October 21, 1805, put an end to these dreams of a cross-channel invasion. Still, Napoleon was left with perhaps the largest, and certainly one of the best trained and most experienced forces the Continent of Europe had yet witnessed.[21]

As dreams of subjugating England eluded him, Napoleon unleashed his army on his continental foes. This conflict culminated in the battle of Austerlitz on December 2 of that year, arguably his most masterful performance on the battlefield. The battle is also known as the battle of the three emperors, since Napoleon, the Austrian Emperor and the Russian Tsar were all present on the battlefield.[22] The only state that remained undecided during the conflict was Prussia.

This proved to be only the beginning of the exploits of the Grand Armée, a force whose deeds would be written across Europe from Moscow to Madrid, leaving no state unaffected. Smaller states like Denmark would have to find some accommodation with the French juggernaut if they hoped to survive.

Through the 1790s, Denmark remained neutral, and as a result spared itself from feeling the ripples of many of the convulsive changes that gripped France. At the same time, the small northern kingdom became in essence a French client.

For Johann von Ewald, the 1790s stood as a decade of work and assimilation. He continued to reform the Danish Jäger Corps. Likewise, he continued to write and publish his ideas on light troops. As noted in the previous chapter, his staunch efforts to improve the defenses of his adopted kingdom slowly won over the Danish nobility, and he achieved acceptance among his brother officers as well.[23] These efforts reached their pinnacle when, in 1802, Johann von Ewald received promotion to Major General in the Danish service.

Ewald's active military service to his new state continued in 1803, when French aggression against the state of Hanover forced the Danish government to take a more active stance concerning its own defenses. It should be pointed out that Hanover remained closely allied to Great Britain, as George III was Hanoverian by descent.[24] Thus, Napoleon's actions in regard to this state should be seen in the context of his overall strategy against Britain. At the same time, French motives were not trusted in Copenhagen, and so the Danish government decided to mobilize part of their army in order to defend the duchies of Schleswig and Holstein. As a result of this policy, General Johann von Ewald received orders to take up a position on the southeastern border of Holstein in command of a force that numbered about four thousand men.[25]

Most of the troops remained deployed in this area over the following year. In October 1805, responding to the battle of Austerlitz, the Danish government concentrated an army of twenty thousand men in the duchies under the command of the Crown Prince. Ewald commanded the vanguard of the force and took up a position at Segenburg.

In the following year, Prussia's stance changed from one of indecision to outright opposition to Napoleon. The state mobilized for war. Still, the Prussian army was merely a shadow of the lions of Rossbach and Leuthen. Their military had failed to reform and stay current with changes in doctrine and organization. In the coming conflagration, they would pay dearly for this neglect.[26]

The French forces swooped across central Europe. Due to the reforms enacted both during the Wars of the French Revolution and during the preceding period of Napoleon's reign, the French were able to move much more rapidly than their Prussian adversaries.[27]

The twin battles of Jena and Auerstädt were fought on 14 October 1806. While Napoleon was present on the field commanding at Jena, the battle of Auerstädt was conducted completely by his subordinates, specifically, the I Corps under Jean-Baptiste Bernadotte and the III Corps under Nicolas Davout.[28] In an age that would later be depicted as one of decisive battles, Jena-Auerstädt stood as one of the few occasions when the reality accorded with the perception, as by the end of the day, the French succeeded in virtually annihilating the Prussian Army as a fighting force.[29]

At Jena, Napoleon bested a Prussian force under Frederick Ludwig zu Hohenlohe-Ingelfingen. Jena stood as the more evenly matched of the two contests, as the French had approximately 40,000 troops to the Prussians roughly 60,000. In this clash, Napoleon spent the morning launching successive attacks on the Prussians designed to drive them back and provide space for the Grand Armée to maneuver. During the fighting, one of Napoleon's marshals, Michel Ney, disobeyed orders and entered the fray.[30] While he drove by the Prussians on his front, he overextended himself and risked being cut off. Napoleon had to commit his entire cavalry reserve to relive his overly-ambitious lieutenant. Likewise, he ordered Marshal Jean Lannes to shift his attack to relieve Ney.[31] This, in turn, caused the French center to weaken. Napoleon deployed the Imperial Guard to hold the French center. Napoleon's moves saved his subordinate from disaster, but the French plan was thrown off. The Prussians failed to take advantage of the situation, a fact which most subsequent commentaries argue led to their defeat.

At approximately one in the afternoon, Napoleon ordered his forces to attack the Prussian flanks and drive them in, thus enveloping the enemy center. The French center would then advance against that of the Prussians. These orders were carried out very efficiently, and the Prussians were defeated. Between casualties and prisoners, the Prussian loss stood at nearly 25,000, while that of the French amounted to 24, 080.

Simultaneously, at Auerstädt, now known as Auerstedt, Marshal Louis Davout and his III Corps fell into an encounter battle with the main Prussian field army and their Saxon Allies. Karl Wilhelm Ferdinand, Duke of Brunswick-Lüneburg commanded this force.

Davout's III Corps consisted of some 28,000 men, organized into two divisions, with some 44 guns. His mission was to delay any attempt by the Prussians to move further along the road in the vicinity and thus hinder their withdrawal to Magdeburg or Leipzig. Brunswick's force, on the other hand, was composed of 48,000 troops and 128 guns.[32] It was organized into five divisions with some light troops for screening the main force as well.

For his part, Brunswick sought to reach the Untrat River at Freyburg in Saxony and make his way across it. He trusted in the Prussian-Saxon force to the south near Hohenlohe to cover his withdrawal.

In the early morning hours of October 14, elements of the advanced forces of both armies collided and a classic encounter battle began to take shape. As the respective commanders realized what was going on, they proceeded to funnel more troops into the fight. During the fighting, the Prussians launched numerous cavalry attacks on the French forces. The assaults were, however, uncoordinated and failed to achieve any purpose. In essence, the Prussians squandered their cavalry against the French.

Once he had driven off the Prussian cavalry assaults, Davout proceeded to grind down their infantry. As a result, by the middle of the day, the Prussian right began to show signs of crumbling. Still, one-third of their army remained uncommitted to the battle. As the right collapsed, a general retreat was ordered. The Prussian general Scharnhorst sought to extricate the bulk of the army.

As the Prussian's withdrew, night began to fall. Troops from the Prussian force at Auerstädt ran into the survivors of Jena on the roads leading away from their respective battlefields. Confusion spread in the ranks as the two forces exchanged tales of mutual woe. The retreat quickly degenerated into a route, and the French managed to capture various isolated groups of prisoners as Prussian forces lost cohesion.[33]

The fact that the French were capable of launching such an organized and successful pursuit of the defeated Prussians after the battle was one of the factors that singled out the twin battles of Jena-Auerstädt from the numerous other clashes of the Napoleonic period. It also sounded the death knell of the Prussian military reputation established under Frederick the Great.[34]

Not only did the French succeed in defeating the Prussians on the day, but they followed up with a relentless pursuit of the vanquished foe.

If strategically decisive battles were a rarity at this time, an after-battle pursuit was nearly unheard of. It was the French chase after the defeated Prussians that brought them to the borders of neutral Denmark, and pitted Napoleon's marshal Jean Bernadotte against Johann von Ewald.

While Denmark had remained neutral throughout much of this period, their neutrality should not be taken to mean that the state existed as a mere French pawn. Zealous to protect his nation's autonomy, when word reached King Christian VII that the French were mustering along the border of Schleswig in preparation to chase down the retreating Prussians, he dispatched Ewald to defend the territory.[35]

Meanwhile, following the twin disasters at Jena and Auerstädt, a Prussian force under General Gerhardt Lebrecht von Blücher retreated with Napoleon in pursuit. They headed in the direction of the Holstein border. Here, Ewald stood guard against any violation of Danish territory. On November 5, Blücher occupied the town of Lübeck in Schleswig, where Ewald had previously served as military governor. Prince Joachim Murat and Marshal Nicholas Soult pursued the retreating Prussians.

Ewald at first attempted to handle the situation diplomatically, with an eye towards preserving Danish neutrality. He wrote a letter to Blücher, asking him to respect Danish territory, but at the same time informing him that he would resist any violations of Danish sovereignty by the retreating Prussians. This came as a fairly bold stance from a Danish general, and perhaps an indication of the first stage in fall of Prussia's perception as a great power in the aftermath of the twin battles.[36]

The French attacked the Prussians on November 6, and some retreating Prussian troops attempted to cross the Holstein border. They were followed by a French column, numbering between three and four thousand men who advanced to Fackenburg. The French demanded free passage into Danish territory. They made this demand believing that the Danes had already granted such rights to the Prussians, which was not the case.

The Danes resisted the French incursion, and fighting broke out between the two sides, with Ewald commanding the Danish contingent. Realizing that his troops were outnumbered and would soon be defeated, Ewald sought a truce to parley with the French commander. First, he tried to stop the firing by waving a white cloth with his hands. On his horse, he rode in front of the forces and jumped a ditch, six feet wide and twelve feet deep.[37]

Ewald succeeded, gaining the attention of a French hussar. The soldier, in turn, conducted Ewald to Baron Andraes von Liliencron, an aide-de-camp to Prince Joachim Murat, Napoleon's brother in law, and the highest-ranking French officer in the vicinity of the fighting.

Joachim Murat was a daring cavalry commander and one of Napoleon's most enduring colleagues. Born in Gascony on 26 March 1767, Murat was initially destined for the priesthood, a vocation toward which he possessed no inclination. While studying at seminary, just before his twentieth birthday, Murat joined the French army serving in the king's cavalry for two years. The outbreak of the French Revolution in 1789 soon offered Murat new opportunities for advancement. He served briefly in the National Guard, where pay and conditions were better, and discipline less strict, but returned to his old regiment.

Murat and Napoleon first met when Murat helped secure the artillery necessary to aid Napoleon in the suppression of the Parisian mob in 1795, the "infamous whiff of grape." For his role in securing the necessary guns, Murat earned a position on Napoleon's staff. Promoted to colonel, he accompanied the latter to Italy in 1797, where through courage and daring he rose to the rank of *general de brigade*. Likewise, Napoleon asked Murat to join him on his expedition to Egypt. He accompanied Napoleon on the Egyptian campaign in 1798, and returned to France with him, aiding in the coup of 18 Brumaire, which helped bring Napoleon to political power in France. The tie between the two grew even more formal when Murat married Napoleon's sister Caroline in January 1800. Murat was part of the first class of Marshals created by Napoleon in May 1804.

Over time, Murat's relationship with Napoleon grew stormy. Much of this resulted from jealousy on the part of the French marshal who felt slighted when Napoleon's blood relations received greater rewards and titles in the newly forged empire than he did.[38]

As befit his reputation, Murat, received Ewald in a very impolite manner. The French cavalryman insisted to Ewald that Prussians troops under Blücher had been given free passage across the Danish border and that they had gone to the town of Fackenburg. For his part, Ewald attempted in vain to persuade the French commander that no such events had occurred. Murat, growing frustrated, yelled at Ewald that he should be shot. Then he asked the Danish general where the Prussians had gone. Now it was Ewald's turn to lose patience, and he replied that he was a Danish general and no French spy.[39]

The preceding exchange ended the interview between Murat and Ewald. Murat left the meeting, and Ewald, along with his aide, had to return to the Danish lines with no escort. This treatment constituted not only an insult, but posed a real threat to Ewald, as during his return, without escort or formal flag of truce, he could have been taken or killed by French troops with impunity. Once again, the experience of years of operating in detached operations paid dividends, as he eluded the French to return to his troops unmolested. The skills of the partisan remained sharp. Taking advantage of the avarice of a French grenadier, he managed to hire the man as a guide to help return him and his horses. At dawn, he arrived at Stockelsdorf, which was crowded with French marauders, the Danes having resisted the French advance for as long as they could, had been forced to withdraw.[40]

As negative as the exchange between Ewald and Murat had been, it did result in some positive outcomes overall. The French were ordered to leave Danish territory by Napoleon. When the Emperor learned of Murat's behavior both during the interview and in Denmark overall, he was not pleased. He well understood that Murat's actions constituted just the sort of thing that could generate a new challenge to his domination of Europe. Even when it was learned that Murat's behavior was due in part to the news of the death of a favorite aide-de-camp, the information did not assuage Napoleon's temper. Ewald, for his part, forgave the marshal his testiness in their interview, but said that he could not accept the breach of military etiquette.[41]

In the days following Ewald's meeting with Marshal Murat, the Danish border returned to quiescence. After the French withdrew, Napoleon made certain that henceforth Danish neutrality was strictly enforced. Ewald remained in the vicinity of Segenburg until November 1806.

While the French may have observed Danish neutrality from this point forward, the same could not be said for the British. In 1807, they bombarded Copenhagen and captured the city.[42] Responding to these actions, the Danish government ordered Ewald to move the vanguard of his forces to the northeast coast of Holstein and occupy the islands of Laaland, Falster and Møen. This constituted a defensive measure on the part of the Danes. Once in position, Ewald's forces continued in readiness for further operations.[43]

Soon thereafter, when the British evacuated Zeeland, Ewald moved in with his troops, setting up his headquarters at Letraburg. Once established in Letraburg, Ewald retained control of the entire area save Copenhagen and Kronborg. Ewald occupied the region until relieved by the crown prince.[44]

Where the British had hoped to use the capture of Copenhagen as the springboard to open up new operations against Napoleon on the continent, it exerted the reverse effect. The surrender of the Danish fleet, and British demands on the government, had the effect of driving the Danes into an open alliance with the French.[45]

Even as a French ally, the Danes retained some autonomy. Over the winter of 1808-09, relations with Sweden grew sour, and the Danes pre-

pared to attack their neighbor to the north. Ewald was ordered to lead
the vanguard of the invasion with his troops, certainly an honor for a
foreign-born officer. They were to proceed over an ice-bridge across the
Soud, which separates the two countries by only two miles at its nar-
rowest point. The men were in high spirits and ready to carry out the
assault when it was discovered that the ice was not thick enough to support the men and their equipment.[46] As a result, the planned invasion
never materialized.

While he did not have the opportunity to engage in active combat operations in 1809, Ewald still received recognition for his services. In that
year, the crown prince, who had worked closely with Ewald in many of
the operations described above, ascended the Danish throne as King Frederick VI. Noting his friend's distinguished service to his adopted homeland, Frederick presented Ewald with the Grand Cross of the Dannebrog
Order.[47] At this point, it could be said that he had truly been accepted in
his new country.

Ewald's last major undertaking as an active field commander occurred
during one of the lesser known, but certainly one of the more colorful
episodes of the Napoleonic Wars, the rebellion of Major von Schill, also
known as von Schill's ride. Ferdinand Baptista von Schill was a renegade
Prussian soldier who sought to lead an uprising that would throw off the
French yoke from central Europe. Born in Wilsdorf-bie-Dresden on 5
June 1776, von Schill entered the Prussian cavalry at 12 or 14. Ironically,
his father had raised a Freikorps during the Seven Years War which had
fought against the Prussians.

Freikorps were irregular units of men, raised at the private expense of
their leader and taken into the service of the state. This method of raising
troops saved the state the time and effort of raising forces itself, and at the
same time provided it with a completed unit. In addition, it offered the
commanders of such units a more rapid path to career advancement than
through the normal chain of command.[48]   The services of the Freikorps
allowed his father, born a commoner, to purchase a title of nobility. This,
in turn, helped the son to enter the aristocratically dominated cavalry.[49]

Ferdinand von Schill was wounded at either Jena or Auerstädt in
1806, the sources are conflicting.[50]   They do agree, however, that his
wounds were serious enough for him to be sent to Kolberg to convalesce.
While recovering from his wounds, Schill received command of a volunteer Hussar unit raised for the defense of the city. In this role, he participated in the defense of the city against a French siege that lasted form 20
March to 2 July 1806. Like his father, he led a unit that was in essence
a Freikorps, which raided behind the French lines.[51] His actions in the

defense of Kolberg, as well as his experiences in the campaign of 1806, encompassed Schill's formative military experiences.

In 1809, Schill received a promotion to Major and took command of the 2nd Hussar Regiment. The regiment included troops he had commanded at Kolberg. Due to their past experiences serving together, the men were very loyal to Schill personally, and this would prove a volatile combination.

At this time, Prussia writhed under the heavy burdens imposed on the state by the Treaty of Tilsit, which significantly reduced the size of the state. In effect, they reduced Prussia to little more than a French vassal.[52] In addition, the defeats at Jean-Auerstädt which led to the treaty constituted nothing short of a national humiliation. Responding to these crises, the government embarked on a series of military reforms geared to rebuild the army and prepare it for a renewed conflict with the French at some time in the future.[53]

For his part, Schill fell under the influence of these reforms, and especially their nationalist ideology. These led him to determine on launching a revolt against French domination of his homeland. Therefore, on 28 April 1809, he led his unit, the 600 man Brandenburg Hussars, out of Berlin. He told his men that he planned to reestablish Prussia's martial glory by leading them on a war of liberation against the French. Schill literally jumped the gun in taking these actions. Prussia's staunchly conservative king, Frederick Wilhelm III ordered the young cavalry leader to return to his post. When Schill refused, the king declared him an outlaw.[54]

At the time von Schill initiated his revolt, he had only a small group of followers. Thus, one of his main tasks lay in recruiting more adherents. As his most recent biographer observes, in order to accomplish this, "Schill had to make as much noise as possible as he went....This, of course, came naturally to him."[55] This author further points out that such a tactic made it much easier to locate the cavalry commander as well. Still, he did manage to attract troops, and whenever he came up against troops from Westphalia or the German Confederation, Schill and his men triumphed and gained new recruits in the bargain. As Sam Mustafa points out, "Unfortunately for Schill, there weren't actually very many Westphalians defending Westphalia."[56] At the outset of his rebellion, most of the Westphalian troops were actually stationed in Spain. As a result, the main forces he had to contend with were the Dutch, Danish and French troops stationed throughout northern Germany. Still, these troops would oppose Schill and his followers with greater commitment than any German forces. Likewise, they began to catch up to the renegade with greater speed and confidence as the pursuit continued.[57]

There existed other important reasons for the rapid response of the French and allied forces to uprising of Schill and his rebels (referred to as the Schill'schen). Napoleon's empire was far from peaceful. There were often revolts against French power throughout his realm. The restive nature of these occupied territories was often exacerbated by the incompetent rule of some of the other members of the Bonaparte clan. None of Napoleon's family members seems to have succeeded more often in stimulating the forces of rebellion than his brother Jerome.[58]

Jerome had recently put down two rebellions, those of Katte and Dörnberg. As a result, he already stood on his guard when Schill's rebellion erupted. Jerome summoned the Third Dutch division under the command of French general Pierre-Guillaume Gratien to augment his own forces. These troops only just arrived at the end of April. In addition, Jerome and his war minister called on a brigade of Dutch troops to aid in the suppression of Schill and his followers.[59] The Danish troops were led by von Ewald, now sixty-five years old. As a result of these alarms, by the middle of May a composite force of over eight thousand French, Dutch and Danish troops hunted von Schill and his followers.[60]

In their movements, the Schill'schen bypassed the important city of Marburg, with its solid defenses. They instead moved northward, parallel to the Elbe River, sending out flying columns as they proceeded. As they made their way along the Elbe in Saxony, their depredations would drive away support from the inhabitants who were already lukewarm to Schill's cause at the outset. When they reached Tangermünde, where one of Schill's close subordinates, Adolf von Lützow declared that he could not continue with the Schil'schen. Lützow therefore remained in Tangermünde, the town he once proposed as the objective of the march.[61] This constituted a significant loss for Schill in that without him, the rebel leader lacked a very capable subordinate, one who could help focus the former's thinking and possibly direct it towards a realizable goal. For instance, shortly after Lützow's departure from the Schil-schen, they dallied for a week in Arneburg, "an unheard of leisure given their normally hectic pace."[62] Even the addition of 300 Prussian infantrymen from Berlin who joined the rebellion out of frustration at the slow pace of reforms there could not compensate for the time wasted. Nor could his capture of the town of Halle soon thereafter, which held the imperial payroll.

After his respite, Schill planned to move on to Stralsund. Sam Mustafa asserts that "The six days he spent in Arneburg represented what was probably the last chance Ferdinand von Schill had to save himself."[63] The problem was that the Schill-schen were still actively engaged in combat during this period of inertia. On 5 May, for instance, they engaged the garrison of the fortress Magdeburg near Dodendorf. While Schill and his men claimed victory against the 4,000 Westphalian and French troops who opposed them, and took 206 of them prisoner, they lost some thirteen officers and seventy men. While their opponents could make good their losses with relative ease, for Schill, every man counted. Even though many of the Westphalians would join the rebel force, it would take time to amalgamate them. Further, Schill had lost veterans troops upon whose loyalty he could count. 13 May witnessed the Schil'schen once more on the move, having left Arneburg, they marched north along the Elbe. Apparently, Schill decided to leave Westphalia and head into Mecklenburg or even make for Pomerania. A likely reason for his move lay in the fact that so few troops came out to support him up to this point. Likewise, some of his officers later stated that he had mentioned the northern port city of Stralsund as a destination as early as the second week in May.[64]

News of Schill's movements spread well in advance of the Schil-schen. Despite this fact, they surprised the garrison commander at Dömitz in Mecklenburg and captured him during his morning ride. As a result, the town fell without a shot being fired.[65] Some read into events such as these as passive support for Schill and his followers. Such support as there was would be fleeting, however, as Schill's men moved out across Mecklenburg and plundered the farms and orchards in the region in order to find food for themselves and their horses. This was the first time Schill resorted to such a tactic. Sam Mustafa attributes this lack of discipline among Schill's men to the large number of recent recruits in his force. Still, it had the consequence of undercutting popular support for the rebel leader. Since the French army often resorted to similar tactics, the Schill-schen's activities in Mecklenburg blurred an important line of differentiation between his troops and those of the occupiers.

Schill sought to create a popular revolt. Now he possessed some idea of what he had set in motion. At the same time, he was unaware of the consequences. On the day that he had taken Dömitz, King Frederick Wilhelm III of Prussia issued a proclamation in which the 2nd Brandenburg Hussar Regiment von Schill was officially struck from the army lists. As a result, von Schill and his men were no longer considered Prussian soldiers, legally, they were merely outlaws.[66]

Meanwhile, the Dutch and Danish forces mustered to suppress Schill's uprising were moving ever closer. For his part, Schill managed to pace himself in a particularly dangerous position with his men dispersed plundering the countryside. To some extent, this was mitigated while he remained on the move. Still, should he ever stop and set up a base of operations, he would be in great peril.[67]

As noted, the formative influence on Schill was his experience during the siege of Kolberg two years previously, therefore, the idea of defending a fixed point appealed to him, at least according to Mustafa.[68] By the same token, as his movements continued, with no clear goal in sight, the morale of his followers began to wane. At Rostock, for example, some of his men considered running away. Even as the support of his early followers declined, however, Schill continued to attract new followers. He gained recruits both at Rostock and Wismar, requisitioning large quantities of weapons and uniforms at both locations as well. In the latter case, this came only after some ferocious fighting against the Danish and Dutch troops sent to oppose him at Damgarten on 24 May. To some extent, the continued infusion of new troops likely masked the deeper morale problems within the ranks of Schill-schen.[69]

Schill and his troops retreated from Damgarten and made for Stralsund in Pomerania. Somewhere during this period, Schill reached out to the English sending emissaries to them in hopes of garnering support.

Stralsund, as it existed during the Napoleonic Wars, sat on an egg-shaped island that composed part of an excellent natural harbor. As with many towns and cities in Europe at this time, it possessed formidable defensive walls.[70] This meant that an attacker who sought to gain the town would most likely have to bring siege artillery and batter down the walls in order to do so. There were three gates in Stralsund's landward walls, the Tribsee Gate, the Frankish Gate and the Knieper Gate. As he made his way to Stralsund, some of the young officers who had flocked to his banner began to abandon him. For his part, Schill boasted that he would make Stralsund a second Saragossa.[71]

Schill took Stralsund in the second week of May. Once he was secure in the town, he mobilized the local militia and began to improve the defenses. The local troops amounted to only an additional 300 men, not really enough to oppose the forces now being sent against him. Likewise, these men were reserves, and not trained and experienced professionals.[72] Add to this the fact that Schill, while he possessed direct experience of siege, that at Kolberg, had never formally studied siege warfare or how to successfully defend a town against an assault.[73] If he had, he would know that once he hunkered down in the town he had effectively given up the initiative to his opponents. Without some kind of naval support, or maritime evacuation, it was only a matter of time until the French defeated Schill and his followers and took the town. While Schill did attempt to send emissaries to England, it does not appear that anything ever came of this gesture.[74]

Not only did Ferdinand von Schill have the French, Danish and Dutch to worry about, his relations with the town leadership quickly grew strained. Their position is understandable, since they would also be held accountable by the French for any aid given to Schill and his rebels. They likely understood better than he the foolishness of his attempt at this point.[75]

On 30 May, Gratien's force arrived in the outskirts of Stralsund. It amounted to 8,500 troops, with substantially more cavalry than Schill possessed. The force branched out quickly and took up positions around the town. Gratien wasted no time, with the attack beginning just after noon on the day of his arrival. Such a rapid deployment and assault occasionally occurred during the opening stages of the siege. If the attacker believed they had caught the garrison unprepared, they might risk an assault in the open in the hopes of taking the town quickly by storm as opposed to the slow attrition of a siege.

Inside the city, Schill deployed his infantry in three more or less even groups to defend the city's three gates. He held his cavalry as a sort of mobile reserve that could be directed quickly to any area that seemed to be buckling under enemy pressure.[76] As for the besiegers, the final plans for the attack on Stralsund were not completed until about one in the morning.[77]

The assault on Stralsund commenced on 31 May. The troops under Ewald's command were Danish Jäger, men whose training he had personally oversaw. Likewise, most were German recruits from Holstein.[78] The attack jumped off, targeting the three gates. As it developed, Schill mistook Gratien's deployments. He focused his defenders on the attack on the Tirbsee Gate to counter what he perceived as Gratien's main assault. As a result, the other two gates were only lightly defended by a combination of militia and sharpshooters. As Mustafa reports, "At the Knieper Gate, Stralsund's western portal, a thin forest stood within two hundred yards of the defenses and thus covered an attacker until his final approach."[79] It was on this flank that Ewald's troops made their move. His force included two battalions of infantry and two companies of Jäger. Ewald held his light cavalry in reserve, ready to exploit any breakthrough should one occur.[80]

Here is a mature Ewald, who had led light troops nearly his entire adult life, pondered and written extensively on their proper use, demonstrating the skill thus acquired through years of experience and study. While this assault presented something of a new experience for him, he had not yet commanded troops in an assault on a walled town, he had certainly seen this sort of activity in his early years as a soldier during the

Seven Years' War. When he joined the action, we see Ewald once again, as on so many previous occasions, leading from the front. Drawing his sword, at age sixty-five, he led his troops into the attack on Stralsund.[81]

One of the Schill-schen, a Lieutenant von der Horst, witnessed the Danish assault develop on the Knieper Gate. Ewald's men charged the position repeatedly with the bayonet. All tolled it required three attempts for them to smash through the defenders. Throughout this period, they came under heavy artillery and small arms fire. Even as the canister shells burst around them, Ewald exuded calm, issuing orders to continue the assault.[82] With most of his forces already committed, only some of the cavalry could be sent to reinforce the troops defending this portal.[83] Quickly, the overall defenses began to crumble. Some of Schill's lieutenants, including von der Horst, sought permission to burn the town, which the leaders refused. While they continued to argue, Ewald's Danes broke through the Knieper Gate, the resistance at that location lasting less than an hour.[84]

Even after they successfully breached the Knieper Gate, the Danes continued to encounter determined resistance. The fighting inside the walls of Stralsund continued house to house.[85]

Somewhere between 1:30 and 2 PM, Schill left Brünnow in charge of the defenders at the Tribsee Gate and set out to see if he could restore the deteriorating situation at the Knieper Gate by rallying the defenders stationed there. He took with him on this mission Lieutenant Wilhelm August von Mosch, one of his most trusted aids and a loyal friend. The two had only ridden about eight blocks when they perceived Danish cavalry in the streets ahead of them. At this point, Schill ordered Mosch to pull some troops from the Frankish Gate to launch a counter-attack. He dutifully road off to fulfill his mission, turning when he was about a block away to see what Schill was doing. The last view von Mosch had of his friend was Schill riding into a part of Ewald's Danish infantry.[86]

As is often the case in the confusion that attends the latter phases of a battle, no one has been able to make a convincing case that they were present at the moment when Schill was fatally wounded. Many were present just afterwards. Schill was in the middle of the Fährstraße or Ferry Street, which climbs up from the harbor and becomes what was then Johannes Strasse, about two blocks away from the Knieper Gate in the Old Market. This is the oldest neighborhood in the town. Mosch saw Schill in the street riding towards the Danish infantry, when he noticed some additional men coming around a corner. It seems that in the confusion, Schill mistook these men for his own troops, when they were in fact Danish Hussars. There may have been some Danish staff officers and light infantry mixed in with the party as well.[87]

Both sides realized the identity of the other simultaneously. One of the Danes supposedly cried, "There is Schill!" and opened fire. Others followed suit. The Major turned to flee, but only made about fifty yards before he fell from the saddle, with a ball in the back of his head. He lay on the ground in front of 21 Fährstraße, where one of the Danish troops stabbed him in the side to be sure he was indeed dead. His body was then carried up the street to the Golden Lion Tavern in the Old Market and laid on a table. Again, no one has ever been able to claim convincingly that they fired the fatal shot.[88]

Likewise, some claim that Schill was actually killed by a sabre blow to the head. While there is clearly a sabre cut visible on Schill's face in the death mask made shortly after the fighting, the overwhelming majority of the accounts describe his being shot and falling from his horse dead on the spot.

While lying at the tavern, Schill's body was plundered by his assailants. It was soon moved the Rathaus on Gratien's order. There it was inspected by the leaders of the occupying force and the identity verified.[89]

The recapture of Stralsund was important accomplishment for Napoleon on the strategic level. Had Schill and his followers managed to retain control of the town, it could have served the British as a staging area from which they could open up a new theater in northern Europe. Clearly, there existed some sympathy in the areas occupied by the French for the uprising. The support of a major power such as Britain may have served to increase the willingness among many in the region to challenge French domination.

In the end, it was not to be. Most of Schill's men were either killed or captured at Stralsund. About two hundred managed to escape from Stralsund. Many of these fortunate ones fled back to Prussia.

Initially, Gratien seemed willing to parole most of the prisoners he had taken among the enlisted men. The arrival of General Ewald and Lieutenant-Colonel Michelin, the latter of whom was to be the new French military governor of Stralsund, altered this verdict. Ever the military professional, Ewald reminded Gratien that the men they had in custody were not viewed as soldiers, but rather as bandits, even by their own king. Given their status, they deserved no mercy and had to be held in custody.

Gratien countered that they did deserve some mercy as they had come under a flag of truce. The resulting middle course adopted prevented the victory at Stralsund from being complete. Two of the officers were allowed to return to the Schilll-schen camp, now under the command of a Major Brünnow. They were under the observation of four squadrons of Dutch cavalry and an artillery battery. However, security seemed lax in the Dutch camp, perhaps due to some assumption that a full surrender was imminent.

Brünnow's men launched a spirited attack against their Dutch guardians and achieved complete surprise. They managed a breakthrough, making their way into Prussia and taking shelter under Blücher.[91] The latter, while officially under orders to aid in the suppression of the rebellion, was a very well-known Francophobe, and seems to simply have looked the other way as deserters returned to the ranks.

As a result, Gratien placed his final prisoner count at some 570, though various accounts offer a range of different figures. Many of these men were marched across Europe to prisons in France.[92]

As a recognition of the part played by Ewald and his troops in suppressing Schill's uprising and liberating the city, they were presented with an official letter of thanks from the city leaders. The letter stated in part, "The name Ewald will never be forgotten by us."[93] One final encomium to cap a long and distinguished military career.

Ewald's role in putting down Schill's uprising should not be seen as open support of the French or of Napoleon's Continental System. Rather, it should be clear that Ewald spent his life in support of legitimate authority. When he was ordered by his Landgraf to put down a rebellion against a foreign king, he did so, with professionalism and valor. Likewise, when the king of his adopted country gave him a similar mission, he again acted accordingly.

Later in 1809, after returning from his efforts in the suppression of Schill's rebellion, the king ordered Ewald to drive the British from their foothold in Cuxhaven and destroy the ships they had sailed up the Elbe River. With this task completed, he was to take part in a joint attack on Helgioland with French support.[94]

Before these movements could be initiated, however the British withdrew to their ships and remained at anchor, just out of reach of the land forces near Cuxhaven. Ewald advanced his forces as far as Bremerlehe on 7 August, however, promised reinforcements from Hamburg and Westphalia did not materialize. Without these additional troops, Ewald had to notify his king that he lacked sufficient manpower to successfully dislodge the British. As a result, Ewald was ordered back to Holstein.

In November of 1812, he received the appointment of Commanding General of the Duchy of Holstein, under the overall command of Field Marshal Charles. His headquarters were located at Kiel.[95]

For his part, Ewald narrowly missed one last opportunity for military adventure, but one that would likely have ended in his death. By 1812, relations between France and Napoleon's nominal ally, Russia, began to fall apart. Napoleon began to plan a massive invasion to bring this adversary to his knees. Since much of the Grand Armée was spread out across Europe maintaining his control, and there was the persistent devourer of manpower, the Spanish ulcer, Napoleon had to turn more than ever before to his satellite kingdoms in central Europe for aid.

Even neutral Denmark could not escape his requisition. In April 1812, the French demanded the Danes furnish a division of ten thousand men. The levee was then divided into two smaller divisions and placed on both Holstein and Schleswig. The troops thus raised were to be attached to Napoleon's XI Corps, under the command of Marshal Pierre Augereau.[96] Since Ewald was in command of Holstein, he likely would have been called upon to lead his troops into the depths of the Russian campaign, especially since he now commanded the Holstein division included in the above levee. Thankfully, this unit was not called upon to make the long march that ended at Moscow and turned around for the nightmarish retreat that has become so much a part of Napoleonic history.

Later in 1812, Ewald received the decoration of the Dannebrog Man from the king. He was now winning fame as a national hero in his adopted country. Some of these accolades certainly stemmed from his willingness to stand up to the French in the aftermath of the Jena-Auerstädt campaign. Likewise, there was his success in putting down Schill's uprising.

Early in 1813, an old chest infection, which had afflicted Ewald intermittently since his service in North America, returned. Diagnosed as dropsy, it could have been any number of different ailments. As the condition worsened, Ewald was forced to retire from active duty. Ewald stepped down on 1 May 1813, after fifty-three years of military service.[97]

He retired to his country estate near Kiel, where he lingered in some pain for nearly two months. Still, he did have the consolation of being surrounded by his son and five daughters as he endured his final illness. He died on 25 June 1813 at noon and was buried on the 29th at St George's cemetery in Kiel. His grave is no longer there however, having been destroyed during the Allied bombing offensive in World War II.[98]

CONCLUSION

This survey of Johann Ewald's life presents the portrait of a soldiers' soldier who lived through times of profound change in the art of warfare. These were not so much alterations in technology or doctrine as of motivation, what drove men to take up arms in the first place. When it came to the soldier's craft, he stood as a consummate professional. As one source described, "His exceptional talents and bravery in small unit combat enabled him in numerous situations to overcome larger combined units."[1]

In many ways, Ewald exemplified the soldier-intellectual that stands as the goal of professional military education today. It is certain, based on the references in his writings, that he read many of the important works on irregular warfare available in his time. He read some of the classics on warfare as well, such as Vegetius. At the same time, he evaluated these works critically through the lens of his own, fairly broad, military experiences. Beginning with the period of peace that followed the Seven Years' War, he reflected on his combat experiences, and began to consider what lessons could be extracted from what he had witnessed. The product was his first short book.

For Ewald, then, the trip to North America was a chance to enhance his military reputation and to practice his craft. Certainly, the American War of Independence encompassed the most active part of Ewald's military career. From the perspective of gaining experience as a partisan fighter, it was the most interesting as well. Ewald profited at this time through commanding units in almost every aspect of eighteenth century land warfare, from major battles, such as Brandywine and Germantown during the 1777 campaign, to countless skirmishes and ambushes throughout his time in America. The captain participated in several major sieges as well, specifically Charleston, South Carolina and Yorktown in Virginia. He therefore had the somewhat unique opportunity to witness siege warfare from the perspectives of both the besieger and besieged.

At this point it is clear that Ewald lived as a thorough military professional to the end of his life. While he served Hessen-Kassel for some twenty-four years, he followed the orders of the Landgraf unquestioningly, even when they took him halfway across the world. Even in his final break, Ewald went through proper military channels, and accepted the advice of the prince to serve in the Danish army rather than the Prussian. A strong sense of honor in word and deed can be detected throughout his life as well. While enemies could be tricked, as this was all in the nature of war, civilians had to be protected and won over through fair treatment as much as possible.

Ewald's service in the American War of Independence provided him with numerous opportunities to participate in a broad spectrum of military actions, from major battles, such as Brandywine and Germantown, to the smaller unit actions and patrols he led in the winter of 1777-78, and again on the approach to Charleston in 1780.

All of these activities provided ample grist for Ewald's intellectual mill, and on his return to Europe, he sought out the cogent lessons imparted by his five years of active fighting. Until the very end of his career, he sought to learn from his experiences. Further, he sought to pass on what he learned as well, either through training the men in his charge, or through his publications. Even in his earliest work, he supplemented his ideas on the conduct of partisan operations with real-life experiences. This factor stood as a characteristic which separated his work from that of many of his contemporaries. Likewise, Ewald saw his writing as a channel through which he could enhance his professional reputation. This proved to be correct on several occasions.

Johann von Ewald died before the German states rose up and through off the French. Still, in some of his correspondence, he did allude to this possibility.

He does seem to have assimilated quite well to his adopted homeland. He never returned to Hessen-Kassel through the rest of his life. His wife and children became the focus of his world outside his work.[2]

In all, perhaps the finest tribute that can be made concerning Johann von Ewald was that he seems truly to have lived up to his personal motto: "Honor is like an island, steep and without a shore. They who once leave can never return."

FOOTNOTES

Notes on Translatations

[1] Peter Paret, "Translation, Literal or Accurate." in the *Journal of Military History*. 78, 3 (July 2014): 1077-1080.

Introduction

[1] On the history of partisan warfare during this period, see the following: Heuser, Beatrice "Small Wars in the Age of Clausewitz: The Watershed between Partisan War and People's War." in *Journal of Strategic Studies*, 33, 1 (February 19, 2010):139-162; James R. Mc Intyre, "Enlightened Rogues: Light Infantry and Partisan Theorists of the Eighteenth Century, 1740-1800." In *The Journal of the Seven Years War Association*, 18, 2 (Fall 2013): 4-28, and British Light Infantry Tactics. Point Pleasant, NJ: Winged Hussar Publishing, 2015. See also Martin Rink "The Partisan's Metamorphosis: From Freelance Military Entrepreneur to German Freedom Fighter, 1740-1815." in *War in History*. 17(1): 6-36; George Satterfield, *Princes, Posts, and Partisans the Army of Louis XIV and Partisan Warfare in the Netherlands (1673-1678)*. Leiden: Brill, 2003.

[2] Carl von Ewald, *Generallieutenant Johann von Ewalds Levnetsløb*. Copenhagen: 1838.

Chapter 1

[1] Concerning the history of Hessen-Cassel, see Walter Horace Bruford *Germany in the Eighteenth Century*. Cambridge: Cambridge University Press, 1935. See also Karl Demandt *Gesichte des Landes Hessen*, 2nd ed. Kassel: Bärenreiter, 1972. See also Peter H. Wilson *Heart of Europe: A History of the Holy Roman Empire*. Cambridge, MA: The Belknap Press of Harvard University Press, 2016. Of particular use for the present study was Charles W. Ingrao *The Hessian Mercenary State: Ideas, Institutions, and Reform under Frederick II, 1760-1785*. Cambridge: Cambridge University Press, 1987.

[2] The name of the state is sometimes given as Hesse-Cassel or Hessen-Cassel. Hessen-Kassel is form utilized by most experts, as well as the official German name of the state. As such, it will be used throughout the remainder of the following work to denote Ewald's birthplace, as well as the homeland of the Hessen-Cassel contingent in the *American War of Independence*.

[3] Wilson *Heart of Europe*, 375.

[4] Charles Ingrao "'Barbarous Strangers': Hessian State and Society during the American Revolution." in *The American Historical Review*. 87,4 (October 1982): 960.

[5] Demandt, *Gesichte*, 125.

[6] Ingrao "'Barbarous Strangers,'"960. On economic conditions in Hessen-Cassel, see also, Atwood, *Hessians*, 12.

[7] Ingrao "'Barbarous Strangers,'"960.

[8] Ibid.

[9] Ibid.

[10] This definition is my own, though it closely parallels that of Peter H. Wilson, who defines the Soldatenhandel as "the practice of the lesser German princes of hiring out their soldiers to other states..." See Peter H. Wilson "The German 'Soldier Trade' of the Seventeenth and Eighteenth Centuries: A Reassessment." *The International History Review*. 18, 4 (November 1996): 757.

[11] There is a long historiography of the soldatenhandel, and it is intricately enmeshed in German political trends. For instance, in the nineteenth century, as German nationalism took hold in central Europe, many historians denounced the subsidy treaties as the result of greed on the part of the petty German princes of the previous century. Some good examples of this early trend is Freidrich Kapp *Der soldatenhandel deutscher fürsten nach Amerika. Ein beitrag zur kulturgeschichte*

des achtzehnten jahrhunderts. Berling: J. Springer, 1874. See also Carl Presser, *Die Soldatenhandel in Hessen.* Marburg: R.G. Einwert, 1900. In the view of these early historians, the troops from Hesse-Cassel and various other German states that were contracted out to other powers were depicted as little more than military chattels. The trend continued through much of the twentieth century in works such as Philipp Losch, *Soldatenhandel mit einem Berzeidnis der Hessen-Kasselischen Gubdfidienvertrage und einer Bibliographie.* Berlag zu Kassel: Barenreiter, 1933. During the 1980s, a more balanced view of the role of subsidies and subsidy troops began to emerge. One of the key works in this regard was Rodney Atwood, *The Hessians Mercenaries from Hessen-Kassel in the American Revolution.* Cambridge: Cambridge University Press, 1980. Following Atwood's work, but expanding on many of the same themes was Charles W. Ingrao, *The Hessian Mercenary State: Ideas, Institutions, and Reform under Frederick II, 1760-1785.* Cambridge: Cambridge University Press, 1987. Published in the interim between these two works, John Childs, *Armies and Warfare in Europe, 1648-1789.* Manchester: Manchester University Press, 1982, 46-48 provides a decidedly traditional and negative interpretation of this practice. In this regards, he merely echoes the description given by those such as Kapp and Presser. The most recent of the works survey here, William Urban *Bayonets for Hire: Mercenaries for Hire 1550-1789.* London: Greenhill Books, 2006, which purports to treat of the history of mercenaries, only touches on subsidies and does not contain any discussion of the soldatenhandel.

12 Ibid. On the more traditional interpretation, see John Childs *Armies and Warfare in Europe, 1648-1789.* Manchester: Manchester University Press, 1982: 46-48.

13 Peter H. Wilson *War, State and Society in Württemberg, 1677-1793.* Cambridge: Cambridge University Press, 1995, 74.

14 Wilson, "Soldier Trade," 758.

15 Peter H. Wilson, *War, State and Society.* 76.

16 Wilson, "Soldier Trade," 775.

17 Ibid, 776.

18 Ibid.

19 Wilson, "Soldier Trade", 777.

20 Atwood, *Hessians,* 1. Concerning the evolution of army structure, see also, John A Lynn, "The Evolution of Army Style in the Modern West, 800-2000." in *The International History Review.* 18,3 (August 1996): 505-545.

21 Wilson, "Soldier Trade," 765.

22 The most recent work on the subject to employ the term subsidientruppen is Daniel Krebbs, *A Generous and Merciful Enemy: Life for German Prisoners of War during the American Revolution.* Norman: University of Oklahoma Press, 2013, 8-9.

23 Ibid.

24 Ibid, 763.

25 Atwood, *Hessians,* 16.

26 Ibid, 16-17.

27 Hoffman, *Hessian Troops,* 75.

28 The War of Jenkins' Ear really requires a new, book-length study. Even the articles surveyed in preparation of the current work are fairly dated. These include: Harvey H. Jackson III "Behind the Lines: Savannah during the War of Jenkins' Ear." in *The Georgia Historical Quarterly.* 78,3 (Fall 1994): 471-492; J.K. Laughton "Jenkins's Ear." in *The English Historical Review.* 4, 16 (Octo. 1889): 741-49; Phinizy Spalding "Oglethorpe, Georgia, and the Spanish Threat." The Georgia Historiacal Quarterly. 78, 3 (Fall 1994): 461-70; Harold W. V. Temperley "The Causes of the War of Jenkins' Ear, 1739." in *Transaction of the Royal Historical Society,* 3rd Series, 3 (1909): 197-236.

29 The conflict is also referred to as the First and Second Silesia Wars. The two most recent works in English on this conflict are: M.S. Anderson *The War of the Austrian Succession 1740-1748.* London: Longman, 1995 and Reed Browning *The War of the Austrian Succession.* New York: St. Martin's Griffin, 1995. The Landgraviate would eventually cease to exist in 1803.

30 Browning, *War of the Austrian Succession,* 20-22.

31 Atwood, *Hessians,* 16. For Hesse-Kassel in the *War of the Austrian Succession,* see M.S. Anderson The War of the Austrian Succession 1740-1748. London: Longman, 1995, 32. See also Dan Schorr "Hessian Colors and Standards, 1740-48." *In Seven Years War Association Journal.* 8.3, (Spring 1994): 4

32 Atwood, *Hessians,* 16.

33 Ibid.

34 Ibid.

35 Ibid. Additional information on the role of the Hessian troops in the War of the Astrian Succession can be found in Major von Dalwigk "Der Anteil der Hessischen Truppen am Österreichen Erbfolgekriege (1740-48)." In *Zeitschrift der Vereins fürhessische Geschichte und Landeskunde*. 42 (1908): 72-139.

36 Daniel Krebs A Generous and Merciful Enemy: *Life for German Prisoners of War during the American Revolution*. Norman: University of Oklahoma Press, 2013, 36.

37 Carl von Ewald *Johannes Ewald: Bilder aus dem Leben eines Soldaten*. Staatarchiv Kassel, Best. C19 Nr. 7217. While this work is often attributed to Johannes Ewald himself, it seems more like that it was the work of his son, or possibly some unknown archivist, as it discusses Johann Ewald's death as well.

38 Friedrich Justinian, quoted in Atwood *Hessians*, 19-20.

39 For basic biographical information on Ewald, see, Tustin, Ewald, *Diary of the American War a Hessian Journal*, New Haven, CT Yale University Press, 1979, xxiv.

40 Ewald, *Diary*, 1.

Chapter 2

1 The conflict is known by all three titles. The primary differentiation seems to be that when referring to the fighting in North America, the name French and Indian is most often applied, while when discussing the European theater, the term Seven Years' War is generally used.

2 On the French and Indian war, the main study is Fred Anderson, *Crucible of War: The Seven Years War and the Fate of Empire in North America, 1754-1766*. New York: Alfred A. Knopf, 2000. On the European theater, there is the recent, but heavily biased Franz J. Szabo, *The Seven Years War in Europe 1756-1763*. New York: Longman, 2008. Finally, the maritime dimension is ably covered in Daniel Baugh, *The Global Seven Years War, 1754-1763*. London: Pearson Education, 2011. Though dated, the essential work on the western theater, the one in which Ewlad fought, remains Sir Reginald Savory *His Britanic Majesty's Army in Germany during the Seven Years' War*. Oxford: Clarendon Press, 1966.

3 On the life of General von Browne, see Christopher Duffy, *The Wild Goose and the Eagle: A life of Marshal von Browne, 1705-1757*. Chatto & Windus, 1964. On the engagement sand its ramifications, see Szabo, *Seven Years War*, 42-44. For a more balanced view of Frederick and his motives in the campaign, see Christopher Duffy, *Frederick the Great: A Military Life*. London: Routledge, 1985, 102-08.

4 The most thorough dissection of these engagements in English is found in Christopher Duffy, *Prussia's Glory: Rossbach and Leuthen 1757*. Chicago: The Emperor's Press, 2003.

5 This rapid shift in the fortunes of the war is often referred to as the miracle of the House of Brandenburg.

6 Concerning Ferdinand's services in the War of the Austrian Succession, see *M.S. Anderson, The War of the Austrian Succession 1740-1748*. London: Longman, 1995 and Reed Browning *The War of the Austrian Succession*. New York: St. Martin's Griffin, 1995. On the role of the European nobility in the military during this period, as well as the expectation that noble youth would receive a military education, see Christopher Storrs and H.M. Scott "The Military revolution and the European Nobility, c. 1600-1800." in War in History, 3, 1 (January 1996):1-41

7 On the surrender at Pirna, See Franz Szabo, , 37-44.

8 On Rossbach and Leuthen, see Christopher Duffy Prussia's Glory: Rossbach and Leuthen, 1757. Rosemont, Ill.: Emperor's, 2004.

9 On the Convention of Kloster Seven, see Szabo, *Seven Years' War*, 78-79.

10 Concerning Ferdinand's command of His Britannic Majesty's Army, see James R. Mc Intyre "A Study in Coalition Command: Ferdinand of Brunswick and His Britannic Majesty's Army" in *Journal of the Seven Years War Association*. 20, 3 (Winter 2015-16): 25-40.

11 Minden is one of the most celebrated engagements in the western theater. Useful secondary accounts include: Sir Lees Knowles *Minden and the Seven Years' War*, London: Simpkin, Marshall, Hamilton, Kent and Co., (1914.), Frank Mc Lynn *1759: The Year Britain became Master of the World*. New York: Atlantic Monthly Press, 2004. On a more current and scholarly level, see Baugh, *Global Seven Years' War* , 444-45. More dated, but useful on the various commanders is Charles Winslow Elliot "The Men That Fought at Minden." *The Journal of the American Military Institute*. 3, 2 (Summer 1939): 80-103. Dated, but still very useful for placing the battle in its wider context is Sir Lees Knowles, *The Battle of Minden and the Seven Years War*. London: Simpkin, Marshall, Hamilton, Kent, and Company, 1914.

12 Knowles *Minden*, 31.

[13] On Maxen, see Christopher Duffy, *Frederick the Great: A Military Life*. London: Routledge, 1985, 193-97, and Szabo, Seven Years War, 251-253.

[14] On Ferdinand's command style, see Mc Intyre "Coalition Command,"

[15] On the French use of western German to supply their armies, see *Childs, Armies and Warfare*, 161-165.

[16] The French strategy described in the text derived from a clear net assessment of their naval weakness in comparison to Great Britain. On the French strategy in the Seven Years' War, see Jonathan R. Dull *The French Navy and the Seven Years' War*. Lincoln, NE: University of Nebraska Press, 2005, 37.

[17] See Ewald, *Bild*, 1. See also Carl von Ewald *Generallieutenant Johann von Ewalds Levnetsløb*. Copenhagen: Riises Boglade,1838, 1-2.

[18] Concerning the battle of Sandershausen, see Alexander Burns, "Hesse-Kassel Stands Alone: The Battle of Sandershausen, July 23rd, 1758." *Journal of the Seven Years War Association* 18, 1 (Spring 2013): 4-19.

[19] Ewald, *Bilder*, 1.

[20] Tustin, *Diary*, xxv. See also Carl von Ewald, *Ewalds Levnetsløb*. 2

[21] Johann Ewald *Gedanken eines hessischen Offiziers uber sa, was man bei Fuhrung eines Detachements im Felde zu thun hat*. Cassel: Johann Jacob Cramer, 1774, 15.

[22] The Regiment von Gilsa was the regiment von Fürstennburg until 1759. It then became the Füsilier-Regiment von Gilsa. As was often the case in eighteenth century army formations, the name of the unit changed following a change in commanders.

[34] Daniel Krebs, *Generous and Merciful Enemy*. On the percentage of the Hessian population who served during the eighteenth century, see *Childs, Armies and Warfare*, 60-61.

[24] Atwood, *Hessians*,

[25] Unless otherwise noted, the preceding derives from Rudolf Witzel *Hessen-Kassels Regimenter in der Alliierten Armee 1762*. N.P.: Norderstedt Books on Demand GmbH, 2008.

[26] The difference between a standing and a converged grenadier battalion was that in the case of the former, the unit was recruited as a grenadier unit. In the case of the latter, or converged grenadier battalion, the grenadiers of other existing companies were taken and merged to form a grenadier battalion. As a result, the converged battalions tended to have a somewhat ad hoc nature.

[27] The preceding description of the Hessian army derives from Mark Henry, "The Hessian Army of the Seven Years War," *Seven Years' War Association Journal*, 7, 3, (Spring 1994): 40.

[28] Ibid, 41.

[29] Born in 1720, he was educated in Geneva, where he came into contact with the burgeoning intellectual movement known as the Enlightenment. Many of its values informed the latter years of his reign. After his return to Hesse-Cassel, he converted to Roman Catholicism, a decision which cost him his marriage, and earned him the distrust of many of the princes of the Holy Roman Empire, at least during the early part of his reign. For biographical information on Frederick II of Hesse-Cassel, see Charle Ingrao *The Hessian Mercenary State: Ideas, Institutions, and Reform under Frederick II, 1760-1785*. Cambridge: Cambridge University Press, 1987.

[30] Luke Mulder "Some Notes on Landgraf Friedreich II of Hessen-Kassel and the Re-Organization of 1760." In *β*, 8, 2 (Winter 2000):18.

[31] R. D. Pengel *German States in the Seven Years' War: Supplement*. Powys, UK: Imperial Press, 1993 reprint of 1984 original, np. The Regiment von Gilsa began as the Hanstein regiment of foot. It was commanded by Lieutenant General von Gilsa from 1759-1765. In 1760, it was converted into a fusilier regiment with attendant alterations being made to its uniform.

[32] Carl von Ewald, *Ewalds Levnetsløb*, 2.

[33] On the details of Ewald's uniform, see Pengel, *German States in the Seven Years' War*.

[34] Carl von Ewald, *Ewalds Levnetsløb*, 2.

[35] Henry, "Hessian Army," 41.

[36] Carl von Ewald *Ewalds Levnetsløb*, 2.

[37] Johan Ewald, *Diary*, xxv.

[38] Carl von Ewald *Johannes Ewald: aus dem Leben eines Soldaten*. Staatarchiv Kassel, Best. C19 Nr. 7217.

[39] Duffy, *Military Experience in the Age of Reason*, 73-74.

[40] Ewald, *Ewalds Levnetsløb*, 2.

[41] These sources include the introductory not in Ewald's Diary of the American War, Tustin, ed. xxiv-xxvi. This is clearly based on the biography of Ewald by his son, Carl. Additional information on the elder Ewald's services in the Seven Years War were gleaned from Carl von Ewald *Ewalds Levnetsløb*, 2-6. Finally, an anonymous pamphlet in the Hessian Archives attributed to Ewald but more like the work of his son as it describes the death of Johan von Ewald in some detail provided some additional information. See Carl von Ewald *Johannes Ewald: aus dem Leben eines Soldaten*. Staatarchiv Kassel, Best. C19 Nr. 7217.

[42] Ewald *Ewalds Levnetsløb*, 2.

43 On military education for officers during the period, see Christopher Duffy, *The Military Experience in the Age of Reason, 1715- 1789.* New York: Scribner, 1987, 47-8. On the tutorial method, see Don Higginbotham *George Washington and the American Military Tradition.* Athens: University of Georgia Press, 1985, 14-15. On the humane nature of training, see Duffy, *Military Experience in the Age of Reason,* 122-23.

44 Ewald *Ewalds Levnetsløb,* 2.

45 Ibid.

46 On the role of the nobility in the armies of the period, See Duffy, *Military Experience,* 35-42. See also Christopher Storrs and H.M. Scott "The Military revolution and the European Nobility, c. 1600-1800." in *War in History,* 3, 1 (January 1996):1-4. Likewise, the opening of the officer class also benefited Friedrich von Steuben during his early services in the Prussian Army. See Paul Lockhart The Drillmaster of Valley Forge: The Baron de Steuben and the Making of the American Army. New York: Harper Collins, 2008, 16-21.

47 Ewald *Ewalds Levnetsløb,* 2.

48 The translators of Ewald's *Treatise on Partisan Warfare* comments that the young man saw field service almost immediately after joining the army. Johan von Ewald, Treatise on Partisan Warfare. Robert A. Selig and David Curtiss Skaggs, trans. New York: Greenwood Press, 1991,1.

49 This period encompassed the end of what some characterize as the Military Revolution. The Military Revolution is tangential to the current topic, but is worth mention. It refers to a series of technological and doctrinal changes which occurred in the period roughly between 1500 and 1800. Proponents argue that these changes drastically altered the manner in which wars were conducted, as well as the means states utilized to support their militaries. Significant works in this discussion include: Parker, Geoffrey *The Military Revolution: Military Innovation and the Rise of the West, 1500-1800.* Cambridge, Cambridge University Press, 1988. See also Frank Tallet *War and Society in Early-Modern Europe, 1495-1715.* London: Routledge, 1992. Jeremy Black challenged the entire concept of the Military Revolution in Jeremy Black *A Military Revolution? Military Change and European Society, 1550-1800.* Basingstoke: Macmillan Education, 1991. Basic themes presented by many of the above historians were developed and expanded upon in Clifford J. Rogers, ed. *The Military Revolution Debate: Readings on the Military Transformation of Early Modern Europe.* Boulder, CO: Westview Press, 1995.

50 This and the following discussion of eighteenth century warfare are based on the following sources: Jeremy Black *Warfare in the Eighteenth Century.* London: Cassell, 1999. Anthony D. Darling *Red Coat and Brown Bess.* Alexandria Bay, NY: Museum Restoration Service, 1971. Somewhat dated, but extremely useful for understanding most aspects of land warfare in the period is *The Military Experience in the Age of Reason, 1715- 1789.* New York: Scribner, 1987. Russell F. Weigley *The Age of Battles: The Quest for Decisive Warfare from Breitenfeld to Waterloo.* Bloomington: Indiana University Press, 1991.

51 While dated, Harold L. Peterson *Round Shot and Rammers.* Harrisburg, PA: Stackpole Books, 1969 remains a comprehensive discussion of artillery in the period. The preceding discussion of the field guns is derived predominantly from his work. See also, B.P. Hughes *Open Fire: The Artillery Tactics from Marlborough to Wellington.* Sussex: Antony Bird Publications, 1983. Concerning the Hessian artillery during Ewald's early career in particular see Mike Partridge "The Artillery of Hesse-Cassel: A Brief Organizational History." In *Seven Years War Association Journal,* 8, 2 (Winter 2000): 14-15.

52 John Ellis Cavalry *The History of Mounted Warfare.* Yorkshire: Pen and Sword Books, 2004 reprint of 1978 original, 77-108.

53 Weigley, *Age of Battles,* xiv-xv.

54 For an excellent discussion of tactics and tactical development during much of the period under investigation, see Brent Nosworthy *The Anatomy of Victory: Battle Tactics 1689-1763.* New York: Hippocrene Books, 1990.

55 Darling *Red Coat and Brown Bess,* 10-12.

56 Concerning lines versus columns and the debate over the musket's role as a shock versus a fire weapons, see Robert S. Quimby *The Background of Napoleonic Warfare: The Theory of Military Tactics in Eighteenth-Century France.* New York: Columbia University Press, 1957.

57 On the role of the bayonet, see Larry H. Addison *The Patterns of War through the Eighteenth Century.* Bloomington: Indiana University Press, 1990, 92-93. See also Matthew H. Spring *With Zeal and Bayonets Only: The British Army on Campaign in American, 1775-1783.* Norman: University of Oklahoma Press, 2008, 216-44.

58 Ibid.

59 On the battle of Corbach, See Knowles, Minden, 31-21, Savory, *His Britannic Majesty's Army,* 216-20, and Szabo, *Seven Years War,* 302-03.

60 On this engagement, see Savory, *His Britannic Majesty's Army,* 227-228.

[61] Ibid.

[62] Ibid.

[63] Szabo, *Seven Years War*, 329.

[64] Ibid, 328.

[65] Ewald, *Bilder*, 2.

[66] Harold L. Peterson The Book of the Continental Soldier Being a Compleat Account of the Uniforms, Weapons, and Equipment with which he Lived and Fought. Harrisburg, PA: Stackpole Books, 1968, 171-72. While this work deals with a slightly later period, advances in medical technology were glacially slow, especially by comparison with the present time.

[67] Ewald, *Bilder*, 2

[68] Ibid.

[69] Ewald *Diary*, xxv.

[70] Savory, Britannic Majesty's Army, 322.

[71] Szabo, *Seven Years War*, 352-53.

[72] George Nafzinger "Order of Battle, Battle of Vellinghausen, July 15-16, 1761" Nafzinger Collenction, U.S. Army Combat Studies Institute, Internet. http://usacac.army.mil/cac2/CGSC/CARL/nafziger/761GAC.pdf Last Accessed November 30, 2016.

[73] Ewald, *Gedanken*, 32.

[74] Ibid.

[75] Ibid, 32-3.

[76] See Peter Paret, *Clausewitz and the State: The Man, his Theories, and his Times*. Princeton: Princeton University Press, 1985, 191-92. See also, chapter 12, n. 122.

[77] Szabo *Seven Years War*, 409-10.

[78] Ewald, *Diary*, xxv.

[79] Anonymous "Militär in alten Mauern" September 13-14, 2003 Internet. https://web.archive.org/web/20031005141352/http://www.hessenmilitaer.de/amoeneburg.htm Last accessed September 28, 2016. See also, Carl Renouard *Geschichte des Krieges in Hannover, Hessen und Westfalen von 1757 bis 1763*. 3 Bände, Cassel, 1863-64 , pp. 784-796.

[80] "Militär in alten Mauern".

[81] Ibid.

[82] Sir Charles Hotham-Thompson, Operations of the Allied Army under the Duke of Brunswick, 1757-1762. London: T. Jeffreys, 1764, reprint, West Chester, OH: The Nafziger Collection, 2016, 165.

[83] "Militär in alten Mauern".

[84] Ibid.

[85] Ibid.

[86] Ewald, *Picture*, 2

[87] Ewald, *Gedanken*, 15-16.

[88] Ibid.

[89] Militär in alten Mauern."

[90] Ibid.

[91] Hotham-Thompson, Operations of the Allied Army under the Duke of Brunswick, 166.

[92] C.T. Atkinson "British Strategy and Battles in Westphalian Campaigns of 1758-1762." In Journal of the United Services Institution. 79, 516 (1934): 739-40.

[93] Savory, Britannic Majesty's Army, 440

[94] Franz Szabo seeks to present Frederick as a sort of proto-Nazi. This assertion is patently false and this bias pervades his work on the Seven Years' War in Europe. Frederick's motives and goals in the conflict seem no better, or worse, than those of the other belligerents. While it is true Frederick did lose hope at times, and even attempted suicide on at least one occasion, in the end, his state survived intact, if heavily damaged by the fighting.

Chapter 3

[1] Duffy, *Experience of War*, 302.

[2] Szabo, *Seven Years' War*, 180.

[3] Georg Heinz Wetzel, Die Hessischen Jager: einer deutche Truppenhistorie in politischen Wandlungsprozess von vier Jahrhunderten (1631-1987). Kassel, Verlag George, 1987, 17.

[4] On the topic of exactions and their role in warfare especially during the Seven Years' War, see Child's, *Armies and Warfare*, 159-170. For a detailed discussion of the practice of contributions, see Col. John W. Wright "Military Contributions during the Eighteenth Century." in Journal of the American Military Institute, 3, 1 (Spring 1939): 3-13.

5 Ingrao, *Hessian Mercenary State*, 57.

6 Taylor, "Military System and Rural Social Change in Eighteenth Century Hesse-Cassel." in *Journal of Social History*. 25, 3 (April 1992):494-95.

7 Wilson, "Soldier Trade." 789. On the use of the army to stimulate the domestic economy, see Ingrao, "Barbarous Strangers," 961.

8 This was the practice in the British army of the period, though not necessarily employed by Continental powers. On the British army, see J.A. Houlding, *Fit for Service The Training of the British Army, 1715-1795*. Oxford: Clarendon Press, 1981.

9 Ewald, *Diary*, xxv.

10 Robert A. Selig, "Light Infantry Lessons from America? Johann Ewald's Experiences in the American Revolutionary War as Depicted in his Abhandlung uber den Kleinen Kreis (1785)." in Studies in Eighteenth Century Culture. 23 (1994): 114.

11 On the debate concerning the efficacy of Landgraf Friedrich's reforms, see Peter K. Taylor, "'Patrimonial' Bureaucracy and 'Rational' Policy in Eighteenth-Century Germany: The Case of Hessian Recruitment Reforms, 1762-93." in Central European History. 22,1 (March 1989): 33-56; and "Military System and Rural Social Change in Eighteenth-Century Hesse-Cassel." in Journal of Social History. 25, 3 (April 1992): 479-504. Peter H. Wilson challenges Taylor's reforms in Wilson "German 'Soldier Trade,'" 768-771.

12 Carl von Ewald, *Ewalds Levnetsløb*, 6

13 Carl von Ewald Johannes Ewald: Bilder aus dem Leben eines Soldaten. Staatarchiv Kassel, Best. C19 Nr. 7217,4.

14 Ibid, 5.

15 Selig, "Light Infantry Lessons," 111-12. On the reaction of other members of the Hessian nobility to his promotion, see Ewald, Diary, xxvi. Finally, on the effect of his non-noble status on his career advancement, see Beatrice Heuser, "Johann Ewald," in Philosophers of War The Evolution of History's Greatest Military Thinkers. vol. 1, Daniel Coetzee and Lee Eystrulid, eds. Santa Barbara, CA: Praeger, 2013, 41.

16 Ferdinand Zwenger "Johann Ewald in hessischen Dienst." Hessenland, VII (1893): 143.

17 Ewald, *Diary*, xxv-vi.

18 Ibid, xxvi.

19 Carl von Ewald, *Ewalds Levnetsløb*, 7

20 Ibid. See also, Zwenger, "Johann Ewald," 144. The above reflects a combination of the quote as rendered in both sources.

21 Zwenger "Johann Ewald," 144.

22 Carl von Ewald, *Ewalds Levnetsløb*, 7-8.

23 Zwenger "Johann Ewald," 144. The possible term of imprisonment is given in Carl von Ewald, *Ewalds Levnetsløb*, 8.

24 On the topic of dueling, see Barbara Holland Gentleman's Blood: A History of Dueling from Swords at Dawn to Pistols at Dusk. New York: Bloomsbury, 2003. On notions of dueling in the armies of Louis XIV, see John A. Lynn "The Embattled Future of Academic Military History." In Journal of Military History, 61, 4 (October 1997): 786-87.

25 Ewald, *Diary*, xxvi.

26 Ewald quoted in Zwenger, "Johann Ewald," 144.

27 Ewald, *Ewalds Levnetsløb*, 8.

28 Ingrao, Hessian Mercenary State, 75-79.

29 Ingrao, "'Barbarous Strangers,'" 960.

30 Zwenger, "Johann Ewald," 144.

31 Ibid.

32 Johann von Ewald, Johann von Hinrichs, Johann Chrittoph von Huyn, The Siege of Charleston. Bernard A. Uhlendorf, ed, and trans. New York: New York Times and Arno Press, 1968, 6.

33 On the development of light infantry theory, see James R. Mc Intyre "Enlightened Rogues: Light Infantry and Partisan Theorists of the Eighteenth Century, 1740-1800." In The Journal of the Seven Years War Association, 18, 2 (Fall 2013): 4-28. On the development of light infantry in practice, see James Mc Intyre British Light Infantry Tactics: The Development of British Light Infantry, Continental and North American Influences, 1740-1765. Point Pleaseant, NJ: Winged Hussar Publishing, 2015.

34 On the topic of petite guerre, see John Grenier, The First Way of War: American War Making on the Frontier. Cambridge: Cambridge University Press, 2005; Sandrine Picaud-Monnerat, La Petite Guerre au XVIIIe Siecle Paris: Economica, 2010; Armstrong Starkey, War in the Age of Enlightenment, 1700-1789. Westport, CT: Praeger, 2003; Otto Zwengel, "Zur Theorie des Kleinen Kriegs." Allegemeine Militarrundschau. 10 (1969): 397-404.

35 Azar Gat The Origins of Military Thought: From the Enlightenment to Clausewitz. Oxford: Clarendon Press, 1989, 25.

36 Ibid, 27.

37 Ibid, 28.

38 Ibid, 29.

39 Johann Ewald, Gedanken eines hessischen Offiziers uber sa, was man bei Fuhrung eines Detachments im Felde zu thun hat. Cassel: Johann Jacob Cramer, 1774, np. Hereinafter, the work will be referred to simply as Gedanken. All page numbers included in these notes are based on the German original.

40 Gedanken, Forward, 2.

41 Ibid, 1-6.

42 Selig and Skaggs,

43 Ewald, Gedanken, 1

44 Schomberg was a unique character, as he was the only man to hold a commission in both the English and French Armies. Ibid, 4-5.

45 On Ewald's use of French, see Urwin "'I have wanted to go see you for a Long Time,'" 1-2.

46 Ewald, Gedanken, 3.

47 Ibid , 3-4.

48 Ibid, 4.

49 Ibid, 8.

50 Ibid, 14.

51 Ibid, 18-19.

52 Ibid, 20.

53 Ibid.

54 Ibid, 20-21. The chaff-mines Ewald speaks of were false mines dug to confuse the enemy when attacking a fortified post.

55 Ibid, 31.

56 Ibid.

57 Ibid.

58 Ibid, 42

59 Jean Charles, Chevalier de Folard (1669-1752) Folard was probably the most celebrated and debated military writer of the first half of the eighteenth century, not least for his ongoing debate with Puységur. Ewald would certainly have found a kindred spirit and possibly an idle in Folard who joined the French army at 16, after attending a Jesuit college. Folard fought in various battles of the War of Spanish Succession in Italy, and kept a notebook of his experiences and his thoughts on the conduct of war. These eventually came into print in his Abrégé des commentaries de M. de Folard sur L'Histoire de Polybe (Commentaries on Polbus). The most recent biography of Folard as of this writing is Jean Chagnoit Le Chavlier de Folard: Le Strategie d'incertitude. Paris: Editions du Rocher, 1997. For more in-depth discussion of Folard's ideas, see Azar Gat, The Origins of Military Thought: From the Enlightenment to Clausewitz. Oxford: Clarendon Press, 1989; Brent Nosworthy The Anatomy of Victory: Battle Tactics 1689-1763. New York: Hippocrene Books, 1990; and Robert S. Quimby, The Background of Napoleonic Warfare: The Theory of Military Tactics in Eighteenth-Century France. New York: Columbia University Press, 1957.

60 Ibid, 47.

61 Ibid.

62 Ibid, 48.

63 Ibid, 48-49.

64 Ibid, 49.

65 Ibid.

66 Ibid, 53-4.

67 Ibid, 57.

68 Ibid.

69 Ibid.

70 Ibid, 61-62.

71 Ibid, 66.

72 Ibid, 73.

73 Ibid, 73-4.

74 Ibid, 75-76.

75 Ibid, 50.

76 Ibid, 51.

77 Ibid, 50.
78 Ibid, 50.
79 Ibid, 2.
80 Ewald, *Diary*, xxvi
81 Carl von Ewald, *Bild*, 4.
82 Georg Heinz Wetzel *Die Hessischen Jäger: einer deutche Truppenhistorie in politischen Wandlungsprozess von vier Jahrhunderten (1631-1987)*. Kassel, Verlag George, 1987, 31. It is worth noting that the term Jäger literally translates as hunter.
83 Ibid.
84 On the development of light troops in the War of the Austrian Succession, see: Mc Intyre, "Enlightened Rouges," 4-6.
85 David Gates, *The British Light Infantry Arm c. 1790-1815*. London: B.T. Batsford Ltd. 1987, 10.
86 Wetzel *Die Hessischen Jäger*, 18.
87 Ibid.
88 Darling, *Red Coat and Brown Bess*, 10-11.
89 Wetzel *Die Hessischen Jäger*, 18.
90 This was the same von Rall who would later be surprised by Washington at Trenton on December 26, 1776. The jägers were first established in Hessen-Kassel in 1631 by Landgraf William V who raised three companies of them from the huntsmen of his estates. The men composing these companies were required to demonstrate that they were able marksmen and familiar with woodcraft, in addition to proof of good reputation. Of these qualities, accurate marksmanship was an absolute must for a jäger. The chief foresters of their respective districts in turn served as commanders of the companies. Throughout the early period of their existence, it appears that the jägers were pressed into the military service of the state on an ad hoc basis. See Selig, "Light Infantry Lessons from America," 113-4.
91 Selig, Ibid, 114.
92 Ibid.
93 Ibid.
94 Zwenger, "Johann Ewald," 158.
95 Wetzel *Die Hessischen Jäger*, 18
96 Zwenger, "Johann Ewald," 158.
97 Ibid.
98 Ibid.
99 Ibid.
100 Wetzel *Die Hessischen Jäger*, 31.
101 Carl von Ewald, *Bild*, 4
102 For a thorouogh discussion of Pontiac's Rebellion and its causes, see William R. Nester, *"Haughty Conquerors" Amherst and the Great Indian Uprising of 1763*. Westport, CT: Praeger, 2000.
103 One of the more recent works on Lexington and Concord at the time of this writing, Walter R. Borneman American Spring: *Lexington, Concord, and the Road to Revolution*. New York: Little, Brown and Company, 2014, stresses the role of strategic communication in the opening stages of the conflict. The author notes how the rebels managed to get their version of events to London first. See specifically, pages 245-251.
104 Rodney Atwood, *The Hessians: Mercenaries from Hessen-Kassel in the American Revolution*. Cambridge: Cambridge University Press, 23-25.
105 Ibid, 26.
106 Ibid 27.
107 Ibid, 28.
108 Ibid, 37.
109 Ewald, *Diary*, 5.
110 Ibid.
111 Ibid, 5-6.
112 Ibid, 6.

Chapter 4

1 In nationalist myth, the British decision to abandon Boston is often attributed to the placement of American artillery on Dorchester Heights, which would have allowed the Americans to bombard parts of the city. In fact, the decision to evacuate the city had already been reached. This move merely served to hasten its implementation.

[2] Sam Willis The Struggle for Sea Power: A Naval History of the American Revolution. New York: W.W. Norton and Company, 2015, 116-17.

[3] John Adams to George Washington, January 6, 1776, quoted in David McCullough, 1776. New York: Simon and Schuster, 2005, 80.

[4] The colonists actually possessed naval forces, though they were inferior in both numbers and quality to those of their British adversaries. There was a small Continental Navy, authorized by Congress in 1775. In additional there were several state navies including those of Pennsylvania, Virginia and South Carolina. There were colonial privateers as well who prayed on enemy merchant shipping. These forces combined could have offered a significant challenge to the British control of the seas in American waters, however, there existed no central authority to enforce such a coordination. On this point as well, see Willis, Struggle for Sea Power,

[5] Mark V. Kwasny Washington's Partisan War, 1775-1783. Kent, OH: Kent State University Press, 1996,65.

[6] Willis, Struggle for Sea Power, 117.

[7] On Faucitt's role in negotiating the subsidy treaties, see Atwood, The Hessians, 25-28.

[8] The notion of sea legs versus land legs is not hyperbole. Atlantic Crossings during the period under consideration could be quite debilitating for those unaccustomed to life at sea. Many would have been sick and/or malnourished on their arrival. Recovery usually took at least a week. It consisted of regaining one's balance on dry land, and changing from the diet of preserved (salted) foods to fresh provisions.

[9] On the Marblehead Mariners, see Christopher F. Magra "'Soldiers…Bred to the Sea': Maritime Marblehead, and the Origins and Progress of the American Revolution." in The New England Quarterly. 77,4 (December 2004): 531-562. See also, George Athan Billias General John Glover and His Marbelhead Mariners. New York: Holt, Rinehart and Winston, 1960.

[10] In a sense, this was akin to the evacuation of the Anglo-French force from Dunkirk in 1940. It was not a victory but allowed the fight to continue.

[11] David Hackett Fischer Washington's Crossing. Oxford: Oxford University Press, 2004, 73-4.

[12] In the eighteenth-century beef, pork and fish were dreid and packed in salt brine as a means to rpeserve them for consumption on sea voyages. After consuming salt provisions for a period of time, it took several days to a weeks for the digestive system to readapt to fresh food.

[13] Ewald, Dairy, 7.

[14] Barnet Schecter, The Battle for New York The City at the Heart of the American Revolution. New York: Walker and Company, 2002, 204-8.

[15] Ewald, Dairy, 8.

[16] On Colonel von Donop's background, see Wilhelm Gottlieb Levin von Donop, Des Obermarschalls und Drosten Wilhelm Gottlieb Levin von Donop zu Lüdershofen, Maspe Nachricht von dem Geschlecht der von Donop. Paderborn 1796, 21-22. See also Rodney Atwood, The Hessians: Mercenaries from Hessen-Kassel in the American Revolution. Cambridge: Cambridge University Press, 1980, 102-3.

[17] Johann Conrad Dohla, A Hessian Diary of the Revolution. Bruce E. Burgoyne, ed. trans. Norman, OK: University of Oklahoma Press, 1990, 44.

[18] Ewald, Diary, 8-9.

[19] Ibid.

[20] On the Howe brothers' dual role and its influence on the development of the 1776 campaign, see Ira D. Gruber The Howe Brothers and the American Revolution. Chapel Hill: University of North Carolina Press, 1972, 54-70.

[21] Ewald, Diary, 9. It is worth noting that Howe's defense of the jägers may have been due, at least in part to his deteriorating relationship with Heister. Howe would eventually have the latter recalled.

[22] Ibid.

[23] Ibid.

[24] Ibid.

[25] Ibid, 10

[26] Ewald, Gedanken, 3-4.

[27] Ewald, Diary, 10.

[28] Ibid.

[29] Ibid.

[30] Leopold von Heister (ca. 1707-1777), then aged sixty-eight, was a veteran of the Seven Years' War, and the overall commander of the Hessian contingent serving in North America. He was second only in seniority to William Howe. As a result of this, Lieutenant-General Sir Henry Clinton was present with a dormant commission to full general. It would only become active should Howe

become incapacitated. This arrangement insured that the British troops would not fall under a Hessian commander.

31 Ewald, *Diary*, 10.

32 On the riff between Howe and von Heister, and the latter's eventual recall, see Gruber, *Howe Brothers*, 111-12. See also, Smith, *William Howe*, 45.

33 Ibid.

34 Ibid.

35 Ibid, 10-11.

36 Ibid, 11.

37 Ibid, 11.

38 On the origins and development of the long rifle, see James Mc Intyre "On the Origins and Development of the Pennsylvania-American Longrifle, 1500-1700." in *Seven Years War Association Journal*. Vol. 14, no.1 Fall, 2005, 40-55. On the abilities of the riflemen themselves, see Mc Intyre "Separating Myth from History: The Maryland Riflemen in the War of Independence." in Maryland Historical Magazine, Vol. 104, no. 2 (Summer 2009): 101-119. See also Michael Cecere *They Are Indeed a Very Useful Corps American Riflemen in the Revolutionary War*. Westminster, MD: Heritage Books, 2006 and Peterson, Continental Soldier,

39 Some Americans developed a solution to the problem by modifying the rifle to make it capable of taking a bayonet, a practice referred to as 'swamping'. On this point, see Lawrence E. Babits *A Devil of a Whipping The Battle of Cowpens*. Chapel Hill: University of North Carolina Press, 1998.

40 Ewald, *Dairy*, 11.

41 Ibid.

42 Ibid.

43 Ibid.

44 Ibid.

45 For an overview of these thinkers, see James R. Mc Intyre, "Enlightened Rogues: Light Infantry and Partisan Theorists of the Eighteenth Century, 1740-1800." In *The Journal of the Seven Years War Association*, 18, 2 (Fall 2013): 4-28.

46 Ibid, 12.

47 Ewald, *Diary*, 11.

48 Ibid, 11-12. Specifically, the unit on the right flank were the Grant Provincials.

49 Ibid, 12.

50 Fischer, *Washington's Crossing*, 110.

51 Ibid, 110-11.

52 Ewald, *Diary*, 13.

53 Ibid.

54 Ibid.111.

55 Ibid.

56 See Fischer, *Washington's Crossing*, 419. Fischer bases his numbers on those provided by Mark Boatner in his *Encyclopedia of the Revolution* and Howard H. Peckham *The Toll of Independence: Engagements and Battle Casualties of the American Revolution*. Chicago: University of Chicago Press, 1974.

57 David M Cullough *1776*. New York: Simon and Schuster, 2005, 234.

58 Ewald, *Diary*, 111.

59 Ibid.

60 Ibid.

61 Ibid, 13-14.

62 Ibid, 14.

63 Ibid.

64 David Hackett Fischer, *Washington's Crossing*, 111.

65 Ibid, 111-13. See also, Willis, Struggle for Sea Power, 133.

66 Ewald, *Diary*, 14.

67 Fischer, *Washington's Crossing*, 113.

68 Ewald, *Diary* 15. In eighteenth century military parlance, debauches referred to the various escape routes from a position. In the present context, the word could be taken to mean approach routes as well.

69 Ibid.

70 Ibid.

71 Andreas Wiederhold, "The Capture of Fort Washington, New York, Described by Captain Andreas Wiederhold of the Hessian 'Regiment Knyphausen,'" in *PMHB*, 23,1 (1899): 95.

[72] Ibid.

[73] Ibid.

[74] Fischer, *Washington's Crossing*, 113.

[75] Ewald, *Diary*, 16.

[76] Fischer, *Washington's Crossing*, 113.

[77] The casualty figures for both sides are derived from Richard M. Ketchum *The Winter Soldiers: The Battles of Trenton and Princeton.* New York: Henry Holt and Company, 1973, 131. It is worth point out that most of those captured in the surrender of the fort later died in the horrific conditions of British prison hulks in New York harbor. On this point, see Larry G. Bowman *Captive Americans: Prisoners during the American Revolution.* Athens, OH: Ohio University Press, 1976, 11-14.

[78] Ewald, *Diary*, 17.

[79] Ibid, 16-17.

[80] Fischer, *Washington's Crossing*, 121.

[81] Ewald, *Diary*, 17. For an excellent short work on how the British conducted amphibious operations in this period, see David Syrett, "The Methodology of British Amphibious Operations during the Seven Years' War." in *The Mariner's Mirror.* 58, (1972): 269-280.

[82] Ewald, *Dairy*, 17.

[83] Ibid, 18.

[84] Ibid, 18.

[85] William M. Dwyer, *The Day is Ours! An Inside View of the Battle of Trenton and Princeton, November 1776-January 1777.* New Brunswick, NJ: Rutgers University Press, 1998, 17.

[86] Ibid.

[87] Cornwallis to Ewald, November 20, 1776, quoted in Ewald, *Diary*, 18.

[88] Ibid.

[89] Ibid.

[90] Ibid.

[91] White in Dwyer, 18.

[92] Ewald, *Diary*, 18.

[93] Ibid.

[94] On the topic of Hessians and looting, see Fischer, *Washington's Crossing*, 175.

[95] Ewald, *Diary*, 19

[96] Ibid. On the behavior of partisan in Europe over the course of the eighteenth century, see Martin Rink, "The Partisan's Metamorphosis: From Freelance Military Entrepreneur to German Freedom Fighter, 1740-1815." in *War in History.* 17(1): 6-36. There are several sources concerning Pandour Trenck, including his own autobiography which highlights his exploits in the War of the Austrian succession, see Francicus von der *Trenck, Memoirs of the Life of the Illustrious Francis Baron Trenck.* London: W. Owen, 1748. See also James R. Mc Intyre "A Scoundrel's Scoundrel: The Life and Exploits of Baron Franciscus von der Trenck, Pandour Leader" in The Journal of the Seven Years War Association, 19,1 (Winter 2014): 27-42.

[97] This is the route given in Arthur F. Lefkowitz *The Long Retreat: The Calamitous American Defense of New Jersey in 1776.* New Brunswick, NJ: Rutgers University Press, 1999. This author renders the place names as they were in 1776. Many of these remain unchanged. Second River is so named as it is the second main tributary to the Passaic River.

[98] The most complete discussion to date concerning this phase of the conflict can be found in Arthur S. Lefkowitz, The Long Retreat: The Calamitous American Defense of New Jersey in 1776. New Brunswick, NJ: Rutgers University Press, 1999. Be certain to recheck this characterization.

[99] Ewald, *Diary*, 19.

[100] Ibid.

[101] Ibid, 20.

[102] Ibid, 21.

[103] Ibid.

[104] Ibid, 22.

[105] For a discussion of the Hessians and their attitudes on plunder during the march through New Jersey, see Fischer, *Washington's Crossing*, 175.

[106] Ewald, *Diary*, 22.

[107] Ibid.

[108] Ibid.

[109] Ibid.

[110] Ibid.

111 Ibid.
112 On the Continental Corps of Riflemen, see Michael Cecere *They Are Indeed a Very Useful Corps American Riflemen in the Revolutionary War*. Westminster, MD: Heritage Books, 2006.
113 Ewald, *Diary*, 23.
114 See chapter 12
115 Ewald, *Diary*, 24.
116 Ibid.
117 Ibid.
118 Fischer comments on this as well in *Washington's Crossing*, 175, 509-10
119 Ewald, *Diary*, 25.
120 Ibid, 25-26.
121 Ibid, 26.
122 Ibid, 27.
123 Ibid.
124 Ibid, 30.
125 Ibid.
126 For a balanced view of Lee's apparent Treason, see Paul Lockhart, *The Drillmaster of Valley Forge: The Baron de Steuben and the Making of the American Army*. New York: HarperCollins Publishers, 2008, 130.
127 Ibid, 31.
128 Ibid, 38.
129 On this point, see Fischer, *Washington's Crossing*, 192-5.
130 Ewald, *Diary*, 38.
131 Ibid. Slabtown was another name used for Blackhorse at this time, it is uncertain as to why this was the case.
132 Ibid.
133 Fischer makes some of these observations as well, see *Washington's Crossing*, 196.
134 Ewald, *Diary*, 38-39.
135 Ibid, 39.
136 Moorestown was Ewald's creating spelling for Morristown. This is the modern town of Morristown in North Jersey, which would become the winter encampment for the Americans on several occasions, beginning just after the Trenton-Princeton campaign. Ewald was sent to an area just northeast of modern Allentown and Bethlehem in Pennsylvania.
137 Ibid.
138 Ibid.
139 Ibid, 39-42.
140 Ibid. 42.
141 Ibid.
142 Ibid, 44.
143 Ibid.
144 Ibid.
145 Ibid.

Chapter 5

1 Ketchum, *Winter Soldiers*, 280.
2 Ewald, *Diary*, 49.
3 Ibid.
4 John Fortescue, *History of the British Army*, vol. 2 *The British Army in North American, 1775-1783*. London: Greenhill Books, 2001 reprint of 1911 original, 53.
5 William S. Stryker, *The Battle of Trenton and Princeton*. Trenton, NJ: The Old Barracks Association, 2001 reprint of 1898 orig., 292, places the number of British prisoners at 14 officers and 216 men. He places the total British losses from Princeton at roughly 400 of all ranks.
6 Ewald, *Diary*, 50.
7 Ibid.
8 Ibid, 48.
9 Ibid, 51.
10 Ibid.
11 Ibid. On the role of the New Jersey militia in this fighting, see Fischer, *Washington's Crossing*, 346-47. For a more thorough discussion, see Kwasny, *Washington's Partisan War*, 113-18.

[12] Zwenger, "Johann Ewald," 160.

[13] Fischer, *Washington's Crossing*, 348-49 contains a useful discussion of this fighting and the purposes behind it from the American perspective.

[14] Ewald, *Diary*, 52.

[15] Ibid.

[16] Ibid.

[17] Ibid.

[18] Ibid, 53-55.

[19] Ibid, 365.

[20] Ewald to Jeannette von Horne, June 10, 1777, Brunswick, NJ quoted in Ibid, m369.

[21] Ibid, 368-69.

[22] Ibid, 370.

[23] Ibid, 374.

[24] Ibid, 55.

[25] Ibid, 56.

[26] Ibid.

[27] Ibid.

[28] Ibid.

[29] Ibid, 57-62.

[30] Ibid. 62.

[31] Ibid, 62.

[32] Ibid.

[33] Ibid.

[34] Ibid.

[35] Ibid.

[36] Ibid, 62-63.

[37] Ibid, 63.

[38] Ibid.

[39] For a contemporary view on this point see, in particular, Jeney, The Partisan, who writes: "In order to establish this Corps upon a solid and respectable Foundation, it will be absolutely necessary to maintain the strictest subordination, from the Commander in Chief to the private Soldier, and that by the most rigid Discipline, the whole may be accustomed to the utmost Vigilance, Patience, and Attention." M. de Jeney, *The Partisan: Or the Art of Making War in Detachments* (English edition, 1760), 4.

[40] Ewald, *Diary*, 63.

[41] Ibid.

[42] Ibid, 64.

[43] On this point, see Thomas M. Barker, and Thomas M. Huey, "Military Jägers, Their Civilian background and Weaponry." in *The Hessians: The Journal of the Johannes Schwalm Historical Association*. 15 (2012) 1-15.

[44] Anonymous, *Journal of the Hesse-Cassel Jaeger Corps and Hans Konze's List of Jaeger Officers*. Bruce E. Burgoyne, trans. Marie E. Burgoyne and Bruce E. Burgoyne, eds. Westminster, MD: Heritage Books, 2008, 1. At the time, the Jäger Corps consisted of one squadron of mounted Jägers, without mounts, and Major Prueschenk's Company, both newly arrived from Europe. These were added to the companies of Ewald and von Wrede and augmented by a 105-man company of Anspach Jägers under the command of Captain Christoph August con Cramon. This made for a complete unit 600 men. Tis, in turn, received a detachment of 30 Hessian grenadiers to serve as defenders for the two 3-pounder canon attached to the Corps. On the preceding reorganization, see *Jaeger Corps Journal*, 1.

[45] Biographical information on von Wurmb is derived from Michael C. Harris, *Brandywine: A Military History of the Battle that Lost Philadelphia but Saved America, September 11, 1777*. El Dorado Hills, CA: Savas Beatie, 2016, xliii.

[46] Ewald, *Diary*, 64.

[47] Ibid. *The pour le merite* was a military order in the Hessian state, patterned after the one introduced by Frederick the Great of Prussia as a recognition for outstanding personal achievement. It is important to recall the Frederick II of Hesse-Cassel was a great admirer of Frederick. On the decoration, see Paul Hieronymussen, *Orders and Decorations of Europe in Color*, New York: The Macmillan Company, 1967.

[48] Ewald, *Diary*, 64-65. Rocky Hill was initially known as the Devil's Feather Bed due to the difficulty of traveling through the region.

[49] Ibid, 65.

[50] This is Bonhamtown in modern Edison Township, Middlesex New Jersey. It is named for a seventeenth century freeholder. Ewald, *Diary*, 65.

[51] Ibid.

[52] This was Alexander Leslie (1740-1794), he had served in the 1776 campaign, seeing action at Long Island and Kip's Bay. He played a prominent role in the battle of Harlem Heights as well, as his were the outposts attacked by American Lt. Col. Thomas Knowlton. See Boatner, *Encyclopedia*, 617.

[53] Ewald, *Diary*, 65-68.

[54] Ibid, 68.

[55] Ibid.

[56] Ibid.

[57] Ibid.

[58] Ibid.

[59] Ibid.

[60] Duffy, *Military Experience*, 104

[61] Ewald, *Diary*, 68.

[62] Ibid.

[63] Anonymous, *Journal of the Hesse-Cassel Jaeger Corps and Hans Konze's List of Jaeger Officers*. Bruce E. Burgoyne, trans. Marie E. Burgoyne and Bruce E. Burgoyne, eds. Westminster, MD: Heritage Books, 2008, 2

[64] Ibid, 3.

[65] On the various iterations of William Howe's plan for the 1777 campaign, see Gruber, *The Howe Brothers and the American Revolution*. Chapel Hill: University of North Carolina Press, 1972, 158-188.

[66] Harris, *Brandywine*, 2.

[67] On this point, see again, Gruber, Command of the Howe Brothers, 158-188. See also Smith, *William Howe*, 106-111.

[68] Gruber, *Howe Brothers*, 230-31.

[69] Smith, *William Howe*, 80, 87-88.

[70] For background information on Knyphausen, see Atwood, *Hessians*, 49-50, and 74-75. See also, Boatner, *Encyclopedia*, 588

[71] Taaffe, *The Philadelphia Campaign*, 28

[72] Christopher Ward, *The War of the Revolution*, 329

[73] Ibid, 331.

[74] On the composition of the Delaware River defenses, see John W. Jackson, *The Pennsylvania Navy 1775-1781: The Defense of the Delaware*. New Brunswick, NJ: Rutgers University Press, 1974. See also Worthington C. Ford, ed. *Defenses of Philadelphia in 1777*. Brooklyn: Historical Printing Club, 1897. Reprint, De Capo Press, 1971, and John W. Jackson, *The Delaware Bay and River Defenses of Philadelphia*. *Philadelphia*: Philadelphia Maritime Museum, 1977. Concerning the decision of the Howe Brothers to turn to the Chesapeake, see Andrew S. Hamond, The *Autobiography of Captain Sir Andrew Snape Hamond, 1738-1828*. W. Hugh Moomaw, ed. MA thesis, University of Virginia, 1947, 73-74. HMS Roebuck was on station in the Delaware Capes maintaining the British blockade. Her captain, therefore, possessed a very thorough knowledge of the defenses the Patriots had developed in the river.

[75] Stephen Taaffe, *The Philadelphia Campaign*, 52.

[76] Hammond, *Autobiography*, 74.

[77] Ward, *War of the Revolution*, 332.

[78] Journal of *Hesse-Cassel Jäger Corps*, 5.

[79] Taaffe, *Philadelphia Campaign*, 53. On the militia fleeing without offering any resistance, see Ward, *War of the Revolution*, 336.

[80] Ewald, *Diary*, 76.

[81] Ibid.

[82] Ibid.

[83] Ibid. 77. Ottendorf's corps was one of the more colorful units of the Continental Army. It was authorized on December 5, 1776 under Major Nicholas Dietrich, Baron de Ottendorf. It was to consist of five companies, including the independent company of Captain John Paul Schott. The unit was organized between December 9, 1776 and June 1, 1777. The unit was to act as a partisan force and engage in all of the activities that usually accompanied that designation. Interestingly, in its original organization, it was to include both regular infantry and riflemen. On the organization

and composition of Ottendorf's Corps, see Robert K. Wright, *The Continental Army*. Washington, DC: Center of Military History, United States Army, 1989, 340-50. See also, Peterson, *Book of the Continental Soldier*, 268-69.

[84] Ewald, *Diary*, 77. See also, *Journal of Hesse-Cassel Jäger Corps*, 7.

[85] On William Maxwell, see Boatner, *Encyclopedia*, 686-88. On the creation of the Corps of Light Infantry to fill the gap left by the assignment of Morgan's Corps to assist Gates, see Cecere, *Brave and Useful Corps*, 131-33.

[86] Ibid, 78.

[87] Ibid.

[88] Ibid.

[89] Ibid.

[90] Ibid.

[91] Ibid, 79.

[92] Ibid, 79-80.

[93] Ibid, 80.

[94] Ibid, 80.

[95] Ibid. For the specific dispositions, see *Journal of Hesse-Cassel Jäger Corps*, 11.

[96] Ewald, *Diary*, 80.

[97] Ibid. 81.

[98] Ibid, 82.

[99] Ibid, 83. See also *Journal of Hesse-Cassel Jäger Corps*, 12.

[100] Ewald, *Diary*, 83.

[101] Ibid.

[102] Ibid, 84.

[103] Ibid.

[104] Ibid.

[105] On this point, see *Thomas J. McGuire The Philadelphia Campaign, vol. 1: Brandywine and the Fall of Philadelphia*. Mechanicsburg, PA: Stackpole Books, 184.

[106] Ibid, 188-9. There have long been rumors, that eventually became accepted myth, of a local patriot providing intelligence to Washington on the danger he was in. Recently, Michael C. Harris has challenged these and demonstrated their inaccuracy. See Harris, *Brandywine*, x-xvii.

[107] Adjutant General Ross, quoted in Ewald, *Diary*, 84.

[108] Ibid.

[109] Ibid, 85.

[110] Ibid.

[111] Ibid.

[112] Ibid.

[113] Ibid.

[114] Ibid.

[115] Ibid, 86

[116] Ibid.

[117] Ibid.

[118] Ibid.

[119] Ibid.

[120] Ibid, 87

[121] Ibid.

[122] Harris, *Brandywine*, 295-6.

[123] Ewald, *Diary*, 87.

[124] Ibid, 82.

[125] Ibid, 88.

[126] Ibid, 89.

[127] Ibid.

[128] On the battle of the Clouds, see McGuire, *Philadelphia Campaign*, vol. 1, 290-91. See also, Harris, *Brandywine*, 404.

[129] Ewald, *Diary*, 89.

[130] Ibid.

[131] Ibid, 89-90.

[132] *Journal of Hesse-Cassel Jäger Corps*, 17, records that the Corps was occupied with skirmishing throughout the day on the 20th.

[133] British reporting of their casualties is always deemed very low.

134 *Journal of Hesse-Cassel Jäger Corps*, 17-18.

135 The most recent, and thorough examination of the battle of Paoli is Thomas J. McGuire, *Battle of Paoli*. Mechanicsburg, PA: Stackpole Books, 2000.

136 Ewald, *Diary*, 90.

137 Ibid.

138 Ibid.

139 Ibid, 90-91.

140 The Palatinate was another one of the hundred or so states that comprised the Holy Roman Empire at this time. It was located in the southern part of the empire, in the region of today's Austria and south Germany. Ewald, *Diary*, 91.

141 The parade is described in thorough detail in McGuire, *Philadelphia Campaign*, vol. 2, 11-14.

142 Ewald, *Diary*, 91-92.

143 McGuire, *Philadelphia Campaign*, vol. 2, 30-35.

144 Ibid, 92.

145 Ewald, *Diary*, 92

146 Ibid.

147 Ibid.

148 Ibid.

149 Ibid, 93.

150 Ibid.

151 The preceding discussion of the reasons for the American failure at Germantown are based on the following: McGuire, *The Philadelphia Campaign*, vol. 2, 123-24. See also

152 Ewald, *Diary*, 96.

153 McGuire, *The Philadelphia Campaign*, vol. 2, 124.

154 Ewald, *Diary*, 93.

155 Ibid, 96.

156 Ibid.

157 Ibid, 96-97.

158 Ibid, 97.

159 George Washington to John Hancock, September 23, 1777, W.W. in Abbot, and Dorothy Twohig, eds. *The Papers of George Washington, Revolutionary War Series*. Volume 11. Charlottesville, VA; University of Virginia Press, 2001, 302.

160 Mark E. Lender, *The River War*. Trenton, NJ: New Jersey Historical Commission, 1979, 16. See also Peebles, John John Peebles *American War: the Diary of a Scottish Grenadier, 1776-1782*. Ira D. Gruber, ed. Strand, Gloucestershire: Published by the Sutton for the Army Records Society, 1997, 140. The latter should be taken with some circumspection as Peebles was not a participant in the attack.

161 Jackson, *Fort Mercer*, 6-7.

162 Jackson, *Pennsylvania Navy*, 140-41.

163 Frank H. Stewart, *History of the Battle of Red Bank with Events Prior and Subsequent thereto*. Woodbury, NJ: Board of Freeholders of Gloucester County, 1927, 9.

164 McGuire, *The Philadelphia Campaign*, vol.2, 154.

165 On the advanced guard skirmishing, see Ewald, *Diary*, 97. Concerning the security precautions of the Hessians see John W. Jackson, *Fort Mercer, Guardian of the Delaware*. Gloucester, NJ: Gloucester County Cultural and Heritage Commission, 1986 and on their limitations, see McGuire, *The Philadelphia Campaign*, vol. 2, 156.

166 For information on du Plessis, see Captain Gilbert Bodinier, *Dictionnaire des officiers de l'armeeroyale qui ontcombattu aux Etats-Unis pendant la guerre d'independence, 1776-1783 suivi d'un supplement a Les Francais sous le triemeetoiles du commandant Andre Lasseray*. Chateau de Vincennes, 1982, 339.

167 Lender, *River War*, 19.

168 Ewald, *Diary*, 98.

169 Ibid, 98-99.

170 Ibid.

171 Ibid.

172 Ibid.

173 Ibid.99.

174 John Hazelwood was a well-known mariner in Philadelphia and conducted the actions of the Pennsylvania Navy with great skill, though he was criticized by the last commander of Fort Mifflin, Colonel Samuel Smith for not providing enough support to the post during the British

bombardment. On Hazelwood, see Josiah G. Leach, "Commodore John Hazelwood, Commander of the Pennsylvania Navy in the Revolution." in *PMHB*, 26, 1 (1902): 1-6.
175 Lender, *River War*, 26-27.
176 Joseph LaBoyle, "The Israel Angell Diary, 1 October 1777- 28 February 1778." in *Rhode Island History*, 58 (2000):113.
177 Anderson, Lee Patrick Forty Minutes by the *Delaware: The Battle for Fort Mercer.* n.l., Universal Publishers, 1999, 131.
178 William S. Stryker, *The Forts on the Delaware in the Revolutionary War.* Trenton, NJ: John L. Murphy Publishing Co., 1901, 20.
179 Anderson, *Forty Minutes*, 130.
180 Ewald, *Diary*, 99.
181 Ewald, *Diary*, 99-102.
182 Ibid, 122.
183 Lieutenant Colonel Donald M. Londahl-Smidt, ed. trans., "German and British Accounts of the Assault on Fort Mercer at Redbank, NJ in October 1777." in *The Hessians: Journal of the Johannes Schwalm Historical Association.* 16 (2013):1-33. Hereinafter Londal-Smidt, *Accounts*.
184 Ibid, 13
185 Ibid.
186 Ibid, 18.
187 Ibid. 23.
188 Ewald, *Diary*, 102.
189 Ibid. Among the minor flaws Ewald described was the manner in which the fascines were utilized, "the men who carried the fascines in a line should have marched in column around to one spot to fill up the ditch; as it was, the men merely threw the fascines in the ditch and no purpose was served."
190 Ibid, 103.
191 Ibid, 103-04.
192 Concerning the fighting on October 23, see,
193 Ewald, *Diary*, 104.
194 Samuel S. Smith, *Fight for the Delaware, 1777.* Philip Freneau Press, 1970, 37.
195 Feilitzsch Diary in Bruce E. Burgoyne, ed. Trans. *Diaries of Two Ansbach Jaegers.* Bowie, MD: Heritage Books, 1997, 26.
196 Ibid, 104.
197 On Simcoe, see Boatner, *Encyclopedia*, 1009-10.
198 Ewald, *Diary*, 104.
199 Ibid.
200 Ibid, 105.
201 Ibid.
202 Ibid, 105-108.
203 Ibid, 108. He had come to Philadelphia from Liverpool with his father in 1747 at the age of thirteen. On their arrival in North America, he went to work in a counting house, and in 1754 became a partner to the concern. He subsequently held an interest in that house and its various successors for over thirty-nine years, holding a leading position in trade in the colonies. He was an early member of the Patriot movement, and served on the Pennsylvania Committee of Safety, the Continental Congress, and the Congress's Secret Committee. Often known as the "Financier of the Revolution," he repeatedly secured funds for the cash-strapped Continental Army, at times dipping into his own personal fortune. For biographical information on Robert Morris, see Boatner, *Encyclopedia*, 742-44.
204 Ewald, *Diary*, 108.
205 Ibid.
206 On the expedition to Edge Hill, see Taaffe, Philadelphia Campaign, 145-6, and McGuire, *Philadelphia Campaign*, vol. 2, 245-54.
207 Ibid.
208 Ibid.
209 McGuire, *Philadelphia Campaign*, vol. 2, 245-46.
210 *Journal of Hesse-Cassel Jäger Corps*, 32.
211 Ewald, *Diary*, 110.
212 Ibid.
213 Ibid.111.
214 Ibid.

Chapter 6

[1] Ewald, *Diary*, 117. On the partisan activities occurring at this time, see also, Wayne K. Bodle and Jacqueline Thibaut, *Valley Forge Historical Research Report*. Volume 1, Washington, D.C.: Department of the Interior, National Park Service, 1980, 88-104. For a more recent discussion of this period, see Ricardo A. Herrera, "'[T]he zealous activity of Capt. Lee': Light-Horse Harry Lee and *Petite Guerre*," *The Journal of Military History*, 79:1 (January 2015): 9-36.

[2] Mc Intyre, "Delaware River Campaign," 20. On the British response to French intervention in the war, see Piers Mackesy, The War for America, 1775-1783. Lincoln, NE: University of Nebraska Press, 1993 reprint of 1964 original, 160. See also, Jeremy Black, "British Military Strategy." in Donald Stoker, Kenneth J. Hagen and Michael T. Mc Master, eds, Strategy in the *American War of Independence*, London, Routledge, 2010, 66-67.

[3] For background on the Franco-American alliance, see Jonathan R. Dull, *The French Navy and American Independence: A Study of Arms and Diplomacy, 1774–1787*. Princeton: Princeton University Press, 1975.

[4] Ewald, *Diary*, 118.

[5] Ibid.

[6] Ibid, 119.

[7] Ibid, 119. See also note 2, 400.

[8] Ibid, 120.

[9] Ibid, 121.

[10] Ibid, 121-23.

[11] On the conditions at the Valley Forge encampment, see Wayne K. Bodle, and Jacqueline Thibaut, *Valley Forge Historical Research Report*. 3 vols., Washington, D.C.: Department of the Interior, National Park Service, 1980.

[12] The most recent biography of von Steuben is Paul Lockhart, *The Drillmaster of Valley Forge*: The Baron de Steuben and the Making of the American Army. New York: HarperCollins Publishers, 2008. On his efforts to train the Continental Army, see 97-115.

[13] Whether or not the Conway Cabal actually occurred is hotly debated amongst historians. The most moderate view is that there was some dissatisfaction in both Congress and the Army with Washington's performance in the 1777 campaign. When this seemed to manifest as a plot, the conspirators, complainers really, lost heart and Washington emerged firmly in command. On the Cabal, see Taaffe, *Philadelphia Campaign*, 158-67. See also Lockhart, *Drillmaster of Valley Forge*, 58-64.

[14] Lockhart, *Drillmaster of Valley Forge*, 97-105.

[15] Ewald, *Diary*, 123.

[16] Ibid.

[17] Ibid, 126.

[18] Ibid.

[19] Ibid, italics in original.

[20] Ibid, 126-27.

[21] Ibid, 127.

[22] Ibid.

[23] Ibid, 128. The college of Philadelphia is now known as the University of Pennsylvania.

[24] Smith, *William Howe*, 85.

[25] On Sir Henry Clinton's reading habits, see Ira D. Gruber, Books and the British Army in the Age of the American Revolution. Chapel Hill: University of North Carolina Press, 2014. Concerning Clinton's character, see Smith, *William Howe*, 29-32.

[26] On the British response to the widening of the war, see Mackesy, *War for American*, 181-86.

[27] The most recent and thorough examination of the relationship between Clinton and Howe may be found in Smith, *William Howe*, 84, 93-4, 112. Smith seems to make the case that much of the difficulty arose from the sensitive nature of Clinton.

[28] Ewald, *Diary*, 129.

[29] Ibid.

[30] Ibid, 130.

[31] On this engagement, see Lockhart, *Drillmaster of Valley Forge*, 120-125. See also Middlekauff, *Glorious Cause*, 419-20.

[32] Ibid, 130.

[33] Ewald, *Diary*, 130. It is worth recalling in connection with the Loyalists, the Joseph Galloway, who served as the commandant of Philadelphia during the occupation, had been instrumental in convincing Howe to come to the area in the first place. Now he was among the refugees forced to flee with the British. For his part, Galloway would eventually have some measure of revenge by giving scathing testimony against Howe's conduct of military operations to a Parliamentary inquiry in London.

[34] Ibid, 130-31. Specifically, the people he mentions here were from Tulpehocken.

[35] Ewald, *Diary*, 131.

[36] Ibid, 132.

[37] Concerning the decision to attack the British army as it withdrew overland through New Jersey, see Lockhardt, *Drillmaster of Valley Forge*,

[38] On Charles Lee's objections, see Ibid, . For general biographical information on Lee, see

[39] Ewald, *Diary*, 132.

[40] Ibid.

[41] Ibid, 132-3.

[42] Ibid, 133.

[43] Ibid.

[44] Ibid, 134.

[45] Ibid, 134-35.

[46] Ibid, 135.

[47] Ibid.

[48] Ibid

[49] Ibid.

[50] Ibid.

[51] The most recent work on the battle of Monmouth is Joseph G. Bilby and Katherine Bilby Jenkins, *Monmouth Courthouse: The Battle that made the American Army*. Yardley, PA: Westholme Press, 2010.

[52] Ewald, *Diary*, 134. .

[53] Ibid.

[54] Ibid, 136.

[55] Ibid. The transport wagons for the army were in the middle of the column.

[56] Ibid, 137.

[57] Ibid, 140.

[58] For Ewald, a mile would equal 9,206 meters or 30, 203 feet. Clearly, this constituted a much longer distance than a modern American miles.

[59] Ewald, *Diary*, 140-41

[60] Ibid. 141.

[61] Ibid.

[62] Ibid.

[63] Emmerich's Chasseurs were led Andreas Emmerich served in the Seven Years' War in Europe, after which he migrated to America. At the beginning of the War of Independence, he returned to Europe and raise a partisan corps for service with the Crown forces. His unit often coordinated with Ewald's jägers and Simcoe's Queen's Rangers. See Ewald, *Diary*, 405.

[64] Ewald, *Diary* ,141.

[65] Ibid.

[66] Ibid.

[67] Ibid, 143.

[68] Ibid.

[69] Ibid.

[70] Ibid, 144. Atwood discusses the declining effectiveness of the Hessians over time, see *Hessians*, 207-15.

[71] Ibid.

[72] Ibid. the attack had been launched by Armand's partisan corps. "who again appeared to be our antagonist in the fortunes of war." This unit was in fact Ottendor's Corps when Lieutenant Colonel Charles Armand Tuffin, Marquis de la Rouerie, a French volunteer, assumed command. Peterson, *Continental Soldier*, 268. See also, Wright, 350 *Continental Army*,

[73] Ibid. Cathcart was Sir William Shaw, Earl Cathcart.

[74] Ewald, *Diary*, 144.

[75] Ibid, 145.

76 Ibid.
77 Ibid.
78 Ibid.
79 Ibid.
80 Ibid.
81 Ibid.
82 Ibid, 145.
83 Ibid, 145-9.
84 Ibid, 149.
85 Ibid, 149.
86 Ibid.
87 Ibid. Ewald's mention of marauders eludes to the fact that there were many gangs of criminals that operated between the lines in the region. They used affiliation to one side or the other as a pretext to conduct criminal activity. On this point, see Harry M. Ward, *Between the Lines Banditti of the American Revolution*. Westport, CT: Praeger, 2002. See also, Allison, 59-60.
88 *Journal of the Hesse-Cassel Jäger Corps*, 51.
89 Ewald, *Diary*, 149. See also Journal of the Hesse-Cassel Jäger Corps,52.
90 Ibid.
91 Ibid, 150.
92 Ibid.
93 Ibid.
94 Ibid, 151.
95 Ibid, 152.
96 Ibid.
97 Ibid, 153. The British legion, led by Lieutenant Colonel Banastre Tarleton, was a mixed force of cavalry and infantry which sometimes included artillery as well. Tarleton's ability to move rapidly and strike hard made him a scourage of the American force, especially in the southern campaigns later in the war.
98 Ibid, 153-56.
99 Ibid, 156.
100 Ibid.
101 Ibid.
102 Ibid.
103 Ibid.
104 Ibid.
105 Ibid.
106 On the Morristown encampment, see Middlekauff, *Glorious Cause*, 508-11, Charles Royster, *A Revolutionary People at War The Continental Army and American Character, 1775-1783*. Chapel Hill: University of North Carolina Press, 1979, 299-307.
107 Boatner, *Encyclopedia*, 285-87.
108 Ewald, *Diary*, 159.
109 Ibid.
110 Ibid.
111 Ibid.
112 Ibid, 159-60.
113 Ibid.
114 Ibid, 160.
115 Ibid.
116 Ibid.
117 Ibid.
118 Ibid, 160-61. As in the regular units, music was often used to transmit orders. As opposed to the drum and fife, which were the common instruments of the regulars, the Jägers used a hunting horn, hearkening back to their roots as gamekeepers.
119 Ibid, 161.
120 Ibid.
121 Ibid.
122 Patrick Fergusson, born in 1744 descended from an illustrious family of Sottish nobles. He entered the Scots Grey at age 14, after attending a military academy in his youth. He is famous for developing an early breech-loading rifle, which impressed the king. He was given permission to raise a special unit which was equipped with the weapon. These men fought in the 1777 campaign.

Fergusson was wounded in the right arm at the elbow at the battle of Brandywine, and spent much of the following year recuperating. He never had complete use of the arm again. At the same time, his unit was disbanded. He returned to duty in October 1778, taking part in the Little Egg Harbor raid. He would go down to an ignominious defeat at the Battle of King's Mountain in South Carolina On October 7, 1780. See M.M. Gilchrist *Patrick Fergusson A Man of Some Genius.* Edinburgh: NMS Publishing, 2003.

[123] Ibid, 161.

[124] On British the storming of Verplank's Point, see, Noah Alexander Trudeau "'The Fort's Our Own.'" In *MHQ* 16, 1 (Autumn 2003): 87-88.

[125] Ewald, *Diary*, 162.

[126] Ibid, 163.

[127] Ibid.

[128] Ibid. the explanation of fleche is my own by derived from definitions found in Christopher Duffy, *Siege Warfare: The Fortress in the Early Modern World, 1494-1660.* And

[129] Ewald, *Diary*, 163-66.

[130] Ibid, 166.

[131] Ibid.

[132] Ibid, 166-67.

[133] Ibid, 167.

[134] The same sort of action was supposedly taken by a British officer on Daniel Morgan in the French and Indian War. Morgan's resistance, he hit the British officer, led to his receiving a flogging. See Don Higginbotham, *Daniel Morgan Revolutionary Rifleman.* Chapel Hill: University of North Carolina Press, 1961, 4-5. On discipline in general in contemporary European armies, see Duffy, *Military Experience*, 98-101.

[135] Ewald, *Diary*, 167.

[136] Ibid, 168.

[137] Ibid.

[138] Ibid.

[139] On abatis, see Christopher Duffy, *Fire and Stone: The Science of Fortress Warfare, 1600-1860.* 183.

[140] Ewald, *Diary*, 168.

[141] Ewald, *Diary*, 168.

[142] *Journal of the Hesse-Cassel Jäger Corps*, 63.

[143] Ibid, 169.

[144] Ibid, 169.

[145] Ibid.

[146] Ibid.

[147] Ibid.

[148] Ibid, 172.

[149] Ibid.

[150] Ibid.

[151] Ibid, 173.

[152] On the storming of Paulus Hook, see Charles Royster, *Light Horse Harry Lee and the Legacy of the American Revolution.* Baton Rouge: Louisiana State University Press, 1981, 21-23. See also John W. Hartman, *The American Partisan Henry Lee and the Struggle for Independence, 1776-1780.* Shippensburg, PA: Burd Street Press, 2000, 110-15.

[153] Ibid, 178.

[154] Ibid.

[155] Ibid, 178.

[156] Ibid.

[157] Ibid.

[158] Ibid, 179.

[159] Ibid, 174-82.

[160] Ibid, 182. In addition, the mounted jägers were quartered on the plantation of one McGowan.

[161] Ibid, 183.

[162] Ibid. The refugees Ewald mentions here were Loyalists who had been drive from their homes by the Continental forces and sought protection with the British army.

[163] Ibid.

[164] Ibid, 189.

[165] Ibid, 189-90. The number eighty is significant in that shows how many men Ewald lost to the fighting in the previous campaign.

166 Ibid, 191-92.
167 David K. Wilson, *The Southern Strategy Britain's Conquest of South Carolina and Georgia, 1775-1780.* Columbia, S.C: University of South Carolina Press, 2005, xi. On the origins of the southern strategy, see also Mackesy, *War for America*, 43-44, 156-59.
168 Wilson, *Southern Strategy*, xv.
169 Ibid.

Chapter 7

1 On the British capture of Savannah, Georgia, see Henry Lumpkin, *From Savannah to Yorktown: The American Revolution in the South.* New York: Paragon House, 1981, 27-29. See also, Stanley D. M. Carpenter, Southern *Gambit: Cornwallis and the British March to Yorktown.* Norman: University of Oklahoma Press, 2019, 53-7.
2 Wright, *Continental Army*, 108.
3 Lumpkin, *Savannah to Yorktown*, 27.
4 Heinrichs to Herr Heinrichs, 10 April 1779, quoted in "Extracts,"156.
5 On d'Estaing's role in the attack, see Willis, *Sea Power*, 319-21 783 Lumpkin, *Savannah to Yorktown*, 39. See also, Borick, *Gallant Defense*, 21
7 Casimir Pulaski has become a celebrate hero of Polish-American nationalism. As a result, he has become the subject of numerous biographies. Among the more recent of these, which approaches the subject from a scholarly vantage point is Leszek Szymański, *Casimir Pulaski: A Hero of the Revolution.* New York: Hippocrene Books, 1994.
8 On the diplomatic effects of the failed siege of Savannah, see John B. Hattendorf, Newport, the French Navy and American Independence, Newport, RI: The Redwood Press, 2005, 37-39; Dan L. Morrill, Southern Campaigns of the American Revolution, Mount Pleasant, SC: Nautical and Aviation Publishing Company, 1993. On the battle of Rhode Island, see Charles Lippitt, *Battle of Rhode Island.* Np: Nabu Press, 2012; Christian McBurney, The Rhode Island Campaign: *The First French and American Operation in the Revolutionary War.* Yardley, PA: Westholme Press, 2011. Dated, but still very useful is Paul F. Dearden, *The Rhode Island Campaign of 1778: Inauspicious Dawn of Alliance.* Providence, RI: The Rhode Island Bicentennial Foundation, 1980.
9 Wilson, Southern Strategy, 63.
10 Carl P. Borick *A Gallant Defense: The Siege of Charleston, 1780.* Columbia, SC: University of South Caroline Press, 2003, 3-5.
11 Borick, *Gallant Defense*, 27
12 Ibid, 49
13 Ewald, *Diary*, 195.
14 Patrick O'Kelley, *Nothing but Blood and Slaughter.* vol. 2, Booklocker Press, 2004, 52.
15 Borick, *Gallant Defense*, 50.
16 Ewald, *Diary*, 196.
17 Ibid, 197. Ewald often utilized slaves as guides as well as source for intelligence on local conditions, usually with greater success than this first encounter.
18 Ibid, 197-98.
19 Ibid, 198.
20 Ibid.
21 Ibid.
22 See chapter 11 following.
23 Ibid.
24 Ibid, 198-99
25 Ibid, 199
26 Ibid.
27 Ibid, 199-202.
28 As the campaign progressed, Ewald would often utilize slaves as guides or sources of information. Tis indicates that he eventually discovered some means of surmounting the barrier in understanding. He does not indicate what it was, however, it seems safe to speculate that being constantly exposed to their dialect, Ewald developed some understanding of it over time.
29 Ibid, 202.
30 Ibid.
31 Ibid.
32 Ibid.
33 Ibid, 202-03.

[34] O'Kelley, *Blood and Slaughter*, Vol. 2, 61.

[35] Ibid, 203.

[36] Ibid.

[37] O'Kelley, *Blood and Slaughter*, vol. 2, 30.

[38] Ewald, *Diary*, 204.

[39] O'Kelley, *Blood and Slaughter*, vol. 2, 34.

[40] Ewald, *Diary*, 204.

[41] Ibid.

[42] Ibid.

[43] Ibid.

[44] O'Kelley, *Blood and Slaughter*, vol. 2, 34.

[45] Ewald, *Diary*, 204.

[46] Ibid.

[47] O'Kelley, *Blood and Slaughter*, vol. 2, 34.

[48] Ewald, *Diary*, 204.

[49] Ibid, 205.

[50] This was colonel James Webster. Born in 1743, Webster had served in various capacities since 1775. Boatner, *Encyclopedia*, 1178-79.

[51] Ewald, *Diary*, 208-09.

[52] Ibid, 209.

[53] Ibid.

[54] Sébastien Le Prestre de Vauban (1633-1707) was a Marshal of France and chief military engineer to Louis XIV. He is considered by most as a master of fortifications and siege warfare. On siege warfare, see. Christopher Duffy, *Siege Warfare: The Fortress in the Early Modern World 1494-1660.* London: Routledge, 1996, 136-39. On Vauban specifically, see James Falkner, *Marshal Vauban and the Defence of Louis XIV's France.* Barnsley, South Yorkshire: Pen and Sword Military, 2011. See also John A. Lynn, *The Wars of Louis XIV 1667-1714.* London: Longman, 1999, 22-40.

[55] I use Charles Town here and throughout as this was the name of the city at the time of the siege. It was renamed Charlestown when it was incorporated in 1783.

[56] For a very useful article on the siege of Havanan, see Syrett, David "The British Landing at Havana: An Example of an Eighteenth Century Combined Operation." in *The Mariner's Mirror.* 55, (1969): 325-332. The most recent account covering the role of the Royal Navy in the siege of Charleston can be found in Willis, *Sea Power*, 347-48.

[57] Ewald, *Diary*, 210.

[58] Ibid.

[59] Ibid, 210-11.

[60] Ibid, 211.

[61] Ibid.

[62] Ibid.

[63] Ibid.

[64] Ibid.

[65] Ibid.

[66] Ibid, 215. This would be William Washington, a cousin of George, who commanded a Continental Cavalry unit that served with distinction in the southern theater. On William Washington, see Stephen E. Haller, *William Washington: Cavalryman of the Revolution.* Bowie, MD: 2001.

[67] Ibid.

[68] Ibid.

[69] Ibid, 216.

[70] Ibid, 216.

[71] Ibid. Ewald would later discuss this same approach in his *Treatise on Partisan Warfare.*

[72] Ibid.

[73] Ibid.

[74] Ibid.

[75] Ibid, 217. The man's son was Peter Horry, who would play a significant role in the fighting in the Carolinas, both during the siege of Charleston and after.

[76] Ibid.

[77] On the violence nature of the fighting in the southern colonies, especially after the fall of Charleston and consequent British occupation of much of the eastern and central parts of South Carolina, see Walter Edgar, *Partisans and Redcoats The Southern Conflict that Turned the Tide of the American Revolution.* New York: Perennial, 2001; Ronald Hoffman, et al., eds. *An Uncivil War: The Southern*

Backcountry during the American Revolution. Charlottesville, VA: University Press of Virginia, 1985; Dan L Morrill, *The Southern Campaigns of the American Revolution.* Mount Pleasant, SC: Nautical Aviation Publishing Company of America, 1993. Jerome D. Nadelhaft, The Disorders of War: The Revolution in South Carolina. Orono, ME: University of Maine at Orono Press, 1981; Patrick O'Kelley, *Nothing but Blood and Slaughter: The Revolutionary War in the Carolinas.* 4 vols. Booklocker, 2004-06; Charles Royster, *A Revolutionary People at War The Continental Army and American Character, 1775-1783.* Chapel Hill: University of North Carolina Press, 1979; and David Keithly, "Poor, Nasty and Brutish: Guerrilla Operations in America's First Civil War" in *Civil Wars* volume IV, number 3, (Autumn 2001):35- 69.

78 Ewald, *Diary,* 218.

79 Ibid. On the distance of a German mile, or for Ewald, most likely a Hessian mile, at this time, see chapter 6, n. 58.

80 Ibid.

81 Ibid, 218-19.

82 Ibid, 219.

83 Ibid.

84 Ibid.

85 Ibid.

86 Ibid, 220.

87 Ibid.

88 Ibid.

89 Ibid.

90 Ibid.

91 Ibid, 221.

92 Ibid.

93 Ibid.

94 Ibid, 221-22.

95 Ibid, 224.

96 Ibid.

97 Ibid.

98 Borick, *Gallant Defense,* 32.

99 Ewald, *Diary,* 224-25.

100 Ibid.

101 Ibid, 225.

102 Ibid.

103 Ibid.

104 Ibid.

105 Ibid, 226.

106 Ibid, 227.

107 Ibid, 226.

108 Ibid, 227.

109 Ibid.

110 Ibid, 228.

111 Ibid, 229.

112 Ibid.

113 Ibid.

114 The major possessed a fairly solid background. A Scot, born in 1744, he entered Woolwich in 1759, and was commissioned an ensign of the engineers in 1762. He left England for Cuba later that same year and arrived in time to take part in the siege of Havana. During the siege, Moncrieff received an appointment as ensign in the 100th Foot. On the conclusion of the Seven Years War, he held various appointments in the Caribbean and East Florida, as well as New York City. While stationed in the latter, Moncrieff made the acquaintance of several prominent Loyalist families. During the northern campaigns, he contributed little of notice, though he did guide the 4th Regiment across a ford during the battle of Brandywine. In addition, he constructed a bridge across the Raritan that was interesting enough in its engineering for a scale model to be preserved at Woolwich. Still, it was in the southern campaigns that Moncrieff truly distinguished himself. He oversaw the construction of the fortifications which allowed Prévost to hold Savanah against the combined Franco-American assault. This action led to his commission as a brevet major in December 1779.The Major later went on to take part in the occupation of Charlestown. When the British evacuated, he sent some 800 slaves off to the Caribbean, an act for which he was later

accused of making a substantial personal profit. He returned to England after the war, band even took part in the early stages of the Wars of the French Revolution. In 1793, he directed the siege of Dunkirk under the Duke of York, where he was mortally wounded. His body was buried at Ostend. On Moncrieff, see Boatner, *Encyclopedia*, 712-13.

[115] Ewald, *Diary*, 230.

[116] Ibid.

[117] Ibid. Coehorns were small mortars designed to lob solid shot or shells short distances.

[118] Ibid.

[119] Ibid. A boyau is the French term for a ditch covered by a parapet as a communication between two trenches. See Ewald, *Diary*, 416, n.12.

[120] Ibid, 231.

[121] Ibid.

[122] Ibid. For the definition of a traverse, see Duffy, *Fire & Stone*, 186.

[123] Ewald, *Diary*, 231. Ewald often uses the expression warm to connote that he and his men were engaged in heavy fighting.

[124] On the use of Native Americans in the southern theater in particular, see Jim Piechuchs, *Three Peoples, One King*

[125] Ewald, *Diary*, 232. Ewald described the chieftain's dress as follows, 'He wore a shirt of course linen and over a blue coat with red lapels and collar, but had neither breeches nor stockings. His feet were clad in sandals. His head was shaved except for the crown and pendants of silver pistols and swards hung from his ears. His face was daubed with red paint in several places, and in his nose he wore a double silver ring. With great skill, he had wound his head with a silk scarf, which was fastened with silver clasps. On his chest he wore a ring-shaped silver collar and around both arms silver shields fastened with red ribbons, which were gifts from England and on which the monogram "George Rex" was engraved.

[126] Ewald, *Diary*, 232.

[127] General Henry Lee, *The Revolutionary War Memoirs of General Henry Lee*. Robert E. Lee, ed. New York: De Capo Press, 1998, 157.

[128] Ewald, *Diary*, 232.

[129] Ibid. The pointed trees were commonly referred to as abatis. This may indicate a gap in Ewald's knowledge of siege warfare.

[130] Ibid, 232-33.

[131] Ibid, 233.

[132] Ibid.

[133] Sun Tzu, *The Art of War*. Samuel B. Griffith, trans. Oxford: Oxford University Press, 1963, 84.

[134] Ibid, 234.

[135] Ibid.

[136] Ewald, *Diary*, 234.

[137] Ibid. A sap was "a narrow siege trench which is established by the panting of gabions or sandbags." See Duffy, *Fire and Stone*, 186.

[138] O'Kelley, *Blood and Slaughter*, vol. 2, 144-5.

[139] Ewald, *Diary*, 234.

[140] Ibid.

[141] Ibid.

[142] Ibid, 235.

[143] Ibid.

[144] Ibid.

[145] Ibid.

[146] Ibid.

[147] Ibid.

[148] Ibid.

[149] Ibid.

[150] Ibid, 235-36.

[151] Ibid, 236.

[152] Ibid. These were akin to modern shot guns, and so allowed for two shots to be fired before having to reload, which could help increase the volume of fire in the short term.

[153] Ibid.

[154] Ibid.

[155] Ibid. For an explanation of gallery, see Duffy, *Fortress*, 185.

[156] Ibid.

[157] Ibid, 236-237.

[158] Ibid, 238.

[159] Ibid, 239.

[160] Ibid.

[161] Ibid, 241.

[162] Ibid, 242.

[163] Probably the most thorough discussion of the change in paroles can be found in Michael C. Scoggins, *The Day It Rained Militia: Huck's Defeat and the Revolution in the South Carolina Backcountry May-July, 1780*. Charleston, SC: The History Press, 2005, 48-50. On the battle of Waxhaws, a very complete dissection of the engagement can be found in Thomas A. Rider, "Massacre or Myth: No Quarter at the Waxhaws." MA Thesis, University of North Carolina, 2002. See also Jim Piecuch, *The Blood be Upon your Head: Tarleton and the Myth of Buford's Massacre*. Lugoff, SC: Southern Campaigns of the Revolution Press, 2010. Both authors view the charges of a massacre at the battle of Waxhaws as inflated to say the least, but they go on to observe that this is less important when set against the effect of the charges of such an event occurring in mobilizing the population.

[164] O'Kelley, *Blood and Slaughter*, vol. 2, 155.

Chapter 8

[1] Ewald, *Diary*, 243

[2] Ibid.

[3] Ewald, *Diary*, 244.

[4] On the battle of Connecticut Farms, see Mark V. Kwasny, *Washington's Partisan War, 1775-1783*. Kent, OH: Kent State University Press, 1997, 258-59

[5] Ibid. Maxwell's nickname can be found in an issue of American Revolution Magazine, which I have but have to locate.

[6] Kwasny, *Partisan War*, 261

[7] Ewald, *Diary*, 244.

[8] Kwasny, Partisan War, 261.

[9] Ewald, *Diary*, 244-45.

[10] Ibid, 245.

[11] Ibid.

[12] Kwasny, *Partisan War*, 261-265.

[13] Ewald, *Diary*, 245.

[14] Ibid.

[15] Ibid.

[16] Ibid.

[17] Ibid.

[18] Ibid, 245-46.

[19] Ibid, 246.

[20] Ibid

[21] Ibid.

[22] Ibid.

[23] Ibid.

[24] Mackesy, *War for America*, 349.

[25] Ibid, 221-2.

[26] Ewald, *Diary*, 246.

[27] The unit most likely referred to here is DeLancey's Brigade, one of the first units of provincials raised by the British when they came to New York. The unit was recruited and commanded by brigadier general Oliver DeLancey, commissioned on September 4, 1776. DeLancey recruited about 2,000 men in three brigades. The unit took part in numerous operations in and around New York. See Thomas B. Allen and Todd W. Braisted *The Loyalist Corps: Americans in the Service of the King*. Tacoma Park, MD: Fox Acre Press, 2011, 32-4.

[28] Ewald, *Diary*, 246.

[29] This was the force of

[30] Ewald, *Diary*, 246-47.

[31] Ibid, 247.

[32] Ibid, 247-48.

[33] Ibid.

[34] Ibid, 248.

[35] Ibid.

[36] Ibid.

[37] Ibid.

[38] Arnold was an early supporter of the patriot movement. Born in Norwich, Connecticut in 1741, he was the con of a merchant. In his youth, Arnold's father abandoned his family to escape his debts, placing the former in dire financial straits. At age fourteen, in 1755, he Arnold was apprenticed to a druggist. His time as an apprentice lasted about three years year, and in 1758 he ran off to join a New York Company and take part in the Great War for Empire. His mother managed to convince the unit to free him as he was breaking an indenture through his service. Arnold ran off again and enlisted in another New York Company in 1760. Quickly tiring of military life, Arnold deserted and made his way home through the wilderness. He completed his apprenticeships and in his early twenties moved to New Haven with his sister, Hannah.

In New Haven, Arnold quickly became a successful merchant and even purchased several ships which he captained himself. He traded in numerous commodities, including horses, with his territory stretching from the West Indies to New England and Canada. His rivals sometimes accused Arnold of gaining the horses he sold through less than legal means, and he developed a reputation for being rather prickly concerning his honor.

When resistance to British policy began, Arnold came out as an early supporter. With the alarm following Lexington and Concord, he sought and was granted permission to raise a regiment by the Connecticut authorities. He then marched on Fort Ticonderoga, and, in coordination with Ethan Allen and his Green Mountain Boys, captured the post.

Later in 1775, Arnold led a force of approximately 1,100 men on a harrowing march across Maine to attack the British garrison at Quebec, part of an ill-conceived plan to make Canada a fourteenth colony. On a more pragmatic level, securing Canada held some strategic merit, it would close the back door to the colonies by bring the western frontier into the rebellion.

The march across Canada is itself the tale of a profound trial of human endurance. Many men deserted and returned to New England. Arnold managed to get the remnants of his column through, and they joined another force already in Canada from New York under General Richard Montgomery. The two decided to coordinate in an attack on Quebec. The preceding derives from the standard biography of Arnold as of this writing, James Kirby Martin, *Benedict Arnold Revolutionary Hero: An American Warrior Reconsidered*. New York: New York University Press, 1997.

Arnold led one of the wings of an assault on December 31, 1775, during which he received a serious wound to his leg. He was carried form the field, and the attack collapsed, with many of the troops taking part being captured. Arnold's action in the campaign against Quebec are well detailed in Arthur F. Lefkowitz, *Benedict Arnold's Army: The 1775 American Invasion of Canada during the Revolutionary War*. New York: Savas Beatie, 2008. Arnold later put up an epic defense of retreating American forces as they made their way down Lake Champlain out of Canada before British forces under the command of Sir Guy Carleton. He put up a bold if ultimately doomed resistance off Valcour Island, buying time for much of the American force to withdraw before a British flotilla. On Arnold's creation of an American flotilla to block the British and the battle of Valcour Island, see James L. Nelson, *Benedict Arnold's Navy: The Ragtag Fleet that Lost the Battle of Lake Champlain but Won the American Revolution*. Camden, ME: International Marine/McGraw-Hill, 2006.

1777 witnessed Arnold once again leading American forces, this time against the invasion from Canada led by General John Burgoyne. He broke orders to remain in his quarters and personally rallied troops at the battle of Freeman's Farm, contributing in no small way to the Patriot victory there. As a result, he was, once again, wounded in the leg, and credit for the victory was usurped by the overall commander of American forces, Horatio Gates, whom Arnold had defied in leaving his quarters. The standard work on the Saratoga Campaign at this time is Max M. Mintz, *The Generals of Saratoga*. New Haven, CT: Yale University Press, 1990. For a fresh perspective, see Theodore Corbett No Turning Point: *The Saratoga Campaign in Perspective*. Norman: University of Oklahoma Press, 2012.

While convalescing from his wounds, Arnold was given the military command over Philadelphia. Debts accrued from his military service, as well as allegations of financial malfeasance from subordinates followed Arnold into his new appointment, and it seems that he took some advantage of his post to secure his own financial gain. It was also during his residence in the Continental capital that he met and began courting the young Peggy Shippen, daughter of a prominent local Loyalist family. Martin, *Benedict Arnold*, 427-31.

Challenged by the local authorities for his administration of the military governorship, Arnold petitioned Washington for a new command while matters were investigated in Philadelphia. He asked for and was granted the command over the American post at West Point. This post, designed to control the traffic on the Hudson River was considered the key to controlling access to the interior of the colonies.

39 Francis Casimir Kajencki, *Thaddeus Kosciuszko: Military Engineer of the American Revolution*. El Paso, TX: South Polonia Press, 1998, 81-120.
40 Ewald, *Diary*, 249.
41 Martin, *Benedict Arnold*, 1-6.
42 Ewald, *Diary*, 250.
43 Ibid, 251.
44 On the efforts of the British to supply their troops and auxiliaries in North America, see
45 Ewald, *Diary*, 250.
46 Ibid.
47 Ibid.
48 All of these areas are in modern Long Island Sound, New York.
49 Ibid. It is worth recalling here that no equivalent has, as yet, been determined for the measures Ewald included in his diary.
50 A complete history of the whale boat wars has yet to be written. Still, there exists some coverage in other sources. Among these, the most useful are Kwasny, *Partisan War, 255-280. See also Robert L. Tonsetic, Special Operations during the American Revolution*. Philadelphia: Casemate, 2013, 194-221.
51 Ewald, *Diary*, 250-51.
52 Ibid, 251.
53 Ibid, 251.
54 Ibid.
55 Ibid, 251-52.
56 Ibid, 252.
57 Biographical information on Leslie can be found in Boatner, *Encyclopedia*, 617.

Chapter 9

1 Concerning both of these points, see chapter 7, note 165.
2 All of these men, as well as their actions in the cause of American independence, have received thorough treatments in biographies. Likewise, there are several specialized studies that focus specifically on their actions as partisan leaders. On Thomas Sumter, the classic biography remains Robert D. Bass, *Gamecock The Life and Campaigns of General Thomas Sumter*. New York: Holt, Rinehart and Winston, 1961. On Francis Marion, the most recent work is John Oller, *The Swamp Fox: How Francis Marion Saved the American Revolution*. New York: DeCapo Press, 2016. Finally, on Andrew Pickens see William R. Reynolds, Andrew Pickens: South Carolina Patriot in the Revolutionary War. Jefferson, NC: MacFarland and Company, Inc., Publishers, 2012 for the most recent biography.
3 The above summary of the Southern Campaign to this point is derived from the following: Walter Edgar, Partisans and Redcoats *The Southern Conflict that Turned the Tide of the American Revolution*. New York: Perennial, 2001. Ronald Hoffman, et al., eds. An Uncivil War: *The Southern Backcountry during the American Revolution*. Charlottesville, VA: University Press of Virginia, 1985; Kristine E. Jacobson, Conduct of the Partisan War in the Revolutionary War South. MA Thesis U.S. Army Command and General Staff College, Fort Leavenworth, KS, 2003; John R. Maass, *Horatio Gates and the Battle of Camden—"That Unhappy Affair" August 16, 1780*. Camden, SC: Kershaw County Historical Society, 2001. Patrick O'Kelley, *Nothing but Blood and Slaughter: The Revolutionary War in the Carolinas*. 4 vols. Booklocker, 2004-06; John S. Pancake, *The Destructive War The British Campaign in the Carolinas 1780-1782*. University, AL: University of Alabama Press, 1985.
4 For the skirmish at Fishing Creek, see O'Kelley, *Blood and Slaughter*, vol. 2, 277-86.
5 On the Maryland Delaware brigade, the best work remains Christopher Ward, The Delaware Continentals. Wilmington, DE: Historical Society of Delaware, 1941. An invaluable collection of primary documents relating to the unit is Thomas Balch, ed. *Papers Relating Chiefly to the Maryland Line during the Revolution*. Philadelphia: T.K. and P.G. Collins, 1857.
6 Oller, *The Swamp Fox*, 54-6.

[7] Currently, the best treatment of Greene is Terry Gollway, *Washington's General: Nathanael Greene and the Triumph of the American Revolution*. New York: Henry Holt and Company, 2005.

[8] Ibid, 307-323.

[9] Ibid, 324-5.

[10] Ibid.

[11] Lockhart, *Drillmaster of Valley Forge*, 238-42.

[12] Though dated, the classic account on this engagement remains Lyman C. Draper, *Kings Mountain and Its Heroes*. Johnson City, TN: The Overmountain Press, 1996 reprint of 1881 original.

[13] On Greene's assumption of command and the condition of the troops under his command, see James R. Mc Intyre "Nathanael Greene: Soldier-Statesman of the War of Independence in South Carolina." In Gregory D. Massey and Jim Piecuch, eds., *General Nathanael Greene and the American Revolution in the South*. Columbia: University of South Carolina Press, 2012, 174

[14] Ibid, 176-7.

[15] Higginbotham, *Daniel Morgan*, 95-7.

[16] Mc Intyre, "Nathanael Greene," 177.

[17] John R. Maass, *The Road to Yorktown: Jefferson, Lafayette and the British Invasion of Virginia:* Charleston, S.C.: The History Press, 2015, 27-31.

[18] Ewald, *Diary*, 255.

[19] Ibid.---

[20] Ibid, 258.

[21] Ibid, 259.

[22] Allison, *American Revolution*, 65.

[23] The recognized basic texts on the American War of Independence have essentially ignored Arnold's raid, or mentioned it only in passing. These include: Don Higginbotham, *The War of American Independence Military Attitudes, Policies, and Practice 1763-1789*. Boston: Northeastern University Press, 1983, and Robert Middlekauff, *The Glorious Cause: The American Revolution, 1763-1789*. New York: Oxford University Press, 1982. Even the most recent general text on the Revolutionary period, Allison's American Revolution provides only a short paragraph. Allison, *American Revolution*, 65.

[24] Ewald, *Diary*, 259.

[25] Maass, *Road to Yorktown*, 29.

[26] Ewald, *Diary*, 259.

[27] Ibid.

[28] Ibid.

[29] Ibid, 259-60.

[30] Ibid, 260.

[31] Ibid.

[32] Ibid.

[33] Ibid.

[34] On this point, see Jason "Dutch" Palmer, "For Cause and Family in the American Revolution." Unpublished paper presented at 75th Annual Meeting of the Society for Military History, Ogden, Utah, April 18, 2008.

[35] Ewald, *Diary*, 260-61. It is clear from the manner in which the English officer gave his American counterpart's reply to Arnold that he was not popular with the English officers either.

[36] Ibid, 261.

[37] Ibid.

[38] Maass, *Road to Yorktown*, 30.

[39] Ewald, *Diary*, 261.

[40] Maass, *Road to Yorktown*, 12.

[41] Ibid, 28.

[42] Maass discusses some of these attempts as well. On Lord Dunmore in particular, see Boatner, *Encyclopedia*, 340-1.

[43] Ibid, 31.

[44] Ewald, *Diary*, 266. The light infantry of the rangers would be those of the Queen's Rangers.

[45] Ibid.

[46] Ibid.

[47] Ibid. Robinson's Corps has not been identified. There is no additional information on it in Tustin's translation of Ewald's diary. Nor is there any mention of a corps by this name in any of the literature consulted on the Loyalist units.

[48] Ibid.

49 Maass, *Road to Yorktown*, 30

50 Ibid, 267.

51 Ibid.

52 Ibid.

53 Ibid, 267-8.

54 Ibid, 268.

55 Ibid.

56 Ibid.

57 Ibid.

58 Maass, *Road to Yorktown*, 30.

59 Ewald, *Diary*, 268.

60 Ibid, 268-69.

61 Maass, *Road to Yorktown*, 31

62 Ewald, *Diary*, 269.

63 Ibid. See also, Maass, *Road to Yorktown*, 31-2.

64 These men would be Thomas Dundas and Beverly Robinson.

65 Ewald, *Diary*, 269.

66 Ibid, 269-70.

67 Ibid, 270.

68 Ibid, 270.

69 Ibid.

70 Ibid. It seems, from the context of this quote, that Ewald was referring to General Robertson.

71 Ibid.

72 Ibid, 270-71.

73 Ibid, 271.

74 Ibid. Ewald provided a description of the ambush the advanced guard had wandered into as well.

75 Ibid, 272.

76 Ibid.

77 For a solid historical discussion of Native American tactics, see Patrick Malone, *The Skulking Way of War Technology and Tactics among the New England Indians*. New York: Madison Books, 1991.

78 Isle of Wight County falls within the modern Hampton Roads region of Virginia.

79 Ewald, *Diary*, 272.

80 Ibid.

81 Ibid, 273.

82 This was a Major James Gordon.

83 Ewald, *Diary* 273.

84 Ibid.

85 Ibid.

86 Ibid.

87 Ibid, 273-274.

88 Ibid, 274.

89 Ibid.

90 Carl von Clausewitz (June 1, 1780-November 16, 1831) Born in the Prussian territory of Magdeburg, the fourth son of middle class parents, Clausewitz entered the Prussian army at age twelve. He saw various service in the Wars of the French Revolution and Napoleon. In 1801, at age 21, he entered the Prussian Kriegs Akademie where he likely read the works of Emmanuel Kant, and came to the notice of the Prussian military reformer General Gerhardt von Scharnhorst. He served in the Prussian army as part of the French invasion of Russia in 1812. He abandoned Prussian service along with the remainder of the army and joined the Russians against Napoleonic France. This act, while one of patriotism to his homeland, forever marked him for disfavor from the ultra-conservative King of Prussia, Frederick Wilhelm III. After the wars, Clausewitz saw a number of staff appointments, and served as an instructor at the Kriegs Akademie, where he worked on his treatise, *Von Krieg or On War*. He died in a cholera epidemic in 1831, before finishing the work. His widow, in order to relieve the financial burden of his death, published the work posthumously in 1832. There is an immense literature on Clausewitz, as well as his work. The best place to begin is Carl von Clausewitz, *On War*. Michael Howard and Peter Paret, eds. and trans. Princeton: Princeton University Press, 1976. This work remains the most accepted translation of Clausewitz's master work, and contains a concise biography of him as well. For further biographical information, see Peter Paret, *Clausewitz and the State: The Man, his Theories, and his Times*. Princeton: Princeton University Press, 1985. More recent, and challenging to the

orthodoxy on Clausewitz is Jon Tetsuro Sumida, *Decoding Clausewitz: A New Approach to One War*. Lawrence, KS: University Press of Kansas, 2008.

[91] Ewald, *Diary*, 274.

[92] Ibid.

[93] Ibid.

[94] Concerning the battle of Cowpens, see Lawrence E. Babits, *A Devil of a Whipping the Battle of Cowpens*.Chapel Hill: University of North Carolina Press, 1998.

[95] On the race to the Dan, see Lawrence E. Babits and Joshua B. Howard, *Long, Obstinate, and Bloody: The Battle of Guilford Courthouse*. Chapel Hill, University of North Carolina Press, 2009, 13-36. See also Lumpkin, *From Yorktown to Savannah*, 163-75.

[96] Ewald, *Diary*, 274.

[97] Ibid, 275.

[98] Willis, *Sea Power*, 445.

[99] Ibid.

[100] Ibid, 276.

[101] Ibid.

[102] Ibid, Great Bridge was the scene of an important engagement early in the war. On December 9, 1775, local Patriot militia forces beat back Governor Dunmore's Ethiopian Legion, a unit composed of former salves, making the reassertion of Crown control over the colony all but impossible. See Benjamin Quarles, *The Negro Soldier in the American Revolution*. Chapel Hill, University of North Carolina Press, 1961, 23, 27-8.

[103] Ewald, *Diary*, 277. Again, this description belies the tensions prevalent between Ewald and Arnold.

[104] Ibid.

[105] This would have been militia general Isaac Gregory.

[106] Ewald, *Diary*, 277.

[107] Ibid.

[108] Ibid, 278.

[109] Ibid.

[110] Ibid.

[111] This was brigadier general Robert Lawson. He had been posted there by von Steuben.

[112] Ibid.

[113] Ibid. This is Beverley Robinson the elder. He was a Virginian who first came to the attention of the British leadership while aiding in the reorganization of the British intelligence network in New York City. His son served as a major in Arnold's force. See Ewald, *Diary*, 422-3.

[114] Ibid, 278-9.

[115] Ibid, 279.

[116] Ibid. In eighteenth century parlance, "close platoons" likely meant that there're was little to no interval between platoons. This would likely have been done to reduce the chances of the men getting lost or separated in the dark of the night as they made their final approach to the enemy position. Under normal circumstances, a prescribed distance or interval was maintained between the troops on a march so as to keep the column from getting bunched up if the men in the front ran into re forced to slow for whatever reason.

[117] Ibid.

[118] Ibid.

[119] Ibid.

[120] Ibid.

[121] Contrast this escapade with the battle of Paoli. See chapter 5.

[122] Ewald, *Diary*, 279.

[123] Ibid.

[124] Ibid, 279-80.

[125] Ibid, 280.

[126] Ibid.

[127] Maass, *Road to Yorktown*, 41. 1126 Ibid, 44.

[129] James R. Gaines, *For Liberty and Glory: Washington, Lafayette and their Revolutions*. New York: W.W. Norton and Company, 2007, 8.

[130] Maass, *Road to Yorktown*, 47.

[131] Lafayette to Washington, March 7, 1781 quoted in Ibid.

[132] Ewald, *Diary*, 280. Interestingly, Ewald notes in connection with this march that his men moved single file. There are several possible reasons for this deployment. One might have been to prevent the troops from getting lost in the darkness. Likewise, the terrain may have been such that they had

no other alternative. It could just as possibly have been a combination of these factors. Ewald does not specify, though he did think the use of a single file for the march significant enough to include as a detail.

133 Ibid.
134 Ibid, 281.
135 Ibid.
136 Ibid.
137 Ibid.
138 Ibid, 284.
139 Ibid.
140 Ibid.
141 Duffy, *Military Experience*, 166-7.
142 Ibid, 184.
143 Ewald, *Diary*, 285.
144 Ibid.
145 Ibid.
146 Ibid.
147 Ibid
148 Ibid.
149 Ibid.
150 Ewald, *Diary*, 285-86.
151 Tustin identifies Walker provisionally, and further states that he was a prominent citizen.in the locality in which Ewald was operation. Ewald, *Diary*, 425, n. 20.
152 Ibid, 286.
153 Ibid, 287.
154 Ibid.
155 Ibid.
156 Ibid.
157 Tustin identifies the American commander as militia general Isaac Gregory, a prominent local Whig. Ewald, *Diary*, 287, 424, n4.
158 Ibid.
159 See Urwin, "'I have wanted to go see you for a Long Time,'" 1-14.
160 Ibid, 288-89.
161 Ibid, 289.
162 Ibid, 289-90.
163 Ibid, 290
164 Ibid.
165 Ibid.
166 Ibid, 290-91.
167 *Journal of the Hesse-Cassel Jager Corps*, 143.
168 On medical treatment in the period, specifically that of wounds, see particularly, Barton Redmon, *For Six Pence a Day: A Collection of Essays on the British Army during the Era of the Seven Years War, 1755-1765*. Pulaski, VA: King Smith Publishing, 2012, 143-54.
169 Ewald, *Diary*, 291.
170 Ibid.
171 Ibid.
172 On this point concerning Arnold, see Martin, Benedict Arnold,
173 The preceding discussion of eighteenth century wound care constitutes a combination of material from several sources, including: Duffy, *Military Experience*, 170-2, 264-5. See also Redmon, For Six Pence a Day, 143-54.
174 Ewald, *Diary*, 294.
175 Ibid.
176 Ibid.
177 Ibid, 294-95
178 Ibid, 296.
179 Martin, *Benedict Arnold*, 430.
180 Lumpkin, *Savannah to Yorktown*, 165.
181 Ibid, 163-5.
182 Ibid, 165.

[183] The most thorough discussion of Guilford Courthouse can be found in Larry Babits and Joshua B. Howard, *Long, Obstinate and Bloody; The Battle of Guilford Courthouse*. Chapel Hill: University of North Carolina Press, 2009.

[184] The preceding reconstruction of the battle of Guilford Courthouse is based on Babits and Howard, Long, Obstinate and Bloody. For an excellent overview of the campaign, see Hugh F. Ranking *Greene and Cornwallis: The Campaign in the Carolinas*. Raleigh, NC: Office of Archives and History, North Carolina Department of Cultural Resources, 2003 (reprint of 1776 original).

[185] Lumpkin, *Savannah to Yorktown*, 222-3.

[186] Oller, *Swamp Fox*, 104.

[187] Maass, *Road to Yorktown*, 31.

[188] Ibid.

[189] Ewald, *Diary*, 296.

[190] Ibid.

[191] Ibid, 297.

[192] Ibid.

[193] Ibid. It is worth noting that at this time, Ewald continued to convalesce from his wound, and did not take a direct role in the operations he describes in his diary. His accounts of these actions are therefore less detailed than those of other exploit he relates in his diary.

[194] Ibid.

[195] Ibid.

[196] Ibid, 299.

[197] Ibid, 298. There is a significant literature on the use of African American troops by both sides in the American War for Independence. Dated but still relevant to any discussion of the topic is Quarles, *Negro Soldier*. It is worth noting that most subsequent works in this sub-genre build on the works of Quarles. See also Michael Lanning, *African Americans in the Revolutionary War*. New York: Kensington Publishing, 2000. The most recent work as of this writing is Alan Gilbert, *Black Patriots and Loyalists: Fighting for Emancipation in the War for Independence*. Chicago: University of Chicago Press, 2012.

[198] Ewald, *Diary*, 299-302.

[199] Ibid, 302.

[200] Ibid.

[201] Sources on Clausewitz have been set out above, see note 134. On Jomini see John Shy, "Jomini" in *Makers of Modern Strategy from Machiavelli to the Nuclear Age*. Peter Paret, ed. Princeton: Princeton University Press, 1986, 143-85.

[202] Ewald, *Diary*, 302.

[203] Ibid.

[204] Ibid, 302-3.

[205] Ibid, 303.

[206] Ibid.

[207] Ibid.

[208] Ibid, 303-4.

[209] Ibid, 304.

[210] Ibid, 304-05.

[211] The most recent discussion of the number of slaves who fled bondage can be found in Maass, *Road to Yorktown*, 98-99.

[212] Lumpkin, *Savannah to Yorktown*, 224.

[213] Ewald, *Diary*, 305.

[214] Ibid.

[215] Maass, *Road to Yorktown*, 51.

[216] Ibid, 55.

[217] Ibid, 57.

[218] Ibid, 58.

[219] Ibid, 306.

[220] Ibid.

[221] Ewald, *Diary*, 306.

[222] Ibid, 307.

[223] Ibid.

[224] Ibid.

[225] Ibid, 308.

[226] Armand's Legion was the successor unit to Ottendorf's Corps.

227 Ibid.
228 Ibid, 308-09.
229 Ibid, 309.
230 On the concept of breaking the determination of the troops, see
231 Ibid.
232 Ibid.
233 Ibid.
234 Ibid, 309-14.
235 Ibid, 312.
236 Ibid.
237 Ibid.
238 Ibid.
239 Ibid.
240 Ibid.
241 On this point, see Duffy, *Military Experience*, 80-2
242 Ewald, *Diary* 313.
243 Ibid.
244 Ibid.
245 Ibid.
246 Mackesy, *War for America*, 407-8. See also Wilson, *Southern Strategy*, 265-6.
247 Ewald, *Diary*, 313-14.
248 Ibid, 314.
249 On Pyle's Hacking match, sometimes referred to as the battle of Haw River, see Lumpkin, *Savannah to Yorktown*, 167-8. See also, Babits and Howard, *Long, Obstinate and Bloody*, 38-9, 42.
250 Ewald, *Diary*, 314-15.
251 On the American plan to attack New York City, as well as the French resistance to the plan, see Herman O. Benninghof II, *The Brilliance of Yorktown: A March of History, 1781* Command and Control, Allied Side. Gettysburg, PA: Thomas Publications, 2006, 33-4. On the reconnaissance of New York, see 1250 Ewald, *Diary*, 315.
253 Willis, *Sea Power*, 447.
254 Ewald, *Diary*, 315.
255 Ibid.
256 Ibid, 315-16.
257 Ibid, 316.
258 This comment seems almost prophetic when the events following Ewald's return to Hesse-Cassel are considered. As will be seen, at that time, his career stagnated once again, and his common status once again stood as a roadblock to his further advancement. It begs the question of whether Ewald felt this way at the time, or if he later added this section when the diary was being edited.
259 Urwin, "'I have wanted to go see you for a Long Time,'" 1-2.
260 On the battle of Greene Spring, see Maass, *Road to Yorktown*, 136-40. See also Lumpkin, *Yorktown to Savannah*, 227.
261 Ibid, 319. It is worth pointing out that Washington was given overall command of this force by order of Louis XVI to Rochambeau. On the allied command structure, see Benninghof, *Brilliance of Yorktown*, 24.
262 Ewald, *Diary*, 317-19.
263 Ibid.
264 Ibid.
265 Ibid, 319-20.
266 Ibid, 320.
267 Ibid. Tustin gives no other information on the colonel than his last name. Furthermore, he could not fully substantiate any connection to the Washingtons, noting only that "locally it was said the families were 'kin'." See 429-30.
268 Ibid, 322.
269 Ibid.

Chapter 10

1 Ibid.
2 Willis, *Sea Power*, 447. On this point, see also Spring, *Zeal and Bayonets*, 35
3 Ibid.

4 Ibid, 322-3.

5 Ibid, 323.

6 This was the plantation belonging to the colonel Whiting whom Ewald had met previously.

7 Ibid.

8 Ibid.

9 Ewald, *Gedanken*, 3-4.

10 W. J. Woods, *Battles of the Revolutionary War, 1775-1781*. New York: DeCapo Press, 1995 reprint of 1990 original, 262. The specific numbers of troops involved were 3, 000 French infantry and 100 cavalry of the Duc de Luzerne's Legion.

11 The real authority on this phase of the campaign, ie its development and the march southward is Benninghof, *Brilliance of Yorktown*.

12 Ibid, 262-63.

13 Ibid, 264. On the description of Graves as useless, see Wilis, *Sea Power*, 449.

14 Ewald, *Diary*, 323

15 Ibid, 324.

16 Ibid.

17 Ibid.

18 Ibid.

19 Ibid, 324-25.

20 Ibid.

21 Willis, *Sea Power*, 451.

22 Wood, Battles, 268-9. See also, John B. Hattendorf, *Newport, the French Navy, and American Independence*. Newport: The Redwood Press, 2005, 102.

23 Willis, *Sea Power*, 450. The planning, organization and march to Virginia are covered in excellent detail in Benninghof, *Brilliance of Yorktown*, 155-84.

24 Ewald, *Diary*, 325. Ewald had previously noted the arrival of De Grasse's squadron. See also, Hattendorf, *Newport*, 102.

25 Ewald, *Diary*, 325.

26 Ibid. In addition, Ewald noted that about 1,000 sailors came ashore that evening form the British ships, some of whom were to act as gunners.

27 Ibid, 325-6.

28 Ibid, 326.

29 Ibid.

30 Ibid.

31 Ibid.

32 Ibid.

33 Ibid.

34 Ibid.

35 Ibid.

36 Wood, *Battles*, 269-70.

37 Ibid, 270.

38 Ibid.

39 Ibid.

40 Hattendorf, *Newport*, 103.

41 Wood, *Battles*, 273.

42 Ibid, 276-77. See also, Willis, *Sea Power*, 453-54.

43 Willis, Sea Power, 454.

44 Ibid, 455.

45 Ewald, *Diary*, 326

46 Ibid.

47 Ibid.

48 Ibid.

49 Ibid, 326-27.

50 Ibid, 327.

51 Ibid.

52 Ibid.

53 Ibid. Fire ships were vessels that had been stripped of their armaments and loaded with combustibles. They would be set adrift on the tides to float towards and enemy fleet with a skeleton crew of volunteers. As they drew close to their opponents, the crew would begin setting fires to their own ship, and when they judged the moment right, they would abandon ship. The goal was

that the fire ship would float into the midst of the enemy fleet, and explode, hurling bits of burning wood at the vessels of their opponents, the result being fires breaking out on a number of vessels of the enemy force.

54 Ewald, *Diary*, 327

55 Ibid, 328.

56 Ibid.

57 Ibid.

58 Ibid.

59 Ibid.

60 Ibid.

61 Ibid.

62 Ibid, 329.

63 Lumpkin, *Savannah to Yorktown*, 336

64 Ibid.

65 Ibid. Lauzun's refers to the unit Lauzun's Legion, founded by the Armand Louis de Gontaur, duc de Lauzun in March 1780. The legion was based on the concept of a small unit that included elements of infantry, cavalry and artillery. In essence, it was a sort of self-contained army. Lauzun formed his legion from various contingents of French and foreign volunteers. The latter are often referred to as mercenaries. They took part in action primarily in the West Indies. Their main action in North America outside of the siege of Yorktown was at White Plains. On the Legion, see Robert A. Selig, "The du de Lauzun and his Legion: Rochambeau's most Troublesome, Colorful Soldiers" at http://www.americanrevolution.org/lauzun.php internet. Lest accessed, 4/15/16. See also Lee Kennett, *The French Forces in America, 1780-1783*. Westport, CT: Greenwood Press, 1977.

66 Ewald, *Diary*, 328-9.

67 Ibid, 329.

68 Ibid.

69 Ibid.

70 Ibid.

71 Ibid, 329-30.

72 Ibid, 330.

73 Ibid.

74 Ibid.

75 Ibid.

76 Lumpkin, *Savannah to Yorktown*, 239.

77 Burke Davis, *The Campaign that Won America: The Story of Yorktown*. New York: Eastern National, 1970, 213.

78 Ibid, 214.

79 Ibid.

80 Lumpkin, *Savannah to Yorktown*, 239.

81 Ewald, *Diary*, 334.

82 Davis, *Campaign that Won America*, 217.

83 Ewald, *Diary*, 334.

84 Davis, *Campaign that Won America*, 218.

85 Ibid, 219.

86 Ibid, 221.

87 Ewald, *Diary*, 334. These men were Commissar General Perkins, and Lieutenant Charles Perekins.

88 Davis, *Campaign that Won America*, 223-4.

89 Ewald, *Diary*, 334

90 Davis, *Campaign that Won America*, 220.

91 Ewald, *Diary*, 334.

92 Ibid, 224, See also Lumpkin, *Savannah to Yorktown*, 241.

93 Ewald, *Diary*, 334.

94 Lumpkin, *Savannah to Yorktown*, 241.

95 Ewald, *Diary*, 335

96 Lumpkin, *Savannah to Yorktown*, 241. See also, *Campaign that Won America*, 225-6

97 Ibid.

98 Davis, *Campaign that Won America*, 227-8.

99 Ibid, 229.

100 Ibid, 230-31

101 Ewald, *Diary*, 335.

[102] Ibid.
[103] Lumpkin, *Savannah to Yorktown*, 242.
[104] Ewald, *Diary*, 336.
[105] Ibid.
[106] Lumpkin, *Savannah to Yorktown*, 242.
[107] Ibid, 243
[108] Ewald, *Diary*, 337.
[109] Ibid.
[110] Lumpkin, *Savannah to Yorktown*, 243.
[111] Ewald, *Diary*, 337
[112] Lumpkin, *Savannah to Yorktown*, 243
[113] Ibid.
[114] Ibid.
[115] Ewald, *Diary*, 339.
[116] Lumpkin, *Savannah to Yorktown*, 244.
[117] Ibid. Charles O'Hara (1740?-1802) is listed as the illegitimate son of James O'Hara, second Lord of Trawley and Colonel of the Coldstream Guards. Charles received a good education at Westminster School. On December 23, 1752, he received his first commission as cornet in the 3rd Dragoons. He was eleven or twelve at the time. At sixteen, he went to the Continental to serve in the Seven Years' War, where he saw action in both Germany, as part of the allied army of Ferdinand of Brunswick, and in Portugal. After the war, he served in Goree as Lieutenant Colonel Commandant of a black unit known as the Africa Corps. He came to America in 1778 as the war expanded due to French involvement. He served briefly in New York. He then went south, serving as commander of the 2nd battalion of Guards throughout the southern campaigns under Cornwallis. He represented the Earl at the Yorktown surrender as the former complained of feeling under the weather. He later served as governor of Gibraltar during the 1790s. See Boatner, *Encyclopedia*, 815-6.
[118] Ibid.
[119] Ibid.
[120] Ewald, *Diary*, 339.
[121] Ibid.
[122] Ibid.
[123] Ibid.
[124] Ibid.

Chapter 11

[1] Ewald, *Diary*, 343-44.
[2] Ibid, 344.
[3] On the whale boats, see chapter 8, note 991.
[4] Ewald, *Dairy*, 344.
[5] Ibid.
[6] See chapter 2.
[7] This is the impression given by most general histories of the conflict. See Don Higginbotham, *The War of American Independence: Military Attitudes, Policies and Practice, 1763-1789*. Boston: Northeastern University Press, 1983, Robert Middlekauff, *The Glorious Cause: The American Revolution, 1763-1789*. New York: Oxford University Press, 1982, Charles P. Neimeyer, *The Revolutionary War*. Westport, CT: Greenwood Press, 2007.
[8] Ibid, 345.
[9] Ibid, 345-46.
[10] Ibid, 346
[11] Germain stood with a promising military career before him, until, he either misunderstood, or disobeyed orders at the battle of Minden. A later court of inquiry found his actions contributed materially to the British loss of the battle, and he was cashiered from the Army, and forbidden ever to serve in the Crown's armed forces ever again. A number of historians have seen in Germain's past the reasons for his decided aggressive approach to the war in North America.
[12] Ibid.
[13] Ibid, 347.
[14] Ibid.
[15] Ibid.

16 Ibid, 348.
17 Ibid.
18 Ibid.
19 Ibid.
20 Ibid.
21 Ibid, 349.
22 *Jaeger Corps Journal*, 180.
23 Ibid, 181.
24 Ibid
25 Ewald, *Diary*, 350.
26 Ibid.
27 Ibid.
28 Ibid.
29 On the effects of the Seven Years' War on Hessen-Kassel, see chapter 3. For more on the civil conflict in and around New York City, see Harry M. Ward, *Between the Lines*. See also Kwasny, Washington's Partisan War,
30 Ibid.
31 Ibid.
32 Ibid.
33 Ibid, 351.
34 Ibid.
35 Ibid.
36 Ibid.
37 Ibid.
38 Ibid, 352.
39 Ibid.
40 Kajencki, *Thaddeus Kosciuszko*, 118.
41 Ibid.
42 McDougall was a long-time Revolutionary. A first generation immigrant, he had come to the colonies from the Hebrides in 1738, when he was four years old. He had held various jobs in his youth, including several stints on merchant seamen. When the French and Indian War broke out, he turned from the merchant service to privateering. This allowed him to expand his small fortune, and after the war, having family to care for on land, he went into land speculation and importing. As the colonial relationship worsened, McDougall, always an outcast form the traditional New York elites, sided with the Sons of Liberty. When fighting broke out, he joined the Continental Army, being made colonel of the 1st New York Regiment on June 30, 1775. He served throughout the war, rising to the rank of Major General. He became involved with New York politics after the war, and died in 1786. He is interred in the family vault at the First Presbyterian Church in New York City. On McDougall, see William McDougall, *American Revolutionary: A Biography of General Alexander McDougall*. Westport, CT: Greenwood Press, 1977.
43 Ibid, 353.
44 Ibid.
45 On Henry Knox, see Mark Puls, *Henry Knox: Visionary General of the American Revolution*. New York: Palgrave Macmillan, 2008.
46 Ewald, *Diary*, 353.
47 Ibid, 353.
48 Ibid.
49 Ibid, 353-4.
50 Ibid, 354.
51 Ibid, 355.
52 This brings up a long-standing debate as to what motivated the troops in the Continental Army. On one hand, a number of historians, including Robert A. Gross, James Kirby Martin, Mark Edward Lender, James Kirby and Charles P. Neimeyer see the motivations for Washington's troops as purely material in nature. Charles Royster alone has countered their assertions, and placed much of the emphasis for soldiers to join and remain in the ranks as ideological in nature. The relevant works are: Robert A. Gros, *The Minutemen and Their World*. New York: Hill and Wang, 1976, James Kirby Martin and Mark Edward Lender, *A Respectable Army: The Military Origins of the Republic, 1763-1789*. Wheeling, IL: Harlan Davidson, Inc. 1982, Charles P. Neimeyer, *The Revolutionary War*. Westport, CT: Greenwood Press, 2007, Edward C. Papenfuse and Gregory A Stiverson "General Smallwood's Recruits: The Peacetime Career of the Revolutionary War

Private." in *William and Mary Quarterly*, 30, 1 (January 1973): 117-132, and Charles Royster, *A Revolutionary People at War The Continental Army and American Character, 1775-1783*. Chapel Hill: University of North Carolina Press, 1979.

53 On the half-pay controversy, see Royster, *A Revolutionary People at War*, 200-04.
54 On the Newburgh Conspiracy, see Higginbotham, *War of Independence*, 405-11 Middlekauff, *Glorious Cause*, 582-4. Royster, *Revolutionary People*, 333-41, gives the best more thorough description of the sentiments of the officers at the time.
55 Ewald, *Diary*, 357.
56 Ibid.
57 Ibid.
58 Ibid.
59 Ibid, 357-58.
60 Ibid, 358.
61 Ibid.
62 *Journal of the Hesse-Cassel Jaeger Corps*, 181.
63 Ibid.
64 Ewald, *Diary*, 359-60. See also Journal of the Hesse-Cassel Jaeger Corps, 182.
65 *Journal of the Hesse-Cassel Jaeger Corps*, 184.
66 Ibid.
67 Ewald, *Diary*, 360.
68 Ibid.
69 Ibid.
70 Ibid.
71 Ibid, 361.
72 *Journal of the Hesse-Cassel Jaeger Corps*, 193.
73 On the damage sustained by Hessen-Kassel in the Seven Years War, see Chapter 3, 48-9. See also Igrao, "'Barbarous Strangers,'" 961.
74 *Journal of the Hesse-Cassel Jaeger Corps*, 193.
75 Ibid, 361.
76 The debate on this issue is covered quite succinctly in H.D. Schmidt "The Hessian Mercenaries: the Career of a Political Cliché." in *History*, 43, 149 (1958): 207-212.
77 Wilson, "Soldier Trade," 764-65.
78 Igrao, "'Barbarous Strangers,'" 961.
79 Ibid.

Chapter 12

1 There is general consensus on this point, though there was variance in degree from one European military to another.
2 Johann Ewald, *Treatise on Partisan Warfare*. Robert A. Selig and David Curtiss Skaggs, trans. New York: Greenwood Press, 1991, 23.
3 Ibid, 64.
4 Ibid.
5 John Graves Simcoe Simcoe's *Military Journal: A History of the Operations of a Partisan Corps, called The Queen's Rangers, Commanded by Lieutenant Colonel J.G. Simcoe, During the War of the American Revolution*. 1781, 7-8.
6 Ewald, *Treatise*, 64-65.
7 The key works that dealt specifically with light troops at the time were:
8 Ewald, *Treatise*, 67.
9 Ibid.
10 Ibid, 68-69.
11 Ibid, 69.
12 Ibid.
13 See chapter 10,
14 Ibid.
15 Ibid, 70.
16 Ibid.
17 Ibid, 71

18 For a solid discussion of the Legion concept and its evolution, especially in the American case, see Andrew J. Birtle, "The Origins of the Legion of the United States." *In Journal of Military History*, 67, 4 (October 2003): 1249- 61.

19 Ibid.

20 Ibid, 72.

21 See Mc Intyre, "Enlightened Rogues," 27-9. See also, James R. Mc Intyre, *British Light Infantry Tactics*. Point Pleasant, NJ: Winged Hussar Publishing, 2015.

22 Ewald, *Treatise on Partisan Warfare*, 73.

23 Ibid, 74.

24 Ibid.

25 Ibid.

26 Ibid.

27 Ibid, 75

28 Ibid.

29 See chapter 7, 234, 236.

30 Ewald, *Treatise on Partisan Warfare*, 76.

31 Ibid, 77.

32 Ibid.

33 Ibid.

34 Ibid.

35 Ibid.

36 Ibid, 79. Zwieback consisted of a small loaf of bread that was cut and toasted until very dry. This allowed it to last longer without going bad. It could be seen as a rough precursor to the infamous hard tack of the civil war.

37 Ibid, 79-80.

38 Ibid, 81.

39 Ibid, 82.

40 Ibid.

41 Ibid.

42 Ibid.

43 Ewald, *Gedanken*, 27-56.

44 Ewald, *Treatise on Partisan Warfare*, 85.

45 Ibid, 85-86

46 On Ewald's intelligence concerning the American attack on Germantown, October 4, 1777, see chapter 5.

47 Ibid, 86.

48 Ibid.

49 Ibid.

50 Ibid.

51 Ibid, 87.

52 Ibid.

53 Ibid.

54 Ibid.

55 Ibid, 88.

56 Ibid.

57 Ibid, 88-9.

58 Ibid, 89.

59 Ibid.

60 Ibid, 90.

61 Ibid, 91

62 Ibid, 93

63 Ibid.

64 Ibid, 94.

65 Ibid, 94-95.

66 Ibid, 95.

67 Ibid.

68 Ibid, 96.

69 Ibid, 97

70 Ibid.

71 Ibid.

[72] Ibid, 98.

[73] Ibid.

[74] Ibid, 101.

[75] Ibid.

[76] Ibid.

[77] Ibid.

[78] Ibid, 102.

[79] Ibid.

[80] Ibid.

[81] Ibid, 103.

[82] Ibid, 104-5.

[83] Ibid, 107.

[84] Ibid, 107-08. For details of this operation see chapter 5. See also, McGuire, *Battle of Paoli*.

[85] Ewald, *Treatise on Partisan Warfare*, 111.

[86] Sun Tzu, *Art of War*, 66

[87] Here, Ewald is referring to Armand François de La Croix and his work *Traité de la Petite Guerre pour les Compagnes Franches*. Paris: A Boudet, 1752. John Grenier notes that this work, published in the 1750s, initiated the second state in the discussion of petite guerre, and was the first widely read word in French dedicated to the subject. See John Grenier, *The First Way of War: American War Making on the Frontier*. Cambridge: Cambridge University Press, 2005, 95.

[88] Ewald, *Treatise on Partisan Warfare*, 111.

[89] Ibid.

[90] Ibid, 113.

[91] Ibid, 114.

[92] Ibid, 116.

[93] Ibid.

[94] Ibid, 117.

[95] Ibid.

[96] Ibid, 117-18.

[97] Ibid, 118.

[98] Ibid.

[99] Ibid.

[100] Ibid, 119.

[101] Ibid.

[102] Ibid.

[103] Ibid.

[104] Ibid.

[105] Ibid.

[106] Ibid, 121.

[107] Ibid.

[108] Ibid, 122.

[109] Ibid.

[110] Ibid.

[111] Ibid, 124.

[112] Ibid.

[113] Ibid.

[114] Ibid, 125.

[115] Ibid, 126.

[116] Ibid.

[117] Ibid, 126-7.

[118] Ibid, 128.

[119] Concerning Ewald's service under Arnold in Virginia, see chapter 9.

[120] Ewald, *Treatise on Partisan Warfare*, 128.

[121] Ibid, 130.

[122] Ibid.

[123] Ibid.

[124] Ibid.

[125] Ibid, 131.

[126] Ibid.

[127] Ibid.

[128] Ibid, 132.
[129] Ibid, 28. For a solid biography of Scharnhorst focused on his intellectual pursuits, see Charles Edward White, *The Enlightened Soldier: Scharnhorst and the Militärische Gesellschaft in Berlin, 1801-1805.* New York: Praeger, 1989.
[130] Ewald, *Diary,* xxvii.
[131] Ewald, *Treatise,* 3.
[132] Peter Paret, *Clausewitz and the State: The Man, his Theories, and his Times.* Princeton: Princeton University Press, 1985, 191-92.
[133] Carl von Clausewitz, *Clausewitz on Small War.* Christopher Daase and James W. Davis, eds. and trans. Oxford: Oxford University press, 2015, 167.
[134] J.F.C. Fuller, "The Revival and Training of Light Infantry in the British Army." in *Journal of the Royal United Services Institution.* 57 (1913): 1208.
[135] Ibid, 1208-09.
[136] Ibid, 1209.
[137] Ibid, 1211.
[138] Tustin, Ewald, *Diary,* xxvii.
[139] On this point, there are many historians. For the most recent discussion, see Jonathan Abel, *Guibert: Father of Napoleon's Grande Armée.* Norman: University of Oklahoma Press, 2016, 27-33.
[140] Ewald, *Diary,* xxvii.
[141] Ibid.
[142] Ibid.
[143] Ibid.
[144] Ibid.
[145] Clausewitz, *Clausewitz on Small War,* 159. [146] Full bibliographic information on these works is as follows: Johann von Ewald *Gesprache eines Husarencorporals, eines Jagers und liechten Infanteristen uber die Pflichten und den Dienst der liechten Soldaten.* Altona: Hammerich, 1794. Johann von Ewald *Belehrunger uber den Kreig, besonders uber den kleinen Krieg, durch Beispiele grosser Helden und kluger und tapferer Manner.* 3 vols. Schleswig: J.G. Schlooss, 1798.
[147] Ewald, *Diary,* xiv-v.
[148] Ewald, *Diary* xxvii. Ewald's previous command, the Jäger Corps, were reassigned to Eckernförde.
[149] Ibid, xxviii.
[150] Ibid.
[151] Ibid.
[152] Ibid.
[153] Ibid.
[154] Ibid.

Chapter 13

[1] This brief sketch of the early stages of the French Revolution draws on the following: Roger Chartier, *The Cultural Origins of the French Revolution.* Lydia G. Cochrane, trans. Durham: Duke University Press, 1991. Dated, but still interesting is Alfred Cobban, *The Social Interpretation of the French Revolution.* 2nd ed. Cambridge: Cambridge University Press, 1999. One of the key works for launching the more recent studies of the French Revolution is François Furet, *Interpreting the French Revolution.* Elborg Forester, trans. Cambridge: Cambridge University Press, 1981. On the period leading up to the Revolution, see Georges Lefebvre, *The Coming of the French Revolution.* Princeton: Princeton University Press, 1947. On the outbreak of mass paranoia in the countryside over the summer of 1789, see Lefebvre, The Great Fear: *Rural Panic in Revolutionary France.* New York: Vintage Books, 1973. Though much out of vogue in its interpretation, Albert Soboul, *The French Revolution 1787-1799: From the Storming of the Bastille to Napoleon.* New York: Vintage Books, 1962, remains magisterial in its narrative. Finally, essentially a primary source, and a must read for anyone interested in the French Revolution is Alexis de Tocqueville, *The Old Regime and the French Revolution.* Stuart Gilbert, trans. New York: Doubleday, 1983 reprint of 1955 original.
[2] T.C.W. Blanning, The French Revolutionary Wars, 1787-1802. New York: St. Martin's Press, 1996, 38-9.
[3] Specifically, here, I am referring to the Marquis de Bouillé, who was paced in charge of Louis XVI's attempted escape from France, commonly known as the Flight to Varennes. See Souboul, *French Revolution,* 219.
[4] On the French army during this period of profound transition, see Samuel F. Scott *From Yorktown to Valmy: The Transformation of the French Army in the Age of Revolution.* Niwot, CO: University

Press of Colorado, 1998. The author's previous work, *The Response of the Royal Army to the French Revolution: The Role and Development of the Line Army, 1787-1793*. Oxford: Clarendon Press, 1978 is quite useful on this period as well.

[5] The amalgam and its implications are best dealt with by John A. Lynn *The Bayonets of the Republic: Motivation and Tactics in the Army of Revolutionary France, 1791-94*. 2nd ed. Boulder, CO: Westview Press, 1996, 57-60.

[6] For the military effects of the levée en masse, see Blanning, *French Revolutionary Wars*, 101. See also Alan Forrest, Soldiers of the French Revolution. Durham: Duke University Press, 1990, 51-53; Lynn, *Bayonets*, 55-7.

[7] For a very solid biography focused on Napoleon's early career, see Philip Dwyer *Napoleon: The Path to Power*. New Haven: Yale University Press, 2007.

[8] Ibid, 177-80.

[9] Ibid, 468-70.

[10] The military aspect of Napoleon's career has garnered the most attention over the years, and works on the subject are certainly plentiful. The standard account of his military career is David G. Chandler. *The Campaigns of Napoleon*. London: Weidenfeld and Nicolson, 1995.

[11] Felix Markham, *Napoleon and the Awakening of Europe: A Study of the Military, Political, and Personal Elements of the Napoleonic Domination of Europe*. New York: Collier Books, 1963, 62.

[12] Ibid.

[13] Robert B. Holtman, The Napoleonic Revolution. Philadelphia: J.B. Lippincott Company, 1967, 89-95. See also Louis Bergeron France under Napoleon. R.R. Palmer trans. Princeton: Princeton University Press, 1981, 122-25.

[14] Concerning the camp at Boulogne, see John R. Elting, *Swords Around a Throne*. New York: The Free Press, 1988, 59, 145. On Napoleon's hopes to develop French sea power, see Alan Schom, *Trafalgar: Countdown to Battle 1803-1805*. New York: Oxford University Press, 1990, 63-96.

[15] Abel, *Guibert*, 24-5. See also, Duffy, *Military Experience*, 157 for a discussion of the manner in which the march was carried out by most states during the period of the Seven Years' War.

[16] Ibid.

[17] Ibid, 25.

[18] Chandler, *Campaign of Napoleon*, 319-27. See also Elting, Swords around a Throne, 55-65.

[19] On this incident, see Charles Esdaile, *Napoleon's Wars: An International History*. New York: Penguin Books, 2008, 190-2.

[20] Ibid, 193-4.

[21] On Napoleon's military reforms, see Esdaile, *Napoleon's Wars*, 9-10. Gunther E. Rothenberg, *The Art of War in the Age of Napoleon*. Bloomington: Indiana University Press, 1978, 126-38. For a thorough discussion of Napoleon's style of warfare, see David Chandler, *Napoleon's Campaigns*, 133-90. Some of Chandler's ideas have been challenged by later scholars. Of particular utility in discussing the tactics of the period are: Paddy Griffith, *The Art of War of Revolutionary France, 1789-1802*. London: Greenhill Books, 1998 and Rory Muir, *Tactics and the Experience of Battle in the Age of Napoleon*. New Haven: Yale University Press, 1998.

[22] The classic work on this campaign is Christopher Duffy, Austerlitz, 1805. London: Seeley Service & Company, 1977. See also, Alistair Horne, *How Far from Austerlitz? Napoleon 1805-1815*. New York: MacMillan, 1996.

[23] See chapter 12, pages, 458-9.

[24] Esdaile, *Napoleon's Wars*, 256-60.

[25] Ewald, *Diary*, xxviii.

[26] H.M. Scott "Introduction: Prussia from Rossbach to Jena." in *German History*, 12, 3 (1994): 279-85.

[27] For a solid overview of the reforms enacted during the period of the French Revolution and Napoleon's early years in power, see Elting, *Swords around a Throne*, 27-65.

[28] Louis-Nicolas Davout (May 10, 1770-June 1, 1823) Born at Yvonne, he went to the military academy at Auxerre before transferring to the Ecole Militaire in Paris. He was commissioned a sous-lieutenant in 1788. When the revolution broke out, he embraced it early on, and served France in the Wars of the Revolution, rising through the ranks. He played a pivotyal role at the battle of Austerltiz as well. See Delderfield, Napoleon's Marshals, 22-45. See also, John G. Gallaher, *The Iron Marshal. A Biography of Louis N. Davout*. London: The Greenhill Books, 2000.

[29] Concerning Jena and Auerstädt as examples of decisive battle, see Weigley, Age of Battles, 390-404.

[30] Michel Ney (January 10, 1769-December 7, 1815). Dubbed by Napoleon as "bravest of the brave," Ney was born in southern France, the son of a master-barrel-cooper. He was educated at the Collège des Augustins and became a civil servant. This calling did not suit him, and Ney joined

the army as an enlisted man, and was present at the Cannonade at Valmy as well as the battle of Neerwinden. Likewise, he served at the battle of Hohenlinden in 1800. He served Napoleon throughout the period of the Consulate and Empire. Physically courageous to a fault, Ney often over-extended himself, as in the present circumstance. His rear-guard action on the retreat from Russia earned him the nom-de-guerre listed at the outset. His loyalty to Napoleon eventually led him to turn on the Louis XVIII during the hundred days, for which he was executed by firing squad on December 7, 1815. Delderfield, *Napoelon's Marshals*, 12-46, 222-3.

31 Jean Lannes (April 10, 1769-May 31-1809). Lannes was one of Napoleon's most talented tactical leaders. The sone fo a Gascon farmer, he had no formal military education until he joined a unit of volunteers in 1792. His men elected him their sergeant major. He saw service in the Pyrenees in 1793-94, and rose to chef de brigade. He was later removed from this rank under the Thermidorian Reaction. He met Napoleon while serving under him the Italian Campaign, and joined the expedition to Egypt as well. He was wounded in the legs by a cannon ball on the second day of Aspern-Essling, May 22, 1809. Both legs had to be amputated. He succumbed to his injuries on May 31, 1809. See Delderfield, *Napoleon's Marshals*, 16-31. 123-4.

32 This figure did not include battalion guns.

33 Ibid, 272.

34 The preceding overview of Jen is derived from Chandler, Napoleon's Campaigns, 479-506. See also Elting, *Swords around a Throne*, 127-45. The most recent account of these battles as of this writing is F.N. Maude, The Jena Campaign: *1806-The Twin Battles of Jena & Auerstadt between Napoleon's French and the Prussian Army*. Np: Leonaur, 2007.

35 Ewald, *Diary*, xxviii

36 Ibid, xxviii-xxix.

37 Ibid, xxix.

38 For this brief biographical sketch of Joachim Murat, see David G. Chandler, ed. *Napoleon's Marshals*. London: Weidenfield and Nicolson, 1995, R. F. Delderfield, *The March of the Twenty-Six*. London: Leo Cooper, 2004, and A.G. MacDonnell, *Napoleon and His Marshals*. London: Prion, 1996.

39 Ewald, *Diary*, xxix.

40 Ibid.

41 Ibid.

42 Esdaile, *Napoleon's Wars*, 312-3.

43 Ibid, xxix-xxx.

44 Ibid, xxx

45 Ibid.

46 Ibid.

47 Ibid.

48 On Freikorps and their role in connection with contemporary military establishments, see Duffy, Military Experience, 269-73. See also, Duffy, *The Army of Frederick the Great*. 2nd ed. Chicago, IL: emperor's Press, 1996, 133-8.

49 Sam A. Mustafa, *The Long Ride of Major von Schill: A Journey through German History and Memory*. Lanham: Rowan and Littlefield, 2008,

50 On Schill's wounds, see Mustafa, *Schill*, 54.

51 Ibid,

52 Esdaile, *Napoleon's Wars*, 295-9.e

53 Weigley, *Age of Battles*, 407-09.

54 On the Prussian military reforms, see Andrew Uffindell, Great Generals of the Napoleonic Wars and their Battles 1805-1815. Gloucestershire, Spellbound, 2007, 183-88.

55 Mustafa, *Schill*, 99.

56 Ibid.

57 Ibid.

58 On the rebellions which occurred in areas under the control of Jerome, see Chandler, Napoleon's Campaigns, 450, 776. See also Elting, Sword around a Throne, 402-3.

59 Mustafa, *Schill*, 99.

60 Ibid.

61 Ibid, 99-100.

62 Ibid, 100.

63 Ibid.

64 Ibid, 101.

65 Ibid.

66 Ibid, 102.

67 Ibid.

68 Ibid.

69 Ibid, 103-04.

70 Ibid, 105-06.

71 Saragossa refers to a fortress town in Spain. The inhabitants of the town successfully resisted a siege by the French in 1808. The city did, however, fall to another French siege the following year. On Schill's boast, see Mustafa, *Schill*, 107.

72 Ibid, 107-08.

73 Ibid, 108.

74 Ibid, 103.

75 Ibid, 108.

76 Ibid, 110.

77 Ewald, *Bild*, 6

78 Ibid.

79 *Schill* Schill, 110.

80 Ibid.

81 Ewald, *Bild*, 6

82 Ibid.

83 Mustafa, *Schill*, 110.

84 Ibid. 111.

85 Ewald, *Bild*, 6

86 Mustafa, *Schill*, 111.

87 Ibid, 111-12.

88 Ibid, 112.

89 Ibid.

90 Ibid, 113. Michelin is given as a Lieutenant Colonel in the Dutch army. No further information was obtainable. See George Barsch *Ferdinand von Schill's Zug und Tod in Jahre 1809*. Leipzig: Brockhaus, 1860, 117.

91 Ibid, 113-14.

92 Ibid, 114.

93 Barsch *Ferdinand von Schill's Zug*, 116-17 quoted in Ibid, 114.

94 Ewald, *Diary*, xxx.

95 Ibid.

96 Ewald, *Diary*, xxx. Concerning Marshal Pierre Augereau, (October 21, 1757-June 12, 1816). Another one of the marshalate whose options were profoundly effected by the Revolution. Augereau was the son of a Parisian fruit seller. He joined a dragoon regiment, where he gained a reputation for his swordsmanship. He became a well-known duelist as well. This latter talent created problems for Augereau as he killed an officer and was forced to flee France. He drifted around Europe for over a decade until Louis XVI announced a general amnesty in 1781, and he was able to return to France once again. With the outbreak of the Revolution, Augereau served in the Royal Army and saw action in the Vendée. He saw action on the Pyrenees front and later joined the Army of Italy, where he met Napoleon. He served throughout the Napoleonic Wars, and even returned to Napoleon for the Hundred Days. After Waterloo, Louis XVIII stripped augereau of his title and pension. He died the following year on his estate. See Delderfield, *Napoleon's Marshals*, 32-5, 268 . See also, Ewalting, Swords around a Throne, 12-19, 647-8.

97 Ibid, xxxi.

98 Ibid.

Conclusion

1 Hans Konze, "The Hessen-Kassel Jaeger Corps in the American War of Independence, 1776-1783," quoted in *Journal of the Hesse-Cassel Jaeger Corps*, 195.

2 Ewald, *Bild*, 7.

BIBLIOGRAPHY

Primary Sources:

Anon. "Battle of Germantown form a British Account." in *Pennsylvania Magazine of History and Biography*, 11,1 (April 1887): 112-14.

_____*The Operations of the Allied Army under the Command of his Serene Highness Prince Ferdinand Duke of Brunswick and Luneberg during the Greatest Part of Six Campaigns beginning in the Year 1757 and ending in the Year 1762*. London: T. Jeffreys, 1764.

_____*Journal of the Hesse-Cassel Jaeger Corps and Hans Konze's List of Jaeger Officers*. Bruce E. Burgoyne, trans. Marie E. Burgoyne and Bruce E. Burgoyne, eds. Westminster, MD: Heritage Books, 2008.

Balch, Thomas, ed. *Papers Relating Chiefly to the Maryland Line during the Revolution*. Philadelphia: T.K. and P.G. Collins, 1857.

Bardeleben, Schlieffen, W. Heikennitz, Junkenn, Wangermann, and Schramm, "Report of the Court-Martial for the Trial of the Hessian Officers captured by Washington at Trenton, December 26, 1776." in *Pennsylvania Magazine of History and Biography*. 7, 1 (1883): 45-49.

Burgoyne, Bruce E. ed. Trans. *Diaries of Two Ansbach Jaegers*. Bowie, MD: Heritage Books, 1997.

Burgoyne, Bruce E. and Mary E. ed. and trans. *Hessian Chaplains: Their Duties and Diaries*, Westminster, MD: Heritage Books, 2003

_____*Revolutionary War Letters Written by Hessian Officers*. Westminster, MD: Heritage Books, 2005.

Clausewitz, Carl von *On War*. Michael Howard and Peter Paret, eds. and trans. Princeton: Princeton University Press, 1976.

_____*Clausewitz on Small War*. Oxford: Oxford University Press, 2015.

Cointe Jean Louis Le *The Science of Military Posts: for the use of Regimental Officers who frequently Command detached parties. In which is shewn the manner of attacking and defending posts. With cuts, explaining the Construction of Field Forts, and Intrenchment. By M. La Cointe of the Royal Academy at Nismes. To which are added some remarks taken from M. Saxe, De La Croix and others serving to the same purpose. Translated from the French. By an officer*. London: Printed for T. Payne, at the Mews Gate, 1761.

Dohla, Johann Conrad *A Hessian Diary of the Revolution*. Bruce E. Burgoyne, ed. trans. Norman, OK: University of Oklahoma Press, 1990.

Ewald, Carl von *Generallieutenant Johann von Ewalds Levnetsløb*. Copenhagen: Riises Boglade1838.

————Johannes Ewald: *Bilder aus dem Leben eines Soldaten*. Staatarchiv Kassel, Best. C19 Nr. 7217.

Ewald, Johann *Gedanken eines hessischen Offiziers uber sa, was man bei Fuhrung eines Detachments im Felde zu thun hat*. Cassel: Johann Jacob Cramer, 1774.

————*Abhandlung von dem Deinst der Leichten Truppen*. Schleswig: J.G. Schloss, 1790 and 1796.

————*Belehrunger uber den Kreig, besonders uber den kleinen Krieg, durch Beispiele grosser Helden und kluger und tapferer Manner*. 3 vols. Schleswig: J.G. Schlooss, 1798.

————*Gesprache eines Husarencorporals, eines Jagers und liechten Infanteristen uber die Pflichten und den Dienst der liechten Soldaten*. Altona: Hammerich, 1794.

————*Vom Dienst im Felde fur Unteroffiziere…* Schleswig: J.G. Rohss, Christiani & Korte, 1802.

————Johann von Hinrichs, Johann Chrittoph von Huyn, *The Siege of Charleston*. Bernard A. Uhlendorf, ed, and trans. New York: New York Times and Arno Press, 1968.

————*Diary of the American War*. Joseph P. Tustin, ed and trans. New Haven, CT: Yale University Press, 1979.

————*Treatise on Partisan Warfare*. Robert A. Selig and David Curtiss Skaggs, trans. New York: Greenwood Press, 1991.

Folard, Jean-Charles, Chevalier de *Abrégé des commentaries de M. de Folard sur L'Histoire de Polybe*. Paris : Chez La veuve Gandouin …, Giffart …, David l'aîné …, Jombert …, Durand …,1754.

Graf, Holger Thodor, Lena Haunert and Christoph Kampmann, eds. *Aldiges Leben am Ausgang des Ancien Regime. Die Tagesbuchaufzeichnungen (1754-1798) des Georg Ernst von und zu Gilsa*. Marburg: Hessisches Landesamt fur gesscichtliche Landeskunde, 2010.

St. Gregory of Tours. *The History of the Franks, Volume II: Text*. Trans. by Ormonde Maddock Dalton. Clarendon Press: 1967.

Hamond, Andrew S. *The Autobiography of Captain Sir Andrew Snape Hamond, 1738-1828*. W. Hugh Moomaw, ed. MA thesis, University of Virginia, 1947.

Hotham-Thompson, Sir Charles *Operations of the Allied Army under the Duke of Brunswick, 1757-1762*. London: T. Jeffreys, 1764.

Jeney, M. de *The Partisan: Or the Art of Making War in Detachments* (English edition, 1760).

Londahl-Smidt, Lieutenant Colonel Donald M. ed. trans., "German and British Accounts of the Assault on Fort Mercer at Redbank, NJ in October 1777." in *The Hessians: Journal of the Johannes Schwalm Historical Association*. 16 (2013):1-33.

Morton, Robert "The Diary of Robert Morton." *Pennsylvania Magazine of History and Biography* 1, no.1 (1877): 1-39.

Muenchhausen, Friedrich von *At General Howe's Side, 1776-1778: The Diary of General William Howe's Aide de Camp, Captain Friedrich von Muenchhausen*. E. Kipping, trans., S. Smith, ed. Monmouth Beach, NJ: Philip Freneau, 1974.

Peebles, John *John Peebles American War: The Diary of a Scottish Grenadier, 1776-1782.* Ira D. Gruber,   ed. Strand, Gloucestershire: Published by the Sutton for the Army Records Society, 1997.

Serle, Ambrose *The American Journal of Ambrose Serle Secretary to Lord Howe 1776-1778.* Tatum, Edward   H. ed. New York: New York Times and Arno Press, 1969 reprint of 1940 edition.

Showman, Richard; Dennis M. Conrad and Roger Parks eds. *The Papers of Nathanael Greene.* 13 vols.   Chapel Hill: University of North Carolina Press, 1976-2005.

Simcoe, John Graves *Simcoe's Military Journal.* New York: Bartlett and Welford, 1844.

Sun Tzu, *The Art of War.* Samuel B. Griffith, trans. Oxford: Oxford University Press, 1963.

Tielke, Johann Gottlieb *The Field Engineer or, Instruction upon every Branch of Field Fortification: Demonstrated by Examples which Occurred in the Seven Years' War between the Prussians,* The   *Austrians and the Russians.* London: J. Walter, 1769.

Trenck, Francicus von der *Memoirs of the Life of the Illustrious Francis Baron Trenck.* London: W. Owen,   1748.

Wiederhold, Andreas "The Capture of Fort Washington, New York, Described by Captain Andreas Wiederhold, of the Hessian 'Regiment Knyphausen.'" *Pennsylvania Magazine of History and Biography,* 23, no. 1 (1899):95-97.

Secondary Sources:

Reference Works:

Boatner, Mark M, III *Encyclopedia of the American Revolution.* Mechanicsburg, PA: Stackpole Books, 1994.

Bodinier, Captain Gilbert *Dictionnaire des officiers de l'armee royale qui ont combattu aux Etats-Unis pendant la guerre d'independance, 1776-1783 suivi d'un supplement a Les Francais sous le trieme etoiles du commandant Andre Lasseray.* Chateau de Vincennes, 1982.

Coetzee, Daniel and Lee Eystrulid eds. *Philosophers of War: The Evolution of History's Greatest Military Thinkers.* 2 vols., Santa Barbara, CA: Praeger, 2013.

Neumann, George *The History of the Weapons of the American Revolution.* New York: Harper and Row Publishers, 1967.

Books:

Abel, Jonathan *Guibert: Father of Napoleon's Grande Armée.* Norman: University of Oklahoma Press, 2016.

Addison, Larry H. *The Patterns of War through the Eighteenth Century.* Bloomington: Indiana University   Press, 1990.

Allison, Robert J. *The American Revolution: A Concise History*. Oxford: Oxford University Press, 2011.

Anderson, Fred *Crucible of War: The Seven Years War and the Fate of Empire in North America, 1754-1766*. New York: Alfred A. Knopf, 2000.

Anderson, M.S. *The War of the Austrian Succession 1740-1748*. London: Longman, 1995.

Baugh, Daniel *The Global Seven Years War, 1754-1763*. London: Pearson Education, 2011.

Babits, Lawrence E. *A Devil of a Whipping the Battle of Cowpens*. Chapel Hill: University of North Carolina Press, 1998.

_____. and Howard, Joshua B. *Long, Obstinate and Bloody; The Battle of Guilford Courthouse*. Chapel Hill: University of North Carolina Press, 2009.

Barsch, George *Ferdinand von Schill's Zug und Tod in Jahre 1809*. Leipzig: Brockhaus, 1860.

Bass, Robert D. *Gamecock, The Life and Campaigns of General Thomas Sumter*. New York: Holt, Rinehart and Winston, 1961.

Bell, David A. *The First Total War: Napoleon's Europe and the Birth of Warfare as we Know It*. Boston: Houghton Mifflin Company, 2007.

Billias, George Athan *General John Glover and His Marbelhead Mariners*. New York: Holt, Rinehart and Winston, 1960

Black, Jeremy *A Military Revolution? Military Change and European Society, 1550-1800*. Basingstoke: Macmillan Education, 1991.

_____*Warfare in the Eighteenth Century*. London: Cassell, 1999.

Bodle, Wayne K. and Jacqueline Thibaut, *Valley Forge Historical Research Report*. 3 vols., Washington, D.C.: Department of the Interior, National Park Service, 1980.

Borick, Carl P. *A Gallant Defense: The Siege of Charleston, 1780*. Columbia, SC: University of South Carolina Press, 2003.

Borneman Walter R. *American Spring: Lexington, Concord, and the Road to Revolution*. New York: Little, Brown and Company, 2014.

Bowman, Larry G. *Captive Americans: Prisoners during the American Revolution*. Athens, OH: Ohio University Press, 1976.

Brown, M. L. *Firearms in Colonial America, 1492-1792*. Washington, D.C.: Smithsonian Institution Press, 1980.

Browning, Reed *The War of the Austrian Succession*. New York: St. Martin's Griffin, 1995.

Bruford, Walter Horace *Germany in the Eighteenth Century*. Cambridge: Cambridge University Press, 1935.

Cecere, Michael *They Are Indeed a Very Useful Corps American Riflemen in the Revolutionary War*. Westminster, MD: Heritage Books, 2006.

Chagnoit, Jean *Le Chavlier de Folard: Le Strategie d'incertitude.* Paris: Editions du Rocher, 1997.

Chandler, David G. ed. *Napoleon's Marshals.* London: Weidenfield and Nicolson, 1987.

_____*The Campaigns of Napoleon.* London: Weidenfeld and Nicolson, 1995.

Chartier, Roger *The Cultural Origins of the French Revolution.* Lydia G. Cochrane, trans. Durham: Duke University Press, 1991.

Childs, John *Armies and Warfare in Europe, 1648-1789.* Manchester: Manchester University Press, 1982.

Clapham, J. H. *The Causes of the War of 1792.* New York: Octagon Books, 1969.

Cobban, Alfred *The Social Interpretation of the French Revolution.* 2nd ed. Cambridge: Cambridge University Press, 1999.

Corbett Theodore *No Turning Point: The Saratoga Campaign in Perspective.* Norman: University of Oklahoma Press, 2012.

Crytzer, Brady J. Hessians: *Mercenaries, Rebels, and the War for British North America.* Yardley, PA:Westholme Press, 2015.

Darling, Anthony D. *Red Coat and Brown Bess.* Alexandria Bay, NY: Museum Restoration Service, 1971.

Dearden, Paul F. *The Rhode Island Campaign of 1778: Inauspicious Dawn of Alliance.* Providence, RI: The Rhode Island Bicentennial Foundation, 1980.

Dederer, John M. *Making Bricks without Straw: Nathanael Greene's Southern Campaign and Mao Tse-Tung's Mobile War.* Manhattan, KS: Sunflower University Press, 1983.

Delderfield, R. F. *The March of the Twenty-Six.* London: Leo Cooper, 2004.

Demandt, Karl *Gesichte des Landes Hessen,* 2nd ed. Kassel: Bärenreiter, 1972.

Draper, Lyman C. *Kings Mountain and Its Heroes.* Johnson City, TN: The Overmountain Press, 1996 reprint of 1881 original.

Duffy, Christopher *The Wild Goose and the Eagle: A life of Marshal von Browne, 1705-1757.* Chatto & Windus, 1964.

_____*Frederick the Great: A Military Life* London: Routledge, 1985.

_____*The Military Experience in the Age of Reason, 1715- 1789.* New York: Scribner, 1987.

_____*The Army of Frederick the Great.* 2nd ed. Chicago, IL: emperor's Press, 1996.

_____*Siege Warfare: The Fortress in the Early Modern World 1494-1660.* London: Routledge, 1996.

_____*Instrument of War vol. 1 The Austrian Army in the Seven Years' War.* Chicago, IL: The Emperor's Press, 2000.

Dull, Jonathan R. *The French Navy and American Independence: A Study of Arms and Diplomacy, 1774–1787.* Princeton: Princeton University Press, 1975.

Dwyer Philip Napoleon: *The Path to Power.* New Haven: Yale University Press, 2007.

Dwyer, William M. *The Day is Ours! An Inside View of the Battle of Trenton and Princeton, November 1776-January 1777.* New Brunswick, NJ: Rutgers University Press, 1998.

Dyke, Samuel E *The Pennsylvania Rifle.* Constantine Kermes, ill. Lancaster, PA: Bicentennial Book, 1974.

Edgar, Walter, *Partisans and Redcoats The Southern Conflict that Turned the Tide of the American Revolution.* New York: Perennial, 2001.

Ellis, John *Cavalry The History of Mounted Warfare.* Yorkshire: Pen and Sword Books, 2004 reprint of 1978 original.

Elting, John R. *Swords Around a Throne.* New York: The Free Press, 1988.

Esdaile, Charles The Wars of Napoleon. London: Longman, 1995.

——————*Napoleon's Wars: An International History.* New York: Penguin Books, 2008.

Flakner, James Marshal Vauban and the Defence of Louis XIV's France. Barnsley, South Yorkshire: Pen and Sword Military, 2011.

Fischer, David Hackett *Washington's Crossing.* New York: Oxford University Press, 2004.

Ford, Worthington C. ed. *Defenses of Philadelphia in 1777.* Brooklyn: Historical Printing Club, 1897. Reprint, De Capo Press, 1971.

Forrest, Alan *Soldiers of the French Revolution.* Durham: Duke University Press, 1990.

Fuller, J.F. C. British Light Infantry in the Eighteenth Century. London: Hutchinson & Co., 1925.

Furet, François *Interpreting the French Revolution.* Elborg Forester, trans. Cambridge: Cambridge University Press, 1981.

Gaines, James R. *For Liberty and Glory: Washington, Lafayette and their Revolutions.* New York: W.W. Norton and Company, 2007.

Gallagher, John J. *The Battle of Brooklyn 1776.* Edison, NJ: Castle books, 2002.

Gallaher, John G. *The Iron Marshal. A Biography of Louis N. Davout.* London: The Greenhill Books, 2000.

Gates, David *The British Light Infantry Arm c. 1790-1815.* London: B.T. Batsford Ltd. 1987.

Gat, Azar, *The Origins of Military Thought: From the Enlightenment to Clausewitz.* Oxford: Clarendon Press, 1989.

Gay, Peter *The Enlightenment.* 2 vols. New York: W.W. Norton, 1966.

Gilbert, Alan. *Black Patriots and Loyalists: Fighting for Emancipation in the War for Independence.* Chicago: University of Chicago Press, 2012.

Gilchrist, M.M. *Patrick Fergusson A Man of Some Genius.* Edinburgh: NMS Publishing, 2003.

Glozier, Matther *Marshal Schomberg, 1615–1690: The Ablest Soldier of his Age: International Soldiering and the Formation of State Armies in Seventeenth–Century Europe.* Brighton: Sussex Academy Press, 2005.

Golway, Terry *Washington's General Nathanael Greene and the Triumph of the American Revolution.* New York: Henry Holt and Company, 2005.

Grenier, John *The First Way of War: American War Making on the Frontier.* Cambridge: Cambridge University Press, 2005.

Griffith, Paddy *The Art of War of Revolutionary France, 1789-1802.* London: Greenhill Books,1998.

Gros, Robert A. *The Minutemen and Their World.* New York: Hill and Wang, 1976.

Gruber, Ira D. *Books and the British Army in the Age of the American Revolution.* Chapel Hill: University of North Carolina Press, 2014.

_____*The Howe Brothers and the American Revolution.* Chapel Hill: University of North Carolina Press, 1972.

Haller, Stephen E. *William Washington: Cavalryman of the Revolution.* Bowie, MD: 2001.

Harris, Michael C. *Brandywine: A Military History of the Battle that Lost Philadelphia but Saved America, September 11, 1777.* El Dorado Hills, CA: Savas Beatie, 2016.

Hartman, John W. *The American Partisan Henry Lee and the Struggle for Independence, 1776-1780.* Shippensburg, PA: Burd Street Press, 2000.

Hattendorf, John B. *Newport, the French Navy, and American Independence.* Newport: The Redwood Press, 2005.

Haynes, Alan *Robert Cecil, First Earl of Salisbury: Servant of Two Sovereigns.* London: P. Owen, 1989.

Hieronymussen, Paul *Orders and Decorations of Europe in Color.* New York: The Macmillan Company, 1967.

Higginbotham, Don *George Washington and the American Military Tradition.* Athens: University of Georgia Press, 1985.

_____*The War of American Independence: Military Attitudes, Policies and Practice, 1763-1789.* Boston: Northeastern University Press, 1983.

_____*Daniel Morgan Revolutionary Rifleman.* Chapel Hill: University of North Carolina Press, 1961.

Hoffman, Ronald, et al., eds. *An Uncivil War: The Southern Backcountry during the American Revolution.* Charlottesville, VA: University Press of Virginia, 1985.

Holland, Barbara *Gentleman's Blood: A History of Dueling from Swords at Dawn to Pistols at Dusk*. New York: Bloomsbury, 2003.

Holtman, Robert B. *The Napoleonic Revolution*. Philadelphia: J.B. Lippincott Company, 1967.

Horne, Alistair *How Far from Austerlitz? Napoleon 1805-1815*. New York: MacMillan, 1996.

Huddleston, Joe D. *Colonial Riflemen in the American Revolution*. York, PA: George Shumway Publisher, 1978.

Hughes, B.P. *Open Fire: The Artillery Tactics from Marlborough to Wellington*. Sussex: Antony Bird Publications, 1983.

Ingrao, Charles W. *The Hessian Mercenary State: Ideas, Institutions, and Reform under Frederick II, 1760-1785*. Cambridge: Cambridge University Press, 1987.

Jackson, John W. *The Pennsylvania Navy 1775-1781: The Defense of the Delaware*. New Brunswick, NJ: Rutgers University Press, 1974.

_____*The Delaware Bay and River Defenses of Philadelphia*. Philadelphia: Philadelphia Maritime Museum, 1977.

_____*Fort Mercer, Guardian of the Delaware*. Gloucester, NJ: Gloucester County Cultural and Heritage Commission, 1986.

Kajencki, Francis Casimir *Thaddeus Kosciuszko: Military Engineer of the American Revolution*. El Paso, TX: South Polonia Press, 1998.

Kapp, Freidrich *Der Soldatenhandel deutscher fürsten nach Amerika. Ein Beitrag zur Kulturgeschichte des Achtzehnten Jahrhunderts*. Berlin: Verlag von Julius J. Springer, 1874.

Kennett, Lee B. *The French Forces in America, 1780-1783*. Westport, CT: Greenwood Press, 1977.

Ketchum, Richard M. The Winter Soldiers: *The Battles of Trenton and Princeton*. New York: Henry Holt and Company, 1973.

Krebs, Daniel A Generous and Merciful Enemy: Life for German Prisoners of War during the American Revolution. Norman: University of Oklahoma Press, 2013.

Kwasny Mark V. *Washington's Partisan War, 1775-1783*. Kent, OH: Kent State University Press, 1996.

LaCrosse, Richard B. *Revolutionary Rangers Daniel Morgan's Riflemen and their Role on the Northern Frontier, 1778-1783*. with introduction by Harry Kels Swan, Bowie, MD: Heritage Books, Inc., 2002.

Lambert, Robert Stansbury *South Carolina Loyalists in the American Revolution*. Columbia, SC: University of South Carolina Press, 1987.

Lanning, Michael *African Americans in the Revolutionary War*. New York: Kensington Publishing, 2000.

Lefebvre, Georges *The Coming of the French Revolution*. Princeton: Princeton University Press, 1947.

_____*The Great Fear: Rural Panic in Revolutionary France.* New York: Vintage Books, 1973.

Lefkowitz, Arthur S. *The Long Retreat: The Calamitous American Defense of New Jersey in 1776.* New Brunswick, NJ: Rutgers University Press, 1999.

Lender, Mark E. *The River War.* Trenton, NJ: New Jersey Historical Commission, 1979.

Lippitt, Charles *Battle of Rhode Island.* Np: Nabu Press, 2012.

Lockhart, Paul *The Drillmaster of Valley Forge: The Baron de Steuben and the Making of the American Army.* New York: HarperCollins Publishers, 2008.

Losch, Philipp *Soldatenhandel mit einem Berzeidnis der Hessen-Kasselischen Gubdfidienvertrage und einer Bibliographie.* Berlag zu Kassel: Barenreiter, 1933.

Lumpkin, Henry From Savannah to Yorktown: The American Revolution in the South. New York: Paragon House, 1981.

Lynn John A. *The Wars of Louis XIV 1667-1714.* London: Longman, 1999.

_____*The Bayonets of the Republic: Motivation and Tactics in the Army of Revolutionary France, 1791-94.* 2nd ed. Boulder, CO: Westview Press, 1996.

Maass, John R. *The Road to Yorktown: Jefferson, Lafayette and the British Invasion of Virginia.* Charleston, SC: The History Press, 2015.

MacDonnell,. A.G. *Napoleon and His Marshals.* London: Prion, 1996.

Mackesy, Piers *The War for America, 1775-1783.* Lincoln, NE: University of Nebraska Press, 1993 reprint of 1964 original.

Malone, Patrick *The Skulking Way of War Technology and Tactics among the New England Indians.* New York: Madison Books, 1991.

Markham, Felix *Napoleon and the Awakening of Europe: A Study of the Military, Political, and Personal Elements of the Napoleonic Domination of Europe.* New York: Collier Books, 1963.

Martin, James Kirby and Mark Edward Lender, *A Respectable Army: The Military Origins of the Republic, 1763-1789.* Wheeling, IL: Harlan Davidson, Inc. 1982.

Maude, F.N. The Jena Campaign: *1806-The Twin Battles of Jena & Auerstadt Between Napoleon's French and the Prussian Army.* Np: Leonaur, 2007.

McBurney, Christian *The Rhode Island Campaign: The First French and American Operation in the Revolutionary War.* Yardley, PA: Westholme Press, 2011.

McCullough, David *1776* New York: Simon & Schuster, 2005.

McDougall, William *American Revolutionary: A Biography of General Alexander McDougall.* Westport, CT: Greenwood Press, 1977.

Middlekauff, Robert *The Glorious Cause: The American Revolution, 1763-1789.* New York: Oxford University Press, 1982.

Mintz Max M. *The Generals of Saratoga*. New Haven, CT: Yale University Press, 1990.

Morrill, Dan L *The Southern Campaigns of the American Revolution*. Mount Pleasant, SC: Nautical Aviation   Publishing Company of America, 1993.

Muir, Rory *Tactics and the Experience of Battle in the Age of Napoleon*. New Haven: Yale University Press, 1998.

Mustafa, Sam A. *The Long Ride of Major von Schill: A Journey through German History and Memory*. Lanham: Rowan and Littlefield, 2008.

Nadelhaft, Jerome D. *The Disorders of War: The Revolution in South Carolina*. Orono, ME: University of Maine at Orono Press, 1981.

Neimeyer, Charles P. The Revolutionary War. Westport, CT: Greenwood Press, 2007.

Nester, William R. *"Haughty Conquerors" Amherst and the Great Indian Uprising of 1763*. Westport, CT: Praeger, 2000.

Nosworthy, Brent The Anatomy of Victory: Battle Tactics 1689-1763. New York: Hippocrene Books, 1990.

O'Kelley, Patrick *Nothing but Blood and Slaughter: The Revolutionary War in the Carolinas*. 4 vols. Booklocker, 2004-06.

Oller, John *The Swamp Fox: How Francis Marion Saved the American Revolution*. New York: DeCapo Press, 2016.

Puls, Mark *Henry Knox: Visionary General of the American Revolution*. New York: Palgrave Macmillan, 2008.

Paret, Peter *Clausewitz and the State: The Man, his Theories, and his Times*. Princeton: Princeton University Press, 1985.

Parker, Geoffrey *The Military Revolution: Military Innovation and the Rise of the West, 1500-1800*. Cambridge, Cambridge University Press, 1988.

Peckham Howard H. *The Toll of Independence: Engagements and Battle Casualties of the American Revolution*. Chicago: University of Chicago Press, 1974.

Peterson, Harold L. *The Book of the Continental Soldier Being a Compleat Account of the Uniforms, Weapons, and Equipment with which he Lived and Fought*. Harrisburg, PA: Stackpole Books, 1968.

_____*Round Shot and Rammers*. Harrisburg, PA: Stackpole Books, 1969.

Piecuch, Jim *The Blood be Upon your Head: Tarleton and the Myth of Buford's Massacre*. Lugoff, SC: Southern Campaigns of the Revolution Press, 2010.

Picaud-Monnerat, *Sandrine La Petite Guerre au XVIIIe Siecle Paris:* Economica, 2010.

Presser, Carl *Die Soldatenhandel in Hessen*. Marburg: R.G. Einwert, 1900.

Quarles, Benjamin *The Negro Soldier in the American Revolution*. Chapel Hill, University of North Carolina Press, 1961.

Quimby, Robert S. *The Background of Napoleonic Warfare: The Theory of Military Tactics in Eighteenth-Century France*. New York: Columbia University Press, 1957.

Rankin, Hugh F. *Greene and Cornwallis: The Campaign in the Carolinas*. Raleigh, NC: Office of Archives and History, North Carolina Department of Cultural Resources, 2003 (reprint of 1976 original).

Redmon, Barton For *Six Pence a Day: A Collection of Essays on the British Army during the Era of the Seven Years War, 1755-1765*. Pulaski, VA: King Smith Publishing, 2012.

Renouard, Carl *Geschichte des Krieges in Hannover, Hessen und Westfalen von 1757 bis 1763*. 3 Bände, Cassel, 1863-64 , pp. 784-796

Reynolds, William R. *Andrew Pickens: South Carolina Patriot in the Revolutionary War*. Jefferson, NC: MacFarland and Company, Inc., Publishers, 2012.

Rogers, Clifford J. ed. *The Military Revolution Debate: Readings on the Military Transformation of Early Modern Europe*. Boulder, CO: Westview Press, 1995.

Rothenberg, Gunther E. *The Art of War in the Age of Napoleon*. Bloomington: Indiana University Press, 1978.

Royster, Charles *Light Horse Harry Lee and the Legacy of the American Revolution*. Baton Rouge: Louisiana State University Press, 1981.

_____*A Revolutionary People at War The Continental Army and American Character, 1775-1783*. Chapel Hill: University of North Carolina Press, 1979.

Satterfield, George *Princes, Posts, and Partisans the Army of Louis XIV and Partisan Warfare in the Netherlands (1673-1678)*. Leiden: Brill, 2003.

Savory, Sir Reginald *His Britanic Majesty's Army in Germany during the Seven Years' War*. Oxford: Clarendon Press, 1966.

Schecter, Barnet *The Battle for New York The City at the Heart of the American Revolution*. New York: Walker and Company, 2002.

Scott, Samuel F. The Response of the Royal Army to the French Revolution: The Role and Development of the Line Army, 1787-1793. Oxford: Clarendon Press, 1978.

_____*From Yorktown to Valmy: The Transformation of the French Army in the Age of Revolution*. Niwot, CO: University Press of Colorado, 1998.

Showalter, Dennis *The Wars of Frederick the Great*. London: Longman, 1996.

Shumway, George *Jaeger Rifles*. York, PA: George Shumway Publisher, 2003.

Smith, David *William Howe and the American War of Independence*. London: Bloomsbury Publishing, 2015.

Smith, Samuel S. *Fight for the Delaware, 1777*. Philip Freneau Press, 1970.

Spring, Matthew H. *With Zeal and Bayonets Only The British Army on Campaign in North America, 1775-1783*. Norman: University of Oklahoma Press, 2008.

Soboul, Albert *The French Revolution1787-1799: From the Storming of the Bastille to Napoleon*. New York: Vintage Books, 1962.

Sonntag, Kurt *Trenck, der Pandur und die Brandschatzung Bayerns*. Munchen: Nusser, 1976.

Starkey, Armstrong *War in the Age of Enlightenment, 1700-1789*. Westport, CT: Praeger, 2003.

Strachan, Hew *European Armies and the Conduct of War*. London Routledge, 1983.

Stryker, William S. *The Battle of Trenton and Princeton*. Trenton, NJ: The Old Barracks Association, 2001 reprint of 1898 orig.

Sumida, Jon Tetsuro *Decoding Clausewitz: A New Approach to One War*. Lawrence, KS: University Press of Kansas, 2008.

Szabo, Franz J. *The Seven Years War in Europe 1756-1763*. New York: Longman, 2008.

Szymański, Leszek *Casimir Pulaski: A Hero of the Revolution*. New York: Hippocrene Books, 1994.

Tallet, Frank *War and Society in Early-Modern Europe, 1495-1715*. London: Routledge, 1992.

Tonsetic, Robert L. *Special Operations during the American Revolution*. Philadelphia: Casemate, 2013.

Tocqueville, Alexis de *The Old Regime and the French Revolution*. Stuart Gilbert, trans. NewYork: Doubleday, 1983 reprint of 1955 original.

Tuck, Christopher *Understanding Land Warfare*. London: Routledge, 2014.

Uffindell, Andrew *Great Generals of the Napoleonic Wars and their Battles 1805-1815*. Gloucestershire, Spellbound, 2007.

Urban, William *Bayonets and Scimitars: Arms, Armies and Mercenaries 1700-1789*. London: Frontline Books, 2013.

Ward, Christopher *The Delaware Continentals*. Wilmington, DE: Historical Society of Delaware, 1941.

Ward, Harry M. *Between the Lines Banditti of the American Revolution*. Westport, CT: Praeger, 2002.

Weigley, Russell F. *The Partisan War: The South Carolina Campaign of 1780-1782*. Columbia, SC: University of South Carolina Press, 1970.

————*The Age of Battles: The Quest for Decisive Warfare from Breitenfeld to Waterloo*. Bloomington: Indiana University Press, 1991.

Wetzel, Georg Heinz *Die Hessischen Jager: einer deutche Truppenhistorie in politischen Wandlungsprozess von vier Jahrhunderten (1631-1987)*. Kassel, Verlag George, 1987.

White Charles Edward, *The Enlightened Soldier: Scharnhorst and the Militärische Gesellschaft in Berlin, 1801-1805*. New York: Praeger, 1989.

Willis, Sam *The Struggle for Sea Power: A Naval History of the American Revolution*. New York: W.W. Norton and Company, 2015.

Wilson, David K. *The Southern Strategy Britain's Conquest of South Carolina and Georgia, 1775-1780.* Columbia, S.C: University of South Carolina Press, 2005.

Wilson, Peter H. *War, State and Society in Württemberg. 1677-1793.* Cambridge: Cambridge University Press, 1995.

_____*Heart of Europe: A History of the Holy Roman Empire.* Cambridge, MA: The Belknap Press of Harvard University Press, 2016.

Witzel, Rudolf *Hessen-Kassels Regimenter in der Alliierten Armee 1762.* N.P.: Norderstedt Books on Demand GmbH, 2008.

Woods, W. J. *Battles of the Revolutionary War, 1775-1781.* New York: DeCapo Press, 1995 reprint of 1990 original.

Wright, Robert K. *The Continental Army.* Washington, DC: Center of Military History, United States Army, 1989.

Articles:

Atkinson, C.T. "British Strategy and Battles in the Westphalian Campaigns of 1758-1762." In *Journal of the Royal United Service Institution.* 79, 516 (1934) 733-40.

Barker, Thomas M. and Thomas M. Huey, "Military Jägers, Their Civilian background and Weaponry." in *The Hessians: The Journal of the Johannes Schwalm Historical Association.* 15 (2012) 1-15.

Birtle, Andrew J. "The Origins of the Legion of the United States." In *Journal of Military History,* 67, 4 (October 2003): 1249-61.

Black, Jeremy "British Military Strategy." in Donald Stoker, Kenneth J. Hagen and Michael T. Mc Master, eds, *Strategy in the American War of Independence,* London, Routledge, 2010

Copeland, Peter F. and Albert W. Haarmann "The Provisional Chasseur Companies of Hesse-Cassel during the Revolutionary War." in *Military Collector and Historian.* 18 (1966): 11-13.

Dalwigk Major von, "Der Anteil der Hessischen Truppen am Österreichen Erbfolgekriege (1740-48)." In *Zeitschrift der Vereins fürhessische Geschichte und Landeskunde.* 42 (1908): 72-139.

Frasche, Louis D. F. "Problems of Command: Cornwallis, Partisans, and Militia, 1780" *Military Review,* 57 (April 1977):60-74.

Fuller, J.F.C. "The Revival and Training of Light Infantry in the British Army." In *Journal of the Royal United Services Institution.* 57 (1913): 1187-1214.

Gallagher, Catherine "The Formalism of Military History." in *Representations,* 104, 1 (Fall 2008): 23-33.

Herrera, Ricardo A. "'[T]he zealous activity of Capt. Lee': Light-Horse Harry Lee and Petite Guerre," *Journal of Military History,* 79:1 (January 2015): 9-36.

Heuser, Beatrice "Small Wars in the Age of Clausewitz: The Watershed between Partisan War and People's War." in *Journal of Strategic Studies,* 33, 1 (February 19, 2010):139-162.

Henry, Mark "The Hessian Army of the Seven Years' War." in Seven Years War Association Journal. 8, no.3, (Spring 1994):40-46.

Higginbotham, Don "Reflections on the War of Independence, Modern Guerrilla Warfare, and the War in Vietnam." in Ronald Hoffman and Peter J. Albert, eds. *Arms and Independence: The Military Character of the American Revolution.* Charlottesville: University Press of Virginia, 1984.

Ingrao, Charles "'Barbarous Strangers': Hessian State and Society during the American Revolution." in *American Historical Review.* 87,4 (October 1982): 954-976.

Keithly, David "Poor, Nasty and Brutish: Guerrilla Operations in America's First Civil War." in *Civil Wars* volume IV, number 3, (Autumn 2001):35-69.

Leach, Josiah G. "Commodore John Hazelwood, Commander of the Pennsylvania Navy in the Revolution." in *Pennsylvania Magazine of History and Biography*, 26, 1 (1902): 1-6.

Lynn, John A "The Embattled Future of Academic Military History." in *Journal of Military History*, 61, 4 (October 1997):773-789.

_____"The Evolution of Army Style in the Modern West, 800-2000." in *The International History Review.* 18,3 (August 1996): 505-545.

Magra, Christopher F. "'Soldiers…Bred to the Sea': Maritime Marblehead, and the Origins and Progress of the American Revolution." in *The New England Quarterly.* 77,4 (December 2004): 531-562.

Mc Intyre, James R. "On the Origins and Development of the Pennsylvania-American Longrifle, 1500-1700." in *Seven Years War Association Journal.* Vol. 14, no.1 Fall, 2005, 40-55.

_____"Separating Myth from History: The Maryland Riflemen in the War of Independence." in *Maryland Historical Magazine*, Vol. 104, no. 2 (Summer 2009): 101-119.

_____"Enlightened Rogues: Light Infantry and Partisan Theorists of the Eighteenth Century, 1740-1800." In *Seven Years' War Association Journal*, 18, 2 (Fall 2013): 4-28.

_____"A Scoundrel's Scoundrel: The Life and Exploits of Baron Franciscus von der Trenck, Pandour Leader" in *Seven Years War Association Journal*, 19,1 (Winter 2014): 27-42.

_____"The Delaware River Campaign of 1777: An Examination of an Eighteenth-Century Joint Operation." in *Journal of America's Military Past*, xxxix, 2 (Spring/Summer 2014): 5-24.

Mulder, Luke "Some Notes on Landgraf Friedrich II of Hessen-Kassel and the Re-Organization of 1760." In *Seven Years War Association Journal*, 8, 2 (Winter 2000): 16-18.

Papenfuse, Edward C. and Gregory A Stiverson "General Smallwood's Recruits: The Peacetime Career of the Revolutionary War Private." in *William and Mary Quarterly*, 30, 1 (January 1973): 117-132

Paret, Peter "Translation, Literal or Accurate." in the *Journal of Military History.* 78, 3 (July 2014): 1077-1080.

_____"Colonial Experience and European Military Reform at the End of the Eighteenth Century," in *Bulletin of the Institute of Historical Research*, XXXVII (1964), 47-59.

Partridge, Mike "The Artillery of Hesse-Cassel: A Brief Organizational History." In *Seven Years' War Association Journal,* 8, 2 (Winter 2000): 14-15.

Raudzens, George "War-Winning Weapons: The Measurement of Technological Determinism in Military History." in Journal of Military History volume 54, number 4 (October 1990): 403-33.

Reichmann, Felix "The Pennsylvania Rifle: A Social Interpretation of Changing Military Techniques." In *Pennsylvania Magazine of History and Biography.* volume 69, no.1 (January 1945): 3-14.

Rink, Martin "The Partisan's Metamorphosis: From Freelance Military Entrepreneur to German Freedom Fighter, 1740-1815." in *War in History.* 17(1): 6-36.

Selig, Robert A. "Light Infantry Lessons from America? Johann Ewald's Experiences in the American Revolutionary War as Depicted in his Abhandlung uber den Kleinen Kreis (1785)." in Studies in *Eighteenth Century Culture.* 23 (1994):111-129.

Schorr, Dan "Hessian Colors and Standards, 1740-48." In *SYWAJ.* 8.3, (Spring 1994): 48-51.

Scott, H.M. "Introduction: Prussia from Rossbach to Jena." In *German History,* 12, 3 (1994): 279-85.

Storrs, Christopher and H.M. Scott "The Military revolution and the European Nobility, c. 1600-1800." in *War in History,* 3, 1 (January 1996):1-41

Syrett, David "The British Landing at Havana: An Example of an Eighteenth Century Combined Operation." in *The Mariner's Mirror.* 55, (1969): 325-332.

_____"The Methodology of British Amphibious Operations during the Seven Years' War" in *The Mariner's Mirror.* 58, (1972): 269-280.

Taylor, Peter K. "'Patrimonial' Bureaucracy and 'Rational' Policy in Eighteenth-Century Germany: The Case of Hessian Recruitment Reforms, 1762-93." in *Central European History.* 22,1 (March 1989): 33-56.

_____"Military System and Rural Social Change in Eighteenth-Century Hesse-Cassel." in *Journal of Military History.* 25, 3 (April 1992): 479-504.

Trudeau, Noah Alexander "'The Fort's Our Own.'" In *Military History Quarterly,* 16, 1 (Autumn 2003): 85-93.

Urwin, Gregory J. W. "'I have wanted to go see you for a Long Time' Notes on the Friendship of Johann Ewald and John Graves Simcoe." Lindsay A.H. Parker, Ph.D. trans. In *Hessians: Journal of the Johannes Schwalm Historical Association.* 17 (2014): 1-14.

_____"Cornwallis and the Slaves of Virginia: A New Look at the Yorktown Campaign." Proceedings of the 28th Congress of the International Commission of Military History, 11-17 August, 2002, 172-192.

Weinmeiser, Oscar K. "The Hessian Grenadier Battalions in North America, 1776-1783." in *The Military Collector and Historian.* 27 (1975): 148-52.

Weller, Jac "The Irregular War in the South." *Military Affairs* number 24, 3 (Autumn1960): 124-136.

Wilkinson, Norman B. "The Pennsylvania Rifle." In *Historic Pennsylvania Leaflet.* 4 Pennsylvania Historical and Museum Commission (1976): 1-4.

Wilson, Peter H. "The German "Soldier Trade' of the Seventeenth and Eighteenth Centuries: A Reassessment." *The International History Review.* 18, 4 (November 1996): 757-792.

Wright, Col. John "Military Contributions during the Eighteenth Century." in J*ournal of the American Military Institute*, 3, 1 (Spring 1939): 3-13.

_____"The Rifle in the American Revolution." in *American Historical Review.* 29 (1924): 26-30.

York, Neil L. "Pennsylvania Rifle: Revolutionary Weapon in a Conventional War." in *Pennsylvania Magazine of History and Biography.* 103 (July 1979): 302-324.

Zwengel, Otto "Zur Theorie des Kleinen Kriegs." *Allegemeine Militarrundschau.* 10 (1969): 397-404.

Zwenger, Ferdinand "Johann Ewald in hessischen Dienst." *Hessenland,* VII (1893): 142-4, 158-60, 194-7, 207-9.

Internet Sources:

Anonymous "Militär in alten Mauern" September 13-14, 2003 Internet.https://web.archive.org/web/20031005141352/http://www.hessenmilitaer.de/amoeneburg.htm Last accessed September 28, 2016.

Hagist, Don N. "The Military Library." in Journal of the American Revolution, November 17, 2014. Internet. https://allthingsliberty.com/2014/11/the-military-library/ Last accessed August 2, 2016.

Nafziger, George "Order of Battle, Battle of Vellinghausen, July 15-16, 1761" Nafziger Collection, U.S. Army   Combat Studies Institute, Internet. http://usacac.army.mil/cac2/CGSC/CARL/nafziger/761GAC.pdf Last accessed November 30, 2016

Selig, Robert A. "The du de Lauzun and his Legion: Rochambeau's most Troublesome, Colorful Soldiers" at http://www.americanrevolution.org/lauzun.php internet. Lest accessed, 4/15/16.

Pamphlets:

Stewart, Frank H. *History of the Battle of Red Bank with Events Prior and Subsequent thereto.* Woodbury, NJ: Board of Freeholders of Gloucester County, 1927.

Unpublished Dissertations:

Andrews, Melody "Myrmidons from Abroad": The Role of the German Mercenary in the coming of American Independence." Ph.D. diss., University of Houston, 1986.

Hoffman, Elliot Wheelock "The German Soldiers in the American Revolution." 2 vols. Ph.D. diss. University of New Hampshire, 1982.

Slagle, Robert O. "The von Lossberg Regiment: A Chronicle of Hessian Participation in the American Revolution." Ph. D. diss., American University, 1965.

Unpublished MA Theses:

Jacobson, Kristine E. Conduct of the Partisan War in the Revolutionary War South. MA Thesis U.S. Army Command and General Staff College, Fort Leavenworth, KS, 2003.

Rider, Thomas A. "Massacre or Myth: No Quarter at the Waxhaws." MA Thesis, University of North Carolina, 2002. Unpublished Conference Papers:

Palmer, Jason "Dutch" "For Cause and Family in the American Revolution." Unpublished paper presented at 75th Annual Meeting of the Society for Military History, Ogden, Utah, April 18, 2008.